CRITICAL INSIGHTS

Jane Austen

CRITICAL INSIGHTS

Jane Austen

Editor
Jack Lynch
Rutgers University

Salem Press
Pasadena, California   Hackensack, New Jersey

Cover photo: The Granger Collection, New York

Published by Salem Press

© 2010 by EBSCO Publishing
Editor's text © 2010 by Jack Lynch
"The *Paris Review* Perspective" © 2010 by Radhika Jones for *The Paris Review*

∞ The paper used in these volumes conforms to the American National Standard for Permanence of Paper for Printed Library Materials, Z39.48-1992 (R1997).

Library of Congress Cataloging-in-Publication Data
Jane Austen / editor, Jack Lynch.
   p. cm. -- (Critical insights)
   Includes bibliographical references and index.
   ISBN 978-1-58765-638-5 (one volume : alk. paper) 1. Austen, Jane, 1775-1817--Criticism and interpretation. I. Lynch, Jack (John T.)
   PR4037.J287 2010
   823'.7--dc22

                                                             2009027640

PRINTED IN CANADA

Contents_____

Career, Life, and Influence_____

Critical Contexts_____

Critical Readings_____

Resources

About This Volume

Jack Lynch

Few authors have inspired the same kind of devotion as Jane Austen. With such a small oeuvre—just six novels, a handful of juvenile writings, and a modest collection of letters—it may seem odd that she has created so many dedicated fans, so many reading groups, so many films, so many television adaptations, so many sequels and continuations. And yet the vividness of her world and the depths of her characters have turned countless people into "Janeites," whether they are academics in tweed jackets or enthusiasts who dress like Emma. As early as 1849, the author of *Outlines of General Literature* referred to "Miss Austen, whose novels may be considered as models of perfection in a new and very difficult species of writing." Generations of readers have agreed.

This collection brings together a selection of recent representative critical essays on Austen from a variety of perspectives. All of them take for granted the brilliance of her achievement, but they also make the case that she deserves to be taken seriously as a major writer and a major thinker. After opening with several short introductory essays, the volume moves on to consider Austen's critical contexts through a series of wide-ranging overviews of her life and works. The section that follows, "Critical Readings," provides samples of critical close readings from a number of schools of thought. The volume is rounded out by a chronology of the important events in Austen's life, a list of her works, and a bibliography with suggestions for further reading.

CAREER, LIFE, AND INFLUENCE

On Jane Austen

Jack Lynch

"The little bit (two Inches wide) of Ivory on which I work with so fine a Brush, as produces little effect after much labour"—Jane Austen's comment to her nephew has become famous as a description of her art. That bit of ivory seems little indeed on first reading. Austen's novels are prepared on a very small plane: each novel describes the domestic relations of upper-class men and women in a few houses in a small English village. But while her characters' lives revolve around marriage, the rest of the world was concerned with events of much greater consequence: the Napoleonic Wars raged only a few hundred miles away; political radicals were charged with sedition; abolitionists challenged the foundation of empire; evangelicals were changing the face of Christian piety; feminists were questioning ancient notions about women's place in society; and pathbreaking poets and essayists were reinventing English literature as a whole. Austen's lifetime was an era of tremendous ferment—and yet all of these revolutionary movements seem to be excluded from her novels.

Some critics have been happy that she shut out the rest of the world; some readers in fact still turn to her works as an escape from the unpleasant realities of modern political life. Others have taken the opposite approach, blaming Austen for concentrating on her little domestic world without paying attention to the revolutionary social changes that were taking place around her—surely, the argument goes, if she was a serious writer, she would have had something to say about these epochal events. But because she never announced to the world her opinion of Napoleon, or women's rights, or Romantic poetry, most have agreed with her characterization of her little bit of ivory.

First appearances can be deceiving, however. Although Austen makes few explicit references to these big external events, they all make their appearances in all the novels, just not in obvious ways. The slave economy, for instance, is the basis of the Bertram family's wealth in *Mansfield Park*—it is the need to manage his West Indian plantation that takes Sir Thomas away from his familiar village to faraway Antigua. Austen almost never alludes to warfare, but why else would the Meryton of *Pride and Prejudice* be filled with dashing soldiers if not for the war going on across the English Channel? It would be reductive to say that Austen's novels are "about" these things, but there is no denying that the wider world makes its appearance even on her little bit of ivory. Her works are domestic, but the domestic life she portrays resonates with the whole of English society of her era.

It may be her failure—or refusal—to engage explicitly with the big political concerns of the day that has permitted many readers to wrench Austen out of her own time. Some have read her as an eighteenth-century novelist, a contemporary of Fielding and Richardson, even though she did not publish a word until 1811. Others have treated her as a Victorian novelist, even though she died two years before Victoria was born. Few have traditionally thought about her in the context of her actual literary contemporaries, including the "big six" Romantic poets—William Blake, William Wordsworth, Samuel Taylor Coleridge, John Keats, Percy Bysshe Shelley, and Lord Byron—as well as Sir Walter Scott, Maria Edgeworth, William Godwin, Elizabeth Inchbald, Thomas Love Peacock, and so on. Only in recent years have critics begun to think of Austen as part of her own age, neither a relic of a past age nor a harbinger of what was to come.

Still, even though she was rarely considered as part of her historical moment, she has long been recognized as one of the great writers in English. Austen may owe her place in the canon to her mastery of style: there is no greater prose stylist among the English novelists. Her remarkable control of tone made her works appealing throughout the twentieth century, when most critics who professed allegiance to the New Criticism preferred lyric poetry to prose fiction—Austen brings to her prose narratives all the precision of a lyric poet. That control is what led Thomas Macaulay to call her "a prose Shakespeare" in 1842. It is most evident in that distinctive narratorial voice, which manages to keep readers perpetually on their toes, trying to figure out when she is speaking ironically. In Wayne C. Booth's *A Rhetoric of Irony* (1974), Austen is cited on page 1—*Pride and Prejudice* is the first work mentioned in that landmark study—and her name comes up over and over again throughout the book, more than virtually any other novelist. And that difficulty of ever pinning her down keeps her works endlessly interesting and open to ever-new interpretations.

Readers of Austen, however, have not felt obliged to confine their attention to formal matters such as the irony of the narratorial voice. Especially since the 1970s, as modes of criticism informed by politics and sociology have become increasingly popular, Austen has been examined by new generations. That is not to say her work has been uniformly well received. As Sarah Emsley explains in this volume:

> There has always been a suspicion among readers—and especially among nonreaders—of Jane Austen's novels, that love is not quite a serious enough topic, even for a novel. Janeites are often caricatured as escapist readers indulging in a guilty pleasure, reading Jane Austen in a dreamworld of fantasy, wish-fulfillment, Regency ball gowns, lace, and perfectly happy marriages. The real world, even the real world of other kinds of fiction, it is suggested, is much more serious than that. Even the best of the recent film adaptations do little to counteract the assumption that Austen novels are preoccupied with the perfect wedding as the culmination of every woman's dream.

"Jane Austen's stature," wrote Julia Prewitt Brown, "has declined with the rise of feminist literary criticism." Austen herself called *Pride and Prejudice* "light, & bright, & sparkling"; to many critics it has seemed that the brightness does not do justice to the social ills of Austen's world.

But some feminists have seen in Austen not a submissive woman's voice in perpetual retreat from conflict but a subversive protofeminist who was every bit as politically engaged as other writers of her day—

though in more subtle ways. And it was not merely feminism. Few have gone so far as Austen herself, who offered this modest (or ironically modest) self-description to J. S. Clarke, the librarian to the Prince Regent: "the most unlearned and uninformed female who ever dared to be an authoress." But many have seemed to believe she was unlearned and uninformed, not well versed in the serious intellectual currents of her day, whether political, social, religious, or philosophical. Just as feminists have begun to discover a more subtle and sophisticated feminist in Austen, however, other critics have begun to discover a more subtle and sophisticated philosopher and social theorist. Many of the essays collected here, therefore, take a second, closer look at Austen's novels, showing that they are not what they seem on first reading.

Perhaps more than almost any other novels, Austen's works repay multiple readings. According to a witticism often repeated in Janeite circles, a figure of some distinction—sometimes it is supposed to be Prime Minister Benjamin Disraeli, sometimes philosopher Gilbert Ryle, sometimes an unnamed "poetry professor"—was asked whether he read novels; his answer was, "Yes, all six of them, every year." The "all six of them" implies that Austen's novels are all that this very important person needs to read. But the "every year" may be even more telling: there really are people who make a point of rereading all six novels every year over the course of a lifetime, and they never run out of new things to observe. And some long so much for more Austen material to read that they make up for her short career by writing new Austen novels. As critic Deidre Shauna Lynch puts it, Jane Austen's "works appear to have proven more hospitable to sequelisation than those of almost any other novelist." The numbers bear her out: no major literary author has prompted as many unauthorized continuations and sequels as Austen, including, most recently, the unlikely *Pride and Prejudice and Zombies* (advertised as "the original text of Jane Austen's beloved novel with all-new scenes of bone crunching zombie action"). Not all of the sequels feature quite so much bone crunching, but there is clearly something in Austen's work that lends itself to imaginative re-creation and expansion.

That "something"—that impression that the world she depicts is real and three-dimensional, as are all the people in it—is what keeps readers coming back to the novels again and again, and what keeps critics writing about them. The richness and complexity of Austen's world, even if it is painted on a little bit of ivory, has made it a subject of perpetual interest. And the essays in this volume, taken together, reveal some of the elements of her fiction that have enthralled generations of readers.

Biography of Jane Austen

Rosemary M. Canfield Reisman

Early Life

Jane Austen was born on December 16, 1775, in Steventon, Hampshire, England, the seventh child and second daughter of George Austen and Cassandra Leigh Austen. Her father was the rector of Steventon and nearby Deane. A member of an old but poor family, he had been reared by a wealthy uncle, who educated him at St. John's College, Oxford, where George was later a fellow. Austen's mother was the daughter of a clergyman of noble ancestry who was also an Oxford graduate and a former fellow.

Although Jane and her older sister, Cassandra Austen, spent several years in schools in Southampton and Reading, their real education took place at home. The Austens loved words and books. The children could roam at will through George Austen's impressive library. As they grew older, they staged amateur theatricals. The environment stimulated their curiosity, whether they were observing their mother's experiments in farming or hearing their aristocratic French cousin talk about life in prerevolutionary France. With an ever-increasing family and a wide circle of friends, the Austen children had ample opportunity to analyze human motivations and relationships; it is not surprising that two of Jane's brothers and her sister Cassandra all did some writing at one time or another.

The Austens also shared in remarkable good looks; Jane and Cassandra were sometimes called the best-looking girls in England. However flattering such comments may have been, it is true that Jane was a tall, slender brunette with brown, curly hair, hazel eyes, a good complexion, and a sweet voice. Although neither Jane nor Cassandra was ever married, it was not for lack of prospects. Indeed, both were engaged: Cassandra for some time, to a young clergyman who died in the West Indies, and Jane only overnight, to a family friend whom she rejected in the morning. There was evidently at least one other serious relationship for Jane, a holiday romance that was not pursued and that terminated when the young man died.

Because Jane never left the family circle, her life has often been called uneventful. In fact, it was so busy that Jane had to snatch time to write. In addition to the normal social activities of her class, there were frequent visits to and from her brothers and their families, including lengthy stays by their children, several of whom were very close to their Aunt Jane. There were births, deaths, marriages, and remarriages; there was anxiety about Jane's cousin, whose husband was executed in the French Revolution, and about two brothers, who were British naval officers. Thus, Jane was immersed in life, grieving and rejoicing with family members and friends, mothering nieces and nephews, worrying about the effects of her unstable times on those she loved. As one may note from her letters, she was also a perceptive observer of human behavior, unimpressed by pomposity, unfooled by pretense, and always alert to the comic dimension of human relationships.

It was this comic sense that first led Austen to writing. Her three notebooks collect jokes, skits, and rudimentary character sketches dating from the time she was eleven or twelve, along with a later comic history of England and a brief, unfinished novel titled "Catherine." By 1795, when she was twenty, Austen had produced "Elinor and Marianne" (which was later revised and published in 1811 as *Sense and Sensibility*). By 1797, she had completed "First Impressions," which the publisher Cadell refused even to read but which, revised, became her most famous novel, *Pride and Prejudice* (1813). Although none of her novels was published until 1811 (six years before her death, when *Sense and Sensibility* made its public appearance), Austen had thus begun her mature work before her twenty-first birthday.

Life's Work

Austen's literary reputation rests on six novels, four of which were published during the last years of her life and two posthumously. Because she revised and retitled her early works before she was able to find a publisher for them, it is difficult to trace her development. Evidently, after a work was rejected, she would put it aside, begin another work, and then later revise the earlier one. Her most famous novel, *Pride and Prejudice*, for example, was the product of twelve or fourteen years of work; *Sense and Sensibility* took at least sixteen years and two revisions between conception and publication.

Austen's creative maturity can be divided into two major periods. During the first, she wrote three novels and vainly attempted to get them published. During the second, she revised, completed, and published two of her early novels and wrote three more, two of which were published before her death. It was only during the last half dozen years of her life, then, that she received the recognition her genius merited.

During her years at Steventon, Austen wrote the first version of what was to be her first published work. "Elinor and Marianne" was the story of two sisters whose lives were governed by two different principles. In every crisis, one tried to be sensible, while the other gave way to uncontrolled emotion. The theme was reflected in Austen's revision a year or two later, when she changed the title to *Sense and Sensibility*. It was under the second title that the novel, again revised, was finally published in 1811.

During 1797, Austen completed "First Impressions," which pointed out how foolish rash assessments of other people may be. Like *Sense and Sensibility*, this work told the love stories of two sisters; in this case, however, the prejudiced sister, with all of her faults, captures the reader, who can hardly wait for her to capture the proud nobleman. Tentatively, Austen's father offered the manuscript to a publisher, but the publisher refused even to read it. Austen put it away. In 1809 she revised it, and in 1813 it was published as *Pride and Prejudice*, which is still one of England's best-known and best-loved novels.

The third novel of the Steventon period, *Northanger Abbey* (1818; originally titled "Susan"), began as a satire of the gothic and sentimental novels that were so popular in the late eighteenth century. Like a gothic heroine, the central character is determined to find a murderer in the country house she visits; her curiosity is interpreted as bad manners, however, and she very nearly loses the eligible man who had invited her. Austen's genius could not be confined in a mere literary satire, however, and like her other works, *Northanger Abbey* is a full-fledged commentary on morals and manners.

Northanger Abbey is also interesting because it was the first novel Austen actually sold for publication. The publisher who bought it in 1803, however, evidently changed his plans, and six years later Austen paid him for its return. It was published the year after her death.

In 1801, George Austen suddenly decided to retire and to move his household to Bath, where he and his family lived until his death in 1805. Despite her reluctance to leave Steventon, Austen was fascinated with Bath, a famous watering place that was the setting both for *Northanger Abbey* and for *Persuasion* (1818). Whether her inability to publish discouraged her or she continued to work on her earlier manuscripts is a matter of conjecture; at any rate, *The Watsons*, begun in 1804, was never completed (although its fragment was published in 1871 in J. E. Austen-Leigh's *Memoir of Jane Austen*). In 1809, Jane, Cassandra, and their mother moved back to Hampshire, to a house in the village of Chawton, which had been made available to them by Jane's brother Edward Knight. Jane spent the remaining years of her life there, years that at last brought her success. In 1809, Jane revised *Sense and Sensibility* and *Pride and Prejudice*. Probably with the encouragement and help of her brother Henry Austen, who lived in London, in 1811 she found a publisher for *Sense and Sensibility*. Like all of her novels printed during her lifetime, it was published anonymously. It was also highly successful. In 1813, it was followed by *Pride and Prejudice*.

By 1813 Henry was too proud of his sister to keep her secret any longer and acknowledged that she was the author of these works. By this point in time she had written another novel, *Mansfield Park* (1814), a serious work dealing with religious and ethical issues, particularly as they relate to clerical life. After its publication, she wrote *Emma* (1816), thought by many to be her best novel, even though Jane worried that her readers might dislike the spoiled, snobbish heroine. Drawing from the world of her naval officer brothers, Jane then wrote her final completed novel, *Persuasion*, whose noble but misled heroine had once rejected her true love, a navy captain. Tragicomic in tone, *Persuasion* has often been considered to be Austen's most moving book.

Happy in her Chawton home, surrounded by family and friends, admired by the public and critics alike, and inspired with ideas for another novel, at the end of 1816 Austen seemed destined for years of happiness. She was struck down, however, by a debilitating and crippling illness. By March 1817, she had put aside her novel; by May, she had moved to nearby Winchester, where her physician lived; on July 18, she died. She was buried in Winchester Cathedral.

From *Dictionary of World Biography: The 19th Century.* Pasadena, CA: Salem Press, 1999. Copyright © 1999 by Salem Press, Inc.

Bibliography

Austen, Jane. *Jane Austen's Letters to Her Sister Cassandra and Others*. Edited by R. W. Chapman. 2 vols. Oxford, England: Clarendon Press, 1932. The first collection of surviving Austen letters is arranged chronologically in two volumes with appendices that give summary identifications of anyone who is ambiguously mentioned in the text of the letters. With corrected spelling and punctuation. Includes a map of eighteenth-century Berkshire and Surrey, England.

Brown, Julie Prewit. *Jane Austen's Novels*. Cambridge, Mass.: Harvard University Press, 1979. Provides a somewhat feminist perspective on Jane Austen as a conscious artist who masterfully employed ironic comedy and satiric realism. Five chapters explore the purpose and subtleties of each novel. Includes an eye-opening chapter on the artist as a woman writer.

Bush, Douglas. *Jane Austen*. New York: Macmillan, 1975. This work, addressed to general readers, shows how Austen re-created themes from many minor eighteenth-century writers. Each of Austen's major works is summarized and briefly analyzed in an individual chapter.

Copeland, Edward, and Juliet McMaster, eds. *The Cambridge Companion to Jane Austen*. New York: Cambridge University Press, 1997. This collection of thirteen new essays on Austen is divided between those concerning her own world and those that address modern critical discourse, such as Claudia L. Johnson's "Austen Cults and Cultures." Some essays focus on Austen's novels; others deal with broad issues in her works such as class consciousness, religion, and domestic economy. Includes a chronology and concludes with an assessment of late-twentieth-century developments in Austen scholarship.

Galperin, William H. *The Historical Austen*. Philadelphia: University of Pennsylvania Press, 2003. This study provides a fresh explication of Austen's work. Examines how Austen used her fiction to serve as a "social and political" tool.

Grey, J. David, ed. *The Jane Austen Companion*. New York: Macmillan, 1986. Collection of sixty-four essays from a wide range of academic and nonacademic lovers of Austen's art. Individual essays cover a great variety of subjects and take diverse approaches. A comprehensive guide to both real and imagined places, people, and literary allusion in Austen's work.

Halperin, John. *The Life of Jane Austen*. Baltimore: The Johns Hopkins University Press, 1984. A biographical study of Jane Austen's life with a focus on the association between the life of the artist and the works she produced. Valuable for a realistic look at the life of a legendary figure. Includes illustrations.

Lambdin, Laura Cooner, and Robert Thomas Lambdin, eds. *A Companion to Jane Austen Studies*. New York: Greenwood Press, 2000. Collection of twenty-two essays provides in-depth discussion of Austen's major works.

Lane, Maggie. *Jane Austen's England*. New York: St. Martin's Press, 1986. Fascinating book is full of illustrations that give Austen's readers a look at the world of her novels, taking the reader to the places Austen would have gone, usually through contemporary paintings. The text is informative; the first chapter, "The England of Jane Austen's Time," gives a good basic summary of social conditions around the beginning of the nineteenth century. Arranged chronologically and includes a map, a short bibliography, and an index.

Le Faye, Deirdre. *Jane Austen: A Family Record*. London: The British Library, 1989. A revision of the 1913 edition of *Life and Letters of Jane Austen*, written by a descendant of Austen's nephew James Edward. In addition, presents the results of extensive contemporary research. Provides a thorough look at Austen's life and the close-knit family on which she was financially dependent. Includes a chronology of Austen's life and an extensive family pedigree. With illustrations.

Lynch, Deidre, ed. *Janeites: Austen's Disciples and Devotees*. Princeton, N.J.: Princeton University Press, 2000. Collection of nine essays explores the novelist's position as an enduring cultural phenomenon.

Menon, Patricia. *Austen, Eliot, Charlotte Brontë, and the Mentor-Lover*. New York: Palgrave Macmillan, 2003. An examination of how Austen, Eliot, and Brontë handled matters of gender, sexuality, family, behavior, and freedom in their work.

Mooneyham, Laura G. *Romance, Language, and Education in Jane Austen's Novels*. New York: St. Martin's Press, 1986. Covers all six of Austen's complete novels with a focus on relationships among language, education, and romance. Asserts that the romance between heroine and hero is in itself educational for the heroine because romance offers the opportunity for open communication. This approach is provocative and useful, especially because it emphasizes Austen's own preoccupations.

Myer, Valerie Grosvenor. *Jane Austen: Obstinate Heart*. New York: Arcade, 1997. Biography emphasizes Austen's self-consciousness, born of her inferior social position and constant money worries.

Nokes, David. *Jane Austen: A Life*. New York: Farrar, Straus and Giroux, 1997. Lively, comprehensive biography provides a frank account of Austen's life.

Selwyn, David. *Jane Austen and Leisure*. London: Hambledon Press, 1999. Examines the manners and customs of Austen's class in her era and how Austen portrays them in her works.

Sulloway, Alison. *Jane Austen and the Province of Womanhood*. Philadelphia: University of Pennsylvania Press, 1989. Attempts to place Austen within a framework of "women-centered" authors such as Mary Astell, Mary Wollstonecraft Godwin, and Catharine Macaulay, to novelists Fanny Burney, Maria Edgeworth, and Charlotte Smith. Counters early views of Austen as a conservative woman upholding the status quo in her novels and suggests that she was a moderate feminist who sought reforms for women rather than outright revolution. A valuable resource; thought-provoking and not overly theoretical.

Tomalin, Claire. *Jane Austen: A Life*. New York: Alfred A. Knopf, 1998. Compelling account of Austen's life is exceedingly well written and attempts to tell the story from the subject's own perspective. Proceeding in chronological order, the book concludes with a postscript on the fates of Austen's family members and two interesting appendices: a note of Austen's final illness and an excerpt from the diary of Austen's niece Fanny.

Waldron, Mary. *Jane Austen and the Fiction of Her Time*. New York: Cambridge University Press, 1999. Puts Austen's writings in the context of other literary output of her era. Includes bibliographical references and index.

The *Paris Review* Perspective

Radhika Jones for *The Paris Review*

Everything you need to know about Jane Austen's style you can learn from the first sentence of her novel *Emma*: "Emma Woodhouse, handsome, clever, and rich, with a comfortable home and happy disposition seemed to unite some of the best blessings of existence; and had lived nearly twenty-one years in the world with very little to distress or vex her." The casual reader could easily come away from these words with the impression that the future looks rosy for our heroine. Yet, on closer inspection, it becomes clear that a few things are amiss. Emma's home and disposition only *seem* to unite the best blessings. And they seem to unite only *some* of these blessings. And if there is very little to distress or vex her, then it is incontrovertibly true that distress and vexation remain mathematical possibilities. In fact, at second glance, it seems a safe bet that the novel will consist of exploiting precisely those moments of distress and vexation. This is, in short, a sentence with a happy disposition on the surface but hidden depths beneath. In that way, it is not unlike Emma herself. And with its wealth of smoothly gilded signifiers, it is a perfect example of Jane Austen at work.

Austen was born to a rector and his wife in Hampshire, England, in 1775, well before the days of the author interview or the celebrity writer. No matter: she is a celebrity now. In terms of canonical heft, Austen's name is often twinned with that of Shakespeare. In the ratio of novels written to novels still widely read, she bats an easy 1.000. (That might not sound like such a singular achievement, but it is hard to get a hit every time, as anyone who has ever read Dickens's epic clunker

Barnaby Rudge knows.) Even her juvenilia is worshipped in Janeite circles, her youthful misspellings lovingly preserved in editions of her early epistolary tale "Love and Freindship." She kept no diary, so we have little more than a telegraph version of her life: birth, death, a few domestic travels, and basic family relationships. Some, but not all, of her correspondence survives. What we know of her writing life has passed into the realm of mythology, a scene worthy of one of her novels: Jane weaving her amusing tales in the drawing room amid the hubbub of family conversation.

As for her personal life, although Austen propelled so many charming (and a few less charming) heroines into the waiting arms of well-matched grooms, she never married. Like the Brontës, George Eliot, and Virginia Woolf, she was childless. Yet as the author of six turn-of-the-nineteenth-century novels that vary only slightly in their perfection (a good way to start a fight in literary circles is to voice a preference for dark horse *Mansfield Park*), Jane Austen is the matriarch of entire prose traditions, from the novel of manners to the narrative mode of free indirect discourse. The marriage or dating self-help book, albeit a bastardized child, has a drop of Austen's blood in it. So does the Harlequin romance. Countless other women were writing novels about young girls seeking love at the time Austen wrote; we know this because she mocks their dark-and-stormy gothic thrillers in her parody of the form, *Northanger Abbey*. But it is Austen who has stuck, because she distilled those romantic impulses into a style that is indisputably literary. If you wonder whether her heavyweight chops were recognized from the outset, know that her near-exact contemporary Sir Walter Scott was a fan; he gave *Emma* a rave review.

Part of what has kept her work alive is the dramatic power of her storytelling. Consider *Pride and Prejudice*, the iconic example of the Austen marriage plot. Its opening sentence—"It is a truth universally acknowledged, that a single man in possession of a good fortune, must be in want of a wife"—foretells the arrival of Mr. Bingley, single and wealthy as billed, and his desire to marry the beautiful, virtuous Jane Bennet. The novel proves to be less about Bingley, however, than about his wealthier and even more single friend, Mr. Darcy, who pairs off with Jane's witty sister Elizabeth. For both couples, the path of true love is made rough by meddling siblings and a debauched elopement. For a while, it looks as if the universally acknowledged truth will not carry the day. But things do finally work out for Bingley and Jane, prompting Mrs. Bennet—as vulgar a mother as you'll find in English fiction—to pronounce happily over her eldest daughter: "I was sure you could not be so beautiful for nothing!" It all reads comically until you realize the deep-seated fear behind that line, that Jane Bennet could very easily have been beautiful for nothing—or worse, for the generations of women who have identified with her, that Lizzy could have been clever for nothing. (I am indebted to D. A. Miller for this observation.) For these two worthy young women, marriage is their only way up and out. And yet it is an institution over which they have barely any agency. Mrs. Bennet's unapologetic attempts to maximize her girls' romantic opportunities are simply survivalist tactics in a cruel and uncertain world, one that cared very little for the fate of its daughters.

This is the world in which Austen trafficked, with a light touch but a serious understanding of its stakes: that virtue and talent could go to waste, that lives could go to waste. Critics who question how a writer of such prodigious gifts could confine herself to mere love and friendship miss that point. In remarking on Austen's general omission of history in her plots, Salman Rushdie, in his 2005 *Paris Review* interview, cites it as indicative of one of her virtues. "The function of the British army in the novels of Jane Austen is to look cute at parties," he says. "It's not because she's ducking something, it's that she can fully and profoundly explain the lives of her characters without a reference to the public sphere." In an Austen novel life is what happens on a small canvas—the meetings and picnics and dances in which her heroes and heroines take part—and the reason for her enduring popularity and power is that even in our modern, interconnected world, that truth about life still holds, as much as the one about the rich guy looking for a wife.

Bibliography

Austen, Jane. *Emma*. 1816.
_____. *Mansfield Park*. 1814.
_____. *Northanger Abbey*. 1818.
_____. *Persuasion*. 1818.
_____. *Pride and Prejudice*. 1813.
_____. *Sense and Sensibility*. 1811.
Grey, J. David, ed. *The Jane Austen Companion*. New York: Macmillan, 1986.
Miller, D. A. *Jane Austen, or, The Secret of Style*. Princeton, NJ: Princeton UP, 2003.
Rushdie, Salman. "The Art of Fiction No. 186." Interview with Jack Livings. *The Paris Review* 174 (Summer 2005).

CRITICAL
CONTEXTS

Jane Austen:
A Cultural and Historical Context_____

Neil Heims

Neil Heims sees in Austen's novels an ongoing struggle—between social propriety on one hand and personal integrity on the other. Social mores pull one way; a need to be true to oneself pulls the other. A similar struggle, Heims argues, was taking place in eighteenth-century Britain as public discourse sought to reckon with the trauma of the seventeenth century's civil wars. Women's place in this discourse was a topic of great discussion in the seventeenth and eighteenth centuries and has remained so through the twentieth and into the twenty-first. In this essay, we get a portrait of Austen as "a writer of novels detailing the careers of women who are torn between defining themselves and establishing their own integrity on one hand and conforming to the socially imposed codes of behavior and propriety on the other."   — J.L.

Concern for integrity is a common value and a recurring theme in the novels of Jane Austen. Integrity, in Austen's work, is a quality that gives the person who commands it moral and human authority. It is a sign of having touched the realm of truth and realized truthfulness in oneself. Austen's concern for determining integrity is a concern for determining truth. Integrity confers on a person who possesses it the power to serve as a model or epitome of a type of virtue and goodness. Austen's characters, as they achieve their proper completeness, soundness, and truthfulness, easily become examples of how readers ought to live, think, and behave. Overcoming error and becoming critically aware of oneself are at the moral center of Austen's novels. They are always about behavior, about what behavior reveals, about what ought and ought not be revealed or tolerated in oneself and others, and about the proper responsibilities individuals have to themselves and owe to others.

Such a concern for integrity underpinning the action of her work suggests that in order to power her plots, Austen sets mutually exclusive, opposing views, attitudes, stances, and desires, embodied in her characters, in conflict with each other in a quest to uncover what constitutes integrity. Austen sets her characters the problem of discovering and dealing with their own and one another's ideals and delusions or failing to do so. In Austen's novels there are rights and wrongs. They are discovered and defined through the agency of the plot and the actions and reactions of the characters. That is what moral fiction, which is what Austen writes, is about, separating what is right from what is not. Certain principles and ways of behaving are correct and acceptable; others are not and cause imbalance in personality and threaten social propriety. Austen's novels constitute, impelled by the problems of their plots, the working out, as in a geometrical demonstration, of just what integrity is and offer demonstrations of its effect or of the effect of the lack of integrity on the individual and in society.

What constitutes individual integrity and social propriety is subject to interpretation. Should integrity be defined by one's adherence to a set of values such as those underpinning this advice by Lord Chesterfield to his son, proffered in 1752?

> Good manners, to those one does not love, are no more a breach of truth, than "your humble servant" at the bottom of a challenge is; they are universally agreed upon and understood, to be things of course. They are necessary guards of the decency and peace of society; they must only act defensively; and then not with arms poisoned by perfidy. Truth, but not the whole truth, must be the invariable principle of every man, who hath either religion, honor, or prudence. Those who violate it may be cunning, but they are not able. Lies and perfidy are the refuge of fools and cowards. (84)

This is practical advice that presupposes a moral context. That moral context is established in the beginning of the passage by the concern demonstrated for guarding "the decency and peace of society" and in the conclusion by condemning "lies and perfidy." In between, however, there is an important equivocation: reserve a part of yourself and your reactions. "Truth, but not the whole truth," is what "every man who hath either religion, honor, or prudence" owes to any other man, Lord Chesterfield says, and that is all that anyone else may properly expect of him. It also seems like a way to maintain social peace and prevent insult or offense. But there is a fine line between such practical virtue and the vice of hypocrisy, between the well-mannered man and the hidden and scheming man lurking beneath the well-mannered gentleman who eschews giving open offense. The problem of the proper degree of transparency is repeatedly explored by Austen.

In contrast to Lord Chesterfield's advice, is integrity the quality of being and behaving as it is defined by Austen's Emma? In criticism of the charming but devious Frank Churchill, Emma describes him by the qualities that are wanting in him. He is "so unlike what a man should be! None of that upright integrity, that strict adherence to truth and principle, that disdain of trick and littleness, which a man should display in every transaction of his life" (*Emma* 290). Implicitly, Emma does not admire the kind of reservation that Lord Chesterfield suggests; that there are times one ought to loosen one's hold on truth and maintain politeness. But in Emma's version of virtue, too, there is a fine line between virtue and fault. When "that strict adherence to truth and principle" ignores the humanity and complexity of the one to whom it is addressed, it can become quite like the "poisoned arms" against which Lord Chesterfield warns. Integrity, then, while achievable as a quality of character, is not something fixed and mathematical. It is a quality shaped by a conscious balancing and harmonizing of possibly conflicting character elements and by awareness of one's effect on others, as Emma herself realizes and as both Elizabeth Bennet and Mr. Darcy learn in *Pride and Prejudice*. It is achieved through balance, as the Dashwood sisters demonstrate in *Sense and Sensibility*.

Austen's concern for integrity comes after a century that can be understood primarily by its awareness of the essential fact of division and conflict in human affairs, a century given its cultural definition by the argumentativeness of its leading figures. It is the century in which ideas were established in print and arguments were carried out publicly in print regarding civil, political, ecclesiastical, economic, literary, behavioral, aesthetic, and moral issues. It was the century filled with the disputes and disputations of such moralists as Daniel Defoe, Jonathan Swift, Alexander Pope, Joseph Addison and Richard Steele, Samuel Johnson, and a host of lesser-known figures who were all dedicated to defining and advancing standards for proper behavior. It was also a century in which a number of women writers wrote mostly, but not exclusively, about manners and duties, openly as women, despite the cultural restrictions placed on women that legally subordinated women to men. But women also wrote novels and sometimes works of scholarship. Between 1763 and 1783, Catharine Macaulay, for example, wrote and published an eight-volume history of England beginning with the ascension of James I to the throne of England in 1601. Austen followed suit at the age of fifteen, when she wrote a mock history of England for her family's entertainment.

The eighteenth century was propelled by the idea that men can construct their lives or ruin them by the quality of their moral choices. Moral choices, as grounds for behavior, were not separable from practical choices, and, together, they could be adduced through reason, experience, argument, and even polemic. Austen's novels are propelled by a similar regard for the importance of moral choices and a belief in their practical manifestations. The great and seminal idea looming over the eighteenth century is that those choices and the men who make them must be in conflict but that conflict can be socially confined to civil arguments and that the medium for those arguments is writing, wherein disputation about matters of life and death, wealth and poverty, pleasure and pain, rights and obligations, independence and subjugation can be contemplated. The ideal of intellectual disputation in conversation or in print, however, was often mocked and subverted by the brutal and bloody military conflicts that marred and shaped the century.

The national military conflicts of the eighteenth century forcefully give authority to the proposition expounded by Thomas Hobbes in *Leviathan*, his treatise on power, government, and social order, published in 1651. Hobbes wrote in a passage that has become well known:

> Hereby it is manifest, that during the time men live without a common power to keep them all in awe, they are in that condition which is called war; and such a war, as is of every man, against every man. For war, consisteth not in battle only, or the act of fighting; but in a tract of time, wherein the will to contend by battle is sufficiently known: and therefore the notion of *time,* is to be considered in the nature of war; as it is in the nature of weather. For as the nature of foul weather, lieth not in a shower or two of rain; but in an inclination thereto of many days together: so the nature of war, consisteth not in actual fighting; but in the known disposition thereto, during all the time there is no assurance to the contrary. All other time is peace.
>
> Whatsoever therefore is consequent to a time of war, where every man is enemy to every man; the same consequent to the time, wherein men live without other security, than what their own strength, and their own invention shall furnish them withal. In such condition, there is no place for industry; because the fruit thereof is uncertain: and consequently no culture of the earth; no navigation, nor use of the commodities that may be imported by sea; no commodious building; no instruments of moving, and removing such things as require much force; no knowledge of the face of the earth; no account of time; no arts; no letters; no society; and which is worst of all, continual fear, and danger of violent death; and the life of man, solitary, poor, nasty, brutish, and short. (84)

This is primarily an account of human nature that condemns humankind to wretchedness because it sees overwhelming self-interest, aggression, and conflict as being fundamental to the human character.

Folded within this depiction of strife and chaos, however, is a catalog of what is stifled by such chaos. Hobbes offers a description of a nicely functioning social order, one based on and allowing industry, navigation, trade, building, science, art, literature, security, and comfort. In order to ensure the social peace that will allow such sociable commerce, Hobbes argues the need for a strong social order reinforced by both a machinery of governance above and beyond individuals and individual dispositions attuned to that external ordering power. Eighteenth-century moralists wrote striving toward that positive model, but the century was a time of extensive military conflict and violent upheaval in the social order and the international order.

The century began with the War of the Spanish Succession, 1701-1714, in which England and other European powers fought to prevent France from taking control of Spain. It was a war waged not only in Europe but, as Queen Anne's War, also between the English and the French in their North American colonies. The English were at war again in 1727, fighting to control Gibraltar. In 1740, the English lost Florida to Spain. In 1744, the English and the French, with the First Carnatic War in India, began a long series of battles for imperial domination that encompassed the globe. They fought a series of wars in India, Europe, and North America, until 1763, when the English achieved apparent but short-lived domination, as the American Revolutionary War against British domination would demonstrate. Throughout the century, too, the English were involved in military and political struggles with Scotland and Ireland over the issue of national and political authority. In addition to external strife, the French faced the upheaval of a domestic revolution beginning in 1789. Although the French Revolution was founded on the desire to advance "the rights of man," it was of an exceptionally brutal and bloody sort. Its very brutality signified that the revolutionary fervor defined "man" as an abstraction rather than as an individual. At its worst, the French Revolution determined that people must be thought of as socially constructed units rather than as particular persons the nature of whose behavior, as in

Austen's novels, determines and defines the nature and quality of their society. In 1792, and continuing until 1815, under Napoleon, France became a powerfully belligerent force on the international scene.

The assertion of power and hegemony within the context of conflict and competition occurred as much in the economic sphere as in the military. In 1708, the United Company of Merchants of England Trading to the East Indies was formed. In 1773, the British East India Company began to smuggle opium into China. Several acts of the English Parliament aimed at increasing revenues for the Crown—such as the Molasses Act of 1733, the Sugar Act of 1764, and the Stamp Act of 1765, directed against England's American colonies—were strong catalysts for the American Revolutionary War.

The eighteenth century—steeped in Hobbes's somber understanding of the violence of human nature and caught in a political situation whose military underpinnings and engagements and whose imperial, mercantile motives and activities seemed to reinforce Hobbes's views—was, just because of its strife, division, and brutality, a century of struggle against that perceived inherent human barbarism. The struggle was mainly one of determining and disseminating a morality of behavior. Eighteenth-century England was programmatically devoted to establishing norms of social politeness and individual decorum. Argument about what is proper became the century's chief discourse in England, whether in regard to religious authority, political power, the rights and obligations of men and women, social intercourse, or Shakespearean texts. That discourse was conducted primarily in print. The idea of print as a vehicle for daily civic intercourse and social conversation was introduced at the very start of the century. In 1701 and 1702, the *Daily Courant* and the *Norwich Post* became the first daily newspapers printed in England.

The importance of public discourse was, in large measure, the result of the political and economic changes that defined the eighteenth century and required the widespread dissemination of information. Despite the restoration of the monarchy in 1660, with the defeat of the Puritan Commonwealth and the return of Charles II to the throne of England, the kind of absolute monarchy that had existed before the revolution of the 1640s was not reestablished. The monarch was no longer at the center of the British state—imperial entrepreneurs were. Court intrigues were giving way to business deals, financial arrangements, and individuals who were endeavoring to relocate themselves in the social hierarchy. Bureaucrats, in their role of raising and distributing revenues, especially for England's expanding military operations, were at the center, and shareholders, composed of landowners, merchants, and tradesmen, were collectively investing capital in commonly held trade companies. This fragmentation, distribution, and reconstitution of power made public discourse essential. The rise of printing and publishing made it technically feasible. The construction of a common culture and a polite language of discourse made it socially possible. The journalists, moralists, and novelists of the eighteenth century were engaged in creating the shared culture and the common discourse that could contain disparate individuals, making them part of something they could consider they were holding in common, a culture and a tradition that they were sharing despite a variety of interests that might even be in competition with one another.

At the vanguard of the effort to create a strong moral personality in the British was a series of books, broadsheets, and pamphlets that constructed a literature of manners. In addition to newspapers and publications such as *The Spectator* and *The Tatler*, there were conduct books. That a book might be written to serve exclusively as a guide for one's behavior was not an idea new in the eighteenth century. An important model of such conduct books was *The Courtier*, written by the Italian poet and diplomat Baldassare Castiglione; this immensely popular and widely translated anatomy of the characteristics that constitute a gentleman was published in 1528 in Venice. Jean de La Bruyère's *Manners of the Age* (1688) was another important instructional manual on how to live, cited and commended by Dr. Johnson in his "Life of Addison." In eighteenth-century England, Addison and Steele, with *The*

Spectator and *The Tatler*, began to lay the foundations for a common British civic culture. In their daily essays they set forth what is appropriate matter for conversation and what is not. They discussed how one ought to dress and became arbiters of taste in literature, the theater, and the opera. Through a series of surrogate, fictional characters, they debated moral and social issues. Such was their influence that Dr. Johnson in the "Life of Addison," in his *Lives of the English Poets,* asserted that "before the Tatler and Spectator . . . no writers had yet undertaken to reform either the savageness of neglect or the impertinence of civility; to show when to speak or to be silent; how to refuse or how to comply. . . . [A] judge of propriety, was yet wanting, who should survey the track of daily conversation, and free it from thorns and prickles" (*Works* 1825, 329). In addition, Addison and Steele laid the foundation for the midcentury conduct books, which were frequently addressed to women. Addison clearly presented the role of women in the emerging order of the eighteenth century in *The Spectator.* "Had our Species no Females in it," Addison wrote, on July 17, 1712,

> Men would be quite different Creatures from what they are at present; their Endeavors to please the opposite Sex, polishes and refines them out of those Manners which are most natural to them. . . . [M]an would . . . be . . . but a rude, unfinished Creature, were he conversant with none but of his own Make. (quoted in Irvine 10, sp. 433)

Women of the emerging middle class were not assigned simply to the domestic tasks while men were occupied in the world but to the *domesticating* tasks that would temper the way men played their roles in the world. This female role required schooling. The idea of schooling for women had been broached in the 1690s. In 1694, Mary Astell published *A Serious Proposal to the Ladies for the Advancement of Their True and Greatest Interest*, calling for religious education on a college level for aristocratic women. Her goal was to render women capable of withstanding the moral challenges of the world. In 1700, Astell's *Re-*

flections upon Marriage appeared, arguing against a husband's institutional right to absolute domination over his wife. In 1697, Defoe advocated in the subsection headed "Academy for Women" in the "Of Academies" section of his *Essay upon Projects*, a more comprehensive education than Astell suggested. "I have often thought of it," Defoe wrote,

> as one of the most barbarous customs in the world, considering us as a civilised and a Christian country, that we deny the advantages of learning to women. We reproach the sex every day with folly and impertinence, while I am confident, had they the advantages of education equal to us, they would be guilty of less than ourselves.
>
> One would wonder indeed how it should happen that women are conversable at all, since they are only beholding to natural parts for all their knowledge. Their youth is spent to teach them to stitch and sew, or make baubles. They are taught to read indeed, and perhaps to write their names, or so, and that is the height of a woman's education. And I would but ask any who slight the sex for their understanding, What is a man (a gentleman, I mean) good for that is taught no more?

In 1790, when Jane Austen was fifteen, Catharine Macaulay published *Letters on Education*. Macaulay had, seven years earlier, published the last of her eight-volume history of England. She was a staunch supporter of republicanism and both the American and the French revolutions. In the *Letters on Education*, Macaulay advocated identical education for girls and boys. She argued:

> Let us devote the first ten or twelve years of life to the strengthening of the corporal faculties, to the giving of useful habits, and to those attainments which can be acquired, without burthening the mind with ideas which it cannot well comprehend. The Latin grammar: geography taught in the easiest and pleasantest manner, such parts of physics as lie open to the attention of children; writing, arithmetic, and the French language. (128)

As children grew older or showed particular interest, Macaulay would add to this load, including a special study of Addison's prose as a guide to good writing.

Macaulay's views were more radical than what had been generally proposed regarding women's education and, consequently, women's social position. The school for women, in eighteenth-century England, was chiefly conducted inside the covers of a number of conduct books. Among them was James Fordyce's *Sermons to Young Women* (1766), which Austen delicately subverts in *Pride and Prejudice*. In chapter 14, priggish Mr. Collins, who disdains to read novels, reads three pages from it aloud, "with monotonous solemnity," to the assembled company after dinner before he is interrupted by the frivolous and garrulous Lydia Bennet. Miffed, Mr. Collins refuses to continue once Lydia is silenced, lamenting that he has "often observed how little young ladies are interested by books of a serious stamp, though written solely for their benefit. It amazes me, I confess;—for certainly, there can be nothing so advantageous to them as instruction" (52). Other such instructive works include Lord Halifax's *Advice to a Daughter* (1688); John Gregory's *A Father's Legacy to His Daughters* (1774), which has chapters headed "Religion," "Conduct and Behaviour," "Amusements," and "Friendship, Love, Marriage"; Hester Chapone's *Letters on the Improvement of the Mind* (1773), which instructs girls in the virtues of religion and includes a syllabus of classical masterpieces; Chapone's *A Letter to a New-Married Lady* (1777); and Thomas Gisborne's *An Enquiry into the Duties of the Female Sex* (1797). These books, no matter how respectful of a woman's capability, and even when the products of female authorship, instruct women to subordinate themselves and their needs to men and theirs.

It was in this moral, intellectual, and cultural climate that Jane Austen pursued her career as a writer of novels detailing the careers of women who are torn between defining themselves and establishing their own integrity on one hand and conforming to the socially imposed codes of behavior and propriety on the other. It was a climate in which women writers, although there were a number of them, were yet regarded as peculiar, as, in Dr. Johnson's words, "Amazons of the pen." "In former times," Johnson wrote in 1753, in *The Adventurer*, "the pen, like the sword, was considered as consigned by nature to the hands of men; the ladies contented themselves with private virtues and domestic excellence" (*Works* 1846, 343). There is a suggestion that a lady writing is going against nature. Yet a lady reading was not considered exceptional, and the two greatest of the eighteenth-century novelists, Samuel Richardson and Henry Fielding, were authors with large female readerships. Their novels, moreover, are much concerned with the manners, morals, and hazards of womanhood and the depredations of the male nature.

The novel as a genre, at least since 1605, with the appearance of Miguel de Cervantes's *Don Quixote*, in which the hero is impelled to take up the practice of knight errantry in his contemporary Spain because of the almost hypnotic influence of the chivalric romances he was in the habit of reading, was regarded with suspicion because of anxiety about the power of its influence to blur in readers' minds the distinction between fantasy and reality or vice and virtue, and to provoke behavior modeled on its content. Richardson and Fielding both took the subjects of moral behavior, social responsibility, and the disturbing effects of sexual passion as matter for their novels. Likewise, both dissimulated their identity as novelists. In novels like *Clarissa* and *Pamela*, Richardson purported to be the editor who was presenting collections of letters he had come to possess. Fielding, in *Tom Jones*, describes himself as a historian and his book as a history. In both cases the authors, aside from feigning to elevate their status as writers performing more respectable and credible tasks than novelists, are endeavoring to blur the line between fiction and reality. In the process, they are attempting to re-create and transmit a sense of the real world and of real people undergoing real trials. But the literary nature of their work is hardly disguised. In direct addresses to the reader in *Tom Jones*, Fielding establishes the literary nature of his narrative and often comments on the problems of composition.

Fielding and Richardson carried on a vitalizing ongoing competition in their novels, parodying each other's work. Fielding's Joseph Andrews is the brother of Richardson's Pamela, and Richardson's *Sir Charles Grandison* was written in response to *Tom Jones*. They added to a literature supposedly true to life a dimension that was entirely defined by its allusiveness to literature. The third in the great mid-eighteenth-century triumvirate of novelists, Laurence Sterne, in *Tristram Shandy*, focused, as Austen usually would, on the domestic life of a family at once typical of middle-class English country gentry and idiosyncratic.

Another sort of novel became popular toward the end of the eighteenth century. It, too, achieved resonance because of its nature as a hybrid. But unlike the faux histories of Fielding, the epistolary compilations of Richardson, and Sterne's psychological convolutions, it sought not to approach realism but to counteract it. It was moral not by precept but by its challenge to morality. The gothic novel combined elements of reality and fantasy, of the natural and the supernatural realms, of decadent landscape and tormented dreamscape, in order to create, inside an ambience defined by menace and horror, a bizarre psychological terrain where the energy of reemerging repressed material, centering essentially on sexuality and on class distinctions, can be represented and released. Gothic fiction first appeared in England, in 1765, with the publication of Horace Walpole's *The Castle of Otranto*. The genre was developed and, in a sense, domesticated by two women, Clara Reeve and Ann Radcliffe. Reeve's *The Champion of Virtue*, a reinvention of *The Castle of Otranto,* appeared in 1777. Radcliffe's *The Mysteries of Udolpho* appeared in 1794. It enjoyed great popularity, especially among women, and is marked by the author's trick of providing natural explanations for what appeared at first to be supernatural occurrences. *Northanger Abbey*, which Austen wrote in 1798 but which was not published until after her death, incorporates a parody of the gothic novel inside a novel of manners and, like all of Austen's work, a novel of enlightenment. It is highly referential not only in its devices but also in the actual references Austen's characters make to books like

Udolpho, Sir Charles Grandison, and *Tom Jones.* Austen is not only drawing from the literary context within which she commences to write, she is also clearing a path for herself through that context and opening up a space for her own work and for a sensibility that is both contained by her context and straining against it. Her heroines are women of their century yet individuals who struggle with its forms. In addition, Austen challenges the value of reading novels and, by bringing the objection forward, implicitly defends the novel as a genre and placates the reader—who is, after all, engaged in the very activity of reading a novel at this moment of intersection.

> Catherine, after listening and agreeing as long as she could, with all the civility and deference of the youthful female mind, fearful of hazarding an opinion of its own in opposition to that of a self-assured man . . . ventured at length to vary the subject by a question which had been long uppermost in her thoughts; it was, "Have you ever read *Udolpho,* Mr. Thorpe?"
>
> "*Udolpho!* Oh, Lord! Not I; I never read novels; I have something else to do."
>
> Catherine, humbled and ashamed, was going to apologize for her question, but he prevented her by saying, "Novels are all so full of nonsense and stuff; there has not been a tolerably decent one come out since *Tom Jones,* except *The Monk;* I read that t'other day; but as for all the others, they are the stupidest things in creation."
>
> "I think you must like *Udolpho,* if you were to read it; it is so very interesting."
>
> "Not I, faith! No, if I read any, it shall be Mrs. Radcliffe's; her novels are amusing enough; they are worth reading; some fun and nature in them."
>
> "*Udolpho* was written by Mrs. Radcliffe," said Catherine, with some hesitation, from the fear of mortifying him.
>
> "No sure; was it? Aye, I remember, so it was; I was thinking of that other stupid book, written by that woman they make such a fuss about, she who married the French emigrant."
>
> "I suppose you mean *Camilla?*"

"Yes, that's the book; such unnatural stuff! . . . I took up the first volume once and looked it over, but I soon found it would not do; indeed I guessed what sort of stuff it must be before I saw it: as soon as I heard she had married an emigrant, I was sure I should never be able to get through it."

"I have never read it."

"You had no loss, I assure you; it is the horridest nonsense you can imagine; . . ."

This critique, the justness of which was unfortunately lost on poor Catherine, brought them to the door of Mrs. Thorpe's lodgings, and the feelings of the discerning and unprejudiced reader of *Camilla* gave way to the feelings of the dutiful and affectionate son, as they met Mrs. Thorpe, who had descried them from above, in the passage. (*Northanger Abbey* 32-33)

Austen's satire is caustic. Mr. Thorpe is, clearly, the lesser intelligence in this colloquy, yet Austen shows, without needing to comment beyond a sly animadversion to Mr. Thorpe as a "discerning and unprejudiced reader," which, clearly, he is not, that his social role allows him to exercise unearned authority over his female interlocutor. She, Catherine Morland, despite (or because of) a freer sensibility than his, is prey to an imagination, like Don Quixote's, that has been heated by the fictions she has read, gothic novels in her case, rather than chivalric romances, and she sees signs of gothic horror in the mundane features of life at Northanger Abbey. Moralist that she is, Austen shows that human disregard for the humanity of others is of more real concern than the prevailing literary Grand Guignol.

The author of *Camilla*, so disesteemed by Mr. Thorpe for her marriage to a Frenchman as well as for that novel, is Fanny Burney (1752-1840), a prolific and very popular writer whose *Evelina* and *Cecilia* as well as *Camilla* were important novels for Austen because they were examples of work by a woman and because they concerned issues that exercised Austen in her novels, particularly with their often satiric focus on the lives and manners of the English gentry and the condition of women.

Although her work is composed and calm despite the turmoil of feelings her characters undergo and despite the upheavals in the greater world that seldom seem to touch their daily lives very strongly, Austen lived in a period of great transition. In her six novels, Austen depicts an era that is ending and its little disturbances, and she hints at an era to come and its great disruptions.

Works Cited and Consulted

Austen, Jane. *Emma*. 1816. New York: Modern Library, 2001.

_____. *Northanger Abbey*. 1818. New York: Cambridge UP, 2006.

_____. *Pride and Prejudice*. 1813. New York: Oxford UP, 2004.

Bradbrook, Frank W. *Jane Austen and Her Predecessors*. New York: Cambridge UP, 1966.

Butler, Marilyn. *Jane Austen and the War of Ideas*. Oxford, England: Clarendon Press, 1975.

Chesterfield, Earl of. *Letters to His Son: On the Fine Art of Becoming a Man of the World and a Gentleman*. New York: M. Walter Dunne, 1901.

Copeland, Edward, and Juliet McMaster, eds. *The Cambridge Companion to Jane Austen*. New York: Cambridge UP, 1997.

Craik, W. A. *Jane Austen in Her Time*. London: Thomas Nelson and Sons, 1969.

Defoe, Daniel. "Of Academies." *An Essay upon Projects*. http://ebooks.adelaide.edu.au/d/defoe/daniel/d31es/part16.html

Hannon, Patrice. *101 Things You Didn't Know About Jane Austen*. Avon, MA: Adams Media, 2007.

Hobbes, Thomas. *Leviathan*. 1651. New York: Oxford UP, 2008.

Honan, Park. *Jane Austen: Her Life*. New York: St. Martin's Press, 1987.

Irvine, Robert P. *Jane Austen*. New York: Routledge, 2005.

Johnson, Samuel. *The Works of Samuel Johnson, L.L.D.* Philadelphia, 1825.

_____. *The Works of Samuel Johnson, LL.D.* New York: Alexander V. Blake, 1846.

Macaulay, Catharine. *Letters on Education*. 1790. New York: Woodstock Books, 1994.

Smithers, David Waldron. *Jane Austen in Kent*. London: Hurtwood, 1981.

Jane Austen:
The Critical Reception

Bonnie Blackwell

Although Austen was little known in her own lifetime, shortly after her death her critical ascent began: in 1830 the *Edinburgh Review* acknowledged that "Miss Austen has never been so popular as she deserved to be," and each succeeding generation has worked to compensate for that early oversight. Today an entire critical industry is devoted to explicating Austen's small canon. A typical year now sees the publication of more than 150 articles and fifteen critical books on Austen's life and works, and every critic who discusses the English novel as a genre has to account for her achievement. She has therefore played a part in virtually every wave of literary criticism. She has been subjected to New Critical investigations of irony; she has been put on the couch by Freudians; she has been critiqued for her class consciousness by Marxists; she has been interrogated by disciples of feminism, queer studies, and gender studies. In this essay, Bonnie Blackwell offers an overview of that long critical tradition, beginning with the readings Austen got from her family and close friends and continuing to the present.   — J.L.

During his 1868 term as England's prime minister, Benjamin Disraeli (1804-1881) was asked if he found time to read novels. In Disraeli's surprising reply—"All six of them, every year"—the PM, himself a novelist since the age of twenty-two, obliterates the whole genre of novels from competition for his attention while asserting the utter centrality of *Pride and Prejudice* (1813), *Sense and Sensibility* (1811), *Mansfield Park* (1814), *Emma* (1816), *Persuasion* (1818), and *Northanger Abbey* (1818) to British heritage, so well known that they and their author need not be named. Disraeli invites us to imagine what about reading Austen has prepared him to be prime minister or consoled him when the job was fatiguing. We need not puzzle too long on what aspect of Austen's prose enabled him to give this precisely crafted answer, for her heroines' reading habits are often subject to impertinent queries. Catherine Morland fares poorly when Henry Tilney disparages her taste for "nice books," by which he supposes she means well-bound ones (*Northanger Abbey* 121). Caroline Bingley attempts to lower Lizzy Bennet in Darcy's estimation by sardonically accusing her of being "a great reader who has no pleasure in anything else" (*Pride and Prejudice* 74). Her reply, that "I deserve neither such praise nor such censure," is a model for Disraeli in how to sidestep the intellectual trap of being judged socially for one's private reading; to her creator he gives all the credit.

In this anecdote, a testimony both to Austen's ability to predict human nature and to her lessons in style, we find the dual nature of Austen's reception throughout the nearly two hundred years since the publication of her first novel, *Sense and Sensibility*, in 1811. Critics address a variety of concerns, from the status of women and the disenfranchised to the price of sugar or barouches, but most critical treatments of Austen fall into two broad camps: those that judge her by a standard of realism, thereby comparing the books to lived experience, either of the Regency or the present; and those that address some aspect of her style, especially her use of irony. Some generations of realist-bound criticism find her books reprehensibly silent on such historical events as the Atlantic slave trade and the Napoleonic Wars. Other critical schools invoke a different strain of realism, the psychological realism of recognizable and nuanced human personalities, and find much to admire in Austen's psychological portraits. Her foolish vicars, more concerned with brokering their own advantageous marriages than with caring for the spiritual lives of their brethren, and her selfish mothers blind to their children's faults continue to resonate with this school.

Biography and Early Reception

Jane Austen has been the subject of numerous biographies, including several written by family members and recent standouts by John Halperin and Claire Tomalin.[1] All note the centrality of her family to the formation of her character. She was the seventh of eight children born to the rector of Steventon, Hampshire, on December 16, 1775. Her family was neither rich nor well connected, but the Austens were literary: her father's library included some five hundred volumes that were sold at his retirement for about £200 (Halperin 127), or approximately $40,000 in today's terms. This was a shocking indulgence on the income of a clergyman who had eight children and who frequently appealed to relatives to cover his debts, but the library was a wonderful resource for a fledgling novelist. By her teens, Austen was an energetic, productive author of arch, knowing prose; reading it, one wonders how she achieved so much worldliness at fifteen. Her pleasure in recording the world's folly continued until her distressingly early death at age forty-one, of symptoms many have interpreted as Addison's disease.[2]

Austen's precocious start in the literary life ripened into a highly fertile period in her early twenties. At twenty-one, she wrote "First Impressions" in 1796-97; she later revised it in 1810 and 1813 into *Pride and Prejudice*. In 1797, Austen began converting a two-year-old manuscript, "Elinor and Marianne," into *Sense and Sensibility*, and in 1798-99, she composed works published posthumously as *Lady Susan* and *Northanger Abbey*. She sold *Northanger Abbey* (then called "Susan," though unrelated to the novella *Lady Susan*) in 1802 for £10 to a publisher, Crosby, who advertised it but never printed it; she was finally able to purchase the work back for the same price in 1816 (Halperin 101). Despite early signs of brilliance, Austen did not see her work in print until age thirty-five, and she enjoyed only six years of moderate financial gain from her works. Her earnings from those six years—£670, or about $130,000—were offset by losses on *Mansfield Park* and family debts, but even in gross they are equivalent only to what Maria

Edgeworth, the most successful woman writer of her day, earned yearly in her career, which spanned several decades. Austen was not, then, the best-paid or the most-celebrated woman writer of her day and, indeed, took some years in accommodating her distinctive ironic voice and her plots to the demands of the Regency publishing world. Edward Copeland regards Austen's own lack of wealth as the reason "money . . . especially spendable income, is the love-tipped arrow aimed at the hearts" of both her heroines and her readers (132). Certainly it is undeniable that she pays enormous attention to the incomes and potential earnings of her marriageable characters and that while her heroines loudly disdain the vulgar bargain of marrying for money, nonetheless they have the very good luck to marry rich men for love.

Jane Austen's family members and small social circle were her earliest critics; their objections and accolades are still raised to this day, so this reception history of her work allows them their say. Her siblings read, and often starred in, her juvenilia, including "The Beautiful Cassandra," a spoof in which her sister indulges in a passion for bonnets and ices, and "Henry and Eliza," a romance named for her brother and first cousin, who later married. Her mother's relations, the Leigh Perrots, were the first to remark that "Darcy and Elizabeth had spoilt them for anything else," a sentiment that sums up a still-burgeoning cottage industry in adapting, updating, and admiring *Pride and Prejudice* (Halperin 289).[3] Her mother was the first of many to dislike *Mansfield Park*'s heroine Fanny Price, whom she found "insipid." Her sister Cassandra offered an ingenious solution to give this excessively moral character some needed nuance and spark: marry her off to her antithesis, Henry Crawford, a suggestion Austen scaled back to an extended pursuit and rejected marriage proposal (Tomalin 225). Other friends and relatives admitted to shameful pleasure whenever the urbane and irreligious Mary Crawford triumphs over Fanny. Jane's brother Henry claimed to like his namesake Crawford, "properly, as a clever, pleasant man," as well as he liked Fanny, a dual allegiance that may not have been repeated since (Halperin 251). Her friend Miss

Sharp, a governess, faulted the psychological dimensions of another considering the trade, *Emma*'s Jane Fairfax. She felt that the would-be governess's secret engagement to Frank Churchill rang false; Frank was selfish and rash enough to carry on a secret engagement and correspondence, but the discreet Miss Fairfax was decidedly not (Tomalin 250).

Austen's family's compliments and objections reveal a high priority for realism, including psychological realism, as the goal of fiction. Austen's brothers scrupulously policed her verisimilitude, sometimes at her request—when she asked them to time journeys she did not have the opportunity to make to ensure that her characters move about England in a reasonably timely fashion—and sometimes quite contrary to her liking. In one instance, her brother Edward Knight remarked after reading *Emma*, "Jane, I wish you would tell me where you get those apple-trees of yours that come into bloom in July," a fairly deflating assessment of four hundred pages undone by one misunderstood subclause.[4] Yet, an exacting critic herself, Austen satirized the hard-to-believe in other novels. In a letter critiquing Mary Brunton's *Self-Control*, she joked that her own books might make more of a splash in the world if she imitated the heroine's solitary journey on a tiny boat down an American river, though in her version, she smirked, the young lady would cross the Atlantic and land in Gravesend in her hand-built canoe (Halperin 267). Her realism has, for many readers, been the chief quality to praise in Austen: her subtle portraits of human folly resonate with many. Given the major themes and developments in Austen criticism, however, we may ask whether the realism question has limited our criticism unduly, preventing us from asking other questions.

Contemporary reviewers of Austen's novels did praise her realism, which they typically called "probability" or "believability," and at times her moral lessons. The first review she ever received, on *Sense and Sensibility* in *Critical Review* (1812), calls the novel both "well-written" and "probable." Three months later, *The British Critic* declared *Sense and Sensibility* to be fortified "with sober and salutary maxims for the conduct of life," chiefly in the chastening of the emotional sister who falls in love "with a male coquet," Willoughby (quoted in Halperin 205). *Pride and Prejudice* was more extravagantly praised by the same publication a year later, when it was declared "far superior to almost all the publications of its kind to come before us" and the first edition sold out within six months (quoted in Halperin 210). *Mansfield Park*, her next novel, was not reviewed at all and lost its publisher money. With the publication of *Emma*, Austen received somewhat tepid reviews: the four major reviews—in *Literary Panorama*, *British Critic*, *Monthly Review*, and *Gentlemen's Magazine*—all found it light and trifling in comparison to the weightier *Sense and Sensibility* and more vivacious *Pride and Prejudice*.

Just when, in 1816, it looked as though Austen would not receive serious critical attention from her peers, her publisher John Murray convinced the powerful Sir Walter Scott to pay the very high compliment of a comprehensive assessment of her work in *Quarterly Review*. In Austen's own favorite review, Scott praised her whole oeuvre, excepting *Mansfield Park*, which he failed to mention. It was some compensation that he rescued the underrated *Emma* from other critical diminishments by extolling what he called its "insight into the human heart." Austen, he writes, has "the art of copying from nature as she really exists in the common walks of life, and of presenting to the reader . . . a correct and striking representation of that which is daily taking place around him" (quoted in Halperin 291). Clearly, this tribute to Austen's palpable skill intentionally diminishes her originality and novelty, and preserves those qualities for Scott's own reputation.

The Rise of the Novel

In his monumental study *The Rise of the Novel* (1957), Ian Watt concedes that the "majority of eighteenth-century novels were written by women," though he limits his book's scope to Defoe, Richardson, and Fielding because, he claims, women's control over the novel was "a purely quantitative dominance" (298). Watt elides female writers from his study and blames the predominantly female readership of the novel for the shortfalls of realism in eighteenth-century fiction (301). Despite the frank misogyny of his critical study, Watt reserves a special, though very limited, place in his pantheon of realist novelists for Jane Austen, who he claims solved most of the "obvious technical weaknesses" troubling the novels of the three male authors who consume his work's study (301). The irony of his compliment to Austen is twofold: the scale of his inquiry—one-tenth the space given to Fielding and one-twentieth that for Richardson—contradicts his ranking of her contribution, and, more troubling still, it neutralizes her own spirited defense of the female-dominated novel form in *Northanger Abbey*, where she asks that female heroines, authors, and readers all openly avow their mutual respect: "Let us not desert one another; we are an injured body!" (59).

Austen's exceptionalism—the careful construction of her as the one female author from three centuries of novel writing worth defending—was a time-honored tradition long before Ian Watt's study. Henry James noted that many found "our dear, everybody's dear, Jane so infinitely to their material purpose," whatever that critical purpose might be (quoted in Johnson, "Austen" 211). Many critics of the novel have posited a clean break between Austen and her female predecessors, one that contradicts her own admiration for Fanny Burney, Maria Edgeworth, and Ann Radcliffe. Yet other critics have put Austen in a context and a genealogy of female influence, and not all are corrections antedating Watt. B. G. MacCarthy published an ambitious study of female writers just after World War II that implicitly sides with Watt in seeing "a flood of mediocrity" in women's writing since 1621 yet also finds not one but more than fifty "cogent influences," as she calls them, among females writing prose. MacCarthy manages to praise the distinctive style of Austen while placing her within the context of her female influences and predecessors, and she does so within Watt's key critical term, realism, which she finds women novelists particularly qualified to create (29).

By the date of publication for Marilyn Butler's *Jane Austen and the War of Ideas* (1975), Austen's ascension to the great pantheon of British writers, once contentious, was no longer controversial. Perhaps it is not surprising, then, that Butler sees Austen as part of the old conservative establishment that Butler's generation of Oxford students sought to critique. Butler places Austen squarely within a repudiated Tory tradition and makes a spirited argument that readers should consider what her values are before idolizing her: "Before Austen could be trusted to assist one's choices in the modern world, we needed to know what hers had been" (xxxiii). MacCarthy admires Austen's moral individualism, writing that "not even the literary patronage of the Prince Regent could persuade her from the right of keeping her own literary conscience" (29), whereas Butler finds Austen's "domestic, home-bound, village bound novels . . . programmatically conservative," a disappointment because she had wanted and expected Austen to be a "non-partisan liberal moralist" (xiv).

Butler's reading of a politically retrograde Austen has been widely critiqued, especially by Julia Prewitt Brown, Elaine Showalter, and Sandra Gilbert, all of whom have disputed her positioning of Austen as regressive. Butler was nonetheless influential in creating an Austen "generally assumed to be the most resistant" to feminist, Marxist, and other progressive readings (Evans 1). Nancy Armstrong's *Desire and Domestic Fiction* (1987), which offers many important feminist revisions to Ian Watt's story of male contributions to the novel, nonetheless inherits the icon of a conservative, Tory Austen. For example, Armstrong contrasts *Northanger Abbey* with what she believes is the more progressive *Jane Eyre*. Quoting a scene in which Henry Tilney shames Catherine Morland for expecting remnants of a murder in his family home—"Remember that we are English, that we are Christians. Consult your own understanding, your own sense of the probable"— Armstrong claims that Austen "teaches the heroine of her first novel to understand the excesses of patriarchal culture as a feature of women and the undisciplined imaginations of women, not as a social reality"

(206). Claudia L. Johnson, in contrast, maintains that Austen is not on the side of Sir Thomas Bertram and General Tilney, repressive patriarchs at home and colonizers abroad: "Austen may dismiss 'alarms' concerning the gothic *machinery* . . . , but alarms concerning the central gothic figure, the tyrannical father, are commensurate to the threat they pose" (*Jane Austen* 35). Postcolonial critics have come to argue that Fanny Price stands in for the absent figure of the slave in *Mansfield Park*, since the naming of the novel is an homage to a landmark abolitionist decision, Lord Mansfield's ruling in the Somerset case in 1772, widely understood to outlaw slavery in Britain. Gary Kelly notes that such names would have been familiar to Austen's contemporary readers, who would not have regarded her as apolitical, given the "obvious references" to the Napoleonic Wars and other social upheavals in her novels (158-59).

Raymond Williams frames a Marxist challenge to the common misconception that Jane Austen ignored or effaced the social realities of her day, obliterating everything from Napoleon to the Atlantic slave trade "with the fiction of purely personal relationships" (113). Williams rejects the false dichotomy between the personal world of Austen's courtship novels and the real-life concerns of Regency England, drawing our attention to her preoccupation with the gentry's struggles to reproduce itself as "an acquisitive high-bourgeois society at the point of its most evident interlocking with an agrarian capitalism that is itself mediated by inherited titles and family names" (115). Williams was one of the first to notice the critical edge to Austen's preoccupation with wealth and status, and his tradition is continued in criticism by Edward Copeland's illuminating work on money in Austen and in Austen adaptations by filmmakers Roger Michell (*Persuasion*, 1995) and Joe Wright (*Pride and Prejudice*, 2005), who resist heritage cinema's aesthetic—"detached capital, detached income, detached consumption . . . in incidentally surviving and converted houses" that no one's labor seems to support and maintain. Michell and Wright reinsert livestock and laborers intrusively, not picturesquely, back into the

Austen landscape and insist on a grubby realism in the makeup, costumes, and lighting of their films' mise-en-scènes. In another, more dominant school of adaptation referred to as "heritage cinema," Austen's limited descriptions of fashion, person, and place—her habit of simply describing Pemberley "as a large modern house on rising grounds"—is "corrected" or supplemented to create visual banquets for audiences seeking "a nostalgic gaze that resists the ironies and social critiques" of the source novels (Higson 109-29).

Cinematic interpretations of Austen deserve special mention here: not only is each film a critical reading of a novel, but also many enfold postcolonial criticism of Austen into their scripts. For example, Patricia Rozema's *Mansfield Park* (1999) seeks to bring the book's quiet subtext on slavery to the forefront of the film. As Troost and Greenfield's edited collection *Jane Austen in Hollywood* observes, Austen adaptations noticeably influence popular perceptions of the original source texts, particularly among students, for whom the films have a demonstrable didactic function. Following a series of E. M. Forster novel adaptations in the 1980s on the part of the filmmaking team of James Ivory and Ishmail Merchant, Jane Austen soon surpassed Forster as the most adapted of English authors in a cluster of adaptations in the mid-1990s, and adaptations continue to be made. *Pride and Prejudice*, first brought to the screen in 1940 by MGM, was remade in 1995 by the BBC's Andrew Davies and in 2005 by Joe Wright. Except for *Northanger Abbey* and *Lady Susan*, all of Austen's novels have had adaptations that have gone into wide release, either in period pieces or in contemporary analogies, such as *Bride and Prejudice* (2004) and *Clueless* (1995). These adaptations have brought new generations of readers to the Janeite cult, and the latest development is in biographical studies of the author, including Julian Jarrold's *Becoming Jane* (2007) and the BBC film *Miss Austen Regrets* (2008), which offer competing explanations of Austen's mysterious spinsterhood, given the primacy of courtship and marriage in her novels.

Austen's spinsterhood has provoked questions about her views on the satisfactions of male-female love, as have the portrayals of married couples throughout her books, whose troubled relationships call into question the very notion of a happily ever after. Mrs. Croft may be the only happily married woman in all of Austen who is likable on her own terms, or who has not made a bargain the heroine rejected herself, like Charlotte Collins (née Lucas).[5] One interpretation of Austen's spinsterhood frames it as her strongest testimony to the belief that one should marry only for love; the fact that Austen never married, then, supports the primacy of the romance plot rather than undermining it for biographer Claire Tomalin and filmmaker Julian Jarrold. Both treat Austen's brief flirtation with Tom Lefroy in 1796 (mentioned exactly thrice in her letters) as the love of her life, a strict analogy to Cassandra's own permanent eschewal of marriage in tribute to the death of her fiancé Tom Fowle. The popularity of Jarrold's *Becoming Jane*, which extends these three brief epistolary references into two thrilling hours of highly convincing chemistry between the leads Anne Hathaway and James McAvoy, will assure that this explanation is influential for some time. A more intricate elucidation of Austen's spinsterhood comes from biographer John Halperin and from the BBC biographical film *Miss Austen Regrets*, both of which construct from Austen's novels, family recollections, and letters not a pining, dejected monogamist but an accomplished flirt who was never able to choose among half a dozen attractive offers of marriage throughout her twenties and thirties, none of which came from Tom Lefroy.

A third cause for Austen's spinsterhood has also been suggested in the last twenty years: when Terry Castle reviewed the Deirdre Le Faye edition of Austen's letters in the *London Review of Books*, the *LRB* chose to run the review under the incendiary banner "Was Jane Austen Gay?" The initial response was shockingly negative; many readers assumed that the author took a prurient view of innocent habits, such as sisters sharing beds and writing emotional letters, that were common and unquestioned in the eighteenth and nineteenth centuries. Castle's inquiry is, in fact, far less inflammatory and definitive than the review title suggests, or than most respondents assumed; she writes elliptically that "were one wanting to make a vulgar case for Austen's homoeroticism," the letters to her niece Fanny would be "the place to look" (82). Castle purposely refuses sweeping claims about Austen's sexual orientation, providing instead a close reading of the correspondence between Cassandra and Jane Austen, which she finds suffused with "a primitive adhesiveness—and underlying Eros—of the sister-sister bond."[6] Castle, like Halperin, asks us to reconsider the conservative promoter of marriage we have inherited in the light of some significant tendencies to mock marriage and child rearing in her letters.

Jane Austen's six courtship novels and one novella marry off a total of twenty couples, parceling even those without reciprocal attractions to their intended mates (such as Reginald de Courcy and Frederica Vernon, or Marianne and Colonel Brandon) into tidy marriages. Given the prevalence of the heterosexual courtship plot as the form of closure in all her novels, Austen may seem, at first blush, like one of the least amenable authors for "queer" readings. Queer theory—a critical rubric fashioned from a former insult—describes any gendered identity representing a challenge to the monolith of two opposite sexes that can express their desires only through compulsory heterosexuality (Sedgwick 8). Closer inspection, however, reveals troubled portraits of marriage in Austen's books as well as very strong same-sex (or "homosocial") bonds, particularly among women. In many Austen novels, a female friend labors to attach another female to her brother: Mary Crawford, Isabella Thorpe, and Georgiana Darcy insist on Fanny, Catherine, and Lizzy being their "sisters" in powerful scenes that eclipse the role of their brothers in completing the courtships; Sophie Croft reassures Anne Elliot about being a naval wife without seeming particularly aware that her words will promote the marriage of Anne and Sophie's brother, Frederick Wentworth.

While Castle's essay may have been an infelicitous calling card for ushering in a new school of Austen studies, queer Austen nonetheless developed into a vibrant academic subspecialty over the past twenty years. Critics working in this tradition generally leave the author's own libidinal investments out of the question and focus on one of two main approaches: examining the rich emotional connections of female homosocial structures in Austen's novels[7] or adopting Oscar Wilde's view that pure style, evacuated of morality, including sexual morality and tedious questions of who sleeps with whom, is the proper sphere of the queer critic. Of this latter group, D. A. Miller leads the pack: over the past twenty-five years, he has authored three of the finest books in Jane Austen studies, *The Novel and the Police*, *Narrative and Its Discontents*, and *Jane Austen, or, The Secret of Style*, as well as a charming *Raritan* article, "The Late Jane Austen." Joseph Litvak's *Strange Gourmets* gives a special place to the light, pleasing, and aphoristic style of *Pride and Prejudice*, so similar to the dandy's taste in well-turned phrases, while Miller points out that Austen's portrait of Robert Ferrars picking out a toothpick case amounts to a merciless parody of a gay man, one that sticks in the readerly subconscious to make the surprise marriage of Robert to Lucy Steele all the more shocking (*Jane Austen* 15).

Critical responses to Austen's style need not fall exclusively under the aegis of queer theory; many things motivate critics to investigate what is distinctive and fascinating in her prose. As Virginia Woolf wrote, "Of all authors she is the most difficult to catch in the act of greatness" (quoted in Stoval 231). Wayne C. Booth's *A Rhetoric of Irony* gives special place to Austen's use of the traditional tropes of irony, providing an invigorating close reading of the famous opening line of *Pride and Prejudice*: a single woman of no fortune is the one in want of a husband, he points out; a single man with money wants nothing at all to complete his happiness. This aphoristic substitution informs the style of all *Pride and Prejudice*, while books such as *Persuasion* and *Emma* rely on free indirect discourse, a subtle incorporation of a particular character's voice into the omniscient narrator's prose that allows the author to satirize without preaching (Finch and Bowen). John F. Burrows examines the distinctive voices of particular characters in a quantitative analysis that posits Mr. Darcy's letter as the most formal, elaborate prose in Austen; Burrows writes that style is "not a belletristic fancy but a real presence," one that is "now responsive to straightforward computational procedures" (186). For many of us, however, the pleasures of reading Austen are not quantifiable in mathematical terms, and we will continue to debate the standards for measuring her imposing talents for many more generations.

Notes

1. The earliest was by her elder, and favorite, brother Henry, "A Biographical Notice of the Author," included in the 1818 edition of *Northanger Abbey* and *Persuasion*. Later biographies include Caroline Austen's *My Aunt Jane Austen: A Memoir*, James Edward Austen-Leigh's *A Memoir of Jane Austen*, Mary-Augusta Austen-Leigh's *Personal Aspects of Jane Austen*, and William and Richard Austen-Leigh's *Jane Austen: Her Life and Letters: A Family Record*.

2. Sir Zachary Cope was the earliest to make this diagnosis, in his 1964 article "Jane Austen's Last Illness."

3. *Pride and Prejudice* was the first of her novels to be adapted for the screen, in 1940, and has spawned more updates than any other, including a Bollywood musical (*Bride and Prejudice*). Perhaps the best-known adaptations are those in Helen Fielding's *Bridget Jones's Diary* franchise.

4. In the Box Hill picnic scene in *Emma*, the title character pauses in the midst of midsummer strawberry picking to survey a view that includes Abbey-Mill Farm, "with all its appendages of prosperity and beauty, its rich pastures, spreading flocks, orchard in blossom, and light column of smoke ascending." Austen's brother Edward Knight pointed out that if ripe strawberries were in the fields, the apple orchard would hardly be in blossom. Critic John Sutherland defends this description from charges of failed realism by supposing that it is meant to cover all four seasons, from flocks in pasture (spring) to cooler fall temperatures (necessitating the smoking chimney, which would hardly be a feature of a day described by Frank Churchill and Jane Fairfax as beastly hot). He supposes that Austen intended this survey and therefore did not change the text at the printer despite her brother's criticism (17-18).

5. For an excellent discussion of Mrs. Croft as a naval wife, see Mary Ann O'Farrell's *Telling Complexions* (45-50).

6. The original essay appeared August 3, 1995; the argument and accompanying letters are reprinted in Castle's "The Austen Papers."

7. See Lisa L. Moore's "Desire and Diminution: *Emma*" and George E. Haggerty's "Sisterly Love in *Sense and Sensibility*."

Works Cited

Armstrong, Nancy. *Desire and Domestic Fiction*. New York: Oxford UP, 1987.

Austen, Caroline. *My Aunt Jane Austen: A Memoir*. London: Spottiswoode, Ballantyne, 1952.

Austen, Jane. *Northanger Abbey*. Ed. Claire Grogan. Toronto: Broadview Press, 2002.

_____. *Pride and Prejudice*. Ed. Robert P. Irvine. Toronto: Broadview Press, 2002.

Austen-Leigh, James Edward. *A Memoir of Jane Austen*. Ed. R. W. Chapman. London: Oxford UP, 1926.

Austen-Leigh, Mary-Augusta. *Personal Aspects of Jane Austen*. London: Murray, 1920.

Austen-Leigh, William, and Richard Austen-Leigh. *Jane Austen: Her Life and Letters: A Family Record*. London: Smith, Elder, 1913.

Booth, Wayne C. *A Rhetoric of Irony*. Chicago: U of Chicago P, 1974.

Burrows, John F. "Style." *The Cambridge Companion to Jane Austen*. Ed. Edward Copeland and Juliet McMaster. New York: Cambridge UP, 1997.

Butler, Marilyn. *Jane Austen and the War of Ideas*. Oxford, England: Clarendon Press, 1975.

Castle, Terry. "The Austen Papers." *Lingua Franca* (Sept./Oct. 1995): 77-82.

Cope, Zachary, "Jane Austen's Last Illness." *British Medical Journal* (18 July 1964): 182-83.

Copeland, Edward. "Money." *The Cambridge Companion to Jane Austen*. Ed. Edward Copeland and Juliet McMaster. New York: Cambridge UP, 1997.

Copeland, Edward and Juliet McMaster, eds. *The Cambridge Companion to Jane Austen*. New York: Cambridge UP, 1997.

Evans, Mary Ann. *Jane Austen and the State*. London: Tavistock, 1987.

Finch, Casey, and Peter Bowen. "The Tittle-Tattle of Highbury: Style in *Emma*." *Representations* 31 (Summer 1990): 1-18.

Haggerty, George E. "Sisterly Love in *Sense and Sensibility*." *Unnatural Affections: Women and Fiction in the Later Eighteenth Century*. Bloomington: Indiana UP, 1998. 73-87.

Halperin, John. *The Life of Jane Austen*. Baltimore: Johns Hopkins UP, 1984.

Higson, Andrew. "Re-presenting the National Past: Nostalgia and Pastiche in the Heritage Film." *Fires Were Started: Cinema and Thatcherism*. Ed. Lester Friedman. Minneapolis: U of Minnesota P, 1987.

Johnson, Claudia L. "Austen Cults and Cultures." *The Cambridge Companion to Jane Austen*. Ed. Edward Copeland and Juliet McMaster. New York: Cambridge UP, 1997.

_____. *Jane Austen: Women, Politics, and the Novel*. Chicago: U of Chicago P, 1988.

Kelly, Gary. "Religion and Politics." *The Cambridge Companion to Jane Austen*. Ed. Edward Copeland and Juliet McMaster. New York: Cambridge UP, 1997.

Litvak, Joseph. *Strange Gourmets: Sophistication, Theory, and the Novel*. Durham, NC: Duke UP, 1997.

MacCarthy, B. G. *The Female Pen: Women Writers and Novelists, 1621-1818.* 1944. Cork, Ireland: Cork UP, 1996.

Miller, D. A. *Jane Austen, or, The Secret of Style.* Princeton, NJ: Princeton UP, 2003.

_____. "The Late Jane Austen." *Raritan* 10.1 (1990): 55-79.

_____. *Narrative and Its Discontents: Problems of Closure in the Traditional Novel.* Princeton, NJ: Princeton UP, 1981.

_____. *The Novel and the Police.* Berkeley: U of California P, 1988.

Moore, Lisa L. "Desire and Diminution: *Emma.*" *Dangerous Intimacies: Toward a Sapphic History of the British Novel.* Durham, NC: Duke UP, 1997.

O'Farrell, Mary Ann. *Telling Complexions: The Nineteenth-Century English Novel and the Blush.* Durham, NC: Duke UP, 1997.

Sedgwick, Eve. *Tendencies.* Durham, NC: Duke UP, 1993.

Stoval, Bruce. "Further Reading." *The Cambridge Companion to Jane Austen.* Ed. Edward Copeland and Juliet McMaster. New York: Cambridge UP, 1997.

Sutherland, John. "Emma." *Is Heathcliff a Murderer? Great Puzzles in Nineteenth-Century Literature.* New York: Oxford UP, 1996.

Tomalin, Claire. *Jane Austen: A Life.* New York: Vintage, 1999.

Troost, Linda, and Sayre Greenfield, eds. *Jane Austen in Hollywood.* Lexington: UP of Kentucky, 1998.

Watt, Ian. *The Rise of the Novel.* Berkeley: U of California P, 1957.

Williams, Raymond. *The Country and the City.* New York: Oxford UP, 1973.

Pride, Prejudice, and Persuasion:
A Comparison of Two Novels by Jane Austen_____

Dominick Grace

Few novelists have been more conscious of their use of language than Austen. When Catherine Morland uses the word *nice* in an unfamiliar sense in *Northanger Abbey*, she is jokingly scolded by Eleanor: "You had better change it as soon as you can, or we shall be overpowered with Johnson." "Johnson," of course, meant Samuel Johnson's monumental *Dictionary of the English Language*, published in a revised edition two years before Austen was born. It remained the most important English dictionary throughout Austen's lifetime.

Austen knew her dictionary well, and she expected the same from her readers. As critic John Wiltshire has argued, we are "continually invited to notice how a word is being used and to assess whether it is being used justifiably, sloppily or mischievously." Her attention to subtle shadings of meaning is unmatched among English prose authors. In this essay, Dominick Grace turns to modern dictionaries to discern the precise shades of meaning of words such as *pride*, *prejudice*, and *persuasion*. The essay offers a model of the kind of close reading that Austen's readers would be well advised to practice themselves.   — J.L.

Jane Austen's best-known novel, *Pride and Prejudice*, first took form under the title "First Impressions" in 1796-97 before being revised, retitled, and ultimately published in 1813. It was the second of her novels to be published, though it was the first one to be offered to a publisher. *Persuasion*, her final completed novel, was written in 1815-16 and published together with *Northanger Abbey* (another early novel revised, polished, and published years after its first composition) in 1818, one year after the author's death. In a mere eight years, Austen published a half dozen of the most accomplished novels in the English language, though her period of creativity extended back some fifteen years prior to her first publication. Though she famously downplayed her artistry, referring in a letter to her nephew James Edward Austen to "the little bit (two inches wide) of ivory on which I work with so fine a brush, as produces little effect after much labour," Austen's novels deal complexly and with sophistication with what she suggests is her narrow range.

Certainly, all of Austen's novels deal with a narrow social circle (the upper echelons of the gentry and the lower end of the aristocracy), all have strong satirical elements in their treatment of social rituals (Austen's novels all can be described as novels or comedies of manners), all focus on female protagonists, and all focus specifically on the romantic and marital adventures (and misadventures) of those protagonists. The novels are all realistic to some degree, at least in their characterization of protagonists, but they all also depend to some extent on caricatures as well as on contrived coincidences of plot. However, characterization rather than plot is Austen's central concern, and all of her novels offer remarkable explorations of their protagonists and of the anxieties of understanding oneself, one's place in society, and one's relationships with others. These concerns intersect interestingly in relation to the terms invoked in *Pride and Prejudice* and *Persuasion*.

As the titles *Pride and Prejudice* and *Persuasion* suggest, Austen is frequently interested in exploring concepts with complex social and moral implications. (It should be noted, however, that the titles of Austen's final two novels were selected by her brother, who brought them to press, so the title *Persuasion*, though appropriate, is not necessarily the one Austen would have chosen had she lived to see the novel published.) Three of her six novels have titles invoking abstract concepts (her first novel, *Sense and Sensibility*, being the third). The earlier titles suggest paired concepts, whereas the later title focuses on a single one, though the book could as easily have been called *Prejudice and Persistence* (thereby more closely echoing the earlier titles), since it juxtaposes those two concepts much as the earlier book juxtaposes pride and prejudice. The later title might seem to suggest more focus on external influences, whereas the earlier title might seem to suggest more focus on personal character traits, and there is some truth to this contrast. However, all three terms have more extensive and suggestive meanings than might at first appear. As John Wiltshire has noted, "The reader of Jane Austen is continually invited to notice how a word is being used and to assess whether it is being used justifiably, sloppily or mischievously" (5).

Pride and *prejudice* are terms with both linked and in some ways contrasting meanings. Prejudice involves judgment of others; pride involves judgment of the self. Just as prejudice involves inaccurate judgment, so too does pride. Here is the primary definition of *pride* from the *Oxford English Dictionary*: "A high or overweening opinion of one's own qualities, attainments, or estate, which gives rise to a feeling and attitude of superiority over and contempt for others; inordinate self-esteem." Such a definition suggests an extremely negative coloration for the word, and such a coloration is attached to it in the book at various points. It is such pride, or apparent pride, in Darcy that leads to Elizabeth's prejudicial judgment of him. This realization might lead us to associate pride with Darcy and prejudice with Elizabeth, and such an association would not be inappropriate; indeed, many critics see the novel in such schematic terms. John Halperin, for instance, finds it "unnecessary to rehearse again the process by which Darcy's pride is humbled and Elizabeth's prejudices exposed," taking this diagrammatic view of the novel as a given (363).

However, *pride* has more than one meaning. For example, though the definition above suggests a negative meaning for the word, its etymological root, the Old Norse *prythe*, meant "gallantry, bravery, stateliness"—all positive senses, associating pride with noble behavior—and the *OED* provides as its third definition for pride the following: "A consciousness or feeling of what is befitting or due to oneself or one's position, which prevent a person from doing what he considers is beneath him or unworthy of him; esp, as a good quality, legitimate, 'honest', or 'proper pride', self-respect; also as a mistaken or misapplied feeling, 'false pride.'" In these senses, pride is a far more ambivalent and complex thing; implicit in the definition is the difficulty of distinguishing between proper and false pride, or pride based on a just and accurate sense of self and pride based on a false sense of self. Elizabeth and Darcy briefly discuss pride in volume 1, chapter 11, in just these terms. Darcy asserts that he has tried to avoid failings that will subject him to ridicule; Elizabeth suggests that such failings might include vanity and pride, and Darcy responds, "'Yes, vanity is a weakness indeed. But pride—where there is real superiority of mind, pride will be always under good regulation'" (50). The distinction between vanity, by definition false pride, and pride is an important one, but also suggested, with ironic humor, is that Darcy supposes himself to be possessed of the proper, well-regulated pride (he is of course prejudiced in his view). Darcy's pride is consistently cited, especially early in the novel, as the trait that disinclines others to like him, but that his pride is false is by no means so clear as his observers might think.

Prejudice is perhaps not as complex a word, but it too carries more implications than might be evident at first. Its roots are from the Latin, *pre* and *judicium*, or prejudgment, and definition of it (again from the *OED*) most obviously applicable to the novel is "a judgement formed before due examination or consideration; a premature or hasty judgement; a prejudgement," a definition fairly evidently applicable to Darcy's judgment of the local populace and to Elizabeth's of Darcy, for that matter. Another evidently applicable definition is "preconceived opinion; bias or leaning favourable or unfavourable," clearly descriptive of Elizabeth's reading of the Darcy-Wickham relationship: her prejudice against Darcy, created as the result of a hasty judgment, prejudices her, or gives her a favorable bias, for Wickham, who also does not like Darcy. Evident in many of these definitions for *prejudice* is its association with the judgment one makes of others. However, another of the word's earliest meanings is "injury, detriment, or damage, caused to a person by judgement or action in which his rights are disregarded," a definition not perhaps of primary relevance to the novel but with applicability nevertheless, as various judgments and actions in the novel do have long-term consequences in the book. That is, the term encompasses not only the negative judgment one might have but also the negative consequences that judgment may have for the prejudged. It is both a personal response and a social phenomenon.

Pride and prejudice also both suggest the larger social context important to the action, since they are not dependent solely on one's individual merits but on one's social position and one's judgment of others. Pride is not only a matter of self-estimation, it is a matter of social status, and it is also often as much a matter of how one is judged by others as it is a matter of how one judges oneself. One's pride can be offended if others do not share one's self-estimation, for instance, just as it can be boosted by the flattery and admiration of others (though false pride, or vanity, is what is likely to be boosted by such blandishments). Prejudice, as well, applies to people in a social context; it involves the judgment of others, often based on their social status—or lack thereof—or on their offenses against perceived social standards of decorum and propriety. Consequently, the title hints not only at traits important to the two protagonists as individuals but also at the importance of forces that go a long way toward defining, even determining, social status.

However, the pairing of the two terms in the title suggests not only contrast between them but also kinship. They form a pair; the conjunction is *and*, not *versus*. Consequently, each term may apply to more than one character, and their pairing hints at the ultimate pairing of the two characters central to the action. Arguably, in fact, the kinship between Elizabeth and Darcy as much as the contrast is crucial to their relationship. While pride is clearly established early on as Darcy's besetting fault (or perhaps rather the fault others perceive in him), Elizabeth's first expression of the antagonism between them involves her *own* pride: "'I could easily forgive *his* pride, if he had not mortified *mine*'" (14). Furthermore, shame, the opposite of pride, is a consistent marker of Elizabeth's character, especially in relation to the behavior of her mother and younger sisters. Susan Fraiman has gone so far as to recast the conventional dichotomy of the novel, seeing its focus instead as being on the pride of *both* protagonists, with Darcy's valorized and Elizabeth's ultimately humiliated: "At the outset, Elizabeth and Darcy are each proud, each sceptical of the other, yet finally they reach" a new balance; "in the end both are sceptical of her, both proud of him" (83). Such a reading offers a useful corrective to critical tradition but itself arguably overstates the case by creating a new, equally restrictive schematism.

The word *persuasion* is not linked etymologically to either of the other terms, but it resonates interestingly with them. The first *OED* definition says persuasion is "the addressing of arguments or appeals to a person in order to induce cooperation, submission, or agreement; the presenting of persuasive reasoning or compelling arguments." Here, the term refers clearly to a pressure from without on an individual to adopt ideas or behavior contrary to his or her current ones. However, a persuasion can also be "something which one believes; a belief, conviction, or opinion"—that is, an internal rather than an external influence over one's beliefs or actions. A persuasion could also be "the fact, condition, or state of being persuaded or convinced; conviction, assurance, certain belief," and though this meaning is now archaic, it was current in Austen's time, and it is a meaning that suggests a persuasion can in fact be a fixed belief rather than the result of a rational or argumentative process; it might be seen as something akin to a prejudice in this sense. From these perspectives, persuasion is often associated— especially by Austen—with things people convince themselves of, with little reference to whether the basis of their self-persuasion is sound; as Ann Molan notes, the idea of persuasion addresses "possibilities within and without the self, what one is persuaded *of* and what one is persuaded *by*" (16). While self-persuasions are not always suspect, they are so frequently enough that, as Wiltshire suggests, this term is one of those in Austen's arsenal that the reader must examine carefully.

In fact, as the De Rose and McGuire concordance to Austen's works reveals, the word *persuade* and variations on it occur more frequently in *Pride and Prejudice* (more than fifty examples) than in *Persuasion* (approximately thirty examples). (Indeed, persuasion is a popular concept in Austen; variations of the word occur multiple times in all her novels, most frequently in *Emma*.) Especially in the senses associated with one's fixed beliefs, persuasion is strongly associated with prejudice throughout Austen's work, but persuasion is also strongly linked to pride, especially in *Persuasion* but in the earlier novel as well. Holding fixedly to one's beliefs, or persuasions, is frequently a matter of pride, so persuasion can suffer from the limits not only of prejudice but also of pride.

The scene in which Darcy is introduced does not use the word *persuasion*, but it offers a remarkable example of how pride can work in concert with prejudice to create almost unswayable persuasions. Darcy first appears, with his friend Bingley, at the Meryton ball:

> Mr. Bingley was good looking and gentlemanlike; he had a pleasant countenance, and easy, unaffected manners . . . but his friend Mr. Darcy soon drew the attention of the room by his fine, tall person, handsome features, noble mien; and the report which was in general circulation within five minutes after his entrance, of his having ten thousand a year. The gentlemen pronounced him to be a fine figure of a man, the ladies declared he was much handsomer than Mr. Bingley, and he was looked at with great admiration for about half the evening, till his manners gave a disgust which turned the tide of his popularity; for he was found to be proud, to be above his company, and above being pleased; and not all his large estate in Darbyshire could then save him from having a most forbidding, disagreeable countenance, and being unworthy to be compared to his friend. (7-8)

The terms of contrast between Darcy and Bingley suggest their different natures by focusing on the aspects of Bingley's nature that are likely to make him appealing to people in general and on the aspects of Darcy's nature that mark his high social rank (note especially his "noble mien," recalling that the word *pride* is linked etymologically with conventionally noble traits).

The progress of the paragraph needs to be followed carefully if the description of Darcy is to be properly understood. Specifically, we need to take note of the ways that two points, Darcy's wealth and Darcy's behavior, suggest not only his own nature but also the nature of those judging him. The initial impression of Darcy's handsomeness, nobility, and so on is to a large extent the result of the knowledge of his wealth: that is, he is judged not on objective grounds but in terms colored by the admiration felt for his wealth. The prejudice in favor of wealth in a man (especially an eligible bachelor), established in the novel's famous opening sentence, "It is a truth universally acknowledged, that a single man in possession of a large fortune, must be in want of a wife" (1), clearly determines how Darcy is initially judged. Certainly, if Bingley's fortune makes him an attractive candidate for marriage, sight unseen, then Darcy's far greater fortune clearly makes him an even more attractive candidate. So the initial description of Darcy is colored positively by the news of his wealth.

The subsequent impression of Darcy is colored by his conduct. Readers might therefore be inclined to grant it more credence, since they may be inclined to see how an individual behaves as a fairly reliable guide to character. However, something that becomes clear as this novel progresses is that an easy, unaffected manner such as Bingley's, the ability to make oneself seem winning and attractive in company, may be a desirable trait, but it is also a trait that one can use for purposes of deception, so what one appears to be need not be a reliable guide to what one is is. Wickham, for instance, possesses charm in abumdance, but he is the most despicable character in the novel. Furthermore, it is already evident that those viewing Darcy and Bingley do so from a particular perspective and with a particular agenda in mind, so their judgments are affected by the extent to which the people they view seem amenable to that agenda. Bingley has easy, unaffected manners; Darcy does not. Bingley mingles easily and naturally; Darcy does not. Bingley, therefore, is far more likely to be persuaded to share his wealth with one of the local daughters.

However, Austen hints that Darcy's behavior at the ball, which is in fact rude and therefore deserving of some censure, is not fully motivated by the pride and self-importance ascribed to him. There is a telling moment when Bingley tries to get Darcy to dance, and Darcy responds, "'You know how I detest it, unless I am particularly acquainted with my partner. At such an assembly as this, it would be insupportable. Your sisters are engaged, and there is not another woman in the room, whom it would not be a punishment to me to stand up with'" (8). One might indeed find such an attitude objectionable, but one should note as well that what underlies it is Darcy's discomfort among strangers; he likes to dance only when he knows his partner well, and the women he does know are already dancing. (The irony here is that the women he knows are much less pleasant than some of the ones he does not know.) And dancing, in this context, is unlike dancing now, which tends not to involve verbal interaction, the music being so loud. Clearly, if Darcy's words are to be taken at face value, his refusal to dance is not an indicator of his pride but rather of what we might call bashfulness or social discomfort.

Pride perhaps makes Darcy believe he need not make any effort to overcome this social deficiency and become more like his friend Bingley, however, and a crucial lesson Darcy learns in the novel is the necessity of modifying his behavior to satisfy not only himself but also the company he is in. Doing so is important both personally and socially. The dangers of pridefully persisting in pursuit of one's own prejudices or persuasions are clearly revealed in the events in both novels. Proper pride does not mean inflexible fixity of purpose, a point amusingly hinted at in the scene in which Bingley's exaggerated amiability and easy persuadability are contrasted with Darcy's apparent preference for obstinate fixity of purpose. Elizabeth is on the side of Bingley and persuadability, finding nothing to admire in Darcy's propensity (as she chooses to construct it, anyway) "'to allow nothing for the influence of friendship and affection. A regard for the requester would often make one readily yield to a request, without waiting for arguments to reason one into it'"; as she sees Darcy, "'To yield readily—easily—to the *persuasion* of a friend is no merit with you'" (34). Here, however, Elizabeth apparently understands "persuasion" to be a very light thing indeed, meaning nothing more than a request; as Darcy argues, why ought one to change one's plans at a friend's request if that friend "'has merely desired it, asked without offering one argument in favour of its propriety'" (34)? Darcy recognizes more at play than mere amiability.

Humor intrudes doubly, first because we have already seen Darcy not yield to persuasion in a circumstance—the Meryton ball—in which that refusal creates negative prejudices against him, but second because Elizabeth herself is unlikely to yield readily to persuasion, either, holding with a tenacity comparable to Darcy's to her own constructed views—of Wickham for quite some time, for instance—despite the evidence. With nothing but unsupported assertions on either side, Elizabeth chooses to believe those favorable to Wickham rather than those favorable to Darcy because of her respective prejudices regarding each man. Even Darcy's letter detailing the facts of his history with Wickham takes some time to persuade Elizabeth to surrender her prejudices against him. And when she does surrender them, the shame she feels at how she has misconstructed events suggests the extent to which pride has been bound up in that misconstruction.

Pride and persuasion intermingle similarly in a pair of key scenes in *Persuasion*. Like Darcy, Anne Elliot's suitor Wentworth is a man well endowed with pride. Sarah Wootton compares the two protagonists with the Byronic hero, noting, "Pride is a ubiquitous trait of the Byronic hero" (35). In the well-known scene in which Wentworth praises the firmness of the hazelnut, pride and persuasion are the underlying issue. Ostensibly, he is praising Louisa Musgrove's character for its "decision and firmness," using the firm, unpenetrated shell of the nut as an analogy for fixity of purpose (58-59). However, their discussion is linked to courtship, as Louisa has just contrasted herself with her sister's dithering indecisiveness about how to proceed with her suitor by asserting, "'I have no idea of being so easily persuaded. When I have made up my mind, I have made it'" (58). Anne is within hearing, and she has earlier accepted and then rejected Wentworth's suit, so Wentworth's praise of Louisa's unpersuadability here is an implicit criticism of Anne's persuadability years earlier, when she allowed Lady Russell to dissuade her from marrying Wentworth. Eight years later, Wentworth still smarts from the rejection, his pride still suffering. He acknowledges this more honest basis for his comments to Louisa much later in the novel, when he confesses that he did not renew his suit much earlier because "'I was proud, too proud to ask again. I did not understand you. I shut my eyes, and would not understand you, or do you justice'" (164). The passage stresses the fact that pride prevents proper perception. Wentworth acknowledges not only that he did not perceive Anne accurately but also that his failure of perception was linked to his own will; he *shut* his *eyes* and *would not* understand. Perception is not neutral or objective but deeply colored by the pride and the prejudices of those perceiving. Though Fraiman's argument that *Pride and Prejudice* ultimately valorizes Darcy's pride and his perceptions overstates the case, Wentworth is very clearly a character much more obviously subject to the limitations of pride and to failures of perception arising from that pride and the preconceptions he brings to his new encounters with Anne Elliot.

Given that Wentworth's praise of Louisa's "firmness" is not grounded in an unprejudiced view, especially since the woman who rejected him is sitting by to overhear him, it is unsurprising that his encomium to fixity of purpose has negative consequences. He assuages his pride by implicitly criticizing Anne, but he thereby inadvertently piques Louisa's pride in her tenacity, ingraining the habit in her more firmly. Due to Wentworth's facetious words of praise for persistence, Louisa, "armed with the idea of merit in maintaining her own way" (63), becomes even more willful and unpersuadable than she was before, first to insist on the trip to Lyme and then disastrously in her insistence on jumping down from the wall into Wentworth's arms. Louisa's pride in her refusal to be persuaded out of pursuing her own whims causes a life-threatening injury when she falls to the ground and strikes her head. The consequences of Wentworth's praise of firmness are dire; as Susan Morgan observes, "Captain Wentworth is wrong in his theory of character as much as in its applications" (180). Austen has Anne consider the question of the general applicability of Wentworth's views and so avoids an overly determined authorial judgment, but it is difficult not to see the author's usual ironic distance narrowing while

> Anne wondered whether it ever occurred to [Wentworth] now, to question the justness of his own previous opinion as to the universal felicity and advantage of firmness of character; and whether it might not strike him, that like all other qualities of the mind, it should have its proportions and limits. She thought it could scarcely escape him to feel, that a persuadable temper might sometimes be as much in favour of happiness, as a very resolute character. (78-79)

Louisa's fall is a transformative moment in the novel. Indeed, it is literally the turning point, occurring at the end of the novel's first volume. It is comparable to a superficially very different moment in *Pride and Prejudice* that is also that novel's center: Elizabeth's refusal of Darcy's proposal. Both novels turn on scenes in which the male protagonist is confronted with a situation he cannot control, and in both cases that situation is a key element in his development, for Austen foregrounds the necessity of accommodation, of flexibility and an ability to change, as essential to one's social development. Characters who allow forces such as pride or prejudice to govern them remain incapable of change. By contrast, characters too susceptible to persuasion may also suffer, but Austen suggests that openness to reasoned and reasonable persuasion is more likely to be beneficial than not.

Elizabeth's rejection of Darcy is motivated by many factors, but the words that influence him the most forcibly concern the characteristic on which he most prides himself, his social status. Elizabeth asserts that no mode of address could have succeeded with her, but his ungentlemanlike behavior not only spares her any concern now over hurting his feelings but has also determined her opinion of him from the outset: since she first knew Darcy, she tells him, "'your manners impressing me with the fullest belief of your arrogance, your conceit, and your selfish disdain of the feelings of others, were such as to form the ground-work of disapprobation, on which succeeding events have built so immoveable a dislike'" (128). Darcy's pride, in short—pride in its most negative manifestations—is at the root of Elizabeth's disdain. Crucially, though the novel makes clear that Elizabeth's understanding of Darcy at this point is significantly inaccurate, it also affirms that it contains elements of truth and puts in motion Darcy's efforts to modify his behavior. When next we meet Darcy, his manner has become significantly more amiable; he later acknowledges the faults in his behavior and their roots in pride: "'I have been a selfish being all my life, in practice, though not in principle. As a child I was taught what was right, but not taught to correct my temper. I was given good principles, but left to follow them in pride and conceit'" (241). Elizabeth's admonition, Darcy explicitly acknowledges, taught him a lesson: "'By you I was properly humbled'" (241). However, unlike other characters who tenaciously hold to their pride, their prejudices, or their persuasions, Darcy acts on Elizabeth's lesson. While arguably she has not acted as a friend or used reason, she persuades him to reevaluate himself and to modify his behavior in order to make himself more agreeable to her.

Wentworth, by contrast, is forced to reevaluate his valorization of persistence over persuasion (and arguably his own self-persuasion) after Louisa's fall, one of the results of which is that Wentworth is able to see Anne in a new light when she competently takes control of the situation. As Tony Tanner notes, "it is the apparently yielding but actually steadfast Anne to whom others turn" (235), not only at this crucial point but in fact throughout the novel. Whereas Wentworth has read Anne's yielding to Lady Russell as a deplorable instance of infirmity of purpose, his response has been an equally damaging fixity of purpose of his own. Persuaded that he has been wronged, he determines to give up Anne Elliot, as we have seen above. As a result, he and she lose eight years in which they could have been together. Ironically, it is Anne's fixity, her unpersuadability on the subject of taking another man as husband, that keeps her available for Wentworth when he finally sees past his own pride and prejudicial persuasion of Anne's inconstancy in the novel's true climax.

The novel's climax is not really the scene in which Anne and Wentworth finally avow their love but rather the earlier scene in which Wentworth, writing a letter, overhears Anne's discussion of constancy in love with Captain Harville. The argument turns on who is more faithful in love, men or women, and Anne of course argues for women, the example of her own persistent passion for Wentworth the subtext. Listening and observing, Wentworth is finally able to adjust his perception of Anne, conquer his pride, reverse his prejudicial judgment of her, and repersuade himself of her love. The direct consequence of this scene is Wentworth's renewal of his addresses to Anne and their ultimate marriage. This happy ending, however, is qualified by the novel's clear recognition of the costs attached to the characters' persuasions. Its final irony is that Anne continues to argue that she was right (in deference to proper authority) to defer to Lady Russell at the time and allow herself to be persuaded out of marrying Wentworth. This clearly is a debatable point; Austen leaves the readers to suspect that Anne must ultimately persuade herself that their eight-year separation was in fact justifiable rather than that it really was.

Pride and Prejudice and *Persuasion* are novels that in many respects differ significantly. However, the incidental similarity between their titles in fact points to a consistent interest in both novels in the complex interplay of the subjective and objective influences on characters' judgments. Pride, prejudice, and persuasion are major motivating forces in both novels, and careful consideration of how they function clarifies the meanings of both books.

Works Cited

Austen, Jane. Letter to James Edward Austen. 16 December 1816. *Letters of Jane Austen: Other Excerpts from Letters in Austen-Leigh's "Memoir."* http://www.pemberley.com/janeinfo/auslet22.html#letter130

_____. *Persuasion*. 1816. New York: W. W. Norton, 1995.

_____. *Pride and Prejudice*. 1813. New York: W. W. Norton, 2001.

De Rose, Peter L., and S. W. McGuire. *A Concordance to the Works of Jane Austen*. 3 vols. New York: Garland, 1982.

Fraiman, Susan. *Unbecoming Women: British Women Writers and the Novel of Development*. New York: Columbia UP, 1993.

Halperin, John. *The Life of Jane Austen*. Baltimore: Johns Hopkins UP, 1984.

Molan, Ann. "Persuasion in *Persuasion*." *Critical Review* 24 (1982): 16-29.

Morgan, Susan. *In the Meantime: Character and Perception in Jane Austen's Novels*. Chicago: U of Chicago P, 1980.

Tanner, Tony. *Jane Austen*. Cambridge, MA: Harvard UP, 1986.

Wiltshire, John. *Jane Austen: Introductions and Interventions*. 2003. New York: Palgrave, 2006.

Wootton, Sarah. "The Byronic in Jane Austen's *Persuasion* and *Pride and Prejudice*." *Modern Language Review* 102.1 (2007): 26-39.

CRITICAL READINGS

Bernard J. Paris

Casual readers have long taken it for granted that *Emma* has a happy ending—that the title character ultimately achieves a kind of self-knowledge, and that all the characters then live happily ever after. A critical tradition exists, however, that questions how seriously we are to take Emma's revelation. In Bernard J. Paris's essay, we are encouraged to look on Emma in two apparently incompatible ways at the same time: first, as a real person, with her own emotional and mental life; second, as a literary creation, "an aesthetic and an illustrative character." Paris goes on to read *Emma* as "a creation inside a creation," which allows him to see the heroine as "an imagined human being whose personal qualities are not always in harmony with her dramatic and thematic functions." In the end he concludes that the "novel's rhetoric is in conflict with its concrete portrayal of life," and that a more psychological reading of the character reveals that "her change is neither complete nor entirely for the better, and that her marriage to Knightley signifies not so much an entrance into maturity as a regression to childish dependency."   — J.L.

1

Emma is, like *Mansfield Park*, a controversial novel. The chief issues are the genuineness of Emma's reformation and the felicity of her marriage to Knightley. Most critics feel that Jane Austen means for us to see Emma's self-knowledge as profound, her education as permanent, and her marriage as perfectly happy, and that the author's interpretation is correct. There are two minority positions. One is that Emma does not grow as much as Austen thinks she does and that the ending is not as happy as the rhetoric makes it seem. The other is that Austen is aware of the limitations of her heroine's growth and happiness and that she does not really mean for us to see Emma's character and situation at the end as ideal.

This controversy becomes intelligible, I believe, when we see that Emma is, like Fanny Price, a creation inside a creation. She is the heroine of the comic action and the character whose education constitutes the novel's thematic center, but she is also an imagined human being whose personal qualities are not always in harmony with her dramatic and thematic functions. Most critics are not troubled by a sense of conflict in the novel because they do not respond to Emma as though she were a person; they see her only as an aesthetic and an illustrative character. The critics who see the ending as open, or ironic, or subtly critical of the society into which Emma is absorbed do respond to her as a person. They then ascribe to the novel a thematic structure which fits their perceptions of her character. I am in agreement with those who feel that the novel's rhetoric is in conflict with its concrete portrayal of life. Both as a comedy and as a novel of education, *Emma* encourages a favorable view of the protagonist's happiness and growth. When Emma is understood psychologically, however, it is evident that her change is neither complete nor entirely for the better, and that her marriage to Knightley signifies not so much an entrance into maturity as a regression to childish dependency.

2

As a comic structure, *Emma* is composed of three love relationships with their corresponding blocking forces. The happiness of Emma and Knightley is threatened by Emma's faults and illusions, by the lovers' unconsciousness of their feelings for each other, and by Mr. Woodhouse's opposition to marriage. Jane Fairfax and Frank Churchill are blocked by Mrs. Churchill. Harriet Smith and Robert Martin are thwarted by the interference of Emma. Each of the protagonists undergoes a period of distress as his or her happiness seems about to be frustrated; the blocking forces are removed by a series of rapid reversals;

and there is a flurry of weddings at the end. All obstacles to happiness are overcome. Mistakes are acknowledged, transgressions are forgiven, and conflicts between love and duty are resolved. The marriages are all socially suitable and based on love. No one, it turns out, has been permanently harmed.

"The humor in comedy," says Frye, "is usually someone with a good deal of social prestige and power, who is able to force much of the play's society into line with his obsession."[1] The most important humor in is Emma herself, who fulfills the role both of romantic heroine and of the *alazon* or impostor who is the major blocking force. Emma's "humors" or obsessions are many, and they give rise to a variety of mistakes and illusions. She is an "imaginist," a snob, an arranger of other people's lives. She prides herself on her own elegance and "Understanding" and is obsessed with her superiority and importance. She imposes an irrational law of celibacy upon herself and insists upon an unsuitably grand marriage for Harriet Smith. "The social judgment against the absurd is closer to the comic norm," says Frye, "than the moral judgment against the wicked" (*AC*, p. 168). Emma becomes more and more absurd as she ritually repeats her obsessions. Her repentances, which she repeats with almost equal frequency, keep her from seeming wicked. She is opposed by Knightley, who plays the role of "the plain dealer, an outspoken advocate of a kind of moral norm who has the sympathy of the audience" (*AC*, p. 176). The comic resolution depends upon Emma's being purged of her humors and brought round to Knightley's point of view. When we respond to the novel as a comedy, we have no doubt that this happens; and, as Frye observes, "whatever emerges is supposed to be there for good" (*AC*, p. 170).

The new society which crystallizes at the end is not only more clear-sighted; it is also better ordered and morally more secure. The mystery of Harriet's birth is removed, and she enters her proper social sphere. The capricious Mrs. Churchill is dead, and the relationship between Frank and Jane can become open and honorable. Most important of all, Emma accepts subordination to a proper authority. She has had too much power and independence. Her marriage to Knightley brings back to Hartfield the moral order which had disappeared with the death of her mother.

The tone of *Emma* is notably different from that of *Mansfield Park*. Both novels have comic structures; but *Emma* is amusing and gay, whereas *Mansfield Park* is serious and somber. *Emma* is full of humors characters who are wittily portrayed and who repeat their obsessions with delightful regularity. It abounds in ironies and misunderstandings and gives us all the fun of a comedy of errors. *Mansfield Park* specializes in the creation and removal of anxiety. Its satisfactions are those which accompany the gradual lifting of a nightmare and its eventual transformation into a wish fulfillment fantasy. There is nothing amusing about Fanny's plight, and the blocking characters are far more ominous than funny. Emma is presented as essentially secure; and we are free to laugh at her difficulties, most of which she brings upon herself. It is only after the Box Hill episode that her discomfiture becomes truly painful. Her subsequent vision of a bleak future is the darkest moment in the book, but it is quickly followed not only by her deliverance but also by a general rejoicing which is in marked contrast to the gloom surrounding Fanny on her return to Mansfield. Fanny's jubilation seems somewhat callous; Emma's seems entirely appropriate.

The new society is achieved in *Mansfield Park* through an expulsion of scapegoats, some of whom seem more attractive, in certain respects, than the hero and heroine. In *Emma*, there is no need for a ritual of expulsion. Emma, who has much in common with the spoiled children of *Mansfield Park*, is, unlike most of them, highly educable. Once she is purged of her faults, the new society becomes possible. She represents, at the end, a combination of "energy and spirits" with propriety and moral awareness which is more attractive than the sober rectitude of Fanny and Edmund.

Even in terms of its comic structure, however, the ending of *Emma* leaves something to be desired. Mr. Woodhouse retains too powerful an influence upon the novel's society. He represents, throughout, the forces opposed to comic values. He dislikes marriage, fears life, and opposes change. Like Emma, he repeats his obsessions and imposes them upon others by virtue of his position. In his presence, honesty, spontaneity, and the healthy enjoyment of life are out of the question. There is no possibility of his changing, of course; and we do not wish to see him expelled from the new society; but we would like to see his influence diminished more than it is. For a time it looks as if Emma and Knightley will not be able to marry until he dies. The irrational law he would impose upon his daughter is circumvented by a manipulation of the plot which makes the marriage harmonize with his obsessions, but the high spirits of the last several chapters are considerably dampened by the prospect of the newlyweds having to humor Mr. Woodhouse for as long as he lives. The reader wishes for his death, and one cannot help imagining that Emma and Knightley will soon be troubled by inadmissible longings for release.

3

Different as it is in tone, *Emma* is not so much a departure from *Mansfield Park* as a variation upon its central theme. *Mansfield Park* shows the advantages of discipline, hardship, and struggle and the evils of excessive liberty and indulgence. *Emma* explores the same theme by making a spoiled child the central figure and showing how she is educated through a combination of suffering, correction, and good example.

The opening pages of the novel present Emma to us immediately as a spoiled child, long before Knightley identifies her as such. She has "lived nearly twenty-one years in the world with very little to distress or vex her." Her mother has been long dead; her father is feeble and indulgent; and, "in consequence of her sister's marriage," she has "been mistress of his house from a very early period." Miss Taylor has been her governess for sixteen years, but "the mildness of her temper [has] hardly allowed her to impose any restraint," and "the shadow of authority" has long since "passed away." Emma does "just what she like[s]" and is "directed chiefly by her own" judgment. Her "power of having . . . too much her own way" and "disposition to think a little too well of herself" are identified as the "real evils of her situation," "disadvantages" which threaten "alloy to her many enjoyments."

We are reminded of the Crawfords, with whom Emma has much in common. Like them, she has "sense and energy and spirits" (I, ii). She is well-endowed by nature, but deficient in nurture. There are crucial differences in her upbringing, however, which make her corrigible, whereas they are not. Miss Taylor has given her principles (II, xvii). Her father's demands for care impose a kind of hardship and discipline and mold her into a dutiful daughter. Living in Highbury, she is insulated from the evils of worldliness and the contagion of corrupt examples. The dominant figure in her world is Knightley, who provides guidance, good example, and rebuke. She has "'the assistance of all [his] endeavors to counteract the indulgence of other people'" (III, xvii).

Emma's deficiencies are, in Jane Austen's view, the fault of her nurture. Her existence has been too privileged; she has been made to feel too important; she has received too much deference and praise. She has not had to earn respect, to submit to judgment, or to acknowledge a higher authority. As a result, she lacks discipline, is indisposed to work, and fails to develop her potentialities. She is arrogant, self-important, and controlling. She overrates her capacities and is too confident of her knowledge, judgment, and perception. Because she is so accustomed to having reality arranged for her convenience, she is given to fantasizing and to assuming that things are probably as she wishes or imagines them to be. She has a weakness for flattering illusions and for people who feed her pride. She tends to avoid competition, to cut down rivals, and to evade unpleasant realizations. Her description of Mrs. Elton fits Emma herself very well: she is "a vain woman, extremely well satisfied with herself, and thinking much of her own importance . . . [who means] to shine and be very superior" (II, xiv).

There is a precise structure by which Jane Austen identifies Emma's faults and traces the progress of her education. Almost every time that Emma errs—in judgment, perception, or behavior—she is corrected by Knightley. He warns her of the impropriety of matchmaking, disapproves of her intimacy with Harriet Smith, is outraged by her objections to Robert Martin and her interference with Martin's proposal to Harriet, disagrees with her view of Harriet's matrimonial prospects, warns her against her designs on Mr. Elton, conveys his suspicions of Frank Churchill's secret relation with Jane, and rebukes her for insulting Miss Bates. On every occasion but the last Emma pridefully rejects Knightley's position. Each episode of rejection is paralleled by a later scene in which she humbly recognizes her error. She not only sees that Knightley was right, but she also recognizes the faulty attitudes and values which produced her mistake and determines to change. She is guilty, of course, of a good deal of backsliding; there are some lessons which she must be taught again and again. But the cumulative effect of these recognition scenes, with their accompanying repentances and resolutions, is to suggest a profound and lasting reformation. Her growth is manifested, moreover, in her actions. She accepts Knightley's rebuke at Box Hill immediately, and she begins to behave toward Miss Bates and Jane as Knightley has always told her she should.

The most important change in Emma, from Jane Austen's point of view, is in her attitude toward herself. The process is slow, but her overinflated ego is eventually reduced to a proper size. The movement is from pride to humility, from self-aggrandizement to self-castigation, from self-delusion to self-knowledge: "With insufferable vanity had she believed herself in the secret of everybody's destiny. She was proved to have been universally mistaken" (III, xi). Her more realistic estimate of herself is manifested not only by her repeated self-accusations, but also by her recognition of Knightley's merit and her submission to his authority: "She had often been negligent or perverse, slighting his advice, or even wilfully opposing him, insensible of half his merits, and quarreling with him because he would not acknowledge her false and insolent estimate of her own" (III, xii). Emma is driven to many of her recognitions by threatening complications; but when all difficulties are resolved and happiness is in sight, she does not revert to her former attitudes: "What had she to wish for? Nothing but to grow more worthy of him, whose intentions and judgment had been ever so superior to her own. Nothing but that the lessons of her past folly might teach her humility and circumspection in future" (III, xviii).

Emma's education is an example of moral growth through suffering. She is instructed not only by Knightley but also by reality, which crushes her pride and forces her to abandon her delusional system. She does not accept Knightley's lessons until reality proves her to have been wrong and threatens to punish her for her errors. At first she suffers chiefly through the evils she brings upon Harriet Smith. She feels humbled and repentant and resolves to reform, but her pride and preeminence remain essentially undisturbed, and she repeats her errors. It is only when she begins to suffer on her own account that the truth sinks in and she realizes that she *must* change. Her behavior toward Miss Bates violates her own standards, as well as Knightley's, and threatens her with the loss both of his respect and of her own esteem. The prospect of Knightley's marrying Harriet Smith convinces her, as nothing else could do, how wrong she was to have neglected Jane, to have become intimate with Harriet, and to have opposed her marriage to Robert Martin. The blows to her ego, combined with the prospect of losing Knightley, cure her of her delusions of self-sufficiency. She realizes how much Knightley has always meant to her and how much she needs him now. She is no longer the prideful woman who sees marriage only as a threat to her power and preeminence.

Emma has a comic education plot. The heroine errs as a result of her faults, suffers as a result of her errors, grows as a result of her suffering, and achieves happiness as a result of her growth. (In a tragic education plot, the protagonist grows as a result of his suffering, but is destroyed as a result of his errors.) From Jane Austen's point of view, there is no reason to doubt that Emma's reformation will be permanent and complete. Every fault has been chastened, every error has been corrected, every illusion has been removed. Emma's humility of spirit and respect for Knightley's authority assure continued growth and a prevailing rectitude of heart, mind, and conduct. Her change has already been so remarkable as to earn Knightley's esteem: they "'have every right that equal worth can give,'" he proclaims, "'to be happy together'" (III, xvii). As Wayne Booth observes, "this will be a happy marriage because there is simply nothing left to make it anything less than perfectly happy. It fulfills every value embodied in the world of the book—with the possible exception that Emma may never learn to apply herself as she ought to her reading and her piano!"[2]

4

"Marriage to an intelligent, amiable, good, and attractive man is the best thing that can happen to this heroine," says Booth, "and the readers who do not experience it as such are, I am convinced, far from knowing what Jane Austen is about" (*Rhetoric*, p. 260). As he is aware, there *are* such readers:

> G. B. Stern laments, in *Speaking of Jane Austen*, "Oh, Miss Austen, it was not a good solution; it was a bad solution, an unhappy ending, could we see beyond the last pages of the book." Edmund Wilson predicts that Emma will find a new protégée like Harriet, since she has not been cured of her inclination to "infatuations with women." Marvin Mudrick even more emphatically rejects Jane Austen's explicit rhetoric; he believes that Emma is still a "confirmed exploiter," and for him the ending must be read as ironic. (P. 259)

The mistakes of these readers arise, Booth feels, from looking "at Emma and Knightley as real people." From this perspective, he acknowledges, the "ending will seem false"; but for him this is an inadmissible perspective.

It is quite possible, it seems to me, both to experience *Emma* from Jane Austen's point of view, to know what she thinks she is doing, and to recognize that the novel which she has actually created does not always support her intentions. If we are guided wholly by her rhetoric, we will miss a large part of her achievement and fail to recover some of her deepest intuitions. Instead of ruling out responses which are in conflict with the author's explicit rhetoric, it may be more fruitful to ask if there is not something in the novel—unperceived, perhaps, by the author—to which these critics are reacting.

What these critics see, without articulating it precisely, is that Emma is more than an aesthetic and an illustrative character. She is an imagined human being whose problems have deep psychological sources. The experience she undergoes does not seem sufficient to cure her, and the conditions of her marriage do not seem to promise the degree of happiness which the ending predicts. Booth is right about Jane Austen's intentions. Those who object to the ending have a correct intuition about the persistence of Emma's problems and the incompleteness of the novel's resolution. Both positions are supported by the text. The conflict between them is sponsored not only by differing critical perspectives, but also by internal disparities between rhetoric and mimesis. To understand these disparities properly we must give as much attention to the analysis of Emma's character and development as critics have hitherto given to Jane Austen's view of these phenomena. By seeing Emma as a creation inside a creation, we shall at once account for the novel's inner tensions and enhance our appreciation of Jane Austen's genius in mimetic characterization.

From a psychological point of view, *Emma* is the story of a young woman with both narcissistic and perfectionistic trends which have been induced by her early environment.[3] She has great pride in her superior position and abilities and in her high moral standards. Her need to reinforce and to protect this pride leads her to be domineering toward her subordinates, competitive toward her rivals, and dutiful toward those for whom she feels a sense of responsibility. She suffers inner conflict when she is supposed to be good to her competitors or when she harms (or is in danger of harming) those whom she is supposed to protect. These conflicts produce psychological distress which ranges from mild discomfort to intense self-hate. Her defensive strategies lead her to misconstructions of reality and to moral errors. The recognition of her mistakes and of their potentially serious consequences crushes her pride and generates feelings of anxiety and self-contempt. No longer confident of her own preeminence and rectitude, she transfers her pride to Knightley and restores her position by submitting to and possessing him. This change signifies not maturation, but the substitution of a new defensive strategy for the ones which have collapsed. Her relation to her father, which has all along prevented her from becoming a mature woman, remains essentially unchanged at the end. She cannot marry Knightley until a twist in the plot removes all parental opposition.

The narcissistic person "is often gifted beyond average, early and easily won distinctions, and sometimes was the favored and admired child" (*NHG*, p. 194). He is "driven by the need for . . . self-aggrandizement or for being on top" (*NHG*, p. 192). He gains the necessary feeling of mastery not by work or vindictive triumphs, but by "self-admiration and the exercise of charm" (*NHG*, p. 212). Narcissism means "being 'in love with one's idealized image'" (*NHG*, p. 194). The narcissistic person "*is* his idealized self and seems to adore it. This . . . gives him the buoyancy or the resiliency entirely lacking in the other groups" (my italics). Beneath his "belief in his greatness and uniqueness," however, there lurks a nagging insecurity: "He may speak incessantly of his exploits or of his wonderful qualities and needs endless confirmation of his estimate of himself in the form of admiration and devotion." His solution tends to divorce him from reality and thereby makes him highly vulnerable: "His plans are often too expansive. He does not reckon with limitations. He overrates his capacities" (*NHG*, p. 195). As a result, "failures occur easily. Up to a point his resilience gives him a capacity to bounce, but . . . repeated failures . . . may crush him altogether.

The self-hate and self-contempt, successfully held in abeyance other-wise, may then operate in full force" (*NHG*, p. 195). The applicability of this description to Emma is striking.

Emma's childhood situation is, like Fanny Price's, unhealthy, but to a lesser degree and in a different way. Unlike Fanny, Emma is well-gratified in many of her basic needs. She is socially secure. She feels loved, has a sense of belonging, and is treated with consideration and respect. She seems to have an abundance of self-esteem. In truth, how-ever, her self-esteem is shaky; and a close examination of her behavior shows that she is busily engaged in warding off threats and in seeking reassurance.

Emma is insecure in her self-esteem because almost everything in her situation has contributed to the formation of an unrealistic self-image. She is the favored child, the cleverest member of the family, the mistress of Hartfield, the first lady of Highbury. Her father praises her constantly, almost everyone treats her deferentially, and her governess devotes "all her powers to attach and amuse" her, adapting herself to Emma's "every pleasure, every scheme" (I, i). All of this inflates Emma's sense of her own power, ability, and importance, while mak-ing it unnecessary for her to earn her rewards through effort and achievement. As a result, she makes great claims for herself; but she lacks real self-confidence, which could have come only from testing herself against reality and knowing that she had deserved whatever she receives in the way of praise and respect. Emma identifies with her ide-alized image, which in her case is not a compensation for low self-esteem but is a product of the inflated estimate of herself which she re-ceives from others. She loves her proud self, feels little need to change, and exuberantly plays out her role. Consciously she has few doubts, but unconsciously she is plagued by anxieties which manifest them-selves in her behavior.

Emma's insecurity is revealed in part by the frequent defensiveness of her behavior. She is competitive toward women like Jane Fairfax and Mrs. Elton, who threaten her position as favored child or first lady of Highbury. Jane is her chief rival for the attention and acclaim of the neighborhood; and her accomplishments make Emma uncomfortably aware of the disparity between her own promise and her performance, between other people's praise of her playing and its true worth. Emma's attitudes toward Jane have many of the characteristics of sibling rivalry. She hates to hear Jane praised, and she is hostile toward Miss Bates partly because the old woman is always talking of her niece. Emma dislikes Jane's presence in the neighborhood, is unfriendly to her when she is there, and cuts Jane down by imagining things to her disadvantage and making sport of her with Frank Churchill. She defends her pride, in other words, by either avoiding Jane or belittling her. Since her moral standards tell her that she *should* be a friend to Jane, she is never comfortable with her own behavior; and she needs to assuage her guilt by periodic self-criticism and resolutions to reform.

The fact that we are meant to share Emma's estimate of Mrs. Elton may obscure our perception that Emma is threatened by this woman who is, in many respects, a vulgar version of herself. Both women seek praise, wish to control others, and need to be recognized as first in importance. When Mrs. Elton's status as a newly married woman gives her precedence over Emma, Emma is genuinely disturbed and thinks that it might be worthwhile, after all, to consider marriage. The competition with Mrs. Elton is not enough, of course, to propel her into marrying; but we should take her discomfort seriously as an indication of the importance which being first has for Emma. If she were more secure, she would not be so jealous of petty distinctions. Emma is severely critical of Mrs. Elton not only because the latter deserves it, but also because she has a powerful need to put down a woman whom she experiences as a rival.

Emma is outraged and indignant when Mrs. Elton offers to sponsor her in Bath by providing an introduction to a friend of hers there: "The dignity of Miss Woodhouse, of Hartfield, was sunk indeed!" (II, xiv). She has a similar reaction, though far more intense, when Mr. Elton proposes marriage: ". . . that he . . . should suppose himself her equal in connection or mind! . . . and be so blind . . . as to fancy himself showing no presumption in addressing her!—It was most provoking" (I, xvi). Emma is "insulted by his hopes" because, by showing that he does not regard her as inestimably above him, they threaten to bring her down from the heights of her illusory grandeur. In order to restore her pride, she carefully rehearses in her own mind all the grounds of her superiority: "Perhaps it was not fair to expect him to feel how very much he was her inferior in talent, and all the elegancies of mind. The very want of such equality might prevent his perception of it; but he must know that in fortune and consequence she was greatly his superior. He must know that the Woodhouses . . . [were] the younger branch of a very ancient family—and that the Eltons were nobody." Emma is so jealous of her dignity, so angry when it is challenged, and so eager to reaffirm it, because she lives largely for the gratification of her pride, which is highly vulnerable. Mr. Elton's proposal, like Mrs. Elton's patronage, is completely incompatible with her idealized image of herself.

Emma's rivalry with Knightley is different from those which we have so far examined. Each of her competitors tends to threaten a different aspect of her idealized image, a different set of claims. She acknowledges Donwell to be the equal of Hartfield in consequence and takes pride in her sister's connection with the Knightleys. She is the first lady of Highbury, and George Knightley is the first gentleman. Her rivalry with Knightley is in the areas of perception and judgment. Since he is a man, older, much respected, and authoritative in manner, she is somewhat in awe of him; but, perhaps for that very reason, she clings to a belief that, on some matters at least, she is his superior in insight and discrimination. When they disagree, she tenaciously maintains her own point of view. She longs for vindictive triumphs, for events to prove her right; but it is invariably he who is shown to have been correct. After a series of mortifications, her pride is broken; and she submits herself entirely to Knightley's guidance.

Emma's insecurity is revealed not only by her competitiveness, but also by her pursuit of reassurance. Not only does she avoid people who threaten her, but she also seeks out the company of those who feed her pride. Harriet, Mrs. Weston, and Mr. Woodhouse constitute her claque; in their presence she can be assured of admiration and applause. The mental deficiencies of Harriet and her father disturb Emma at times, but usually she welcomes them as a confirmation of her own superiority. Mrs. Weston is intelligent, but deferential. This combination makes her an excellent source of reinforcement, and it is easy to understand why Emma is so often at Randalls. Critical of almost everyone and contemptuous of many, Emma tends to ignore the faults and to overrate the virtues of this trio. To deprecate them would diminish the value of their exaltation of herself.

Emma's scheming should be seen as, in part at least, an expression of her need for reassurance. It is an effort to repeat the triumphs of her childhood; it is an aspect of her search for glory. The search for glory is usually compensatory in nature. The individual has been made to feel weak, worthless, and, in various ways, inferior. He compensates for all this by creating, with the help of his imagination, an idealized image which raises him above others; and he embarks upon the project of actualizing his idealized image, of attaining in reality the glory which he feels he deserves and which he has already experienced in imagination. Emma's case is different. In this, as in all her defensive strivings, she seeks not to make up for childhood deprivations, but to hold on to the exalted status which she has already been accorded. She is, at the beginning of the novel, already in possession of her glory. Her project is not so much to actualize her idealized image as to find ways of maintaining it.

This presents a considerable difficulty. What is Emma to do? What adult role is she to play? She cannot rely upon her "accomplishments" to provide confirmation, for she has never attained excellence. One reason for this, as we have seen, is that she has never had to prove herself; she has always been surrounded by praise. Another reason, I suspect, is that she protects her pride by leaving her projects unfinished and doing less than she can. She cannot risk being judged on her best effort. It is safer to remain a promising but undisciplined child who could do great things if she tried. In the presence of so challenging a competitor as Jane Fairfax, her lack of effort provides an excuse for not being first in accomplishments.

Emma could seek to reaffirm her glory through a grand marriage. But marriage, she feels, has little to offer: "'Fortune I do not want; consequence I do not want: I believe few married women are half as much mistress of their husband's house, as I am of Hartfield; and never, never could I expect to be so truly beloved and important; so always first and always right in any man's eyes as I am in my father's'" (I, x). Marriage presents itself to Emma less as an opportunity for fulfillment than as a threat. She would have to give up her domestic power and her status as the favored child. There are additional reasons, as we shall see, for her rejection of marriage. The question remains then: what is Emma to do? How is she to preserve the domestic situation which is so necessary to her pride and at the same time discover an activity, suitable to her years, which will maintain the sense of mastery and mental superiority that has been fostered by her experience as a spoiled child?

Emma's solution is to live through other people, to imagine their destinies, and to manage their lives. She will be a matchmaker. As the novel opens, she has just had a great success: Miss Taylor has married, and Emma "'made the match'" herself (I, i). When Mr. Woodhouse asks her not to make any more matches, Emma promises to make none for herself, "'but I must, indeed, for other people. It is the greatest amusement in the world. And after such success you know!'" This project has given her an occupation and a sense of direction for four years, and the happy result confirms her sense of power and perspicacity. But the completion of her project and the departure of Miss Taylor leave a void in her life. It is soon filled by Harriet Smith, who has, like Miss Taylor, the compliant disposition which Emma likes in other people. Emma will be Harriet's sponsor, her mentor. Everything that Harriet becomes she will owe to Emma. Her improvement, her triumphs, and, finally, her superior marriage will all redound to the glory of her maker. It is no wonder that Emma does not want Harriet to marry Robert Martin. This would deprive her of occupation and deny her a splendid opportunity to exercise her powers.

Emma's plans for Harriet and her plans for Mr. Elton quickly coalesce. She has far too much pride invested in the success of her project and far too much confidence in her powers of judgment and control to perceive that she is encouraging Mr. Elton and that it is she, and not Harriet, who is his object. As she herself comes to see, she takes "up the idea . . . and [makes] everything bend to it" (I, xvi). When she brings Harriet and Elton together in the Vicarage, she feels, "for half a minute, . . . the glory of having schemed successfully"; but Elton, of course, does not "come to the point" (I, x). His proposal to her instead is such a blow, not only because it insults her dignity, but also because it deprives her of glory, challenges her sense of mastery, and calls into question the superiority of her "Understanding." His scorn of Harriet, in whom she has now invested her pride, is an offense to herself. The bitterness of this experience makes her wish to avoid a repetition, and she resolves "to do such things no more" (I, xvi).

Emma is far too resilient, of course, to be permanently discouraged by a single setback. In addition, her unconscious compulsions continue to operate. Driven by her needs to protect her pride and to reaffirm her idealized image, she fastens upon one ill-conceived idea after another and makes everything bend to it. Repeated disillusionments and failures eventually puncture her narcissism and produce a change in her behavior, the exact meaning of which I shall discuss later.

Emma needs not only to be great, but also to be perfectly good. Her expansiveness takes the form not only of narcissism, but of perfectionism as well. The perfectionistic person "identifies himself with his standards" and makes "strenuous efforts to measure up to his shoulds by fulfilling duties and obligations, by polite and orderly manners" (*NHG*, p. 196). He "feels superior because of his high standards . . . and on this basis looks down on others." He hides his "arrogant contempt of others," however, "because his very standards prohibit such 'irregular' feelings." He defends his pride by equating "standards and actualities— knowing about moral values and being a good person," by denying his own deficiencies, and by externalizing his self-condemnation. He is harsh upon others when they fall below his standards or display failings which he cannot afford to recognize in himself. His pride in his good qualities is intense but vulnerable. It tends to be broken by misfortune and by "his recognition of an error or failure of his own making" (*NHG*, p. 197). When he realizes "his own fallibility," "self-effacing trends and undiluted self-hate, kept in check successfully hitherto, then may come to the fore."

It is Emma's perfectionistic tendencies which gain her a large measure of approval from Jane Austen even before her pride is broken near the end, for the author has strong perfectionistic elements in her own personality. Emma is no callous manipulator. Her resolution, after the Elton affair, "to do such things no more" is motivated in part by feelings of guilt and concern for the harm she has done to Harriet. She has a strong sense of duty toward her father, her guests, her friends and dependents, and the poor of the neighborhood. We often see her working very hard to perform her various roles in an exemplary fashion. When she lives up to her standards, she experiences a self-approbation which often manifests itself in high spirits and gracious behavior. When she is conscious of failure, she is always distressed, sometimes exceedingly; and she usually attempts to remedy the situation as far as she is able.

Emma's perfectionism demands not only that she be good, but also that she be the ideal lady, the model of elegance, good taste, and fine manners. She tends to measure everyone on a scale of refinement and to be contemptuous of those who fall below her own standards. Her criticism of others is a reaffirmation of her own superiority.

Emma's perfectionism, like her narcissism, is induced not by deprivation but by an excess of approbation. Having always been told that she is perfect, and having derived immense satisfaction from such praise, Emma is under strong pressure to live up to this exalted image of herself. Her narcissism gives rise to a great many claims; she experiences her perfectionism largely as shoulds. She may not work at her piano and her painting, but she does her best to be perfect in her moral relations. The chief threat to her self-regard is Knightley, whose standards are even higher than her own and who has a kind of authority because of his social position and the similarity of his character structure. When subjected to his criticisms, Emma must either defend her pride or be crushed.

Emma's perfectionism manifests itself in its most striking and compulsive form in her relationship with her father. It derives, indeed, chiefly from their pathological interaction. Emma may seem to be in control of the situation at Hartfield; but she manages her father—and, indeed, her own life—only in small matters. It is Mr. Woodhouse who dictates the life style of Hartfield and who determines the possibilities of Emma's existence. He presents himself as a man on the verge of extinction who can be kept alive and in tolerable comfort only by the rigid observance of his wishes. He manipulates Emma through a combination of dependency and praise. She receives from him two complementary messages. The first is that if she does not cater to his weakness and respect his obsessions, he will become nervous and depressed and may, indeed, die. The second is that she is wonderful for being so good to him. The result, for Emma, is that she cannot do anything that will disturb her father. If she did, she would have to take the risk of destroying him and of losing her status as the perfect daughter. The resulting guilt and shame would be unbearable.

Jane Austen depicts Emma's relation with her father in brilliant mimetic detail, but she seems quite blind to its destructiveness and to the compulsive nature of Emma's "goodness." She is indulgent toward Mr. Woodhouse, softens his role as a blocking force, and approves of Emma's hypersensitivity to his needs and wishes. She does not see that Emma is severely constrained by his embeddedness and that she is forced by the combination of his praise and demands into a self-alienated development. Emma is not free to feel her own feelings and to consult her own wishes. She is compelled, much of the time, to repress her resentment, to disguise her feelings, and to act a part. In her father's presence, her lack of spontaneity, congruity, and transparence is striking and nearly complete.

I do not mean to suggest that Emma's acting is for her father only. She is motivated in almost all of her relationships by her need to maintain the various components of her idealized image. As a result, she is almost always, to some extent, insincere. The burdensomeness of this becomes clear when she begins to look forward to a relatively frank relationship with Knightley. His having seen through her pretenses is in some ways a relief. She can abandon her pride and, with it, the necessity of playing a role. Mr. Woodhouse remains, however; and it is not pleasant to imagine the constant hard labor of pretending which living with him will entail.

As we have seen, Emma's narcissism is partly responsible for her attitude toward marriage, which seems to her a state which will threaten rather than enhance her power and preeminence. The chief reason for her lack of interest in marriage, however, is that it is incompatible with her relation to her father. "'I must see somebody very superior to any one I have seen yet,'" she tells Harriet, "'to be tempted . . . and I do *not* wish to see any such person. I would rather not be tempted'" (I, x). If she were to be tempted, she would experience, as she knows, a painful conflict. In order to accept a husband, she would have, it must seem, to kill her father and to become the worst instead of the best of daughters.

Even when she realizes that Knightley must marry no one else, she still does not want him to marry her: "Marriage, in fact, would not do for her. It would be incompatible with what she owed to her father, and with what she felt for him. Nothing should separate her from her father. She would not marry, even if she were asked by Mr. Knightley" (III, xii). After Knightley proposes, "a very short parley with her own heart produced the most solemn resolution of never quitting her father.—

She even wept over the idea of it, as a sin of thought. While he lived, it must be only an engagement . . ." (III, xiv).

The conflict in which she finds herself because of her relationship with her father produces a strong tendency toward detachment in Emma. The most important feelings and activities for a woman of her age and culture are simply inadmissible to her. In order to avoid guilt and conflict she represses her sexual nature and renounces her aspirations for an adult, autonomous, fruitful existence. "'Were I to fall in love,'" she tells Harriet, "'indeed, it would be a different thing! But I have never been in love: it is not my way or nature; and I do not think I ever shall'" (I, x). As "'objects for the affections,'" she will have her sister's children. She will be Aunt Emma! There will be enough children "'for every hope and every fear; and though my attachment to none can equal that of a parent, it suits my ideas of comfort better than what is warmer and blinder.'" There is a reserve, even a frigidity about Emma which is entirely explicable in the light of her bond with her father. Since all warm and intimate relationships threaten that bond, Emma cannot allow herself to experience even the desire for them, which would be a sin of thought, but must settle for what is cooler and more comfortable. She renounces not only her sexual and maternal feelings, but also the active living of her own life. She becomes an onlooker. She lives vicariously, through protégées and other people's marriages.

Emma *is* attracted to the idea of being courted by Frank Churchill, but she never wishes their relationship to become serious. What transpires between them is mostly in her imagination (though Frank, for his own purposes, is attentive); and she arranges everything, his feelings and her own, to suit her various psychological needs. Her "imagination" gives him "the distinguished honour . . . if not of being really in love with her, of being at least very near it, and saved only by her own indifference" (II, vii). It is important for her to feel that she has him in her power, that he would be hers if she wished it; but "her resolution . . . of never marrying" requires that she be indifferent and that his passion not be so strong as to produce painful scenes and a disappointment which would expose her to reproach. Eventually she comes to feel that she, too, is in love, but only a little: "'I must be in love; I should be the oddest creature in the world if I were not—for a few weeks at least'" (II, xii). Emma's detachment has evidently made her feel odd; being in love assures her that she is a normal woman. She is pleased, however, to feel no temptation to accept his proposal:

> the conclusion of every imaginary declaration on his side was that she *re-fused him.* Their affection was always to subside into friendship. Every thing tender and charming was to mark their parting; but still they were to part. When she became sensible of this, it struck her that she could not be very much in love; for in spite of her previous and fixed determination never to quit her father, never to marry, a strong attachment certainly must produce more of a struggle than she could foresee in her own feelings. . . . "I do suspect that he is not really necessary to my happiness. So much the better. . . . I am quite enough in love. I should be sorry to be more." (II, xiii)

Everything is working out for Emma in the best possible way. She imagines Frank to be in love with her, which satisfies her pride. She feels that she is in love with him, which attests to her normality, but not so much that she will be tempted to sins, either of thought or of deed, against her father. Having been in love, moreover, gives her a feeling of security for the future: "'I shall do very well again after a little while—and then, it will be a good thing over; for they say everybody is in love once in their lives, and I shall have been let off easily'" (II, xiii). Apparently, Emma has been afraid of love as overwhelming passion which would throw her into painful inner conflict. Having had a mild case of the disease, to which everyone, it seems, is subject, she feels safe against its more virulent forms. Frank's absence cools her completely; and when she hears of his return, she is determined not "to have her own affections entangled again" (III, i). She is afraid that his feelings might produce "a crisis, an event, a something to alter her present composed and tranquil state" and is relieved to find him decidedly less attentive than before. There is little reason to believe, I might add, that Emma has been in love with Frank at all. Her feelings have been governed by conventional expectations and by her various defensive needs.

The change in Emma is precipitated largely by two events: the Box Hill episode and the discovery that Harriet hopes to marry Knightley. To appreciate the significance of the Box Hill episode, it is important to understand three things: (1) why Emma insults Miss Bates, (2) why, after Knightley's rebuke, she is so depressed, and (3) what effect this experience has upon her feelings toward Knightley.

Emma's insult has been foreshadowed earlier in the novel. She displays an aversion toward Miss Bates throughout and mocks or disparages her many times behind her back. Her attitude toward Miss Bates has a number of sources. She resents her constant praise of Jane; she has a "horror . . . of falling in with the second rate and third rate of Highbury, who were calling on [her] for ever" (II, i); and she finds Miss Bates "'too good natured and too silly'" to suit her (I, x). Miss Bates is a poor spinster with a mother to care for who secures the charity and affection of her neighbors by a strict course of self-effacing behavior. She has "universal good-will" and a "contented temper" (I, iii). She approves of everything without discrimination, constantly expresses her gratitude, and has nothing but praise for everyone. As Emma observes, "'nobody is afraid of her; that is a great charm'" (I, x). As is typical of an expansive person, Emma has a good deal of disdain for such self-effacing qualities. When she encounters them in people like Mr. Woodhouse, Isabella, Mr. and Mrs. Weston, and Harriet Smith, she has strong motives for repressing her contempt. It is more easily felt toward Miss Bates. Even here, however, she is not free of discomfort. She believes, like Knightley, in noblesse oblige; and she has a continual nagging guilt about her sins of omission toward Miss Bates. She has, moreover, a self-effacing component in her own personality which leads her to honor "warmth and tenderness of heart," qualities in which she knows herself to be deficient, especially toward Miss Bates. Insofar as she makes Emma feel cold-hearted or undutiful, Miss Bates is a threatening figure. As such, she arouses in Emma guilt and hostility which are not felt by Miss Bates's more genial neighbors.

Emma's insult to Miss Bates results from the slipping out, under the cover of wit, of a contempt which she had felt frequently but which she had hitherto expressed only privately or indirectly. I have discussed so far some of the reasons for a buildup of hostility toward Miss Bates, but there is yet another source which I believe to be the chief motivation behind the insult. What Emma is saying, as her victim well under-stands, is that Miss Bates is exceedingly "dull" and that her "society" is "irksome" (III, vii). As Emma explains to Knightley, "'I know there is not a better creature in the world: but you must allow, that what is good and what is ridiculous are most unfortunately blended in her.'" What Emma feels most of all toward Miss Bates is an irritability in her pres-ence, an impatience of her silliness, a resentment at being obliged to humor this "tiresome" woman (II, i). She rebels by staying away, by thwarting Miss Bates when she can, by mocking her behind her back, and, finally, by insulting her to her face. Her reactions are fully intelli-gible, I believe, only when we see that Emma is discharging onto Miss Bates feelings which she has, but cannot admit, toward her father.

To a dispassionate observer, Miss Bates and Mr. Woodhouse seem much alike. Like Miss Bates, Mr. Woodhouse is "everywhere beloved for the friendliness of his heart and his amiable temper" (I, i); and, like her, he is an unfortunate blend of the good and the ridiculous. Comic as they may be when they are encountered in a book, it would be impossi-ble to enjoy their society or to find them less than oppressive as people to live with. Emma's heart goes out to Jane Fairfax at Donwell when she thinks that her distress is because of her aunt:

Her parting words, "Oh! Miss Woodhouse, the comfort of being some-times alone!"—seemed to burst from an overcharged heart, and to describe somewhat of the continual endurance to be practiced by her, even toward some of those who loved her best.

"Such a home, indeed! such an aunt! . . . I do pity you. And the more sensibility you betray of their just horrors, the more I shall like you." (III, vi)

Emma is mistaken about Jane, but her response indicates what her own feelings would be if she had to live with Miss Bates. More than that, it indicates what Emma's feelings *are*, unconsciously, about having to live with her father. She cannot stand being with Miss Bates because of "the continual endurance" which she must practice toward Mr. Woodhouse. She has no patience left. What Knightley sees as Miss Bates's harmless absurdities produce in Emma an almost phobic reaction.

Because of her need to be a perfect daughter, Emma must repress any irritation with her father; but the motives for repression are not strong enough to prevent such feelings from being displaced onto Miss Bates and released, from time to time, in relatively safe ways. She can feel on Jane's behalf emotions which would be completely inadmissible if she were to experience them on her own account. Emma behaves toward her father with an unfailing grace and carefully avoids sins even of thought. Her exasperation with Miss Bates, culminating in the insult at Box Hill, betrays her unconscious feelings of oppression and hostility.

As Jane Austen makes clear through Knightley's rebuke, the insult to Miss Bates is inexcusable. Even so, Emma's reaction seems out of proportion to her offense: "Never had she felt so agitated, mortified, grieved, at any circumstance in her life. . . . She had never been so depressed" (III, vii). She cries almost all the way home, in Harriet's presence, and that evening, looking back upon the day, feels it "more to be abhorred in recollection, than any she had ever passed." Emma is so distressed because she has seriously violated her perfectionistic shoulds and can find no way to protect her pride. Knightley has reproached her before, sometimes severely; but she has always been able to maintain the correctness of her own position. Now, however, his values and her own coincide; and after a few attempts at self-defense, she cannot deny "the truth of his representation." Her depression is produced, to some extent, by the collapse of her idealized image. Her self-esteem is sinking. She feels that the "degree" of her father's "fond affection and confiding esteem" is "unmerited." She feels ashamed before Knightley, guilty toward Miss Bates, and angry with herself. How could she have behaved in this way? Her sense of the heinousness of her crime may be related to the fact that Miss Bates is partly a surrogate for her father, toward whom she has the most compulsive feelings of duty. Miss Bates's dependency and compliance are also a factor; Emma has struck a defenseless person.

Emma begins to work almost immediately at restoring her pride. While recognizing that she is not as perfect as her father thinks her to be, she takes comfort in attending to him and in reflecting upon her general conduct toward him: "As a daughter, she hoped, she was not without a heart. She hoped no one could have said to her, 'How could you have been so unfeeling to your father?'" (III, viii). She assuages her guilt toward Miss Bates by self-condemnation and a determination to reform: "She had been often remiss, her conscience told her so; remiss, perhaps, more in thought than fact; scornful, ungracious." As she pays her penitential visit, she hopes to encounter Knightley, but he does not appear. When he learns of her visit, however, he understands at once "all that had passed of good in her feelings" (III, ix). They part "thorough friends," as his manner assures her that she has "fully recovered his good opinion."

Emma is comfortable once more, but things are not as they were before. An important change has taken place in her pride system and in her relation to Knightley. The self-hate and humiliation which she has experienced as a result of her own error have made her afraid of her pride and uncertain of her ability to live up to her shoulds. As a means of self-protection, she submits to Knightley's judgment and authority. If she acts and feels as he would wish, she will be certain of maintaining both his esteem and her own. She makes him an omniscient observer of her moral life, adding in this way the fear of his judgments to her own shoulds as a motive for the repression of all unacceptable impulses. She begins not only to act, but also to feel properly toward Jane and Miss Bates. When Jane rejects her kind attentions, she is "mortified" at being "given so little credit for proper feeling, or esteemed so little worthy as a friend." But she has "the consolation of knowing that her intentions were good, and of being able to say to herself, that could Mr. Knightley have been privy to all her attempts of assisting Jane Fairfax, could he even have seen into her heart, he would not, on this occasion, have found any thing to reprove" (III, ix). Emma is still proud of her goodness, but she experiences her pride now through Knightley's imagined approval rather than through a direct identification with her idealized image.

The Box Hill episode marks the beginning, I believe, of Emma's tender feelings for Knightley. As Horney observes, an expansive person often cannot love until his pride is broken. Emma's humiliation at Knightley's hands arouses feelings of weakness, anxiety, and self-hate. She becomes dependent upon his approval to relieve these feelings and upon his reinforcement to prevent their recurrence. When Knightley hears of her visit to Miss Bates, he looks at her "with a glow of regard":

> She was warmly gratified—and in another moment still more so, by a little movement of more than common friendliness on his part.—He took her hand;—whether she had not herself made the first motion, she could not say—she might, perhaps, have rather offered it—but he took her hand, pressed it, and certainly was on the point of carrying it to his lips—when, from some fancy or other, he suddenly let it go. (III, ix)

Emma is disappointed that he did not complete the motion. There are earlier signs of Knightley's attraction to her, but this is the first instance of a tender impulse on her part toward him. Emma is not aware of the change in their relationship, but this scene prepares for the recognition which is to follow.

Emma's pride receives a devastating blow when she learns of Harriet's hopes of winning Knightley. The two things most important to her, her self-esteem and her preeminence, are severely threatened by this discovery. When Harriet indicates that Frank Churchill is not her object, Emma waits speechless and "in great terror" to learn the truth (III, xi). When all is revealed, including the fact that Harriet has some reasonable hope of a return, it darts through Emma, "with the speed of an arrow, that Mr. Knightley must marry no one but herself!" This intuition is in part a recognition of her own love and her need for his affection. It is mainly, however, a response to threat. If Knightley marries Harriet—or anyone else, for that matter—Emma will lose her position of preeminence, both as first lady of Highbury and, insofar as Knightley is in some respects a father substitute, as favored child. Now that she is "threatened with its loss," Emma discovers how much of her happiness depends "on being *first* with Mr. Knightley, first in interest and affection" (III, xii). She need not marry him, but he must not marry anyone else: "Could she be secure of that, indeed, of his never marrying at all, she believed she should be perfectly satisfied.—Let him but continue the same Mr. Knightley to her and her father . . . and her peace would be fully secured." Given her bond to her father, this would, indeed, be the best solution. What she cannot stand is the thought of Harriet being "the chosen, the first, the dearest." When Knightley proposes, Emma's earliest distinct thought is "that Harriet was nothing, that she was everything herself" (III, xiii).

The discovery of her latest mistake about Harriet is the culminating blow to Emma's pride in the superiority of her values and perceptions. Immediately following her realization that Knightley must marry no one but herself comes a recognition of her own faults. She finds every "part of her mind," other than "her affection for Mr. Knightley," to be "disgusting." Her mistakes strike her now with such "dreadful force" because they have brought upon her a real possibility of disaster. They can no longer be juggled away by an internal process of rationalization or denial, and there seems to be nothing she can do to restore her position. Her realization that Knightley has been right all along and that she could have avoided her present troubles by following his advice makes him assume all the more the aspect of an infallible authority, and she is full of remorse at her earlier impiety. She hates herself and reveres Knightley.

Knightley's proposal enables Emma to rebuild her pride. Her social position is now secure, and she has won a man who is clearly superior to the husband of her chief rival, Jane. She maintains a low estimate of herself, but at the same time she derives reassurance from the fact that so upright and discriminating a man has found her worthy of his love. Since Knightley approves of it, her self-abasement becomes a virtue in which she can take satisfaction. Her many errors of heart and head have made her profoundly distrustful of herself, but she hopes to maintain her perfection in the future by reminding herself of Knightley's superiority and her own past folly (III, xviii).

At the beginning of the novel, Emma identifies with her idealized image. Reality seems to be honoring her narcissistic claims, and she is conscious of fulfilling her perfectionistic shoulds. In the course of the action she receives a series of blows, as her schemes misfire and her perceptions and judgments are proved to have been wrong. She restores her pride in a variety of ways; but her pride system becomes more and more vulnerable as she confronts, again and again, the disparity between her idealized image and reality. The blows which she receives at Box Hill and in her interview with Harriet penetrate her defenses, crush her pride, and generate paroxysms of self-condemnation. Her anguish passes, as events prove favorable; but a significant change takes place in her pride system. She feels weak and unworthy rather than powerful and perfect, and she defends herself against the resulting self-hate and anxiety by transferring her pride to Knightley and experiencing it vicariously through him. Her needs for power and perfection remain unchanged, and she pursues them as compulsively as before, but in a different manner. She idealizes Knightley now, instead of herself, and depends upon his rectitude and preeminence to sustain her worth.

The crushing of Emma's pride and the substitution of compliant for expansive trends seem like growth to Jane Austen because of her own glorification of the self-effacing solution. But when Emma is understood psychologically, there is no reason to believe that she is moving significantly toward self-actualization. This is not to deny that Emma learns from her experiences and makes a better adaptation to her society. She discovers the independence of external reality and gains a knowledge of her inability to control it. She is forced to give up her narcissistic claims and to recognize the immorality of many of her expansive attitudes. Insofar as it made her averse to marriage, her striving for power had cut her off from any meaningful role in her society. The emergence of self-effacing trends leads her to desire marriage and qualifies her for the role of wife. At the beginning of the novel, Emma is an unusual figure in her world; by the end she has the feminine personality which was most commonly induced and most strongly approved by the society of her time.

Given Emma's psychological needs at the end, we must agree with Wayne Booth that marriage to Knightley is "the best thing that can happen to this heroine"; but if we look at it closely, the Emma-Knightley marriage seems far from ideal. The relationship is not based on mature love on the part of either member. Emma is drawn to Knightley by the needs and anxieties which arise when her pride is broken. She has been a spoiled child; now she is a chastened and compliant one who seeks safety through submission to a wise authority.

Knightley will keep her wayward impulses under control, but he will not help her to grow. He is himself a perfectionist who, unlike Emma, succeeds in living up to his own standards. He is attracted to Emma by both her perfectionism and her narcissistic pride and immaturity. He approves of her dutifulness, especially toward her father, but he also enjoys being superior to her in wisdom and maturity. Her pride arouses his competitiveness, and her faults, which give him the victory, are part of her charm. He takes pleasure in being proved right and is most impressed by Emma when she submits to his lecturing. He has found her physically attractive for a long time. The fancied competition with Frank Churchill makes him realize, perhaps unconsciously, how much he enjoys his role of mentor and how important it is to him to be *first* with Miss Woodhouse. When Emma submits to him, he must play down her deficiencies in order to maintain the value of his prize. She is the "sweetest and best of all creatures, faultless in spite of all her faults" (III, xiii). To satisfy his own pride, he needs at once to exalt Emma and to keep her inferior to him. Since she needs at once to receive his approval and to remind herself of his superiority, their relationship promises to be mutually satisfying. That does not, however, make it healthy. It is difficult to see Emma, under Knightley's tutelage, outgrowing her dependency. If she did, there might be trouble.

In one respect Emma does not change at all. She remains completely bound to her father. After Knightley's proposal, the conflict which she has always feared between love and duty confronts her, but it is quickly resolved: she determines never to quit her father, weeps over the idea as a sin of thought, and decides that "while he live[s], it must be only an engagement" (III, xiv). Her conflict is easily disposed of because she does not really have to choose between the two men: Knightley is hers, whether she marries him or not. The problem is really Knightley's. How is he to gain Emma in marriage without violating his (and her) sense of duty toward Mr. Woodhouse? The solution which he proposes is to make Hartfield his home. We are supposed to feel, with Mrs. Weston, that this involves "no sacrifice on any side worth the name" (III, xvii). Emma recognizes, however, as have many readers, "that in living constantly with her father, and in no house of his own, there would be much, very much, to be borne with" (III, xv).

Knightley's solution, involving, as it does, an insistence on marriage, makes Emma's conflict more severe. Not only has she no rational ground for opposing the union, but she also has a strong emotional need to comply with Knightley's wishes. But she knows that even with Knightley's sacrifice Mr. Woodhouse will be unhappy about her marrying. In her relations with her father, Emma has no power of self-assertion. Her need to be the perfect daughter is so compulsive that she cannot do anything, however justified, that will disturb him. She is a slave to his irrational claims. Even though Knightley is eager and Mr. Woodhouse is beginning to be resigned, Emma is paralyzed:

> Still, however, he was not happy. Nay, he appeared so much otherwise, that his daughter's courage failed. She could not bear to see him suffering, to know him fancying himself neglected; and though her understanding almost acquiesced in the assurance of both the Mr. Knightleys, that when once the event were over, his distress would be soon over too, she hesitated—she could not proceed. (III, xix)

Then Mrs. Weston's turkey coop is robbed, and the problem is resolved.

The manipulated ending is in complete accord with the laws and spirit of comedy. It saves Emma from having to make a painful choice, and it reconciles Mr. Woodhouse to the marriage. It serves Jane Austen's thematic purposes by maintaining the illusion of Emma's maturation. By arranging the world to fit Emma's defensive needs, she obscures the psychological realities which she has portrayed so vividly. She does not want us to see, nor can she afford to see consciously herself, the severity of Emma's father problem and the fact that it is unresolved.

Through Emma and through Frank Churchill, Austen dramatizes brilliantly the damaging effects of manipulation by sick, life-denying parental figures. The novel seems, at one point, to promise a thematic exploration of this problem (I, xviii); but Austen has, understandably, no wisdom to offer. All that she can propose is to follow the self-effacing (or the perfectionistic) route of doing one's duty. Frank should have stood up to Mrs. Churchill in the name of his obligation to his father. But he can only get what he wants for himself (and has a right to have) if Mrs. Churchill dies. The dilemma he faces, and the frustrations he has had to endure, account for his dishonorable behavior, which is treated (perhaps because Austen sympathizes) with a surprising mildness.

As the Knightleys' assurances indicate, Emma is not forced by her situation to suspend the marriage. It would have been perfectly moral for her to proceed, expressing all the while her love and concern for her father. His unhappiness would have passed. Jane Austen's amused tone suggests that she has some awareness of the irrationality of Emma's decision, but she seems, nevertheless, to be basically sympathetic toward her heroine's self-sacrificial behavior. She could not have had Emma behave differently, of course. Emma behaves as she must. But it was within the power of her rhetoric, if she had had a clear enough vision, to suggest the destructiveness of Emma's solution and the preferability of the Knightleys' alternative. As we have seen, Emma is in this instance saved from the consequences of her psychological problems by authorial manipulation of the plot. Form and theme work well together here. The comic action accords with the picture of the world which accompanies the self-effacing solution. Reality is antagonistic to Emma's wishes as long as she is proud. When she becomes humble and unselfish, fortune turns in her favor. Virtue is rewarded.

It is difficult to say whether Emma and Knightley have (theoretically) any acceptable alternative to living at Hartfield. As Jane Austen presents the situation, it is unthinkable either for Emma to leave her father or for Mr. Woodhouse to move to Donwell. Either course, we are made to feel, would result in his death. The only solution which the author can sanction is to have Emma and Knightley submit to Mr. Woodhouse's claims, to sacrifice their autonomy, and to live a life of "continual endurance." This may be, in fact, the only way of reconciling the demands of morality with the actualities of the situation; but, as some readers have felt, it is hardly a happy ending. Since the death of Mr. Woodhouse is the only possible source of relief, the reader is left wishing for it, and imagining the suppressed impatience of Emma and Knightley, at the end of the novel. Emma's oversolicitude about her father may well be, in fact, a defense against unconscious desires for his disappearance. The only way she can remain free of guilt when he dies is to hover about him, protecting him from every disturbing influence.

Emma Woodhouse and Fanny Price are, for the most part, opposite psychological types. It is impressive that Jane Austen could enter into the inner lives of such different characters equally well. Given her own character structure, it is not surprising that Austen could judge Emma's narcissism much better than she could see the destructiveness of Fanny's self-effacing solution. She had more distance from Emma's solution, and she could identify its sources and its inadequacies with considerable precision, as she did with the spoiled children in *Mansfield Park*. Austen's combination of empathy with insight gives rise to the sympathetic mockery, so agreeable to the modern sensibility, which sets the tone for much of *Emma*. She has blind spots in *Emma*, however, just as she does in *Mansfield Park*. She overestimates the educative value of suffering and the nobility of compulsive goodness, whether it be perfectionistic or self-effacing in origin. She interprets Emma least satisfactorily toward the end, as she becomes more self-effacing; she is not sufficiently disturbed by the embeddedness of Hartfield; and she is blind to Emma's father problem, which is the source of much of her difficulty and which remains unresolved at the end.

Notes

1. Northrop Frye, *Anatomy of Criticism* (Princeton: Princeton University Press, 1957), p. 169; hereafter referred to in the text as *AC*.
2. Wayne Booth, *The Rhetoric of Fiction* (Chicago: University of Chicago Press, 1961), p. 259.
3. Karen Horney, *Neurosis and Human Growth* (New York: Norton, 1950); hereafter cited as *NHG*. Horney has written only a few pages about the narcissistic and the perfectionistic strategies (pp. 193-97). While they have helped me to understand Emma, my study of Emma has given me far more insight than Horney offers into the dynamics of these solutions.

Jane Austen and Female Reading

Robert W. Uphaus

To what kinds of written works should women be exposed? What should they be allowed, or encouraged, to read? This issue exercised generations of moralists and educators in the eighteenth and nineteenth centuries, as more and more women became literate, and as more and more women began publishing their own works. Novels in particular had to overcome tremendous prejudices against them; they were held to be trivial, frivolous, and fundamentally unserious—the sort of thing usually written and read by women, but a waste of time for all involved. Mr. Collins, in *Pride and Prejudice*, sums up that conventional wisdom when he declares self-righteously that he never reads novels.

We might assume that Austen, a novelist herself, would find the whole discussion absurd, and yet, as Robert W. Uphaus points out, she was drawn to the works of Thomas Gisborne, who warned women away from novels. This insight allows Uphaus to read *Northanger Abbey* not merely as a parody of Gothic absurdity but also as a critique of "female reading generally." Austen, he argues, "uses her own novel to reshape the prior conventions of female reading." And it is more than *Northanger Abbey*—*Sense and Sensibility* too "deals with the practice of female reading," as does *Pride and Prejudice*. Where many men in the eighteenth century accused women of lacking "constancy," saw their true character only in marriage, and considered women's virtue inferior to that of men, Austen challenged the widespread prejudice. Uphaus examines "how Austen both challenged and revised a view of women that disabled their moral status, and how, through her fiction, she established a new practice of female reading and writing."   — J.L.

In a letter to Cassandra Austen, dated 30 August 1805, Jane Austen writes: "I had almost forgot to thank you for your letter. I am glad you recommended 'Gisborne,' for having begun, I am pleased with it, and I had quite determined not to read it."[1] The 'Gisborne' referred to is Thomas Gisborne, and the work is most likely, as R. W. Chapman assumes, *An Enquiry into the Duties of the Female Sex* (1797). Three years earlier Gisborne had published *An Enquiry into the Duties of Men*, but it seems far more probable, in light of Austen's interest in female reading and all that it implies, that she was both reading and impressed by Gisborne's *Enquiry into the Duties of the Female Sex*.

On the subject of female reading Gisborne says a number of things about women and fiction that either coincide with, or perhaps exerted an influence on, Austen's concept of fiction. In a chapter entitled "On the Employment of Time," Gisborne recommends to "every woman, whether single or married, the habit of regularly allotting to improving books a portion of each day."[2] Significantly, Gisborne does not include novels (a term he used interchangeably with romance) among the improving works women should read. Though he readily acknowledges the popularity of novels/romances, he nevertheless laments that they obtain "from a considerable proportion of the female sex a reception much more favourable than is accorded to other kinds of composition more worthy of encouragement" (p. 214). One here recalls the episode in *Pride and Prejudice* when Mr. Collins is invited to read aloud. Austen writes: "a book was produced; but on beholding it, (for every thing announced it to be from a circulating library), he started back, and begging pardon, protested that he never read novels." Eventually, they choose Fordyce's *Sermons*, but not without Collins observing "how little young ladies are interested by books of a serious stamp."[3]

Even the best of novels (none of which Gisborne names)—those, that is, "deemed to have on the whole a moral tendency"—still are "liable to the disgraceful charge of being contaminated occasionally by incidents and passages unfit . . . to be perused by the eye of delicacy" (p. 215). Gisborne bases his condemnation of novels as unfit for women on the general idea that "a practice of reading romances is . . . liable to produce mischievous effects" (p. 216). In his view, novels become a habit-forming vice—one, as he says, "at first, perhaps, of limited indulgence, but a habit that is continually found more formidable and more encroaching" (p. 216). This habit of female reading leads to such "mischievous" consequences as the "secret corruption" of mind, an "aversion to reading of a more improving nature," and the creation of "a susceptibility of impression and a premature warmth of tender emotions" (p. 217).

At this point, one might well wonder what Austen, as a novelist, finds so "pleasing" in Gisborne. On first appearance Gisborne's damning view of women reading, not to say writing, novels might well explain Austen's quite genuine and historically illuminating complaint in *Northanger Abbey* that novelists "are an injured body . . . no species of composition has been so much decried. From pride, ignorance, or fashion, our foes are almost as many as our readers . . . there seems almost a general wish of decrying the capacity and undervaluing the labor of the novelist, and of slighting the performances which have only genius, wit, and taste to recommend them" (V, 37). Austen's complaint appears in a novel initially composed in 1798-99, or around the time Gisborne's work was published. She is almost certainly responding to the general view of the novel represented by Gisborne and others, and she is correct to assert that "our foes are almost as many as our readers."[4]

Viewed within the context of Gisborne's commentary, *Northanger Abbey* may be approached as a calculated response not only to Gothic fiction specifically but also to female reading generally. That is, Austen mocks Catherine for being a stereotypical kind of female reader, about whose practice of reading Austen early remarks: "provided that nothing like useful knowledge could be gained from them, provided they were all story and no reflection, she had never any objection to books at all" (V, 15). In the end, Austen uses her own novel to reshape the prior conventions of female reading. For example, one of the "mischievous effects" Gisborne attacks is what he calls a premature warmth of tender emotions depicted by lovers. Austen, however, claims that her representation of love is unique, for she must "confess" that Henry

Tilney's affection for Catherine "originated in nothing better than gratitude, or, in other words, that a persuasion of her partiality for him had been the only cause of giving her a serious thought." Austen continues, "It is a new circumstance in romance, I acknowledge, and dreadfully derogatory of an heroine's dignity; but if it be as new in common life, the credit of a wild imagination will at least be all my own" (V, 243).

Austen clearly insists that what her novel does is "new"—new not only in its representation of a heroine, but new in its substitution of gratitude for "tender emotions."[5] But just how new is Austen's early fiction? And why, in 1805, when Austen was reading Gisborne, didn't she feel as threatened by his views of female reading and the novel as she must have apparently felt when she was writing *Northanger Abbey*?[6] Let me backtrack briefly and look at what the consensus view of female reading was, and how Austen shaped this view into a new kind of female reading, one that provided both story and reflection.

Gisborne was not so much initiating as summarizing the negative view of women as consumers of fiction. From the mid-eighteenth century onwards there occurs a steady attack on women as the principal readers of fiction—an attack whose advocates are, to a very great degree, women. These attacks, by women in behalf of women, constitute an important and largely unexamined influence on Austen's fiction.[7] In *An Unfortunate Mother's Advice to Her Absent Daughters* (1761), Sarah Pennington cautions her daughters about "some reading Ladies," reminding them that "a sensible Woman will soon be convinced, that all the Learning her utmost Application can make her Mistress of will be, from the Difference of Education, in many Points inferior to that of a School-Boy."[8] Still a few pages later she does provide her daughters with an impressive reading list that includes the sermons of Tillotson, Hoadly, Sherlock, Clarke, and individual works by—among other authors—Locke, Wollaston, Seneca, Cicero, Epictetus, Pope, and Thomson (p. 39).

However, one notices that this list includes no novels, about which

Pennington tells her daughters, "never give yourself the Trouble of reading" (p. 39). Pennington's charges against the novel are several, and anticipate Gisborne's later commentary. First, novels excite an "idle Curiosity," and thus produce "useless knowledge"; second, they represent a "Loss of Time"—a view echoed years later by Coleridge when he comments that reading novels "is not so much to be called pass-time as kill-time."[9] Third, and most serious, Pennington asserts that novels are apt "to give a romantic Turn to the Mind, that is often productive of great Errors in Judgment." This last accusation against female reading can be traced as far back as Richard Allestree's *The Ladies Calling* (1677), where Allestree writes that "the reading [of] Romances . . . seems now to be thought the peculiar and only becoming study of young Ladies." He condemns such reading on the grounds that romances elicit "amorous Passions . . . which are apt to insinuate themselves into their unwary Readers, and by an unhappy inversion, a coppy [sic] shall produce an Original."[10]

In the view of Allestree and Pennington, women are particularly susceptible to reading passionately, a view dramatized in Charlotte Lennox's *Female Quixote* (1752). Women are imitative readers who, evidently, tend to repeat in life what they read in fiction. Late in the eighteenth century the condemnation of female reading focuses specifically on woman's susceptibility to sensibility, so much so that the term "sensibility" acts as a surrogate not just for a specific way of seeing or feeling, but for a practice of reading principally (but not exclusively) associated with women. This practice of reading draws attention from such women writers as Mary Wollstonecraft and Maria Edgeworth— writers who identified sensibility with a female reading practice, and who yet wrote novels to enact an alternative program of female reading, one that would later be most successfully implemented by Jane Austen.

If we look at some sample observations by Wollstonecraft and, perhaps more important, Maria Edgeworth, we shall see that a novel like *Sense and Sensibility* deals with the practice of female reading. As I shall demonstrate shortly, Marianne Dashwood represents precisely the kind of female reader of sensibility whose romantic turn of mind, to borrow from Pennington, does indeed produce "great Errors in Judgment." In *Thoughts on The Education of Daughters* (1787), Mary Wollstonecraft clearly distinguishes between a kind of female reading that is sensible and one that produces the mistakes of sensibility. She observes that many novels "give a wrong account of the human passions," and then describes how the imitative female reader is affected by such misrepresentations: "Sensibility is described and praised, and the effects of it represented in a way so different from nature, that those who imitate it must make themselves very ridiculous. A false taste is acquired, and sensible books appear dull and insipid. . . . Gallantry is made the only interesting subject with the novelist; reading, therefore, will often co-operate to make his fair admirers insignificant."[11] Here is an early version of Marianne Dashwood—how she reads with and responds to her man of gallantry, Willoughby. Indeed, Wollstonecraft provides a revealing context for understanding the significance of Marianne's rejection of "second attachments," for Wollstonecraft comments that "It is too universal a maxim with Novelists, that love is felt but once" (p. 85).

No less striking, Maria Edgeworth's remarks on sensibility and the novel provide a compelling context for, if not a direct influence on, Austen's formulation of female reading in *Sense and Sensibility*. The consensus view is that *Sense and Sensibility* was begun as *Elinor and Marianne* around 1795, then recast in non-epistolary form in November of 1797, and revised and prepared for publication between 1809-1811.[12] Edgeworth herself published *Letters for Literary Ladies* in 1795 and, with her father, *Practical Education* in 1798. In her correspondence, Austen only comments on Edgeworth's novels, humorously declaring to Anna Austen: "I have made up my mind to like no Novels really, but Miss Edgeworth's, yours & my own" (28 September 1814). If she respected Edgeworth as a novelist, perhaps she was also aware of Edgeworth's previous commentaries on female reading—

commentaries that bear a striking resemblance to Austen's representation of female reading in *Sense and Sensibility.*

Edgeworth, for instance, lays out the following defensive program for the regulation of the female imagination. She warns:

> Much prudence and ability are requisite to conduct properly a young woman's literary education. Her imagination must not be raised above the taste for necessary occupations . . . her mind must be enlarged, yet the delicacy of her manners must be preserved; her knowledge must be various, and her powers of reasoning unawed by authority; yet she must *habitually* feel that nice sense of propriety, which is at once the guard and the charm of every feminine virtue. By early caution, unremitting, scrupulous caution in the choice of the books which are put into the hands of girls, a mother, or a preceptress, may fully occupy, and entertain their pupils, and excite in their minds a *taste* for propriety, as well as a taste for literature.[13]

This is exactly the sort of defensive program Elinor Dashwood promotes with Marianne, for Elinor recognizes Marianne's susceptibility to sensibility and all that it entails. But the way Austen dissociates her own practice of fiction from what passed for female reading is by arranging for Marianne to fall prey to what Edgeworth quite strikingly condemns as the "moral picturesque" encouraged by so much previous female reading.

Recall some of Austen's comments about Marianne Dashwood, such as: "[Willoughby's] person and air were equal to what her fancy had ever drawn for the hero of a favorite story" (I, 43); Willoughby "read [from Marianne's view] with all the sensibility and spirit which Edward had unfortunately wanted" (I, 48); and Edward's remark that Marianne "would have every book that tells her how to admire an old twisted tree" (I, 92). There is a strong similarity between Austen's description of Marianne's sensibility and Edgeworth's condemnation of "sentimental stories":

This species of reading cultivates what is called the heart prematurely, lowers the tone of the mind, and induces indifference for those common pleasures and occupations which, however trivial in themselves, constitute by far the greatest portion of our daily happiness. . . . We know, from common experience, the effects which are produced upon the female mind by immoderate novel-reading. To those who acquire this taste every object becomes disgusting which is not in an attitude for poetic painting; a species of moral picturesque is sought for in every scene of life, and this is not always compatible with sound sense, or with simple reality. (I, 332-33)

This is a wholly accurate description of Marianne's early predicament. Austen represents Marianne as, among other things, a typical victim of the kind of female reading both Wollstonecraft and Edgeworth attacked. Edgeworth's later observation helps us to understand the thematic significance of Marianne's initial rejection of Colonel Brandon and her preference for Willoughby. Edgeworth writes: "Sentimental authors, who paint with enchanting colours all the graces and all the virtues in happy union, teach us to expect that this union should be indissoluble. Afterwards, from the natural influence of association, we expect in real life to meet with virtue when we see grace, and we are disappointed, almost disgusted, when we find virtue unadorned" (I, 297).

Brandon and Elinor are portraits of virtue "unadorned," and so is Fanny Price, that much maligned heroine about whom Alasdair MacIntyre has astutely commented: "Fanny's lack of charm is crucial to Jane Austen's intentions. For charm is the characteristically modern quality which those who lack or simulate the virtues use to get by in the situations of characteristically modern life."[14] "Gallantry," "elegance," and "charm" are the essential components of a kind of female reading that played on the moral picturesque and tended, as Wollstonecraft observes, "to make women the creatures of sensation."[15] Even Elizabeth Bennet mistakes charm for virtue. She responds to Darcy's letter about Wickham by reflecting about the latter: "As to his real character, had information been in her power, she had never felt a wish of enquiring.

His countenance, voice, and manner, had established him at once in the possession of every virtue" (II, 206). But Austen pounds home the lesson about the moral picturesque once Elizabeth recognizes Darcy's real virtue.

> If gratitude and esteem are good foundations of affection, Elizabeth's change of sentiment will be neither improbable nor faulty. But if otherwise, if the regard springing from such sources is unreasonable or unnatural, in comparison of what is so often described as arising on a first interview with its object, and even before two words have been exchanged, nothing can be said in her defence, except that she had given somewhat of a trial to the latter method, in her partiality for Wickham, and that its ill-success might perhaps authorise her to seek the other less interesting mode of attachment. (II, 279)

Austen's new program of female reading, already evident in such early novels as *Pride and Prejudice*, *Northanger Abbey*, and *Sense and Sensibility*, depends on the rejection of the female reader as a "creature of sensation." No less important, her concept of female reading implements what Mary Wollstonecraft strongly wished for—namely, the consideration of women not as moral objects of decorum and propriety, but as "moral beings" (*Vindication*, p. 25). Just how radical a departure this was for female reading (*Clarissa* notwithstanding) can be seen if we look briefly at what Wollstonecraft means by "[giving] a sex to virtue" (*Vindication*, p. 11).

We saw earlier how Austen evidently read Gisborne, and it is just as important to notice that Wollstonecraft, in *A Vindication of the Rights of Woman*, repeatedly quotes from Adam Smith's *The Theory of Moral Sentiments*. I stress this point because Smith and Gisborne, in the most striking ways, identify virtue with gender. They establish a moral context within which one can measure Austen's clear departure from the assumption that women lacked a full moral character. The issue here, as I understand it, is not simply limited to the question of whether

Austen was or was not a feminist. Rather, my concern is with how Austen both challenged and revised a view of women that disabled their moral status, and how, through her fiction, she established a new practice of female reading and writing.[16]

The prevailing moral view of women is best summarized by Pope's lines in "Of the Characters of Women" that "Most Women have no Character at all," or Chesterfield's assertion that "Women, then, are only children of a larger growth."[17] Both authors subscribe to the stereotype that women lack the constancy necessary for the exertion of moral conduct. However, the view of women that Austen responds to most strongly and subsequently challenges is that stated in Lord Lyttelton's lines addressed to women: "Seek to be good, but aim not to be great:/ A Woman's noblest station is retreat."[18]

Lyttelton bases his distinction between "good" and "great" on the idea that women, at best, have a second order of virtue. Women have this status because their sphere is domestic, rather than public, and because the character of women is "naturally" designed for a second order of virtue. Put another way, the only suitable context within which women may display their second order of virtue—their "goodness"—is marriage. For example, Jane West observes: "Marriage may be said rather to open than to close the eventful period of female life; since it is by that means that we enter on a scene of enlarged usefulness, activity, and responsibility."[19] Or, as Juliana-Susannah Seymour writes, "There is only one Path by which a married Woman can arrive at Happiness, and this is by conforming herself to the Sentiments of her Husband."[20]

Now conformity of will, both within and without marriage, is a matter of great interest in Austen's fiction. Austen treats this subject in a variety of ways for a variety of purposes. Elizabeth Bennet and Emma Woodhouse are very strong-willed, but even as they later revise their behavior they do not abdicate their will in order to conform to the desires of their prospective husbands. Conversely, Fanny Price is very compliant, and yet she rejects Henry Crawford's marriage proposal, failing to conform to Sir Thomas Bertram's will. Indeed, the moral surprise of Fanny's behavior, seen within the context of woman's secondary moral status, is that Fanny, like Elinor Dashwood and Anne Elliot, practices constancy, about which MacIntyre has remarked: "in some ways constancy plays a role in Jane Austen analogous to that of *phronesis* in Aristotle; it is a virtue the possession of which is a prerequisite for the possession of other virtues" (pp. 170-71).

What Austen's fiction repeatedly challenges is, first, the idea that women lack constancy; this is precisely the moral issue debated in *Persuasion* by Captain Harville and Anne Elliot, with Anne claiming for her "own sex" the constancy "of loving longest, when existence or when hope is gone" (V, 235). Second, in Austen's fiction women need *not* be married to realize their moral character; this, in fact, is Anne Elliot's point when she reminds Captain Harville that she believes men are "capable of every thing great and good in your married lives . . . I mean, while the woman you love lives, and lives for you" (V, 235). In Austen's fiction, it is women who face the moral challenge of being single, rebuffed, or abandoned. Third, Austen resists the moral view that women can only display a second order of virtue—what Adam Smith calls "humanity." One should recall such characters as Elinor Dashwood, Fanny Price, Anne Elliot, Mrs. Smith, and Mrs. Croft before reading Smith's distinction between humanity and generosity:

> Humanity is the virtue of a woman, generosity of a man. The fair-sex, who have commonly much more tenderness than ours, have seldom so much generosity. . . . Humanity consists merely in the exquisite fellow-feeling which the spectator entertains with the sentiments of the persons principally concerned, so as to grieve for their sufferings, to resent their injuries, and to rejoice at their good fortune. The most humane actions require no self-denial, no self-command, no great exertion of the sense of propriety. . . . But it is otherwise with generosity. We never are generous except when in some respect we prefer some other person to ourselves, and sacrifice some great and important interest of our own to an equal interest of a friend or of a superior.[21]

In her fiction, Austen quietly goes about demolishing the idea that women are incapable of exerting generosity—that is, those actions requiring self-denial, self-command, and propriety. Austen's strongest women display a recognition, to borrow from Gisborne, that "Fortitude is not to be sought merely on the rampart, or the deck, or the field of battle. Its place is no less in the chamber of sickness and pain, in the retirements of anxiety, of grief, and of disappointment" (p. 25). One recalls Anne Elliot's initial astonishment when she first visits Mrs. Smith. We are told that Anne "could scarcely imagine a more cheerless situation in itself than Mrs. Smith's. . . . Yet, in spite of all this, Anne had reason to believe that she had moments only of languor and depression, to hours of occupation and enjoyment" (V, 153-54). Anne, we are told, "watched—observed—reflected"—all cues for the reader to do the same; and she "finally determined that this was not a case of fortitude or of resignation only . . . but here was something more; here was that elasticity of mind, that disposition to be comforted, that power of turning readily from evil to good, and of finding employment which carried her out of herself, which was from Nature alone" (V, 154). Austen assigns many of Adam Smith's moral characteristics of "generosity" to a woman, and she does so in a passage that looks very like a challenge and an announcement to those who think of women as capable only of "humanity."

There are further examples of Austen's efforts to establish the authentic moral character of women. In *Mansfield Park*, Sir Thomas Bertram, a man who fancies himself an exemplar of propriety, condemns Fanny for rejecting Henry Crawford's proposal of marriage. However, his condemnation reveals the limitations of his moral assumptions at the same time that it displays Fanny's authentic moral strength. Sir Thomas asks, "Have you any reason, child, to think ill of Mr. Crawford's temper?" Fanny responds, "No, Sir"; and Austen continues, "She longed to add, 'but of his principles I have'" (III, 317). By introducing the term "principle" and associating it with Fanny's decision—that is, Fanny's act of self-denial and self-command—Austen sets up Sir Thomas as an exponent of the moral stereotype that assumes women are incapable of being "generous" in Smith's sense of the word. When Sir Thomas berates Fanny for her "wilfulness of temper, self-conceit and every tendency to that independence of spirit . . . which in young women is offensive and disgusting" (III, 318), we should see that Austen is, in fact, praising Fanny's exertion of principle and challenging Sir Thomas's moral assumption that Fanny's "independence of spirit" is offensive and disgusting. Indeed, Fanny's conduct conforms exactly to Thomas Gisborne's caution to women that they should remember "these two plain and momentous rules of conduct at which we have arrived. First, that on every occasion you are to act precisely in that manner, which you believe that moral rectitude would of itself require you to adopt independently of any reference to effects which may be produced by your example: and secondly, that, whatever may be your station in life, there is no case in which your example cannot do harm; nor any in which it may not do good" (pp. 158-59).

Similar challenges to Adam Smith's ideas that women are incapable of "generosity" occur in *Sense and Sensibility* and *Persuasion*. Elinor Dashwood undergoes severe moral tests, and she is the clear moral equal of Colonel Brandon. These tests are designed to display not only her "humanity" but her "generosity." Here is Austen's description of Elinor's reflections after she learns of Edward Ferrars's engagement to Lucy Steele:

> She was silent.—Elinor's security sunk; but her self-command did not sink with it. . . . Her resentment of such behaviour, her indignation at having been its dupe, for a short time made her feel only for herself; but other ideas, other considerations soon arose . . . but if he had injured her, how much more had he injured himself. . . . She might in time regain tranquillity; but *he*, what had he to look forward to? . . . she wept for him, more than for herself. . . . She was stronger alone, and her own good sense so well supported her, that her firmness was as unshaken, her appearance of cheerfulness as invariable, as with regrets so poignant and so fresh, it was possible for them to be. (I, 131, 139-41)

Viewed within the context of Smith's moral formulation, Elinor is clearly acting morally as only a man is expected to do. Austen undermines the stereotypes of previous female reading by displaying some of her central women characters in the act of exercising "generous" moral actions.

Finally, Anne Elliot, too, represents a challenge to the assumption that women in fiction lack moral strength. Examined in the light of Adam Smith's moral assumption that "Where little self-command is necessary, little self-approbation is due" (p. 147). Anne Elliot's exchange with Captain Wentworth takes on added importance. Addressing Wentworth as her prospective husband, Anne defends her past submission to Lady Russell's judgment, arguing that "I must believe that I was right, much as I suffered from it." She then continues: "But I mean, that I was right in submitting to her, and that if I had done otherwise, I should have suffered more in continuing the engagement than I did even in giving it up, because I should have suffered in my conscience. I have now, as far as such a sentiment is allowable in human nature, nothing to reproach myself with; and if I mistake not, a strong sense of duty is no bad part of a woman's portion" (V, 246). Anne's version of "a woman's portion," like Austen's, implicitly redefines the traditional content of female reading—that is, the customary feminine attributes of sensibility and "humanity" (in Adam Smith's sense); at the same time, Anne explicitly challenges the assumption that women have a second-class moral status by asserting her own strength of character and "generosity" (in Adam Smith's sense). In making a declaration of both literary and moral principle, Anne clearly sums up her author's view of women *and* the novel, as well as women *in* the novel.

From *Studies in the Novel* 19, no. 3 (1987): 334-345. Copyright © 1987 by The University of North Texas. Reprinted by permission.

Notes

1. *Jane Austen's Letters*, collected and edited by R. W. Chapman, 2 vols. (Oxford: Clarendon Press, 1932), 1, 47. All further references are cited within the text.

2. Thomas Gisborne, *An Enquiry Into the Duties of the Female Sex* (London: T. Cadell and W. Davis, 1797), p. 212. All further references are cited within the text.

3. *The Novels of Jane Austen*, ed. R. W. Chapman, 6 vols. (London: Oxford, 1960, 1965), II, 68-69. All further references to Austen's novels are to this edition and will be cited by volume and page number. In my essay I have assumed that Austen was initially addressing an audience of women readers. Of the twelve contemporary reviews and notices collected in B. C. Southam's *Jane Austen: The Critical Heritage* (London: Routledge & Kegan Paul, 1968), the majority explicitly assume that Austen was writing for "female friends" (p. 40) and "fair readers" (pp. 36-37, 46, 70, 79). Significantly, in his review of *Emma* Sir Walter Scott makes no such assumption (pp. 58-69); moreover, in 1821 Richard Whately clearly views Austen as an author who ought to be read by "men of sense and taste" (p. 87).

4. Austen's comments on novels in *Northanger Abbey* coincide with her report to her sister, Cassandra, that "As an inducement to subscribe [to her circulating library] Mrs. Martin tells us that her Collection is not to consist only of Novels, but of every kind of Literature. . . . She might have spared this pretension to *our* family, who are great Novel-readers & not ashamed of being so" (*Letters*, I, 38). The date of this letter is 18 December 1798, around the time Austen was drafting *Northanger Abbey* (then called *Susan*).

5. For a more extensive gloss on the importance of "gratitude" as a replacement for tender emotions see *Pride and Prejudice*, where Austen variously comments: "It was gratitude.—Gratitude, not merely for having once loved her, but for loving her still well enough, to forgive all the petulance and acrimony of her manner in rejecting him [Darcy]. . . . If gratitude and esteem are good foundations of affection, Elizabeth's change of sentiment will be neither improbable nor faulty" (II, 265, 279).

6. One should recall that in the advertisement to *Northanger Abbey* Austen entreats the reader "to bear in mind that thirteen years have passed since it was finished, many more since it was begun, and that during that period, places, manners, books, and opinions have undergone considerable changes" (V, [12]).

7. It is surprising that so wide-ranging a collection as the recently published *Fetter'd or Free?*, ed. Mary Anne Schofield and Cecilia Macheski (Athens: Ohio Univ. Press, 1986), should not contain an essay that explores the repeated attacks on women reading fiction.

8. Sarah Pennington, *An Unfortunate Mother's Advice to her Absent Daughters* (London: S. Chandler, 1761), pp. 26-27. All further references are cited within the text. The subsequent quotations are on pp. 39-40.

9. Quoted in John Tinnon Taylor, *Early Opposition to the English Novel* (New York: King's Crown Press, 1943), p. 106.

10. Richard Allestree, *The Ladies Calling*, 5th impression (Oxford: 1677), pp. 164-65.

11. Mary Wollstonecraft, *Thoughts on the Education of Daughters* (London: Joseph Johnson, 1787), pp. 50-51. All further references are cited within the text.

12. I am here relying on A. Walton Litz's useful chronology of composition in *The Jane Austen Companion*, ed. J. David Grey et al. (New York: Macmillan, 1986), pp. 47-52.

13. *Practical Education*, 2 vols. (London: Joseph Johnson, 1798), 2:550. All further references are cited within the text.

14. Alasdair MacIntyre, *After Virtue* (Notre Dame: Univ. of Notre Dame Press, 1981), p. 225. All further references are cited within the text.

15. *A Vindication of the Rights of Woman*, ed. Carol H. Poston (New York: Norton, 1975), p. 61. All further references are cited as *Vindication* in the text. There is an interesting flipside to the "moral picturesque," one that Austen associates with men. In *Sanditon*, it is the "gallant" Sir Edward Denham, whom Austen says "had read more sentimental Novels than agreed with him," who professes a love for novels that "display Human Nature with Grandeur—such as show her in the Sublimities of intense Feeling—such as exhibit the progress of strong Passion from the first Germ of incipient Susceptibility to the utmost Energies of Reason half-dethroned,—where we see the strong spark of Woman's Captivations elicit such Fire in the Soul of Man as leads ... to hazard all, dare all, atcheive [sic] all, to obtain her" (VI, 403). Charlotte Heywood appears to be speaking for Austen when she curtly replies to Sir Edward Denham, "If I understand you aright ... our taste in Novels is not at all the same" (VI, 404).

16. I would not presume to describe the spectrum of debate regarding Austen's "feminism." However, I would recommend for examination such works as Mary Poovey, *The Proper Lady and the Woman Writer* (Chicago and London: Univ. of Chicago Press, 1984); Sandra M. Gilbert and Susan Gubar, *The Madwoman in the Attic* (New Haven: Yale Univ. Press, 1979); the essays by Margaret Kirkham and Margaret Doody in *The Jane Austen Companion*; two essays by Marian E. Fowler, "The Feminist Bias of *Pride and Prejudice*," *Dalhousie Review* 57 (1977), 47-64, and "The Courtesy-book Heroine of *Mansfield Park*," *University of Toronto Quarterly* 44 (1974), 31-46; and Lloyd W. Brown, "Jane Austen and the Feminist Tradition," *Nineteenth-Century Fiction* 28 (1973), 321-38.

17. *Letters to His Son and Others* (London: Dent, 1984), p. 66.

18. These lines are quoted, approvingly, as part of the epigraph on the title page of Elizabeth Griffith's *Essays Addressed to Young Married Women* (London: T. Cadell, 1782). The lines themselves come from Lyttelton's "Advice To a Lady" (1731).

19. *Letters To A Young Lady*, 3 vols. 2d ed. (London: Longman, 1806), 2:451.

20. *The Conduct of a Married Life* (London: R. Baldwin, 1753), p. 2.

21. *The Theory of Moral Sentiments*, ed. D. D. Raphael and A. L. Macfie (Oxford: Clarendon Press, 1979), pp. 190-91. All further references are cited within the text.

Why There's No Sex in Jane Austen's Fiction_____

Susan Morgan

"The passions are perfectly unknown to her," said Charlotte Brontë about Jane Austen in the 1850s. Not all critics have agreed; in the mid-1990s, several critics began exploring the eroticism, homoeroticism, and autoeroticism of Austen's novels. But on this question, at least, Susan Morgan sides with the traditionalists: "The romantic encounters" in Austen's novels, she writes, "are not sexual, not literally sexual, but also not metaphorically sexual." For her the question is *why*.

She dismisses two common answers as too facile: "the assumption that because there was no sex in Austen's life, there is no sex in her books," and the other assumption "that Austen was a rationalist who did not like sex." Neither does justice to the richness of the novels. Morgan instead finds her answers both in the literary-historical context of Austen's fiction and in the formal nature of her genre, the realistic novel. By asking "what British novels were like when Austen started writing, what narrative conventions had developed," especially in the works of Frances Burney and Samuel Richardson, Morgan offers "a defense of that absence, a defense cast in the form of tradition and the individual talent." In that earlier novel tradition, seduction often took the form of rape, and sex often indicated what she calls "depressingly patriarchal relations between the sexes."   — J.L.

A Writer who follows nature and pretends to keep the Christian System in his Eye, cannot make a Heaven in this World for his Favorites.

—Richardson

The Sky will be much friendlier then than now,
A part of labor and a part of pain
And next in glory to enduring love,
Not this dividing and indifferent Blue.

—Stevens

The question of why there is no sex in Jane Austen's fiction has long fascinated many of her readers. The question matters, apart from the fact that things having to do with sex usually matter, because its absence in Austen's novels has been held against them, has been seen as limiting their greatness. Instead, I offer a defense of that absence, a defense cast in the form of tradition and the individual talent. I begin by sketching what British novels were like when Austen started writing, what narrative conventions had developed by the end of the eighteenth century.

There is a lot of attempted (and achieved) rape in eighteenth-century British fiction. The plots of novels are littered with endangered virgins.[1] As Nancy K. Miller puts it in her study of some eighteenth-century British and French novels, "the heroine's text is the text of an ideology that codes femininity in the paradigms of sexual vulnerability."[2] This pattern certainly speaks to us of what I would call depressingly patriarchal relations between the sexes in eighteenth-century England. Ruth Perry has discussed in fascinating detail how the educational training of and social expectations for women led to lives of enforced leisure filled, and justified, by sexual and romantic fantasies.[3] And Mary Poovey's analysis of eighteenth-century conduct books underlines the extent to which the social concern with propriety was based on the pervasive and oppressive assumption that "women are fundamentally sexual" and thus need to be kept under control.[4] Sexual dominance, at least in the invented stories in novels, is obviously a satisfying way of doing that.

But I want to argue that the prevalence of sex and seduction in eighteenth-century novels also speaks in a less ominous voice, a voice having less to do with the injustices of society and more to do with the equalities of art. For this recurring pattern in eighteenth-century novels also speaks to what was the relatively new narrative problem of a relatively new genre: the possible relations between character and plot created by the novel form itself. Along with this aesthetic problem, it also speaks to the real problem of a general, and perhaps Christian, sense that life is a danger to self. The literary conventions of virgin and rake and whore are not entirely, or even primarily, the result of the oppressive social situation of eighteenth-century women in Britain.

In the first place, the novels tend to side with the heroine, at least until late in the century, when the gothic hero-villain begins to sing his siren song. The good, in these novels, means to be untouched by events. It means to remain as we were born, innocent and pure. Therefore action, event, plot, is an attack on character. What better image for this state of affairs, this hostile encounter between plot and character, than an insidious seduction or aggressive rape? Experience, and plots, can only violate characters, violate them by changing their identity, the very essence of who they are. If coming to life, coming of age, is imaged as a sexual violation, what better representation of the self who must stand against the transforming, and thereby corrupting, power of experience than as a woman and a virgin?

There are distinctive narrative consequences of imaging life as assault and humanity as female. The generative point, for both heroines and plots, is that heroines can move from being good to being corrupt or they can stay good. And that is all they can do. What characters like Clarissa, Sophia Western, Goldsmith's Olivia Primrose, Burney's Evelina, Smollett's Lydia Melford, Walpole's Isabella or Radcliffe's Emily St. Aubert cannot do, except by mere willingness, is initiate the changes in themselves. In other words, to represent a character's change as sexual violation means that it must be accomplished by a man. Perhaps the most significant literary point about eighteenth-century British novels is that most plots can only be initiated by a fallen woman or a man. And this is true even of the racy fiction written near the beginning of the century. Such erotic novels as Aphra Behn's *Love Letters Between a Nobleman and His Sister*, Mary Delarivière Manley's *The New Atalantis*, or Eliza Haywood's early fiction, though offering heroines with experience rather than virginity, still define them in sexual terms.[5]

In this relatively new genre, then, the inventions of art present themselves as the inevitabilities of nature. Once narrative action is dramatized in the form of sexual action, then female characters, who cannot force the matter, can only try to charm the men into initiating or not initiating that action. As J. M. S. Tompkins long ago noted, "in many books the heroine is entirely passive."[6] Heroines are relegated necessarily to being the material out of which life and fiction will be made. And the maker is male. The line between virgin and whore, as Haywood and Cleland and Fielding and so many others represented it, is the line between has not and has, a line drawn—in writing and in life— by men.

If Lady Booby appears to initiate the action between herself and Joseph Andrews, her conduct highlights two essential points. First, like Moll Flanders, Lady Booby has become the kind of character who can make such a move only because at some earlier time a man made such a move on her. Her identity was long ago shaped by another than herself, that other necessarily male. Just as important, what she initiates she does not complete. Lady Booby cannot change Joseph's identity along with his clothes. Whatever the woman's experience or the man's lack of it, whatever her precedence in age and class, whatever her economic power over him: realizing the action, having the power to change that identity, can only be up to the man.

The other side of the exclusively male sexual power to change a woman totally is to change her not at all. No one is a bit of a virgin. If women can make nothing happen, this has a double sense. For what they can do is to make *nothing* happen. And that would constitute a happy ending. Yet even that passive resistance, that dramatic role as immovable object, can be undermined. Heroines, at the last resort, can always be raped. It does not matter so much whether they actually are. It only matters that they, and the reader, are always aware of the possibility, are always aware of their ultimately vulnerable identity. Of all the eighteenth-century heroines I recall, only Clarissa Harlowe is grand enough really to make nothing happen, no matter what a man can make happen. And the effort kills her.

Given the physical basis of this eighteenth-century idea of plot and character, a specific given is the greater physical strength of men. Always lurking in these novels is the fact that a man can literally dominate a woman—if he chooses. Therefore, there must always be a limit to how much a virginal heroine can like the physical world. As Clarissa so grandly taught us, to counter the man's literal superiority by asserting the woman's spiritual superiority can ultimately be done only at the price of denying the value of physical life itself. If the vessel is frail, the vessel, like the rest of mere matter, can be declared to be without intrinsic worth. Finally, the only move left to the permanently vanquished is to deny the validity of the game.

Less radically, when heroines in eighteenth-century fiction begin as good and are not violated, they can still be transformed. But that transformation is external, a change in style rather than in essential character. With Burney's ingenues, being good turns out to be informational, a matter of learning how to be good gracefully. Lord Orville shapes the unformed Evelina on her entrance into the world. He must protect her from the villain she could not physically withstand. Her virginity is in his hands. But since her purity is a given, his pedagogic and creative power does not take the form of changing her identity but rather of maintaining it and making it visible, of giving it an appropriate external form. In an essential sense, he does not change her at all. Nothing happens. For Pamela or Evelina or Belinda, becoming experienced ultimately means no more than getting to play Audrey Hepburn, dressed beautifully, behaving perfectly, and dancing with a prince at a ball.

Before we post-Freudians smoothly explain the eighteenth-century literary parade of frosty ingenues as projections of their authors' bad attitudes to women or of their secret desires, we might ask why any heroine should love sex while it signifies the measure of a hero's physical, social, and economic power over her. That point will surely take the bloom off the rose. Rape is not fun. But neither is a seductivity which demands a heroine's consenting gratitude for the implicit fact that it is generous enough, restrained enough, not to be rape. All good virgins prefer death to dishonor, as characters prefer stasis to change—

or ought to. God help the ones who have so abandoned themselves as to like it. Aphra Behn's Silvia, Moll Flanders, Fanny Hill, all go on to live immersed in the substantial pleasures of the sexual universe. But pure or fallen, for all of them biology, and therefore men, determine fate.

Clarissa offers both a rich representation and a damning critique of the convention of the pure heroine in the British sexual novel. In exploring the meaning of the convention, Richardson's novel offers what remains to this day the most profound analysis in British fiction of the human and literary consequences of, and the human and literary motives for, defining a woman in essentially sexual terms.[7] And those consequences, those motives, are evil. Reading *Clarissa*, turning to the limiting alternative offered in *Sir Charles Grandison*, we can surely see why new life for the novel would next lie in a radically different fiction which could define character in other than sexual terms. The sexual novel continued after *Clarissa*, was certainly inspired by it, and continues even now. But *Clarissa*'s significance in literary history must surely include its power to decry the very genre of which it is the most sublime representative.

The move from innocence to experience, which will become the richest metaphor in nineteenth-century fiction for exploring the interaction of character and plot, for representing the dynamic relations between self and world, in eighteenth-century fiction is generally a suspect act. It means just one thing for heroines: the loss of virginity. And that in turn means the loss of self. No wonder that near the end of the century Blake was so impatient with the limitations of imaging a woman's life as the pale virgin shrouded in snow. No wonder that he foresaw a better future for both masculine and feminine precisely through ejecting from imagination the idea of purity, and thus the idea of violation. And as Austen's fiction was so soon and so brilliantly to demonstrate, Blake was both accurate and prophetic in terms of the history of the novel.

* * *

If character change in eighteenth-century sexual novels cannot be imaged as gradual growth but only as a crude and sudden metamorphosis, and if it can only be recounted as a chronicle of victorious assault, it still is change. Virgin ingenues, in fiction as well as out, grow tiresome by thirty, perhaps even by twenty-five. What may be more relevant, novels about the moment of growing up, about a young lady's entrance into the world, are severely restricted in their inventiveness by a narrative convention which evaluates a successful rite of passage as undesirable. And marriage, after all, is just a less dramatic form than rape of terminating a heroine's original identity. There is life after virginity. There is even life for heroes beyond their sexual obsessions with someone else's virginity. But how does one write stories about it?

At the beginning of the new century, in a move still viewed by many liberated modern readers as an obstacle to claims for her high seriousness, Austen got rid of the sex. And I do not mean only those endless rapes, near rapes, seductions, threats of seductions, rumors of seductions, rencontres, suspected rencontres, or just extremely unlikely rencontres which must, nonetheless, be guarded against. While most of the sexual energies in eighteenth-century novels are the energies of power and aggression, there are a few heartbeats of more appealing desires. Along with Lady Booby's physical appreciation of Joseph Andrews balanced by his blushing admiration of Fanny's cleavage, a few memorable instances might be Tom Jones eating oysters, the Widow Wadman's interest in Uncle Toby Shandy's spot, Tabitha Bramble's shocked focus on Humphry Clinker's bare posterior, and even a page or two of *Clarissa*.

But Austen has none of this. And readers have not been slow to decide why. She was, after all, unmarried and respectable. How utterly familiar to us all is the assumption that because there was no sex in Austen's life, there is no sex in her books. But this shaky biographical principle limits art to the experiences of life. The more sophisticated critical version, that Austen was a rationalist who did not like sex, is just cheap psychology. Still, the general conclusion has been that

Austen's fiction, without sex, without the symbols of sex, is without passion. And that is the great limitation of the work and the author. For one hundred and fifty years readers have been looking at Austen's work and claiming with Charlotte Brontë that "the Passions are perfectly unknown to her."[8] Where, they have in some form or another asked, is the sex? Where, in George Moore's grander phrase, is the "burning human heart in English prose narrative?"[9] Instead of "Clarissa, Lovelace, and passion," all we get are evasions like the infamous proposal scene in *Emma*, which outrageously announces, "what did she say?—Just what she ought, of course. A lady always does."[10]

My purpose here is not to defend the presence of passion in Austen's novels, though I would certainly argue that it is there. I will only say in passing that for Austen, as for Blake, sexuality is a part of full humanity. In Alice Chandler's words, Austen's fiction "fuses the physical with the emotional and the intellectual to create a sense of total human relationships."[11] The feelings between lead characters such as Elizabeth Bennet and Fitzwilliam Darcy, or Elinor Dashwood and Edward Ferrars, do unite a range of emotions including those we call the sexual. Sex is not something distinct that can be broken off from other feelings like a leg from a torso.

And if sex is not a leg that stands on its own, it is also not the heart of the matter, the essential human desire and act, of which all other desires and acts are somehow symbols, sublimations, or denials. It is sexuality as a phallic leg, and sexuality as a vaginal heart, the kernel of Captain Wentworth's "beautiful glossy nut" (p. 88) of character, that Austen banishes from her fiction. When I claim that Austen has gotten rid of the sex, I refer specifically to a literary sexuality, the notion of sexuality in much of eighteenth-century fiction, the notion of sexuality which defines character, and plot, in sociobiological terms. That notion does, of course, occur outside novels, and outside the eighteenth century, a dark fact which brightens the continuing radicalism of Austen's work.

The romantic encounters between Austen's leading characters are not sexual, not literally sexual, but also not metaphorically sexual. The landscape around Netherfield or Hartfield contains no such natural projections as Penistone Crags in *Wuthering Heights*; the rooms are littered with no item as evocative as the "woman's little pink silk neckerchief" in *Adam Bede*. For those readers who cannot accept the idea of an art which leaves out such a fundamental matter as sex, no matter how sound the literary and historical purpose, no matter how original and influential the result, I remind them that there is sex after Austen. No lasting prohibition was enforced. Sex does not disappear from English fiction, even is there all along in the gothic novels of the first two decades of the nineteenth century. And I am glad. I too enjoy the burning human heart, Hetty's pink neckerchief and Tess's red ribbon, and various characters forgetting themselves in a boat. All I claim for Austen is that its absence, its temporary and localized absence, was a great boon for British fiction, and should be understood as a great achievement.

All Austen's heroines are virgins, including the one aged twenty-seven. But the enormous difference, which will transform ideas of character and suddenly and immeasurably enrich the novel form, is that Austen does not define their innocence in sexual terms. With one stroke of that vaginal, virginal, pen, Austen renders irrelevant what in previous English novels enjoyed a place of central relevance, that the heroine is a virgin. Perhaps Austen's own virginity, her status as a spinster, so long held to be a measure of her limitations as a writer, should instead be regarded as the catalyst for one of her most profound achievements. Perhaps it required a virgin woman novelist to introduce into British fiction the simple and endlessly influential point that women can grow, can be educated, can mature, without the catalyst of a penis. Austen merely conceives the inconceivable. She erases the physical basis of character. She abandons the fiction of nature for the fiction of art. And thus she holds a heroine responsible for herself. Even Clarissa, that most fully responsible of eighteenth-century heroines, found herself hemmed round, and pierced, by a man. One way to describe Austen's place in British literary history is to say that her work introduces an entire canon of brilliantly individual, highly visible, imaginatively influential women characters for all of whom it is effectively insignificant that they have never been laid.

* * *

The radical premise of Austen's novels, what distinguishes them so essentially from previous novels and makes them the original ancestors of so many later novels, is that plot is not a threat to character. Event is not an assault on self. Instead, character and plot can be dynamically intertwined. And central to Austen's subject is how that relation can most positively be created and sustained. This may only be to say that Austen's work celebrates life, a point which generations of readers have known quite well. But we also need to know its significance, to see the originality in that choice of celebration and also the extensiveness of its implications for British fiction.

Austen's heroines usually do lose their innocence, and the point is that they should. For the premise of the novels is that experience is good. Austen's heroes and her villains are not depicted as physically able to protect her heroines or, on the other hand, physically able to overpower them. They all, heroes as well as heroines, have to find something else to do. And we must measure their value in terms of what they choose. Since the terms of value can be almost anything a novelist chooses, the possibilities for character and for narrative suddenly explode.

This new sense of narrative possibility in developing character implies a new dimension to the narrative artist, as a creator rather than as a mimic or reproducer of the given patterns of human nature and society. That acknowledgment of creativity, of making character, applies both to the writer and to the characters themselves. For what else are they engaged in but the making of their characters? We know from the opening moments of *Northanger Abbey*, when we are told that Cather-

---

ine Morland is "in training for a heroine" (p. 15), that the narrative question is what she will make of herself and the narrative problem is that she begins by choosing the wrong thing. That question and that problem are radically different from those confronted by Clarissa or Evelina. But the startling point is that even an ignorant seventeen-year-old like Catherine has some creative power to make herself into something. And the question she must answer, of how to use that power, is very much the question her author must answer as well.

This is not to claim that Austen's novels were entirely alone in offering new portraits of heroines.[12] There would, of course, be Scott's Jeanie Deans in *The Heart of Midlothian*. In a minor key, there would also be Susan Ferrier's first novel in 1818, *Marriage*. Ferrier's long-suffering heroine, Mary Douglas, is threatened by an unattractive marriage rather than a rake, and her main opponent is not the man but her ambitious mother. Even more than Burney's *Evelina*, Ferrier's novel uses but also devalues sentimental conventions, with their sexual definitions of worth. It offers an extensive social analysis which does not define the moral character in simple, sexual terms. The limitation may simply be that Ferrier's work, though innovative, is just too slight to contain either the radical vision or the power of influence that Austen's would.

In more substantive, and earlier, novels, Maria Edgeworth also used sentimental conventions that defined most of her heroines in predictable sexual terms. But she then created plots which, through their narrative point of view, did more than play out the limited possibilities contained in those terms. The plots do not create new kinds of stories. But they do place each favored heroine, Belinda Portman in *Belinda*, Helen Stanley in *Helen*, at a distance from the center of the action. The center offers the traditional sexual ingenue and her traditional plot. The lead heroine stands to the side, as visitor, as observer, as repairer of other people's lives. But Edgeworth did not tell a major story of how that new heroine would work out her own possibilities. The result is heroines who never quite come to life. It is as if Edgeworth could create them, and even give them power, but not over their own plots. Edgeworth did not allow her heroines the issues which would empower them to generate stories of their own making. Austen did. And the formal possibility Austen introduced so lavishly into British fiction became a matter of content, became, indeed, the major content of many of the great novels of the nineteenth century.

* * *

What did female sexuality mean in British fiction before Austen? It meant male sexual power. And it also meant limited plots. Consider then what banishing that defining sexuality might mean. I understand why many traditional critics, normatively masculine if not always literally male, condescended to Austen for doing away with the sexual, and thereby physical, definition of heroism, why they emphasized the critical portrait of Austen as a spinster writer, inexperienced and cold and repressed. They knew their enemy and, as it were, attacked her work in *ad hominem* terms. But feminist critics should be wary of engaging, in the name of modernism or feminism or the sexual revolution, in the same old phallacy.

When, as modern liberated readers, we criticize as limited or even patriarchal a fiction which has removed a heroine's meaning from the level of her sexual attractiveness to and sexual relations with a man, we are hardly as liberal, or Austen as conventional and repressed, as we may think. The passivity inherent in so many late nineteenth- and early twentieth-century socially-conscious portraits of heroines, stressing their oppressive situation as victims even while acknowledging their own sexual appetites, invokes the simpler categories of eighteenth-century heroines. That early virgin ingenue, the would-be victim of the bad man, saved by the good, is really a kind of twin of many a sexually experienced twentieth-century heroine, who, while already a victim of the bad man and knowing that the bad man is the same as the good, still cannot save herself except by exile and seclusion. In many modern and early modern novels, male characters are still attempting to define female characters, still offering them a form of rape. And the fact that this rape is now sophisticatedly social and psychological as well as literal, and that the heroine now knows or comes to know that the white knight is probably more dangerous than the black, must surely invoke the nineteenth-century insights of Hardy's *Tess of the D'Urbervilles* or Eliot's *Mill on the Floss*, and also move back to the insights of *Clarissa*.

But Hardy and Eliot were able to explore the evils of a woman being sexually defined by her culture in part because Austen had banished from fiction, and thus effectively revealed as a fiction, the fiction of a woman being sexually defined by nature. Hardy's and Eliot's novels may also invoke the limiting point about *Clarissa*, that finally the woman is a victim, however charming, however heroic, however sublime. Granted the brilliance of many such portraits in three centuries of fiction, there is yet no critical or moral ground to claim them as somehow more radical or more politically acceptable than Austen's insistent visions of female responsibilities and power. Neither position is really the more radical or progressive, either socially or historically.

For many women, and even some men, the coming to political consciousness in the last two decades, and resultant sense of victimization and horror at our male-dominated culture, have directed our literary values as well. The revitalization of the women's movement in the 1960's meant that *The Mill on the Floss* or *The Awakening* or *The Yellow Wallpaper* spoke to many of us more powerfully than *Mansfield Park* or the sparkling *Pride and Prejudice*. Yet our proper outrage about the situation of women in our culture should not damage our ability to admit and enjoy the powerful images of women's potential and fulfillment in nineteenth-century British fiction written by both men and women. Nor should it obscure our recognition of the extent of Austen's achievement in her portrayals of women characters. Suddenly, overwhelmingly, in English fiction, women are expected to have high expectations. They are, in fact, morally required to do so. Failing to believe in their own abilities to make a future, falling back on their own weakness and the external measures of materiality or male admiration, which for Austen is also a falling back on old fictional modes of defining heroines, is treated virtually as a crime. Let us not confuse that with prudery. Austen's heroines are not allowed to define themselves sexually precisely because, in contrast to the limited and powerless heroines of the previous century, they are required to define themselves.

The absence of sex in Austen's work represents neither a moral absolutism nor an historical conservatism nor a psychological limitation. It represents a literary innovation. The change from previous fiction is more accurately a matter of replacement than of loss. It redefines the nature of power and the power of nature in British fiction, by turning away from their physical, and therefore masculine, base. It is an original narrative response to the naturalistic use of sex in eighteenth-century novels, a liberating absence relative to what had become a limiting presence, a matter of tradition and the feminine talent, a brilliant breakthrough in ideas of character and plot, a cause for celebration, a grand literary and historical event. For what it liberates is the role of women in British fiction. After Austen, heroines, and heroes, and novels, could never be quite the same.

Notes

1. The point was made as early as 1936, in R. P. Utter and G. B. Needham, *Pamela's Daughters* (New York: Macmillan). See also Ian Watt, *The Rise of the Novel: Studies in Defoe, Richardson and Fielding* (Berkeley: Univ. of California Press, 1967).

2. *The Heroine's Text: Readings in the French and English Novel, 1722-1782* (New York: Columbia Univ. Press, 1980), p. xi.

3. See particularly her chapter on "Romantic Love and Sexual Fantasy in Epistolary Fiction," *Women, Letters, and the Novel* (New York: AMS Press, 1980), pp. 137-67.

4. *The Proper Lady and the Woman Writer: Ideology as Style in the Works of Mary*

Wollstonecraft, Mary Shelley, and Jane Austen (Chicago: Univ. of Chicago Press, 1984), p. 19.

5. The constancy of sex in eighteenth-century novels has been noted by many readers, some of whom have guided my own reading in the field. See J. M. S. Tompkins, *The Popular Novel in England 1700-1800* (Lincoln: Univ. of Nebraska Press, 1961); John J. Richetti, *Popular Fiction Before Richardson: Narrative Patterns 1700-1739* (Oxford: Oxford Univ. Press, 1969); Jerry C. Beasley, *Novels of the 1740's* (Athens: Univ. of Georgia Press, 1982).

6. *The Popular Novel in England*, p. 135.

7. For excellent discussions of sexuality and gender in *Clarissa*, see Leo Brandy, "Penetration and Impenetrability in *Clarissa*," in *New Approaches to Eighteenth-Century Literature*, ed. Philip Harth (New York: Columbia Univ. Press, 1974); Terry Castle, *Clarissa's Ciphers: Meaning and Disruption in Richardson's "Clarissa"* (Ithaca, NY: Cornell Univ. Press, 1982); and Terry Eagleton, *The Rape of Clarissa: Writing, Sexuality and Class Struggle in Samuel Richardson* (Oxford: Basil Blackwell, 1982).

8. Quoted by John Halperin, "Introduction: Jane Austen's Nineteenth-Century Critics: Walter Scott to Henry James," in *Jane Austen Bicentenary Essays*, ed. John Halperin (New York: Cambridge Univ. Press, 1975), p. 8.

9. Quoted by Marvin Mudrick in "Jane Austen's drawing-room," *Bicentenary Essays*, p. 252. Moore's answer seems to be that the burning human heart went to France and Russia.

10. *The Novels of Jane Austen*, 3d ed., ed. R. W. Chapman (Oxford: Oxford Univ. Press, 1933), 4:431. All further references to Austen's novels are to the volumes in this edition.

11. Alice Chandler, "'A Pair of Fine Eyes': Jane Austen's Treatment of Sex," *Studies in the Novel 7* (Spring 1975), 94.

12. For a useful discussion of the kinds of fiction being written, see Neal Frank Doubleday, *Variety of Attempt: British and American Fiction in the Early Nineteenth-Century* (Lincoln: Univ. of Nebraska Press, 1976).

Liberty, Connection, and Tyranny:
The Novels of Jane Austen and the Aesthetic Movement of the Picturesque_____

Jill Heydt-Stevenson

The word *picturesque* is little used in casual conversation these days, and when it does appear, it usually refers loosely to any pretty scene. But the late eighteenth century took the idea of the picturesque seriously and developed an entire aesthetic philosophy around it. William Gilpin, the age's most influential theorist of the picturesque, saw in a properly picturesque scene the smoothness characteristic of the beautiful commingling with the roughness of untamed nature. And "among all the objects of art, the picturesque eye is perhaps most inquisitive after the elegant relics of ancient architecture; the ruined tower, the Gothic arch, the remains of castles, and abbeys. These are the richest legacies of art. They are consecrated by time; and almost deserve the veneration we pay to the works of nature itself."

Jill Heydt-Stevenson, noting that "readers have not taken seriously Austen's comprehensive knowledge of this aesthetic," argues that "she was, in fact, lucidly informed about the picturesque controversies among various landscape gardeners and aestheticians." More important, Austen saw the connections between this aesthetic discourse and a larger discourse about liberty itself. Her work "explores the junction between the boundaries of personal liberty allowed to women and those allowed to the landscape itself, privileging for her own heroines bonds with the wilder, unornamented, picturesque landscape."   — J.L.

How liberated should a landscape be from the regulating hands of improvers or the unconstraining hands of picturesque design? Should the landscape be belted or free; should curves be severely serpentine or careless and easy? Should avenues five miles long be cut down to clear the way for new plantings? Should a landscape architect alter the course of a river and plant a pleasure garden on English soil "in the style of Watteau"? (Aslet 1936-37).[1] How much freedom of movement, either through the land or through the network of social classes should the individual—especially a woman—be permitted? Should a heroine have the freedom to express emotions so violently that they almost kill her (*Sense and Sensibility*); to disobey her guardian by marrying the man she loves (*Persuasion*); to marry her cousin (*Mansfield Park*); to marry out of her financial class or change her mind about an engagement or walk across the fields and get her petticoats muddy and her cheeks pink and completely outrage her neighbors and future relatives (*Pride and Prejudice*)?

In Austen's novels, arguments about the construction of a national identity converge with arguments about the construction of womanhood and the construction of landscape. When we examine this convergence, we find that Austen explores the junction between the boundaries of personal liberty allowed to women and those allowed to the landscape itself, privileging for her own heroines bonds with the wilder, unornamented, picturesque landscape. I will argue here that we can more fully understand this convergence and better address some of the questions listed above when we examine the aesthetic debates concerning the picturesque that occurred between (roughly) 1790 and 1811. Recognizing Austen's affiliation with picturesque aesthetics— and particularly with the theorists Uvedale Price and Richard Payne Knight—reveals a complex nexus among the novels, the nation, the picturesque, and Romantic aesthetics. And although critics have suffered from several blind spots when they have tried to assess Austen's relationship to the picturesque,[2] she was, in fact, lucidly informed about the picturesque controversies among various landscape gardeners and aestheticians that were played out during her lifetime. Austen lived fully in the world of landscape architecture, witnessing at firsthand the impact of picturesque improvement and the conflict between the preservers and the improvers: her wealthy relatives living at

Godmersham Park and Goodnestone Farm had their land improved in the style of Capability Brown, and Repton himself transformed Stoneleigh Abbey, much to the family's dismay.[3]

Simply put, readers have not taken seriously Austen's comprehensive knowledge of this aesthetic.[4] Further, they have failed to differentiate between picturesque aesthetics and picturesque improvement. Although the latter distinction is crucial, it is one that is rarely, if ever, acknowledged in discussions of the picturesque, where the two kinds of landscape styles tend to get lumped together under one umbrella term, picturesque. This essay begins with the convictions, first, that the picturesque is far too complicated to be summarily dismissed as the hackneyed third in the triumvirate of the sublime, beautiful, and picturesque, and, second, that Austen, well aware of aesthetic debates, deliberately endorses picturesque aesthetics and satirizes picturesque improvement.[5]

Picturesque Improvement

. . . a thraldom [*sic*] unfit for a free country
——Sir Uvedale Price 1: 338

It is now, I believe, generally admitted, that the system of picturesque improvement, employed by the late Mr. Brown and his followers, is the very reverse of picturesque.

——Knight, *Landscape* 1. 17

In order to see how Austen's heroines are linked to the debates about English nationalism and the appearance and treatment of the landscape, it is important to have a clear sense of the differences among the various landscape styles. The debate centered on whether to preserve or alter, and thus whether to maintain or to use, though both camps believed they were preserving what was distinctly English. The picturesque theorists called for a wilder beauty; in contrast, the improvers claimed that those who wanted to tell them to keep their land undomesticated were directly compromising an owner's ability to make use of his property. Reacting to the charge of the improver, Humphry Repton, Price, and Knight contended that their own version of the aesthetic was powerfully nationalistic, that they were *protecting* the British landscape from improvements that would "disfigure" the face of the land (Price, *Essays* 1: 331-32). And Knight lamented the "sacrilegious waste/ Of False improvement, and pretended taste" (*Landscape* 2. 317-19).

Brown and Repton's designs—termed the modern system of gardening—signified for Austen, Price, and Knight a "fashionable" outlook, divorced from the guidance of history and destructive of traditional community. The "preservers" (Knight and Price) endorsed a looser, less fastidious garden design that emphasized verdant, overshadowing trees, and density of shrubbery. This did not mean, however, as some have charged, that they wanted the lawn to look like a Salvator Rosa painting—that Knight or Price had, in short, "gothic Fantasies" (Hunt 154). Instead, Knight petitioned for "just congruity of parts combined/ To please the *sense*, and satisfy the *mind*" (*Landscape* 2. 39-40). In arguing against Repton, he was arguing for a less formal landscape, one whose design takes its cue organically from the nature of the landscape itself, rather than from preconceived rules: "No general rule of embellishment can be applicable to all the varieties of natural situation; and those who adopt such general rules, may be more properly said to *improve by accident*, than either Mr. Price or myself" (11n; Knight's italics).[6]

Humphry Repton did drastically improve the landscape: we find (in his early work) a formal, minimalist design that favors sweeping lawns and scattered trees, and often the removal of villages and commons for the sake of the prospect. According to these principles of improvement, the landscape architect clumps trees and bushes into distinct patches, circles the entire property with a "belt," and shaves the grass so that it sweeps smoothly up to the very base of the estate. Thus the house sits at the top of a rise, unmediated or unmodulated by trees or shrubbery.

A reader/viewer studying Repton's Red Books (hand-painted "before and after" views of his proposed alterations) will see that his aesthetic transformations of the landscape, though often beautiful, are dependent upon the eradication of commons, of signs of commerce, and of laborers' homes. For example, in his "before and after" view of the fort, near Bristol, the "before" view shows thirty-six adults and six playing children, primarily dressed in brown, dark red, and dark blue, walking on the common; nearby are many rows of brown homes. In the "after" picture there are only two ladies and one child, dressed in white with a touch of pink, walking by several chairs charmingly and intimately grouped under the trees. The brown houses are gone and replaced with three handsome white dwellings in the distance behind trees. In other words, a beautiful *private* park replaces a common area and eradicates the urbanized scene, supplanting it with a spacious property that the few privately appreciate. Repton explains that "the late prodigious increase of buildings had so injured the prospect from this house, that its original advantages of situation were almost destroyed" (8). Repton's editor, J. C. Loudon, argues that the improver "may be considered as combining all that was excellent in the former schools . . . with good taste and good sense" (vii). Yet Loudon's estimation of Repton ignores the question of who is privileged to remain in the landscape.

Fundamental to the debates between the picturesque theorists and the improvers is the question of control, and it is this issue of control that is also central to Austen's *Mansfield Park*: the question of what and who is privileged to remain in the landscape is the pivotal one in the novel. Critics have long recognized how in *Mansfield Park* and in other novels Austen satirizes Capability Brown and Humphry Repton's schools of picturesque landscape improvement, but no one has explored in detail the important fact that in so doing she sympathizes with Uvedale Price and Richard Payne Knight and thus refrains from satirizing the picturesque as a *whole*.[7]

Let us now look specifically at *Mansfield Park*. During an evening dinner party, the company discusses the improvement of Sotherton and other estates: Rushworth claims, "It is the most complete thing! I never saw a place so altered in my life. I told Smith I did not know where I was" (53).[8] Rushworth has already disconnected the landscape from the house, from the inhabitants and from the past—leaving it only to the memory of many—by having had "two or three fine old trees cut down that grew too near the house" (55). But such mutilation is nothing compared to the projected destruction of the old avenue. In an often-cited quotation, Fanny expresses distress at this prospect when she quotes Cowper: "'Ye fallen avenues, once more I mourn your fate unmerited'" (56).[9] Yet Austen is not just attacking improvement; her sympathies connect intimately to those of Uvedale Price, who observes that "the destruction of so many of these venerable approaches" is the "fatal consequence" of fashion. "Even the old avenue, whose branches had intertwined with each other for ages, must undergo this fashionable metamorphosis" (1: 249, 256). Price narrates: "At a gentleman's place in Cheshire, there is an avenue of oaks; . . . Mr. Brown absolutely condemned it; but it now stands, a noble monument of the triumph of the *natural feelings* of the owner, over the narrow and systematic ideas of a professed improver" (1: 249-50n; italics mine). Rushworth, clearly a man of no great "natural feelings," points out that "Repton, or anybody of that sort, would certainly have the avenue at Sotherton down" (Austen 55), an avenue that we learn later is "oak entirely and measures *half a mile long*" (82-83, italics mine).

Indeed, in Austen's novels, the issue of how much control one should exert over a landscape is not a localized aesthetic issue, but instead directly impinges on the treatment of and expectations for women; Austen links debates about the freedom of landscape to debates about the freedom of woman. For example, Fanny, like the avenue Rushworth will cut down, is expendable and must be made to fit into the overall "aesthetic" plan. The picturesque theorists argued that such an emphasis on the "plan" over the organic layout atomized the natural world, severing relations between trees and between the house and the landscape. Price observes that picturesque improvement not only disconnects but is despotic: trees and other bushes are clumped together or

> are *cut down without pity*, if they will not range according to a prescribed model; till mangled, starved, and *cut off from all connection*, these *unhappy* newly drilled corps "Stand bare and naked, trembling at themselves." (1: 256, 338; italics mine)

Fanny, herself, is "cut off from all connection" and "cut down without pity," first, when she arrives as a child, and second, when she is expected to marry Henry Crawford. Let me examine these moments in some detail.

When she is first deposited at Mansfield Park, Mrs. Norris and Sir Thomas harbor the despotic fantasy that they can mold and fashion Fanny without themselves or anyone else being affected. Austen dramatizes this by implementing the metaphor of landscape design in the language describing Fanny's literal and psychological placement in the household. Fanny's bedroom is chosen literally to "keep her in her place": Mrs. Norris argues that the "little white attic will be much the best *place* for her, so near Miss Lee, and not far from the girls, and close by the housemaids. . . . Indeed, I do not see that you could *place* her any where else" (9-10, italics mine). Both Mrs. Norris and Sir Thomas's sketches of Fanny's domestic landscape exclude her from any liberty or equality. He defines Fanny by fixing her in a place of subordination and endeavors to keep her both literally and psychologically depressed: "There will be some difficulty in our way . . . as to the distinction proper to be made between the girls as they grow up; . . . without depressing her spirits too far, [we will] make her remember that she is not a *Miss Bertram*" (10). Sir Thomas fantasizes that he can control Fanny's impact on the family by cutting his niece off from equal connection with his children.

His system for such custodial "gardening" fails: Fanny shows that she will "grow" where she will when she refuses to marry Crawford—when she refuses to accede to her uncle's "prescribed model" for matrimony; significantly, he condemns her because she has indeed attempted to exercise her own taste and judgment: He says, "I thought you free . . . from that independence of spirit, which prevails so much in modern days. . . . But you have now shewn me that you can be wilful and perverse, that you can and will decide for yourself, without any consideration or deference for those who have surely some right to guide you" (318). And later when Fanny takes her own private walk in the shrubbery, Mrs. Norris says, "She likes to go her own way to work; she does not like to be dictated to; she takes her own independent walk whenever she can" (323).

Price and Knight draw a parallel between the political tyrant and the improvers, who advocate "a species of thraldom [*sic*] unfit for a free country":

It seems as if the improver said, "you shall never wander from my walks; never exercise your own taste and judgment, never form your own compositions; neither your eyes nor your feet shall be allowed to stray from the boundaries I have traced." (Uvedale Price 1: 338)

Sir Thomas himself resembles Price's description of the "despotic" improver, who, in attempting to "improve" Fanny by forcing her to marry Henry Crawford, will not let her "wander from [her] walks" or "exercise [her] own taste and judgment" or "form [her] own composition"—that is, her own life plans. As Price says, "There is, indeed, something despotic in the general system of improvement; all must be laid open; all that obstructs, levelled to the ground; houses, orchards, gardens, all swept away" (Uvedale Price 1: 338).

Fanny's depression is a measure of just how "successful" Sir Thomas has been, for the very lack of compositional "disposition" in the family structure powerfully affects her personal disposition. William Gilpin, the picturesque theorist and travel guide, explains that—in picturesque terms—"disposition" is "the art of grouping and combining the figures, and several parts of a picture" and is "an essential, which contributes greatly to produce a *whole* in painting"—in short, to create harmony and repose (*An Essay on Prints* 9-10). In contrast, Sir Thomas and Mrs. Norris are concerned with a kind of unity based only on what Gilpin would call the "design," or the way that each part, "*separately taken*" (Gilpin's italics), produces a whole; thus the individual parts remain "scattered" and "have no dependence on each other" (7). What is ironic about Sir Thomas and Mrs. Norris's compositional strategy, of course, is that organizing the family by "design" rather than by "disposition" disconnects yet reconnects the members together in a pathological way. For example, the family remains atomized while competition and rivalry bond them together: sister against sister, brother against brother, sisters against cousin, aunt against niece, children against father, and so on. To use the theatrical term, each individual wants "center stage," or, to use Gilpin's picturesque term, each one wants the focus of "catching lights" (xi). Like a picture with too many subjects, the characters, as disconnected parts, compete with each other for prominence.

Fanny and Edmund are ultimately able to find such connection based on harmony and repose in their retreat to the retired little village between gently rising hills where they will live protected in a parsonage just "a stone's throw of the knoll and church." The deeply conservative plea for preservation over improvement in the novel leads to the eradication of the ones who represent newness and change: Maria, Mrs. Norris, Mary and Henry; as their absence "improves" Mansfield Park, so will the repudiation of picturesque improvement and the endorsement of picturesque aesthetics "improve" the landscape of England itself: Knight, like Austen, will "Protect from all the sacrilegious

waste/ Of False improvement, and pretended taste,/ One tranquil vale
. . ." (*Landscape* 2. 313, 317-19).

However, a central irony emerges here if we interpret Austen as only
conservative in this rejection of improvement, for her apparently conservative plea for preservation honors Fanny's connection to the natural world and functions as a subversive plea for the necessity of
women's freedom and liberty.

Landscape and the Discourse of the Body

> Limbs . . . never taught to move by rules,
> But free alike from bandages and schools.
> —Knight, *Landscape* 1. 44, 49-50

In "The Ideology of the Aesthetic," Terry Eagleton argues that "aesthetics . . . has little enough to do with art. It denotes instead a whole
program of social, psychical and political reconstruction on the part of
the early European bourgeoisie. . . . Aesthetics is born as a discourse of
the body" (327). I want to argue that picturesque aesthetics constitute
an instance in which the issues of the body, of sexuality, of women, and
of the desire for liberty intertwine.[10] In fact, the sometimes overt, sometimes covert feminism and liberation this aesthetic introduces did not
go unnoticed by its contemporaries, though it is significant that in recent years literary critics have focused primarily on the opposite—
what they see as repressive and oppressive tendencies in this movement and in these theorists. In other words, the picturesque that contemporary Marxist critics see as a system that dispossessed the poor of
human sympathy, some of Knight's contemporaries saw as a system
that would cause a revolution.[11]

In *The Landscape*, Knight makes explicit the connection between
the emancipation of the body, the mind, and the landscape from "iron
bonds," and urges that England adopt a style of landscape gardening

that will allow nature to be "unfetter'd," her body "free and unconfined," and her "Limbs . . . never taught to move by rules,/ But free
alike from bandages and schools" (1. 44, 49-50). Knight describes the
landscape in specifically female terms, not only employing the feminine pronoun to speak of nature—conventional, after all—but invoking in his analogies the experience of women. For example, abhorring
the tortures that fashion forces women and the landscape to endure,
Knight writes in his *Analytical Inquiry* that because women, like the
unaltered landscape, possess inherent appeal, they have least need of
those that are artificial; he goes on to describe the fashions in women's
clothing, which closely resemble the current fashion in landscape improvement:

> Yet art has been wearied, and nature ransacked; tortures have been en-
> dured, and health sacrificed; and all to enable this lovely part of the cre-
> ation to appear in shapes as remote as possible from that in which all its na-
> tive loveliness consists. (2-3)

It was, in fact, the shaping, arranging, and improving of the landscape—
whose function is analogous to the confining clothing—that disturbed
the picturesque theorists most; controlling nature by trimming, shav-
ing, cutting, pruning, or uprooting it violates and abuses the landscape.[12]

Price and Knight's criticisms of the improved landscape resemble
those of feminist critics who argue that a comparison between women
and the landscape both exploits and excludes women, while using their
bodies as metaphors of erotic interest—where the male gaze "tends to
. . . freeze the flow of action in moments of erotic contemplation"
(Mulvey 19). For example, Annette Kolodny argues in *Lay of the Land*
that there have been two responses to the American landscape—the
desire to violate it and the desire to regress psychologically in its presence. She argues that we are still "bound by the vocabulary of a feminine landscape and the psychological patterns of regression and viola-

tion that it implies" (146). The picturesque, however, does allow us to conceive of the landscape in feminine terms without reducing it to this binary opposition. Kolodny's description of "the images of abuse" that are heaped upon the virgin landscape resemble Price and Knight's complaints about Brown's "improvements," which they maintained consisted of assault and plunder:

> . . . — See yon fantastic band,
> With charts, pedometers and rules in hand,
> Advance triumphant, and alike lay waste
> The forms of nature, and the works of taste!
> To improve, adorn, and polish, they profess;
> But shave the goddess, whom they come to dress;
> Level each broken bank and shaggy mound,
> And fashion all to one unvaried round;
>
> (Knight, *Landscape* 1. 275-82)

Here Knight describes how improvement, in attempting to smooth surfaces ("shave" and "level"), actually "lay[s] waste" any singularity in nature. We can understand that the improver's frantic effort to "fashion to one unvaried round" strives to create a landscape representative of the "ideal" mother in whose presence "we are unwilling to move, almost to think" (Uvedale Price 1: 88). Thus picturesque aesthetics counter both passive regression to the mother and rape of the virgin bride.

The development of the picturesque thus had an unintentional yet powerful impact on relaxing and liberating the gender limitations that Burke imposed on the system of the sublime and beautiful, based as it is on highly conventional and rigid masculine and feminine characteristics. Price and Knight wanted to establish that there were more than two kinds of aesthetic experience (the sublime and the beautiful), and by introducing the picturesque (as I have explained), they hoped to correct the system of improvements initiated by Brown and continued by

Repton, improvements they felt were grounded in a debased version of the beautiful that was insipid and diminished in its simplicity.[13] Thus the picturesque entered into the famous Burkean dichotomy of the sublime and the beautiful as a destabilizing and mediating term, taking the energy from the sublime and the languor from the beautiful and intermixing them. What we see is a landscape that, in contrast to the beautiful and sublime, is erotic, for it transforms "Mother nature," as it were, into a lover: characterized as the "coquetry of nature," the picturesque makes "beauty more amusing, more varied, more playful, but also, '[l]ess winning soft, less amiably mild'" (Uvedale Price 1: 89).[14] This playful and complex landscape invites action and response, for its visual and textural intricacy "reveals and conceals, and this excites and nourishes curiosity" (1: 22). And curiosity provokes our own energy: it "prompts us to scale every rocky/ promontory, to explore every new recess, [and] by its active agency keeps the fibres to their full tone" (1: 88-89). In promoting the picturesque, which mediates between two extremes and which is feminine but founded on energy and vitality, Knight and Price break down Burke's binary oppositions and they champion an aesthetic that describes the feminine as active, varied, and powerful.

Burke's system, as we know, is based on the opposite, on the necessity of a weak feminine principle, for the feminine beautiful is characterized by "easiness of temper," while the masculine sublime is characterized by "immense force and labor" (Burke 110, 78).[15] Clearly, Burke's system already contained within it strongly eroding forces, of which he seemed supremely unaware. Burke's—and his contemporaries'— inability to transcend the social construction of nature leads to gender biases that are far less objective than Burke himself believed. His conception of these categories as opposites is flawed, for while he touts the beautiful as the place of safety and security, it is in fact a very dangerous aesthetic experience: "It is . . . the deceptive *par excellence*" (Ferguson 75). Yet the picturesque secured this erosion by breaking down the bipolar system of beauty versus sublimity, a binary system in which women are associated with beauty and thus with vulnerability.[16] The picturesque thus takes us out of that gender-based "cat-and-mouse game" in which "an enervated feminine beauty must be regularly stiffened by a masculine sublime whose terrors must then be instantly defused, in an endless rhythm of erection and detumescence" (Eagleton 330-31).[17]

I am explicitly arguing against the widely held notion that it is always politically and critically reactionary to associate a female character with landscape, and that, specifically, picturesque descriptions of nature are only patriarchal fantasies in which male theorists transform the female body into a fetish (Fabricant). It is significant, though I do not have the time here to discuss the issue fully, that women were the "first to perceive the picturesque" and continued to participate in picturesque viewing.[18] Thus I take issue with the notion that the picturesque is a "rather bourgeois taming of the sublime," or a domestication of the sublime into the "orderly and cultivated," or a "manipulation of flux into form, infinity into frame" (Stewart 75). First of all, this aesthetic emphasizes not form but fluctuation; second, it eschews the orderly and cultivated for lush texture, abundant foliage, and rich contrasts of light and shade; and third, it highlights not "framing" but the play between the frame and chaos: in the aesthetic and in the novels, the paradox of the copy and the original is unresolvable, for we cannot determine whether the landscape or the landscape sketch came first, since art and nature are engaged in a process of reflexive influence. Further, the picturesque troubles the opposition of culture and nature as well: by combining culture and nature simultaneously, rather than empowering one side at the expense of the other, this aesthetic consistently upsets the hierarchical rigidity that favors culture over nature. What can be said, however, is that the critics have placed the picturesque in opposition to the system of the sublime and the beautiful as a whole; Hussey places it in opposition to Romanticism and other critics in opposition to authentic artistic experience—and in each case, it takes on the "feminine" role of the weaker, or lesser category, movement, or experience. Along these lines, W. J. T. Mitchell argues the point in *Iconology* that in interdisciplinary studies in general, art and literature are placed in binary opposition, and that when the sign (art) is opposed to the word (literature), the sign becomes symbolic of nature, the feminine, the passive, and the weaker of the pair, but ultimately the most dangerous because of its potentially subversive power (43). Thus a feminist point of view reveals to us that only a privileging of male power could interpret the picturesque as "taming" and "domesticating" the sublime, rather than noticing the power it potentially offers to women.

I am not ignoring what cultural materialism has taught us about aesthetics (Copley), and I am not idealizing the picturesque theorists: while containing in it the seeds of feminism (both woman and landscape should be free of artificial constraints), the picturesque also offers (to quote Toril Moi) one of those "paradoxically productive aspects of patriarchal ideology (the moments in which the ideology backfires on itself, as it were)" (64). Both inadvertently and deliberately, Knight and Price break down the binary gender opposition in Burke's system, link the picturesque to personal liberation, and thereby offer in picturesque landscape a liberating model for the female body.[19] Their championing of the "natural," "unfettered" landscape, a championing that also celebrates the "natural" and "unfettered" woman, offered writers of this era a fresh vision of woman and of the landscape.[20] When theorists write in sexual terms about a landscape that should be free from "iron bonds," using women's confinements as negative examples, they implicate the body, women, the body politic, and the land.[21]

How then do these issues play themselves out in Austen's conception of a woman's power and position? The heroine's connection with nature differs from novel to novel; for example, in *Persuasion* Austen emphasizes the grief and loss associated with the picturesque, while in *Pride and Prejudice* she highlights the vitality and energy of this kind of landscape.[22] Elizabeth's unconventional beauty, witty playfulness, physical energy, and decorous flirtatiousness dramatize the way in which her mind, like the picturesque landscape, seems "unfetter'd," her body "free and unconfined," and her "limbs . . . never taught to move by rules,/ But free alike from bandages and schools" (Knight, *Landscape* 1. 43, 49-50). In aligning Elizabeth with the values of landscape design that favor energy, playfulness, and sensuous appeal, Austen creates a character whose physical and mental presence challenges traditional and patriarchal assumptions about beauty, decorum, and class.[23] Elizabeth's vitality demonstrates Austen's preference for energy over control and rigidity, a selection that suggests her partiality for the picturesque as opposed to the improved landscape. Like the picturesque, Elizabeth overcomes dichotomies between beauty and sublimity, passivity and aggression, intellect and emotion, by embracing both sides of these oppositional principles.

Austen's incorporation of picturesque theory interfuses the issues of liberty, control, and license for landscape and for woman. Elizabeth arrives at Netherfield "glowing" from having walked alone across open country (32), obviously having asserted both her liberty (by traveling alone) and her desire for connection (in wanting to see her ill sister). When Elizabeth walks into the room, the Bingley sisters focus on her independence by fixating on her (apparently) muddy petticoat rather than on her vitality, a vitality so emphatic that they can barely "keep their countenance,"[24] can just barely screen their emotions, that is, until she's out of the room:

> "She really looked almost wild . . . her hair so untidy, so blowsy!"
> "Yes, and her petticoat; I hope you saw her petticoat, six inches deep in mud, I am absolutely certain; and the gown which had been let down to hide it, not doing its office." (35-36)

It is significant that Darcy, though attracted to her beauty, is plagued by the similar anxieties as to when liberty becomes license: he "was divided between admiration of the brilliancy which exercise had given to her complexion and doubt at the occasion's justifying her coming so far alone" (33). The conflict Darcy feels in enjoying Elizabeth's appearance is based on what he perceives as a possible discordance between vitality and decorum and between liberty and license, because Elizabeth, like the picturesque landscape, redefines manners, redefines the equation between beauty and passive torpor. He resolves this conflict in part by acknowledging that in fact her health is improved by this act of assertion:

> "I am afraid, Mr. Darcy," observed Miss Bingley, in a half whisper, "that this adventure has rather affected your admiration of her fine eyes."
>
> "Not at all," he replied; "they were brightened by the exercise."—A short pause followed this speech. (36)

This episode dramatizes the argument between picturesque theorists and landscape improvers: the improvers believed that to include natural energy, liberty, and spontaneity in garden design, one must sacrifice seemliness and propriety. The improver Humphry Repton claimed that the picturesque would reject "propriety and convenience" (Uvedale Price 3: 6) and asserted the concern that in picturesque design "health, cheerfulness, and comfort" must be sacrificed to the "wild but pleasing scenery of a painter's imagination," a place where one would find not beauty but a "ragged gipsy . . . [a] wild ass, [a] Pomeranian dog, and [a] shaggy goat" (3: 7, 8).[25] And Anna Seward argues that Knight's system in *The Landscape* is the "Jacobinism of taste," an aesthetic that will lead to living in "tangled forests, and amongst men who are unchecked by those guardian laws, which bind the various orders of society in one common interest"; she longs for the improved landscape, with "lawns . . . smoothed by healthful industry."[26]

Yet, picturesque theorists argued that landscape design could be more playful and spontaneous without "neglecting" health, "convenience and propriety" (3: 49). In landscape, this means that, coinciding with picturesque aesthetics, one would have a formal garden by the house and wild nature in the Park (3: 53), a design we see manifested at Pemberley itself, where Elizabeth "had never seen a place for which nature had done more, or where natural beauty had been so little counteracted by an awkward taste" (245). Specifically, Elizabeth's connection to Darcy and his connection to Pemberley reinforces custom and moral heritage, as did the Price and Knight picturesque.

Further, picturesque aesthetics declare that decorum and the integrity of the English landscape did not have to be sacrificed to improvements that would leave every estate and garden looking the same—cut out of one mold, one frame, "fashion[ed] all to one unvaried round" (Knight 1. 282). Unlike the improved landscape or improved beauty (Caroline being a good example), Elizabeth does not conform to cookie-cutter ideals of beauty, for her beauty has not been "vitiated by false ideas of refinement" (Uvedale Price 3: 40), and this Darcy acknowledges: "In spite of his asserting that her manners were not those of the fashionable world, he was caught by their easy playfulness" (23). Freedom for the landscape and for woman become intertwined. The health of the nation and of woman depends upon a dual emphasis on liberty and connection: the picturesque therefore pushes the borders that define what Eagleton calls "that meticulous disciplining of the body which converts morality to style, aestheticizing virtue and so deconstructing the opposition between the proper and the pleasurable" (Eagleton 329).

Austen thus associates Elizabeth with the Price and Knight picturesque and differentiates her from the complete wildness of Lydia, for Elizabeth's beauty combines formality with energy. And yet, critics of Austen's novels have tended to interpret her texts precisely as if they consist of such binary oppositions as those between decorum and vitality or "the individual and society" or "freedom and responsibility, or liberty and license."[27] In contrast, I am asserting that the presence of picturesque aesthetics in this particular episode at Netherfield underscores how the novel breaks down such dualisms. Elizabeth Bennet is not the wild Lydia; neither is she the docile, passive Jane—she mediates between extremes that never do get resolved. Even at the end, she is elbowing the borders of wifely decorum by sending money surreptitiously to her sister.

We find in all of her novels that Austen shows how disconnection and tyranny are inextricably bound and demonstrates how the fate of the national landscape is linked to women's autonomy and self-expression. Lady Catherine, Sir Thomas, Mary, Emma, and Mrs. Norris are among the most extreme improvers (or as Price would call them, "deformers"), for, like the landscape improvers, they dictate to others in their urge to impose on others, mandating that "all that obstructs should be levelled to the ground." As we see in so early a work as *Northanger Abbey*, General Tilney's garden, where every square inch is improved, resembles a miniature Versailles: tyrant that he is, his garden contains "walls . . . countless in number, endless in length," and "a whole parish [seemed] to be a work within the inclosure"; indeed, his gardens, he believes, "are unrivalled in the kingdom" (178).

That Austen is intolerant of the despotic tendency to "improve" the lives of others by dictating to them becomes even more significant when we realize that she historically contextualizes this "personal" distaste for tyranny within the specific political/aesthetic conditions of her own time. This congruence between Austen and the picturesque theorists has significant consequences for our understanding of her novels: scholars have, on the whole, described her as a conservative Tory. And it is true that by endorsing picturesque aesthetics and sympathizing with the aesthetic values of Price and Knight, Austen positions herself as fundamentally conservative in her view of the land: preserve but don't alter the landscape and, especially important, emphasize the importance of social and moral heritage and the preservation of customary ways over new and fashionable landscape innovations. Yet an ironic twist emerges here, for in associating herself with Price and Knight's position on landscape, Austen, the conservative Tory, endorses what was the Whig position (as represented by Knight and Price).[28] Moreover, the theorists' stance, while it may appear to us as fundamentally conservative, was a radical one to take in the 1790s: Price and Knight's position on freeing the landscape from "the iron bonds" of tyranny was linked in the minds of some with Jacobin sympathy (Liu). Finally, and most important, Austen's conservative position on landscape in turn leads to a liberal and feminist attitude toward women, for in identifying her heroines with the landscape of picturesque aesthetics, she associates them with freedom, playfulness, introspection, and connection to others, to their landscape, and to their nation.

Notes

1. This can be found in Humphry Repton's *Red Book for Stoneleigh* (1809), quoted in Clive Aslet's article on Stoneleigh Abbey.

2. Most critics have been loath to associate Austen with an aesthetic that has become notoriously synonymous with art for art's sake (Martin Price), hackneyed tourism (Andrews), a patriarchal fantasy (Fabricant), and class oppression (Bermingham). In order to justify its presence in her novels, they have seen her merely as a satirist of the aesthetic (Llewelyn, Craik, Lascelles, Bermingham), or they have seen both sympathy and criticism but found themselves unable to explain why she should have a dual reaction (Mansell, Litz). Finally, a very few critics have acknowledged her sympathy for the picturesque without contextualizing it historically (Synder).

3. For example, the *Red Book for Stoneleigh* (1809) shows that Repton altered the course of the river, bringing it nearer the south end of the house and sought to preserve an island Leigh wanted removed. Significantly, the family did not approve of these extensive changes. The correspondence between Leigh and Repton reveals strong differences of opinion over the nature of these improvements and suggests that his transformation caused direct conflict (see Aslet 1937). Invented by Repton, Red Books were created individually for each project. By simply lifting a flap, the owner could see hand-painted "before and after" pictures of the landscape renovations Repton envisioned for the property.

4. In this sense, my work is in theoretical alignment with that of Claudia Johnson, whose recent book, *Jane Austen, Women, Politics and the Novel*, argues that "Historical scholars . . . deny [Austen] any direct access or pondered relation to [pressing social and political issues]. Whether linking her to Shaftesbury, Rousseau, or Burke, for ex-

ample, critics shuffle in fear of granting Austen too much, and taking away with one hand what they have given with the other, they couch their arguments about her intellectual antecedents and leanings in the vaguest possible terms of 'affinity,' 'temperament,' or 'unconscious awareness'" (xvii).

5. R. W. Chapman says that Austen "was no doubt acquainted with Price and Payne Knight, and with other polemical writers on landscape and landscape gardening" (26). John Halperin states that Austen read Price and Knight, but he offers no documentation (26). Park Honan is silent on the subject. It does seem reasonable and probable to me that she would have read these works in the lending library at Bath, which she used and which was quite extensive, or that these books would have been in the libraries at Godmersham Park or Goodnestone Farm or at Chawton Manor. On the lending library at Bath, see Margaret Kirkham, who explains that there were "good book shops" and "ten circulating libraries in Bath . . . filled with new books in French and Italian, as well as in English. . . . In Bath, Jane Austen must have had access to virtually any author she wished to read and a quiet reading-room too if she wanted it" (64).

6. Marilyn Butler observes that the followers of Brown tended to see nature as a place where one finds "greater opportunities for sober usefulness" while the followers of Price and Knight (whom she calls progressive) are "liable to see [the country] as a place for the individual to expand in freedom, cultivating the self" (97).

7. See Alistair Duckworth, who argues that it is "misleading" to assume that Austen's "distaste for Repton" implies a "preference for the more naturalistic styles of Price and Knight . . ." (41-42).

8. All quotations from Jane Austen's novels are taken from the Oxford edition, ed. R. W. Chapman.

9. Gilpin also quoted these lines. See his *Observations on the Western Parts of England* 542. Repton would take down the avenue because it would have been unfashionably associated with seventeenth-century French gardening styles, such as one might find at Versailles.

10. However, this focus on liberation can only check the potentially sexist nature of the eroticism of the picturesque if it implies liberation for women as well as for men. Mary Poovey argues that during the French Revolution freedom for the individual did not apply to both men and women, and in fact "intensif[ied] the paradoxes already inherent in propriety: discussions of the inequality of women's position and the complexity of female 'nature' almost completely disappeared from polite discourse . . ." (30). Marilyn Butler backs up the notion of a "conservative backlash," for the anti-Jacobin novel of the 1790s focuses on the inevitable destruction of the heroine who is deluded into ruin by the coupling of political and sexual liberation.

11. This context illustrates just how controversial it was for Price and Knight to attack Brown in the late 1790s. Bermingham, for example, describes Knight (whose mother, by the way, was a servant) as a man whose "class-bound prejudices . . . dispossessed the poor of human sympathy and imagination" (71); Knight's contemporaries branded him a Jacobin and accused him of supporting the French Revolution in his didactic poem *The Landscape*. And Frank Messmann points out that Knight's "advocacy for greater freedom in gardening . . . cannot be separated from views which he expresses elsewhere on greater individual freedom" (84).

12. Alison Sulloway catalogs the fashionable constraints young women were subjected to: starving, purging, standing in stocks with backboards strapped over their shoulders and iron collars; steel busks, bands that forced the shoulder blades to meet, steel rods up the back, stays, and so on (194). Sulloway's chapter "Reconciliation in the Province of the Garden" discusses the oppression of the women and the symbolic resonance of the garden in terms of such matters as obedience, oppression, and sexuality, but she does not contextualize these ideas in terms of landscape debates of the period.

13. It is important to explain that Price and Knight, although having different reactions to Burke, appreciate the beautiful, such as one would find in a Claudian landscape. Price, for example, admired Burke and believed he was expanding, rather than overturning, Burke's system: "I have ventured indeed to explore a new track, and to discriminate the causes and the effects of the picturesque from those of the two other characters: still, however . . . it is a track I never should have discovered, had not [Burke] first cleared and adorned the principal avenues" (Uvedale Price 2: 197). Knight, in contrast, found Burke's *Philosophical Enquiry* to be "brilliant, but absurd and superficial" (*Analytical Inquiry* 197).

14. Here Uvedale Price is quoting from *Paradise Lost*: "less winning soft, less amiably mild" are actually Eve's words of criticism directed at Adam's appearance. She has looked from her image to his and finds him "less winning soft, less amiably mild" than she is. Thus in using this quotation, Price interjects a powerful element of the masculine into the picturesque (which is described mostly in female terms) and thereby breaks down the binary opposition between the masculine and the feminine. Milton's Eden is described in terms of the aesthetic category of the beautiful, as is Eve (4.1.479).

15. From a feminist point of view, Burke's obvious misogyny and quest to naturalize cultural biases and psychological fears and project them onto the landscape degrades women and nature. Frans De Bruyn does note that Burke's involvement in the affairs of India led him to revise significantly this original estimate of the superiority of men over women and the sublime over the beautiful. De Bruyn argues that Burke, in his *Speech on Mr. Fox's East India Bill*, "excoriat[es] the East-India company for disregarding the customary 'reverence paid to the female sex in general, and particularly to women of rank and condition'" (430). De Bruyn interprets this as Burke's belief that "any viable civil order must be founded on positive affection rather than primarily fear or terror, and [Burke] concludes that the degree to which a given society values beauty serves as an accurate measure of the adequacy of its social institutions" (433). However, De Bruyn points out that "Burke's defence of the beautiful and the sentimental idealization of women thus ironically serve as pretexts for the exercise of sublime power" (431); thus, his underlying purpose in idealizing them as exemplars of civilized values is to justify and defend the existing order.

16. The sublime and the beautiful line up according to Hélène Cixous's analysis of patriarchal binary thought (binary oppositions such as activity/passivity; sun/moon; culture/nature; and so on), an oppositional system whereby the "feminine" side is powerless (Moi 104).

17. Eagleton does not connect this to the picturesque, and of course his overall

point of view differs from mine; he argues that "the aesthetic is at once eloquent testimony to the enigmatic origins of morality in a society which everywhere violates it" (338).

18. Elizabeth Wheeler Manwaring argues this point (171). Most of the records, however, were of a private nature and never published. The very fact that the Bluestockings approved of this aesthetic suggests that they found some kinship, as women and as individuals, in an informal, less fettered world (see 171-75 for examples). Further, when they describe picturesque scenes, women clearly identify as women with the natural world at a very personal level, and like men, women who write about nature use gendered language, with parts of the female body as descriptive nouns and verbs ("bosomed high in tufted trees"; 219). See Sarah Scott, author of *Millennium Hall* (1762) and Elizabeth Diggle, who records the Highland scenery she travels through in distinctly female terms by giving a "recipe" for a picturesque scene in the Highlands (qtd. in Andrews 216 [*Journal*, 1788], Glasgow University Library, MS. Gen.738).

19. It is significant that Price did not acknowledge that Burke's conception of the beautiful resembles the picturesque improver's conception of the beautiful—both are weak and diminished: And here is a case of the patriarchal world view unwittingly undermining itself.

20. Although her emphasis is different, Jeanne Moskal makes a similar point in her article on Mary Wollstonecraft (1992); our joint conclusion about Burke and the feminism of the picturesque seems to have been conceived at the same time (see my dissertation, "*Verbal Landscapes*").

21. In *Representations of Revolution*, Ronald Paulson argues that the aesthetic categories of the picturesque, beautiful, sublime, and grotesque became ways to process the revolution (150).

22. I have discussed these issues in other places; see "First Impressions and Later Recollections: The 'Place' of the Picturesque in *Pride and Prejudice*"; my dissertation, "Verbal Landscapes and Visual Texts: Jane Austen and the Picturesque"; and "'Unbecoming Conjunctions': Mourning the Loss of Landscape and Love in *Persuasion*."

23. Certainly it is now admissible, without preamble, to discuss the sexual energy underlying Austen's "cool" surfaces. See Alison Sulloway and Alice Chandler.

24. See Roger Sales, who demonstrates that Austen is continually keeping and losing her "countenance" (31), as evidence that her texts are "open and unresolved" (145).

25. See also Kim Ian Michasiw, who claims that I am arguing that an association with Price and Knight implies that one is "going native" or going over to Matthew Arnold's barbarians (98).

26. Quoted in Marilyn Butler (p. 91). From Anna Seward to J. Johnson, Esq., *Letters of Anna Seward*, 1784-1807, 6 Vols., Edinburgh, 1811, iv. 10-11.

27. Exceptions to this approach can be found; see Susan Morgan and Roger Sales.

28. See also Everett's *Tory View of Landscape*, a valuable new study that resists any easy alignment of Whig with progressive and Tory with reactionary views.

Works Cited

Andrews, Malcolm. *The Search for the Picturesque: Landscape Aesthetics and Tourism in Britain, 1760-1800*. Stanford: Stanford UP, 1989.

Aslet, Clive. "Stoneleigh Abbey, Warwickshire—I-II: The Seat of Lord Leigh." *Country Life* (13 Dec. 1984): 1844-48 and (20 Dec. 1984): 1844-1937.

Austen, Jane. *The Novels of Jane Austen*. Ed. R. W. Chapman. 5 vols. Oxford: Oxford UP, 1988.

Bermingham, Ann. *Landscape and Ideology: The English Rustic Tradition 1740-1860*. Berkeley: U of California P, 1986.

Burke, Edmund. *A Philosophical Enquiry into the Origin of Our Ideas of the Sublime and Beautiful*. Oxford: Oxford UP, 1990.

Butler, Marilyn. *Jane Austen and the War of Ideas*. Oxford: Clarendon, 1975.

Chandler, Alice. "'A Pair of Fine Eyes': Jane Austen's Treatment of Sex." *Studies in the Novel* 7 (1975): 88-103.

Chapman, R. W. *Jane Austen: Facts and Problems*. Oxford: Clarendon, 1948.

Copley, Stephen, and Peter Garside, ed. *The Politics of the Picturesque*. Cambridge: Cambridge UP, 1994.

Craik, W. A. *Jane Austen in Her Time*. London: Nelson, 1969.

De Bruyn, Frans. "Edmund Burke's Gothic Romance: The Portrayal of Warren Hastings in Burke's Writings and Speeches on India." *Criticism* 29 (1987): 415-37.

Duckworth, Alistair. *The Improvement of the Estate: A Study of Jane Austen's Novels*. Baltimore: Johns Hopkins UP, 1971.

Eagleton, Terry. "The Ideology of the Aesthetic." *Poetics Today* 9.2 (1988): 326-38.

Everett, Nigel. *The Tory View of Landscape*. New Haven: Yale UP, 1994.

Fabricant, Carole. "Binding and Dressing Nature's Loose Tresses: The Ideology of Augustan Landscape Design." *Studies in Eighteenth-Century Culture* 8 (1979): 100-35.

Ferguson, Frances. "Edmund Burke, or the Bathos of Experience." *Glyph, Johns Hopkins Textual Studies* 8 (1981): 62-78.

Gilpin, William. *An Essay upon Prints*. London, 1768.

—————. *Observations on the Western Parts of England, Relative Chiefly to Picturesque Beauty*. 1798.

Halperin, John. *The Life of Jane Austen*. Baltimore: Johns Hopkins UP, 1980.

Heydt, Jill. "First Impressions and Later Recollections: The 'Place' of the Picturesque in Pride and Prejudice." *Studies in the Humanities* 12.2 (1985): 115-24.

Heydt-Stevenson, Jill. "Verbal Landscapes and Visual Texts: Jane Austen and the Picturesque." Ph.D. Diss. U of Colorado, 1990.

—————. "'Unbecoming Conjunctions': Mourning the Loss of Landscape and Love in *Persuasion*." *Eighteenth-Century Fiction* 8.1 (1995): 51-71.

Honan, Park. *Jane Austen: Her Life*. New York: Fawcett Columbine, 1987.

Hunt, John Dixon. *Garden and Grove: The Italian Renaissance Garden in the English Imagination, 1600-1750*. Princeton: Princeton UP, 1976.

Hussey, Christopher. *The Picturesque: Studies in a Point of View*. Hamden, CT: Archon Books 1967.

Johnson, Claudia. *Jane Austen, Women, Politics, and the Novel*. Chicago: U of Chicago P, 1988.

Kirkham, Margaret. *Jane Austen and Feminism*. New York: Methuen, 1986.

Knight, Richard Payne. *The Landscape: A Didactic Poem*. 2nd ed. London: Bulmer, 1795.

_____. *An Analytical Inquiry into the Principles of Taste*. 4th ed. London: Hansard, 1808.

Kolodny, Annette. *The Lay of the Land: Metaphor as Experience and History in American Life and Letters*. Chapel Hill: University of North Carolina Press, 1975.

Lascelles, Mary. *Jane Austen and Her Art*. London: Oxford UP, 1939.

Litz, A. Walton. "The Picturesque in *Pride and Prejudice*." *Jane Austen Society of North America* 1 (1979): 15-21.

Liu, Alan. "The Politics of the Picturesque." *Wordsworth: The Sense of History*. Stanford: Stanford UP, 1989. 61-137.

Llewelyn, Margaret. *Jane Austen: A Character Study*. London: Kimber, 1977.

Loudon, J. C., ed. *The Landscape Gardening and Landscape Architecture of the Late Humphry Repton, Esq., Being His Entire Works on These Subjects*. London, 1840.

Mansell, Darrel. *The Novels of Jane Austen: An Interpretation*. New York: Barnes and Noble, 1973.

Manwaring, Elizabeth Wheeler. *Italian Landscape in Eighteenth-Century England*. New York: Oxford UP, 1925.

Messmann, Frank. *Richard Payne Knight: The Twilight of Virtuosity*. Paris: Mouton, 1974.

Michasiw, Kim Ian. "Nine Revisionist Theses on the Picturesque." *Representations* 38 (1992): 76-100.

Mitchell, W. J. T. *Iconology*. Chicago: U of Chicago P, 1986.

Moi, Toril. *Sexual/Textual Politics: Feminist Literary Theory*. New York: Routledge, 1985.

Morgan, Susan. *In the Meantime: Character and Perception in Jane Austen's Fiction*. Chicago: U of Chicago P, 1980.

Moskal, Jeanne. "The Picturesque and the Affectionate in Wollstonecraft's Letters from Norway." *Modern Language Quarterly* 52. 3 (1991): 269-94.

Mulvey, Laura. "Visual Pleasure and Narrative Cinema." *Screen* 16.3 (1975): 15-24.

Paulson, Ronald. *Representations of Revolution*. New Haven: Yale UP, 1983.

Poovey, Mary. *The Proper Lady and the Woman Writer: Ideology as Style in the Works of Mary Wollstonecraft, Mary Shelley, and Jane Austen*. Chicago: U of Chicago P, 1984.

Price, Martin. "The Picturesque Moment." *From Sensibility to Romanticism*. New York: Oxford UP, 1965. 259-92.

Price, Sir Uvedale. *Essays on the Picturesque, As Compared with the Sublime and Beautiful; and, on the Use of Studying Pictures, for the Purpose of Improving Real Landscape*. 3 vols. London: 1794, 1795, 1810.

Repton, Humphry. *Observations on the Theory and Practice of Landscape Gardening*. London: T. Bensley, 1805.

_____. *Red Book*: May 1809. Private Collection. Photocopy in Warwickshire C.R.O.

Sales, Roger. *Representations of Regency England*. New York: Routledge, 1993.

Stewart, Susan. *On Longing: Narratives of the Miniature, the Gigantic, the Souvenir, the Collection*. Baltimore: Johns Hopkins University Press, 1984.

Sulloway, Alison. *Jane Austen and the Province of Womanhood*. Philadelphia: U of Pennsylvania P, 1989.

Synder, William. "Mother Nature's Other Natures: Landscape in Women's Writing, 1770-1830." *Women's Studies* 21 (1992): 143-62.

Of Woman Borne:
Male Experience and Feminine Truth
in Jane Austen's Novels_____

Sarah R. Morrison

Feminist critics have long been fascinated by Austen, one of the few female writers who has long been securely placed in the canon of great English writers. But those feminists have divided over how best to read her. Are her novels fundamentally conservative, propping up the status quo, or subversive, undermining traditional gender relations? Sarah R. Morrison argues that most critics have been asking the wrong questions: in reading Austen for her attitudes toward patriarchy, they have limited themselves to "a masculine framework of values." Morrison encourages them to look instead for specifically female concerns in the novels.

Much earlier criticism has been predicated on the notion that something is *missing* from Austen's works. As Morrison writes, "We still so often read the novels as if the consciousness of the heroine is merely an aperture through which we get a glimpse of a more significant or interesting story than Austen was willing or able to relate." True, they are courtship novels in which men inevitably feature prominently, but, for Morrison, "Austen exerts considerable artistry to keep the love relationships within bounds. . . . She is far more concerned with what such a relationship shares with other kinds of intimate relationships." At the heart of her reading is this observation: "Men are of secondary importance in the novels, however useful they may be to the plot, and male experience becomes relevant only in so far as it confirms 'feminine' truth." Austen's novels, Morrison concludes, "assert the primacy of feminine experience by reducing the characterization of men . . . to their roles in the private domestic circle."   — J.L.

Although Austen's novels have always been open to widely divergent interpretations, the two basic stances taken by critics are to view her as a conservative holding the values of the landed gentry in the late eighteenth century or as a subversive who undercuts the very premises upon which English society rests.[1] Most feminist studies have represented Austen as a conscious or unconscious subversive voicing a woman's frustration at the rigid and sexist social order which enforces women's subservience and dependence, though many feminist critics, as Julia Prewitt Brown notes, are distinctly uncomfortable with what they see as Austen's "cowardly accommodations" with the patriarchal order.[2] What these rival camps share, however, is a tendency to make the patriarchal order itself Austen's essential subject matter. Austen, placed as she is historically, is perhaps most often seen as a pivotal figure, looking both backward and forward; but whether critics emphasize her eighteenth-century roots or stress her affinities with Romanticism, almost always the big question is her valuation of the established patriarchal order. I do not mean to suggest that this is not a question worth asking. I merely wish to suggest that other avenues, perhaps equally worth pursuing, are obscured by our failure to step outside a masculine framework of values.

Alistair Duckworth, who has long and eloquently articulated the conservative case for Austen, offers as a safe generalization this distinction between the novelists who precede Austen and those who follow:

> whereas the eighteenth century novelist . . . can accept society whole, as a given structure within whose terms the individual must act, the nineteenth century novelist tends to question the ethical constitution of society and to set against it a morality generated by the interaction of two people or a small group. . . . From Fielding's comprehensive affirmation of society, the English novel, we may say, moves . . . to Dickens' circumscribed ethic in which a small enclave is purified through love amid a world of wickedness.[3]

Duckworth goes on to assert that "Jane Austen's affiliation is with Fielding rather than Dickens." However useful this schema might be, it unreasonably assumes that an emphasis upon the personal rather than upon the larger social order necessarily translates into a modern disillusionment with society. I align myself with feminist critics who find in Austen an emphasis upon the personal which springs rather from a distinctly feminine perspective; this study assumes, with Susan Morgan, that "Austen's 'social' concerns are with human relations, not society."[4] My interest here, however, is in the nature of Austen's feminism and in a possible explanation for the polarization of Austen studies within the feminist camp as well as across the whole body of criticism dealing with the novels. I approach these questions through a consideration of the use she makes of male characters.

Jane Austen has long been credited with being a keen observer of human nature and a creator of vital and convincing characters of both sexes. Critics, however, have down through the years regularly found fault with one group of characters in particular in her novels, the young men who appear as likely suitors for the heroines—the "heroes" and "villains." In many ways the ongoing complaint that certain of these male figures are inadequately characterized or crudely utilized merely manifested a masculine resistance to Austen's marginalization of male experience, but even recent feminist criticism exhibits a tendency to overemphasize the role of the "important" male characters, often in a misguided attempt to assert Austen's historical relevance and the profundity of her art.

Critics contemporary with Austen, of course, charged her with triviality of subject, and even her most earnest admirers have adopted a defensive stance. The attendant anxiety of her apologists has greatly affected the lines of developing argument to be found in the body of criticism dealing with the novels. In particular, the regrettable tendency in much Austen criticism to stress the role of individual characters as representatives of a particular class or social orientation is born of the desire to make Austen's subject matter more significant and comprehensive. The practice, defended by David Monaghan, of reading the novels as "social allegories" is an approach that broadens the novels' scope with the added advantage of inflating the importance of male characters.[5] Darcy in *Pride and Prejudice* is no longer one man possessing the advantages and prejudices of a particular class: he becomes the quintessential great landowner with ties to the nobility, synonymous with an entire class and a distinct way of life. Similarly Captain Wentworth in *Persuasion* as a self-made man must signal Austen's endorsement of an enterprising middle class that displaces a decayed aristocracy. Suddenly we are more focused on sweeping societal forces, and the roles of the male characters gain greatly in significance. But because this emphasis is largely unjustified, the heroes and villains who figure importantly in the plot are that much more likely to appear too puny to support the thematic burden assigned them.

Critics, whether inclined to read *Sense and Sensibility* as Marianne's or as Elinor's story, have generally seen something lacking in the portrayal of Edward Ferrars and Colonel Brandon. Male critics in particular have revealed an alarming tendency to fall in love with Marianne, and readers of both sexes generally bemoan Austen's pairing of Marianne in the conclusion with staid, middle-aged Colonel Brandon in his flannel waistcoats. Marianne's admirers and Elinor's partisans alike admit that Edward, who because of his secret engagement must remain a distant and shadowy figure, is flat and uninteresting. But the male characters in *Sense and Sensibility* have not been singled out for such criticism. Mr. Knightley in *Emma* is seen as too stuffy for lively Emma, Edmund Bertram in *Mansfield Park* as too much of a prig even for Fanny Price, and Darcy in *Pride and Prejudice* as stiff and unconvincing. The villains, it has often been observed, are never allowed close enough to the heroines to pose much of a threat. Katharine M. Rogers offers what might serve as a partial explanation for the seeming inadequacy of Austen's heroes and villains when she looks at the eighteenth-century feminine novel before Austen. She notes that "Both heroes and heroines were flattened by the conventions appropriated to women's novels"[6] and goes on to observe that "In general, the female novelists do better with less important male characters, who can reflect keen social observation without being distorted by the fantasy requirements bearing on the hero or villain."[7] However true this may be as a general observation, it does not seem a satisfactory explanation for the comparatively scanty portrayal of Austen's less-than-ideal lovers and not-so-threatening rakes.

Pointing to what he deemed a sign of Austen's emotional immaturity, Edmund Wilson long ago observed that "the experience behind the relationships imagined by her in her novels is always an experience of relationships of blood, of which that between sisters is certainly the most deeply felt."[8] Noting that other critics had seen "Marianne's love for Willoughby in *Sense and Sensibility*" as "the most passionate thing in Jane Austen," he went on to assert the greater significance of Elinor's love for Marianne:

> but isn't it rather the emotion of Elinor as she witnesses her sister's disaster than Marianne's emotion over Willoughby of which the poignancy is communicated to the reader? The involvement with one another of the sisters is the real central theme of the book, just as the relation of Elizabeth to her sisters is so vital a part of *Pride and Prejudice*.[9]

Although a number of more recent critics have asserted the importance of relationships between women in the novels—Brown, for instance, argues that "relations between older and younger women are central to the generational structure of Austen's fiction"[10]—many still see as a flaw Austen's slighter characterization of key male figures.[11] Readers' assumptions often lead them to *expect* the relationship between the heroine and the hero to dwarf all others, and at least some of the enduring dissatisfaction with the portrayal of the heroes and anti-heroes stems from an unreasonable puzzlement that they are *not* featured more prominently.

Even some fine recent feminist criticism in some ways seems to be committing the errors of the past. Susan Morgan in "Why There's No Sex in Jane Austen's Fiction" offers an explanation for Austen's departure from what was standard practice in the eighteenth-century novel, the plot revolving around sex—specifically around threats to the heroine's virginity. Morgan describes Austen's break with the past as "a great achievement"[12] and "a literary innovation"[13] that paved the way for writers such as

> Hardy and Eliot [who] were able to explore the evils of a woman being sexually defined by her culture in part because Austen had banished from fiction, and thus effectively revealed as a fiction, the fiction of a woman being sexually defined by nature.[14]

Morgan certainly does not minimize Austen's achievement: she credits her with both great originality and a tremendous influence upon the developing English novel. Yet her argument still seems to be predicated on the assumption that Jane Austen was forced to omit something significant from her art. Judith Wilt in "Jane Austen's Men: Inside/Outside 'the Mystery'" acknowledges that "Jane Austen's women are the glory of her fiction"[15] but goes on to detect something vital lacking in her novels because Austen as a woman—and particularly as a woman of her class and time—is inevitably "turned out from the Mysteries" (as, to be fair to Wilt, men are outside the "Mysteries" belonging to womanhood) and can only approach by indirection and guesswork the all-important initiation of the young male into the adult world of work and fixed identity.[16] We still so often read the novels as if the consciousness of the heroine is merely an aperture through which we get a glimpse of a more significant or interesting story than Austen was willing or able to relate.

In one obvious sense, of course, men are at the center of Jane Austen's novels. The novels are, at least superficially, love stories, ending with the marriage of the hero and heroine. In each of the novels, the narrative interest is concentrated in the central story of courtship—in whether or not the heroine gets her man—and the novel ends with their marriage, but this is not to say as much about the novels as we might think. Such a comment could be said with equal truth of *Tom Jones* or *Great Expectations*. (One *might* say of Melville's masterpiece that the narrative interest is concentrated in whether or not Moby-Dick gets his man.) In reading what is termed a "female" novel, we expect (with some justification) that the love interest will be paramount. But although the coming together of the heroine and hero is undeniably the point toward which the plots of her novels yearn, Austen exerts considerable artistry to keep the love relationships within bounds—as any number of admirers and detractors of the novels have noted in one way or another, from Charlotte Brontë, to D. H. Lawrence, to Marvin Mudrick, to Susan Morgan.[17] Austen deliberately glosses over what is distinctive about a passionate sexual relationship, I believe, because she is far more concerned with what such a relationship shares with other kinds of intimate relationships, whether between siblings, child and parent, or friends. And it is a mistake to demand equal time for the inner life of Austen's heroes and villains, for these characters are dramatized as convincingly as they need to be to fulfill their primary function, which is, as Margaret Lenta argues, to dramatize the female protagonists' experience of them.[18] Their stories (always kept clearly subordinate) echo or underscore the heroines' experience with others of both sexes.[19]

Men are of secondary importance in the novels, however useful they may be to the plot, and male experience becomes relevant only in so far as it confirms "feminine" truth. And by this I mean not a truth for women alone but what for Austen is a universal truth reflected more clearly in women's experience. Elizabeth A. Say agrees with Patricia Meyer Spacks in characterizing the feminine moral ideal offered in women's novels as one of "being" rather than "doing."[20] If, as Nancy Armstrong suggests, it is largely generated by the rise of a feminine domestic consciousness among the newly evolving middle class, it carries such great moral authority primarily because this feminine ideal embodies long-celebrated Christian values impossible to be reconciled with the classical masculine ethic of action that dominates western society. Society had long enjoined upon women a humility and meekness that in Christian terms paradoxically granted them a moral ascendancy, and the historical development charted by Armstrong similarly grants a new moral authority to traditional feminine (i.e., domestic, personal, unworldly) values.[21] It is thus not surprising that the values endorsed by Austen seem to some to hearken backward to a more stable, coherent order and to others to undermine the patriarchal order. Citing "Chodorow's conclusion that men's social orientation is positional while women's is personal," Carol Gilligan suggests that we ask "not why women have conflicts about competitive success, but why men show such readiness to adopt and celebrate a rather narrow [i.e., emphasizing prestige, wealth, victory in war, business, love, etc. over personal happiness] vision of success."[22] Austen implicitly raises this question as she posits a distinctly feminine view of social interaction. In the novels the emphasis is insistently and unapologetically upon the personal. Her art is feminine in its very assumption that personal relationships define one's being, and a traditional feminine vision of success informs her novels.

Like the "less equal" (*MP*, p. 468) punishment attending a man's adultery or fornication, the restrictions society places upon men are not as great as those under which women labor—and Austen everywhere implicitly recognizes this injustice—but her vision extends well beyond some feminist political agenda that envisions a world of different proportions to instead offer a balanced view of life's inherent limitations and the modest possibilities afforded individuals whose lives are necessarily bound to others. Men, in fact, are in this regard actually hampered by the illusion of freedom which their culture grants them. While acknowledging how many women novelists regard pain as "the human condition," Patricia Meyer Spacks nonetheless argues that a special kind of pain is to be found in novels by women that recount a young woman's coming of age: "Lacking a sense of their free will, of full participation in the human franchise, they learn to know that their suffering derives from gender rather than from common humanity."[23] Yet Spacks also acknowledges that "Social facts . . . provide no excuse for a woman, from Jane Austen's point of view" and that Austen "betrays no sense of grievance."[24] I find the explanation for these oddly conjoined ideas not as Spacks does in Austen's belief that the "role of wife and mother" will otherwise "[compensate] for all the hardships of girlhood"[25] but in the direct benefits of the enforced subservience: in the ability to place the subject in another and the object in oneself and in the acceptance of inescapable human dependency. Austen, perhaps unforgivably for some, is not particularly concerned with the struggle of woman to achieve subjectivity; she is far too aware of the need to step outside oneself. As Spacks herself observes in writing of George Eliot's Maggie Tulliver, "the feminine capacity for suffering need not be mere self-display or self-torment, but may provide a medium for moral insight."[26] This burden of consciousness carried by women inflicts its special torments, certainly, precisely because this awareness is not shared by the economically and politically dominant male sex, but it nonetheless affords—from one perspective, at least—a distinct advantage over the more limited vision of men. The very inequality of their condition, the constraints placed upon them, their dependence, the actual condition of being female helps Austen's heroines to a realization that the "female condition" more nearly reflects the essential truth of the human condition. The idea may be anathema to many a modern-day feminist, but for Austen it was an enduring moral truth.

If Austen is not alone among women novelists in her endorsement of such feminine values, she reaches beyond them in a number of respects. Patricia Meyer Spacks has shown how Ann Radcliffe's gothic novels had earlier depicted the clash between a masculine power ethic that celebrates force and a feminine ethic that meets and defeats that force through an effort of the will alone. In Radcliffe's novels, Spacks notes, the "danger of the masculine sublime, embodied in supernatural appearances, is finally illusory," though "Men's *social* power remains both real and dangerous."[27] But in Austen's *Sense and Sensibility*, Spacks finds an even "more pessimistic view than Radcliffe's":

Phallic power is hardly at issue here. Radcliffe debunks it, Austen barely acknowledges it. But men's social power, recognized though not dwelt on by Radcliffe, in this Austen novel appears as a central fact in female lives.[28]

Radcliffe, however, works to demonstrate what Austen's novels assume as a given. Austen's matter-of-fact detailing of male social power effectively demystifies phallic power at the onset. And if she seems more concerned to expose men's social power than Radcliffe, she does not rail against it. A more apt comparison for my purposes would perhaps be with Fanny Burney's realistic novels, and yet, there one detects an attraction to male power not to be found in Austen. In puzzling over the irreproachability of Charlotte Brontë's feminist credentials and Austen's dubious standing, Brown observes "how much colder to male authority Austen is than Brontë, how much less attracted to it, how disinclined to sentimentalize and make excuses for it."[29] Austen, in contrast to other women novelists, resists romanticizing the battle between the sexes. Rather than viewing society from a militant feminist perspective or sentimentalizing the victimization of women in a way that adds a certain lustre to male domination and reinforces the masculine mystique, she succeeds (where others do not) *in making woman the normative center.*

In portraying men, Austen focuses more on the ways in which men's lives are like women's. Why do we not see men without women in the pages of her novels? Why does Austen not follow Darcy or Mr. Knightley into a man's world of business from which women are excluded? It is not enough to counter with the usual argument—that the private, domestic sphere is ideally suited to her subject. In fact, the deliberate and consistent marginalizing of exclusively male experience is perhaps the only realistic technique that could so effectively establish the centrality of women's experience in Austen's fictional world. Critics bent on reasserting Austen's claims to greatness have accumulated considerable evidence from the novels themselves of Austen's awareness of the current political scene both at home and abroad and of social issues such as slavery and the reform movement within the Anglican Church, her knowledge of the military, and her acquaintance with contemporary radical thought. The puzzle has always been, Why such coyness? Why this art of indirection which merely glances sidelong at important issues, ideas and events as it concentrates directly on her "3 or 4 Families in a Country Village"?[30] I would argue that the framework provided by such subdued references actually underscores the significance of the central events in each novel. Precisely because Austen gives this larger world its due, her choice to focus rather upon the personal and domestic asserts in no uncertain terms the centrality of women's experience. Paradoxically perhaps, the message conveyed is that this alternative vision can hold its own: it does not depend upon its tangential relationship to the world of men for its significance.

What largely sets Austen apart from other women novelists is the conceptual ability to move beyond a preoccupation with male power and the technical skill to create the form her vision requires. Everything *but* the plot, it would seem, conspires to circumscribe carefully the roles of male characters in Austen's novels. Deborah Kaplan draws some striking parallels between familiar narrative strategies in Austen's novels and the stance frequently adopted by women letter-writers of Austen's class and time. In these private documents, Kaplan finds just such an inversion of the "value structure of the domestic ideology . . . rendering the greater importance of women's private over men's public experiences through *point of view*"[31] and "us[ing] *irony* to invest women's experience with more significance than men's"[32] [italics mine]. Austen makes use of the trappings of earlier novelists, but as has often been noted, she deliberately reduces, or flattens, such elements as the stock seduction-plot. The rather whimsical note Austen strikes in those famous concluding chapters and the narrator's sudden discreet withdrawal as we seem to be gearing up for a love-scene contribute to a pattern that deflates the love story in the interest of larger thematic concerns. Austen would appear to be deliberately sinking the lover in the man. Significantly, the heroes in Austen's novels are not presented as the professed lovers of the heroines. Rather the heroine spends the better part of the novel observing the hero's conduct in his relations with others, very often as he pays court to another woman— as do Edward Ferrars (*SS*), Edmund Bertram (*MP*), and Captain Wentworth (*P*). Elizabeth Bennet assumes Darcy is destined to marry his cousin (*PP*); and in *Emma*, not even the principals envision the possibility that Emma and Mr. Knightley could become more than "brother" and "sister."

Significantly, all of the heroines marry men whose station in life automatically involves them in inescapable and enduring ties to numerous individuals, as it affords them greater opportunity for self-expression and service to others beyond the immediate domestic circle. Elinor Dashwood (*SS*), Fanny Price (*MP*), and even Catherine Morland (*NA*) marry clergymen; Marianne Dashwood (*SS*), Elizabeth Bennet (*PP*), and Emma Woodhouse (*E*) marry men with large estates; and Anne Elliot (*P*) joins a close-knit community of navy men and their wives which fosters the sharing of both domestic duties and hazards at sea. Marriage is only one tie among many. And Austen can so confidently predict her heroines' happiness at the end of the novels because their happiness depends upon so much more than the character, disposition, or continued affection of their husbands.

Although Austen's novels reflect an awareness of social injustice and sexual stereotyping, these are not of the same significance to Austen that they are to a late twentieth-century sensibility. It is not merely that Austen lacks our rather naive faith in political machinery. More importantly, Austen's work is predicated on the conviction that for men as well as for women the domestic circle of family, friends, and neighbors among whom one spends life's most private moments is of paramount importance. It is here that Austen would judge the success or failure of an individual life. The fantasy embodied in many female novels shows the well-heeled hero in his disinterested choice of a marriage partner embracing this "feminine" truth—that despite the other avenues open to him, domestic life and emotional bonds to parents, siblings, wife and child, and family intimates contribute more to happiness and fulfillment than success measured according to traditional male values.

Austen does not flinch as she avers that in many respects marriage is as significant an act for a man as for a woman.[33] Conventional wisdom tells us that a man who makes a disastrous marriage and finds himself unhappy in his personal life can escape the environs of home in a way not possible for an unhappily married woman. Men may, after all, without apology retreat behind newspapers or bury themselves in business; become avid sportsmen like Willoughby and Sir John Middleton (*SS*) or, like Mr. Hurst, "[live] only to eat, drink, and play at cards" (*PP*, p. 35); seclude themselves in the library, as does Mr. Bennet (*PP*); or indulge in authoritarian posturing, as do General Tilney (*NA*) and Sir Thomas Bertram (*MP*). Certainly the ease with which men are able to escape domestic responsibility and avoid intimacy is fully dramatized in Austen's novels, but so is the price they pay for their emotional withdrawal, and Austen takes the moral measure of her characters largely by the degree and nature of their participation in this domestic world. Men are in this respect rather pitiable creatures, too prone to leading a partial existence. For all the exclamations over Lady Bertram's vacuousness and Mrs. Bennet's vulgarity, a look at the male washouts in the novels should suggest that men are more liable than women to disengage emotionally. Sir Thomas' cold-blooded approach to parenting may finally be worse than Lady Bertram's passivity—certainly many have puzzled over the narrator's failure to chastise Lady Bertram. Even Mrs. Bennet has a kind of integrity not possessed by Mr. Bennet, whose sardonic stance, rather than preserving his dignity, only makes him a more ridiculous figure than many another sensible man with a silly wife. Mrs. Bennet can at least be said to be in earnest as she determinedly goes about what she considers the serious business of her life. In this moral universe, it is a feminine ethic that predominates and men rather than women who are in greatest danger of remaining on the fringes of meaningful experience.

Perhaps the truth is that men are not as important in the novels of Jane Austen as many critics would like to have them and that the function of the love story at the heart of each novel is roughly analogous to the function of the love story to be found in many a novel with a male protagonist—it is important as a sign or indicator and rounds out a comic conclusion, but it is not where the real story lies. The real story is the value of those human links that in some ways appear so fragile but in reality remain indestructible. Austen's "flawed" heroines—Marianne Dashwood, Elizabeth Bennet, and Emma Woodhouse—discover this truth. Her more circumspect heroines—Elinor Dashwood, Fanny Price, and Anne Elliot—consciously strive to maintain their connectedness to others.

Historically feminism embraces two conflicting impulses: the impulse to condemn stereotypical and limiting roles for women, with the rather paradoxical goal of achieving full participation and equality for women on a male-dominated society's terms; and the impulse to validate and elevate traditional women's roles and concerns, placing these in opposition to entrenched patriarchal values. Elaine Showalter identifies two corresponding strains in feminist criticism. The first, which she terms the "feminist critique," is "male-oriented," focusing primarily on "stereotypes of women, the sexism of male critics, and the limited roles women play in literary history."[34] By contrast, what she terms "Gynocritics begins at the point when we free ourselves from the linear absolutes of male literary history, stop trying to fit women between the lines of the male tradition, and focus instead on the newly visible world of female culture."[35] As a feminist Austen falls into the second camp. Her novels assert the primacy of feminine experience by reducing the characterization of men in the novels to their roles in the private domestic circle and by confining their movement to a restricted social scene as viewed from a distinctly feminine perspective. Men count first according to the impact they have upon the lives of their wives, daughters, sisters, lovers, and casual female acquaintance: they are potential husbands with uncertain dispositions or habits "dangerous to a wife's happiness" (*MP*, p. 363), clumsy dance partners, unreliable guardians and protectors, charming companions, and incomes of so many thousand pounds a year. But male experience in so far as it is significant in the novels underscores the universality of the "feminine" truth the novels embody. Showalter complains that "The radical demand that would yoke women writers to feminist revolution and deny them the freedom to explore new subjects would obviously not provide a healthy direction for the female tradition to take. But the denigration of female experience, the insistence that woman deal with 'the real business of the world,' is also destructive."[36] Austen is so difficult to label because her art succeeds in presenting a truly feminine vision. Her novels are not directed at men: she does not envy them.

From *Studies in the Novel* 26, no. 4 (1994): 337-349. Copyright © 1994 by The University of North Texas. Reprinted by permission.

Notes

1. Jane Austen, *The Novels*, 5 vols., 3rd ed., ed. R. W. Chapman (London: Oxford, 1932-34). Parenthetical references are to this edition and employ the following short form of the titles: *NA* (*Northanger Abbey*), *SS* (*Sense and Sensibility*), *PP* (*Pride and Prejudice*), *MP* (*Mansfield Park*), *E* (*Emma*), and *P* (*Persuasion*).

2. Julia Prewitt Brown, "A Feminist Depreciation of Austen: A Polemical Reading," *Novel* 23 (1990): 304.

3. Alistair Duckworth, *The Improvement of the Estate: A Study of Jane Austen's Novels* (Baltimore: Johns Hopkins Univ. Press, 1971), p. 27.

4. Susan Morgan, "Intelligence in *Pride and Prejudice*," *Modern Philology* 73 (1975): 55.

5. David Monaghan, "The Decline of the Gentry: A Study of Jane Austen's Attitude to Formality in *Persuasion*," *Studies in the Novel* 7 (1975): 73.

6. Katharine M. Rogers, "Dreams and Nightmares: Male Characters in the Feminine Novel of the Eighteenth Century" in *Men by Women*, ed. Janet Todd (New York: Holmes and Meier, 1981), p. 13.

7. *Ibid.*, p. 20.

8. Edmund Wilson, "A Long Talk About Jane Austen" in *Jane Austen: A Collection of Critical Essays*, ed. Ian Watt (Englewood Cliffs: Prentice-Hall, 1963), p. 39.

9. *Ibid.*, p. 39.

10. Brown, *Jane Austen's Novels: Social Change and Literary Form* (Cambridge: Harvard Univ. Press, 1979), p. 159.

11. Terming Wilson's essay "a classic of sexist literary criticism," Brown goes on to draw a comparison between Austen's portrayal of friendships between women and the "many novels with male protagonists" in which "the hero's relationship with other boys or men is an obvious and instrumental element in his growth" (*Jane Austen's Novels*, p. 159). In a more recent book, *Jane Austen Among Women* (Baltimore: Johns Hopkins, 1992), Deborah Kaplan takes a biographical approach, exploring the significance for Austen's artistic development of the network of female friends and relations among whom Austen lived and with whom she shared her work.

12. Morgan, "Why There's No Sex in Jane Austen's Fiction," *Studies in the Novel* 19 (1987): 351.

13. *Ibid.*, p. 355.

14. *Ibid.*, p. 354.

15. Judith Wilt, "Jane Austen's Men: Inside/Outside 'the Mystery'" in *Men by Women*, ed. Janet Todd (New York: Holmes and Meier, 1981), p. 59.

16. *Ibid.*, p. 67.

17. Charlotte Brontë's complaint that "the Passions are perfectly unknown to her" [*Jane Austen: The Critical Heritage*, ed. B. C. Southam (London: Routledge and Kegan Paul, 1968), p. 128] and Lawrence's intense dislike of what he termed her "sharp knowing in apartness" are well known ["A Propos of *Lady Chatterley's Lover*" in *Sex, Literature, and Censorship* (New York: Viking, 1953), p. 109]. Mudrick contends that Austen was distinctly uncomfortable dealing with the topic of sex and could only approach the subject indirectly and ironically [*Jane Austen: Irony as Defense and Discovery* (Princeton: Princeton Univ. Press, 1952)].

18. Margaret Lenta, "Jane Austen's Feminism: An Original Response to Convention," *Critical Quarterly* 23:3 (1981): 30.

19. Note the degree of agreement—despite the different assumptions underlying their critical judgments—between Lenta and earlier critics who found fault with the very things that Lenta praises. W. A. Craik (*Jane Austen: The Six Novels*; London: Methuen, 1965), for example, complained that "When Edward Ferrars appears, he is what he should be, but we do not see enough of him for him to seem Elinor's equal in importance" (p. 42) and "it is one of [Edmund Bertram's] deficiencies that he, like Edward Ferrars, appears more through what effect he has on the heroine than through what he is in himself" (p. 112).

20. Elizabeth A. Say, *Evidence on Her Own Behalf: Women's Narrative as Theological Voice* (Savage, Maryland: Rowman, 1990), pp. 71-72.

21. In *Desire and Domestic Fiction: A Political History of the Novel* (New York: Oxford Univ. Press, 1987), Nancy Armstrong charts the historical shift in attitude regarding the traditional feminine virtues of "modesty, humility, and honesty": whereas seventeenth and eighteenth-century conduct books view these as "inherently female qualities" to be "cultivate[d]," Armstrong notes that "In earlier writing, these conspicuously passive virtues were considered the antidote to natural deficiencies that had been the female's heritage ever since the Fall of Man" (p. 66).

22. Carol Gilligan, *In a Different Voice: Psychological Theory and Women's Development* (Cambridge: Harvard Univ. Press, 1982), p. 16.

23. Patricia Meyer Spacks, *The Female Imagination* (New York: Knopf, 1975), p. 158.

24. *Ibid.*, p. 134.

25. *Ibid.*, p. 110.

26. *Ibid.*, p. 57.

27. Spacks, *Desire and Truth: Functions of Plot in Eighteenth-Century English Novels* (Chicago: Univ. of Chicago Press, 1990), p. 160.

28. *Ibid.*, p. 206.

29. Brown, "Feminist," p. 305.

30. Austen, *Letters to Her Sister Cassandra and Others*, 2nd ed., ed. R. W. Chapman (London: Oxford Univ. Press, 1952), p. 401.

31. Deborah Kaplan, *Jane Austen Among Women* (Baltimore: Johns Hopkins Univ. Press, 1992), p. 74.

32. *Ibid.*, p. 75.

33. Feminist critics rightly point out that in choosing a mate a heroine is making a choice of life, and this argument has often been made to justify women novelists' preoccupation with courtship and marriage. In *A Literature of Their Own: British Women Novelists From Brontë to Lessing* (Princeton: Princeton Univ. Press, 1977), Elaine Showalter observes that as early as 1909 in *Marriage as a Trade*, Cicely Hamilton had

> explored the theory that women writers viewed "romance" from an economic perspective, so that their love stories were not frivolous fantasies, but accounts of female survival: "To a woman, a woman in love is not only a woman swayed by emotion, but a human being engaged in carving for herself a career or securing for herself a means of livelihood. Her interest in a love story is, therefore, much more complex than a man's interest therein, and the appreciation which she brings to it is of a very different quality." (p. 225)

Brown, however, reminds us of the inadequacy of this argument when it stands alone:

> True to the paradox that ends Shakespeare's comedies, the novels end in a beginning—that is, a marriage—which in Austen as in Shakespeare is conceived of as a charm against the passage of seasons, against aging, and (in her last, most personal novel) against the sense of oncoming death. To complain that the novels "all end in marriage," therefore, is to remain deaf to the lyricism of her later work . . . and blind to the darker regions of comedy; to impose, in effect, a narrow ideology on an imagination that extends far beyond such boundaries. ("Feminist," p. 307)

34. Elaine Showalter, "Toward a Feminist Poetics" in *The New Feminist Criticism: Essays on Women, Literature, and Theory*, ed. Elaine Showalter (New York: Pantheon, 1985), p. 130.

35. *Ibid.*, p. 131.

36. Showalter, *Literature*, p. 318.

Rank and Status
Christopher Brooke

Our own democratic era tends to look on any strict adherence to social niceties as mere snobbery—we are all supposed to be equals, at least in principle. But in Austen's lifetime, an age when "democratic" was regarded as an insult, social subordination was the organizing principle of many interactions, both public and private. Thomas Jefferson's declaration that "all men are created equal," written before Austen turned one year old, was still tremendously controversial.

That is not to say the class system was rigid. Economic changes over the course of the eighteenth and nineteenth centuries made it more possible than ever before for people to move up and down the social ladder. It was also an age when the class structure was undergoing real crises. The French Revolutionaries had taken to executing aristocrats, and their movement threatened to tear down the traditional hierarchy on the English side of the Channel. Conservative Britain responded by shoring up the traditional hierarchy and treating any questioning of the "natural order" as tantamount to treason.

Austen, of course, was a careful observer of these phenomena, and her observations on social rank are always penetrating. The portrait gallery of characters in her novels includes both pretentious snobs, who treat the system with too much deference, and thoughtless boors, who do not give it the respect it deserves. In this wideranging essay, Christopher Brooke examines some of the ways that understanding the social hierarchy of England in the 1810s can influence our reading of Austen.   — J.L.

Rank and status are the themes of an immensely rich and complex learned literature. Their role in Jane Austen's life and novels has been used to justify the idea that she was traditional and hierarchical—or alternatively, liberal and revolutionary—in her views. In particular, especially since the publication of W. Roberts's *Jane Austen and the French Revolution* in 1979, there has been much debate on the effect of the French Revolution on the society in which she lived and on Jane Austen herself. I do not doubt that she was influenced by the French Revolution. It came on her when she was about the same age that I was when we learned about the Holocaust, which deeply affected me and coloured my attitudes on many things—though I have no Jewish relations, whereas Jane's cousin-in-law was guillotined. But discussions of such influences, though interesting, are purely speculative. My purpose is to look, quite simply, at the texts, and ask what they reveal of the range of attitudes in Jane Austen's world which she chose to illustrate in her novels—and which are revealed by her letters, and those of her circle.

Emma's Snobbery

One of the most striking features of *Emma* is the contrast between the heroine's snobbery and Mr Knightley's readiness to mingle with all about him on relatively equal terms. He is the squire of Highbury, though the word is never used of him: 'the landed property of Hartfield', the seat of Mr Woodhouse, 'certainly was inconsiderable, being but a sort of notch in the Donwell Abbey estate [Mr Knightley's], to which all the rest of Highbury belonged'.[1] The Woodhouses were 'the younger branch of a very, ancient family'; they 'had been settled for several generations at Hartfield'; they were wealthy—but clearly their main wealth lay elsewhere—where, is not specified.[2] While Mr Knightley remains a bachelor, Emma sets herself up as the first lady of Highbury: 'the Woodhouses were first in consequence there'. There is perhaps a little confusion here—more probably a deliberate ambiguity: Mr Knightley is clearly the squire and leader in the parish, yet Donwell Abbey is technically in a neighbouring parish.[3] In any event, Mr Knightley never puts on lordly airs—save that his candid nature makes it natural for him to lay down the law to Emma and his friends; but he always talks as one who is first among equals. Emma, at the start of the book, is a fearful snob—though not in all respects: both she and Mr Knightley treat Mrs Weston, her former governess, as an equal. Some of the best dialogue early in the book (chapter 5) is between Mr Knightley and Mrs Weston on her role as governess and their relations with Emma. Emma is happily at ease with her equals, patronises whom she will—and visits the poor. But when Harriet Smith reveals that Robert Martin, Mr Knightley's favourite tenant farmer, has proposed to her, and reluctantly agrees to reject him, Emma observes that Harriet's marriage to him would have cut them off from one another: 'I could not have visited Mrs Robert Martin, of Abbey-Mill Farm.'[4] In the denouement, when Harriet finally does become engaged to Robert Martin, Emma looks forward to meeting him; but meanwhile, the contrast of her and Mr Knightley's social attitudes forms a major theme in the book.

Emma's snobbery impinges again and again in the first half of *Emma*. Frank Churchill proposes a ball: but to collect sufficient dancers will mean collecting families with whom Emma would not normally associate.

> He seemed to have all the life and spirit, cheerful feelings, and social inclinations of his father, and nothing of the pride or reserve of [the Churchills of] Enscombe. Of pride, indeed, there was, perhaps, scarcely enough; his indifference to a confusion of rank, bordered too much on inelegance of mind. He could be no judge, however, of the evil he was holding cheap. It was but an effusion of lively spirits.

Or so she thought, little knowing he was engaged to Jane Fairfax, whose aunt and grandmother were among her lowlier acquaintances.[5] Soon after, Emma was contemplating the possibility of accepting an invitation to dine with the Coles, who 'had been settled some years in Highbury, and were very good sort of people—friendly, liberal, and unpretending; but, on the other hand, they were of low origin, in trade, and only moderately genteel'. After a while they had become more prosperous and with it very sociable, and Emma was determined not to let them think they could entertain Miss Woodhouse. But when they did plan a large dinner party—and invited Mr Knightley and the Westons, and so also Frank Churchill, but not herself—she began to regret it. 'Her being left in solitary grandeur, even supposing the omission to be intended as a compliment, was but poor comfort.' In the end the invitation came, and Emma went, very conscious of the favour she bestowed.[6]

One significant effect of harping on Emma's snobbery is to set in relief her romantic notions of Harriet's origin and destiny. The only thing known at the outset about Harriet's birth is that she was illegitimate; and this seemed to Mr Knightley to make it the more commendable in Robert Martin to be so keen to marry her. He regarded Emma's notion that she must be a gentleman's daughter (which indeed proves false in the end) as unlikely to be true and certainly not relevant.[7] What is interesting—and left for the readers to interpret as they will—is that Emma regards Harriet's birth as of little, or almost no, consequence: having brought her forward as her own intimate companion, she marries her off in imagination to Mr Elton, Mr Churchill and (in anguish) to Mr Knightley—to a clergyman, to the heir of a great estate, to the squire. This seems highly commendable to a modern reader: what is noteworthy is that it seemed reasonable to a highly intelligent young woman of strict principles in the 1810s. It may show Emma dwelling in a world of fantasy; or it may not.

In the end, Emma finds through her love of Mr Knightley that much of her snobbery is false and superficial. We see the layers of it peeling off, especially when she learns that Harriet is—after all—engaged to Robert Martin. What she had dismissed earlier as degradation—as separating Harriet from herself for ever—she greets now with nothing but delight and relief, to such a degree that she has to disguise her 'most unreasonable degree of happiness' from Mr Knightley. She has come to realise to the full how her romantic attempts to marry Harriet to this man and that have done nothing but harm; that she has bred in Harriet such fantasies as to imagine Mr Knightley in love with her; that the ideas of social hierarchy which Emma had fostered are fantasy. Emma sees at last through Mr Knightley's eyes, perceives Robert Martin's virtues, and all his eligibility for Harriet. 'Now there would be pleasure in [Harriet's] returning.—Every thing would be a pleasure. It would be a great pleasure to know Robert Martin.'[8]

Equality and Hierarchy

Without imputing the opinions of either Mr or Mrs Knightley to their creator, it is sufficiently clear that Jane Austen is puncturing any too rigid views of social hierarchy. Some critics have seen her as a social revolutionary: but it is hard to find much connection between the tiny, peaceful social world of Highbury and the storming of the Bastille. Others have seen her as a subtle defender of the status quo. In any literal sense, that is equally improbable: her remorseless satire on human folly and wickedness—her social categories, however humorously devised, of the bright young Wykehamists, as 'future heroes, legislators, fools, and villains'[9]—run counter to mere passive acceptance. Her portrait even of Mr Knightley is not uncritical. But she makes clear that it is as much his sense of responsibility, his good nature, his gentlemanly behaviour as his birth and inheritance which make him first— with Emma—in Highbury society.

Social historians love to discover evidence of change and novelty in the fields they cultivate: it is a natural temptation in too specialised research. There are many honourable exceptions, but many too who see in the very modest tendency towards egalitarianism in the novels a feature of a society grown more liberal.[10] That view would not have appealed to her niece Fanny Knight—daughter of her brother Edward who became a rich country gentleman by being adopted as the heir of Mr Knight, whose name he later took.

'They were not rich' wrote Fanny to one of her sisters about her aunts, and the people around with whom they chiefly mixed, were not at all high bred, or in short anything more than *mediocre* and they of course tho' superior in *mental powers* and *cultivation* were on the same level as far as *refinement* goes—but I think in later life their intercourse with Mrs Knight [Mr Knight's widow] (who was very fond of and kind to them) improved them both and Aunt Jane was too clever not to put aside all possible signs of 'commonness' (if such an expression is allowable) and teach herself to be more refined, at least in intercourse with people in general.[11]

We can sense from this a little of what the poor relation had to put up with, even among close relations who loved and admired her.

The truth is that the issue of hierarchy versus equality is as old as the recorded social history of the human race. To take it no further back, St Paul had declared to the Galatians: 'There is neither Jew nor Greek, there is neither bond nor free, there is neither male nor female: for ye are all one in Christ Jesus'[12]—an utterance which has found echoes in all parts of Christendom in every age, and been sadly at variance with the facts of life. And not only with the facts: for that great theologian, the pseudo-Denis, a Syrian Greek of about 500 A.D. whose work was deeply influential among most of the theologians of the late Middle Ages, propounded a notion of hierarchy as of the very nature of heaven and of God's world. This remained a commonplace, eloquently and cynically expounded by Ulysses in pagan language in Shakespeare's *Troilus and Cressida*:

> Take but degree away, untune that string,
> And, hark! what discord follows.[13]

Hierarchy, like all concepts of social order, is profoundly ambiguous. In human terms, it may reflect a social order based on birth—with kings, nobles, gentlemen and commoners arranged in order. But in the medieval church—and in the eighteenth-century church too—the peerage, the House of Lords, comprised lords spiritual as well as lords temporal, who came there not by inheritance but by attaining office. In the English Church—both medieval and modern—the proportion of noblemen-bishops has always been small: an aristocratic clergyman doubtless had an advantage in the pursuit of higher offices, but it was rarely decisive—or there were too few of them to hinder men from other walks of life from climbing the ladder.

> 'But why are you to be a clergyman? [asked Miss Crawford of Edmund Bertram] I thought *that* was always the lot of the youngest, where there were many to choose before him.'
> 'Do you think the church itself never chosen then?'
> '*Never* is a black word. But yes, in the *never* of conversation which means *not very often*, I do think it. For what is to be done in the church? Men love to distinguish themselves, and in either of the other lines [as lawyer, or soldier, or sailor], distinction may be gained, but not in the church. A clergyman is nothing.'[14]

No peasant is known to have become archbishop of Canterbury; but only women were wholly excluded. No doubt politics played its part, as it always has in every arrangement and rearrangement of social hierarchy—but even politics were never alone decisive in determining the promotion of the English clergy, even in the eighteenth century. True, the bishop of Winchester through most of Jane Austen's life was Brownlow North, son of an earl and brother of a prime minister; but a bishop of more characteristic origin had held sway earlier in the century, Benjamin Hoadly, son of a schoolmaster.[15]

Yet perhaps the greatest of all qualifications to notions of hierarchy at any time—save for the uncertain play of human affection, which must be reserved for the chapter on marriage—has been the acquisition of wealth. A duke who fell into poverty in the fifteenth century was demoted; impecunious lords in the eighteenth century might find secret service funds (in other words the royal privy purse) placed at their disposal.[16] But broadly speaking the nobility had to be and stay rich; and wealth was the key to social and political influence. For that very reason, a hierarchical society has commonly voiced a deep prejudice against *mere* wealth, not accompanied by noble ancestry and gracious manners—while many highly born have scrambled to acquire it, especially by marrying their sons and daughters to heiresses and heirs of wealth. There are frequent references in Jane Austen's novels to the respectable, and not-so-respectable, ways of acquiring wealth. Land, inheritance, marriage in one's own sphere, an honourable profession—army, navy, law and church—all were respectable. Jane's references to money-making are full of irony; and many which cannot be shown to be ironical may be so. But there can be no mistaking her approval of the way sailors made money, by winning prizes in war—however difficult it may be for us to distinguish this from piracy. On the other hand the country attorney, such as Mr Phillips, Mrs Bennet's brother-in-law, or Mr Shepherd, in *Persuasion*, was of a lower order; and Mr Elliot's first wife is described by Anne Elliot as 'a very low woman'—a phrase her friend Mrs Smith agrees to. 'Her father was a grazier, her grandfather had been a butcher'—but all Mr Elliot wanted at that time was money. 'She was a fine woman, had had a decent education'—yet these attributes, in Mrs Smith's eyes, cannot compensate for her origin.[17] We may doubt that Jane herself would have accepted the notion of Mrs Elliot as a 'very low woman'—even though Anne Elliot is as little a snob in other ways as Mr Knightley. But Mr Gardiner in *Pride and Prejudice* lives hard by his warehouses in Gracechurch Street, and though he prospered in 'a respectable line of trade', the City was not a part of London the fashionable of the west end much cared to visit. Yet he and his wife are deemed by the end of the book those among Elizabeth's relations most worthy to visit Pemberley.[18] The point in *Persuasion* is not to denigrate Mrs Elliot, who is a cipher, but to underline Mr Elliot's love of mammon. There are many such ambiguities in the novels; and Jane rarely makes the rich as vulgar as the highly born. The nobility in her books are unfailingly vulgar or dull.

The issue whether poor and rich, and those of different status, can marry one another is a major theme in *Sense and Sensibility*, *Pride and Prejudice* and *Mansfield Park*, and a minor issue in *Emma* and *Persuasion*. Jane took sardonic pleasure in detailing the dowries of her characters, only too aware of her own poverty. Behind the marriage of partners rich and poor lay a very long literary tradition which more or less faithfully reflects some of the eternal facts of social history. Marriage, indeed, is central to all the novels, and the theme of another chapter. But it cannot be wholly separated from social hierarchy, even, or especially, in imaginative literature.

The two issues are marvellously combined in Shakespeare's *All's Well that Ends Well*, which reveals these problems in a discussion of immense power two hundred years or so before Jane Austen's time, and bears a curious resemblance to *Pride and Prejudice*, which is not at all likely to have occurred to her. The resemblance lies solely in its themes, for the play has a story as far removed from Jane's domestic scenes as one could imagine; and seduction is a crucial element in it, in a form perhaps more allied to *Mansfield Park* than to *Pride and Prejudice*. A king has long suffered from a fearful illness; he is cured by Helena, a young woman whom he rewards by offering her a husband of her choice from his court. She chooses Count Bertram, with whom she has long been secretly in love—she had been given lodging and patronage by his mother, and so knew him well—though as she is a woman of inferior status and no wealth (even if a gentlewoman by birth) he has never given her a thought. She is not low enough to be fair game for his lust, nor high enough to tempt him to marriage. Helena chooses him in the court and the king commands him to marry her. Under protest, he submits to a church wedding, but swears he will never consummate the marriage. Disguised as a pilgrim Helena makes a plot with a woman of similarly gentle origin but in very humble circumstances, Diana, whom Bertram plans to seduce. Helena takes Diana's place when Bertram visits her, and their marriage is consummated. Then all is revealed before the king, and Bertram takes Helena to wife: the audience is left to take its choice of Helena's 'All's well that ends well yet' and the king's 'All yet *seems* to be well.'[19]

What converts the play from its superficially absurd plot to one of Shakespeare's most haunting achievements is the plainness of the exposition in contrast to the folktale romance of the plot. In my understanding of the play I am much indebted to the late N. S. Brooke, who calls the quality naturalism, with full awareness of the ambiguity of the term. But what he describes is language unadorned—not ordinary, since Shakespeare was its author—and plain human sentiments.[20] The point is made very early in the extraordinary scene in which Helena and Parolles discuss virginity: this is no heroine of romance, but a witty, earthy, intelligent woman such as abound in Shakespeare's comedies. Bertram is too much of a snob to see her as such: he is a mere man, and as such, predatory. But Helena manages to catch him engaged in seduction, and turn his folly against himself. She wins him after a fashion in the end; but the conclusion is brilliantly managed to be at once moving and unconvincing. We are moved, with the old lord Lafew, to tears, but we are inclined to agree with the king's perplexity— all *seems* to be well.

Equality in *Pride and Prejudice*

There are no such doubts in *Pride and Prejudice*. Darcy's first instinct is to look at Elizabeth as Bertram looks at Helena, with scant attention: she is beneath him. But as Darcy sees more of Elizabeth he becomes infatuated, and being a decent and honest man (unlike many men in the novels) he sees no alternative but to marry her—and proceeds to expound his perplexities in making his first proposal to her at Hunsford. He has to learn, painfully and slowly, that his marriage cannot be an unequal partnership. Elizabeth herself believes that because her father is a gentleman they are really equals; however that may be, it is Elizabeth's combination of personality and intelligence with beauty which makes Darcy realise that rank and status form no barrier between them; he has to accept that in some senses and qualities, she is his superior. This is difficult: he has grown up with many male chauvinist assumptions. Her quality is all the more remarkable, since in some folks' eyes, women, like tradesmen, were inferior anyway. This was not the case with Mr and Mrs Darcy, though in other marriages Jane Austen allows the ambivalences of human experience freer play.[21]

Money: *Northanger Abbey* and *Sense and Sensibility*

It is striking that in both *Northanger Abbey* and *Sense and Sensibility* the main barrier to the heroines' marriage is money. General Tilney comes of an old Gloucestershire family and lives in an ancient house, however much provided with modern amenities. But his idea of marriage is entirely unromantic and mercenary: he delights to bring Catherine Morland and his second son Henry together, and invites her to Northanger, because he thinks she comes of prosperous family and is an heiress. When John Thorpe contradicts his first estimate of her wealth—enlarges on the throng of her brothers and sisters and sinks her chances of Mr Allen's estate—the General is seized with panic, banishes Catherine from his house, and tries to banish her from Henry's thoughts. It may well be that he would look for family as well as dowry in his eldest son's marriage; and he is himself exceedingly rich, and under no necessity to plan mercenary alliances. But money plays a large role in all his plans.

It is much the same with Mrs Ferrars in *Sense and Sensibility*. She is a very stupid as well as disagreeable woman, and so prefers her second son Robert, a conceited coxcomb, to the subtler, deeper, superficially duller Edward; she is fair game for the wiles of Lucy Steele. Jane Austen distributed folly and stupidity among her characters with a lavish hand, but in *Sense and Sensibility* these qualities are particularly to be found among the rich and highly born—as Mrs Ferrars and Sir John

Middleton bear witness. Mrs Ferrars determines that if Edward will not go into Parliament or join some grand profession, the only hope for him is to marry Miss Morton, who is to be sure the daughter of the late Lord Morton, and so from the ranks of the aristocracy, but whose chief attraction seems to be her £30,000. For a different reason, Marianne's affair with Willoughby is terminated by the purse. Willoughby is deeply in debt and needs to marry a rich wife to mend his fortunes. So he repudiates one of Jane's most enchanting heroines, and marries Miss Gray, for the sake of her wealth. It is only too clear that money is the key to Elinor's and Marianne's troubles, for they are by ancestry and birth fully the equals of the men who woo them. Mr Ferrars had died very rich:[22] how he came by his money is not clear, though some of it had evidently been invested in land. But there is no suggestion that he or his wife came of ancient families; and the Dashwoods were an old family of country gentlefolk.

Pride and Prejudice and the Equality of Gentlemen

The concept of a gentleman has always been ambiguous: it has been used, time out of mind, both to denote a certain measure or kind of courtesy—both 'gentle' and 'courteous' were words with a long history in the courtly, romantic world of medieval literature, a world no less inspiring and absurd than the fantasies of Emma—and a certain kind of social inheritance. Both meanings are fundamental in *Pride and Prejudice*. Elizabeth rebukes Darcy for his ungentlemanly conduct when he first proposes to her: her concept of courtesy thus begins to alter his.[23] He is driven to discourtesy by the conflict between his love for her and the sense of social difference between them—and his snobbery puts an edge on her reaction, for she is exceedingly sensitive to any imputation on her family's standing. Near the end of the book, in a scene of high melodrama, Lady Catherine de Bourgh outbids his discourtesy— one might almost say, parodies his ungentlemanly conduct—by calling Elizabeth an upstart.

'What is to divide [Darcy and her daughter, whom she hopes he will marry]? The upstart pretensions of a young woman without family, connections, or fortune. . . . If you were sensible of your own good, you would not wish to quit the sphere, in which you have been brought up.'

'In marrying your nephew, I should not consider myself as quitting that sphere. He is a gentleman; I am a gentleman's daughter; *so far we are equal.*'[24]

Elizabeth here pronounces the classic statement of a powerful doctrine: all gentlemen were equal. It is to her a crucial fact in her debate with Lady Catherine—and in her much longer and deeper debate with Darcy—that her father and his were alike in social standing. She does not disguise that in other respects they were very different: Darcy was far richer, his other connections were with the aristocracy, hers with trade and the lower professions. But all this is turned upside down by the fact that she avoids the manifest vulgarity of Lady Catherine's conduct and Darcy's snobbery. Jane Austen does not portray a world of equals, but one of paradoxes.[25]

Mansfield Park, Emma and Women

It was possible for women of fortune in Jane Austen's time to hold positions of wealth and independence, and two of them appear in her novels. Mrs Ferrars in *Sense and Sensibility* had free use of a large fortune—save for the inconvenience of annuities to a few old retainers—and abused her position as only the stupid and arrogant can do; and Emma is so much superior to her father in intelligence and initiative that she can do pretty much what she likes. 'The real evils indeed of Emma's situation were the power of having rather too much her own way, and a disposition to think a little too well of herself.'[26] Jane Austen herself had only too clear a view of the disabilities of women in her age; but that did not lead her to present independent women in altogether too favourable a light. Far from it: it was the salvation of Emma that she fell in love with Mr Knightley. Jane's most forceful women are the heroines who are fully the equals of strong husbands—Emma and Elizabeth.

Allowing that her characters—or those who play any serious part in the novels—are all genteel or gentlefolk, it is noteworthy that three of her mature novels turn on women in circumstances of particular disadvantage, and a fourth on the lot of a poor relation. Fanny Price is at once downtrodden and happy, frightened of and devoted to all that pertains to Mansfield Park: hers is an immortal portrait of one poor relation composed by another.[27] In *Pride and Prejudice* Mr Bennet's estate is entailed to heirs male, and his five daughters must shift for themselves when he is dead: the estate goes to his cousin Mr Collins. In *Persuasion* Kellynch Hall and the baronetcy must go to Mr Elliot, cousin of Sir Walter Elliot, since he has only daughters—and their predicament is all the worse because their father is feckless: instead of putting by reserves for their dowries he accumulates only debts. In *Sense and Sensibility* the old Mr Dashwood leaves his estate and his wealth to his nephew—but only for his lifetime; thereafter it becomes wholly the property of the nephew's son by a first marriage and his son; the second wife and her three daughters are left very modestly provided for. In this case, Jane attributes such extraordinary injustice to a preference on the old man's part for his great-nephew, who

> had so far gained on [his] affections . . . by such attractions as are by no means unusual in children of two or three years old: an imperfect articulation, an earnest desire of having his own way, many cunning tricks, and a great deal of noise.[28]

In *Mansfield Park*, Sir Thomas's estates will one day fall wholly to the unworthy Tom.[29]

But this kind of disposition would commonly have been inspired, in part at least, by the desire of a landowner to keep together a notable estate. It is to us the strangest of ambitions: the natural course of human affection looks to provide for all children equally—or as near equally as circumstances allow; where there is too little to divide, the weakest, often the youngest, have commonly been favoured.[30] But the notion that an estate, like a title, should pass from father to *eldest* son, or to the eldest *male* relative—the rule of primogeniture—was one of the absurd legacies of medieval society; and many aspects of contemporary life in Jane Austen's time served to perpetuate it. Norland Park and Mansfield Park were great houses, immensely expensive to preserve or rebuild or refurnish; they were supported by great estates, but these in their turn needed to remain large if the traditional status and privileges and obligations of their owners were to be preserved—or so most of the owners thought.

Jane knew about estates and wills. Her brother Edward was a rich country gentleman; but he had eleven children, and so little to spare for his impecunious mother and sisters—though he did settle them comfortably in Chawton. Her aunt and uncle Leigh Perrott were rich; but their will gave no direct benefit to their poorest relations—a discovery which Jane, now terminally ill, received with undisguised bitterness. 'A few days ago', she wrote to her brother Charles,

> my complaint appeared removed, but I am ashamed to say that the shock of my uncle's will brought on a relapse, and I was so ill on Friday and thought myself so likely to be worse that I could not but press for Cassandra's returning. . . .[31]

Thus in book after book Jane Austen shows us the woman's predicament: marriage or permanent dependence. Even the relatively prosperous *Mansfield Park* offers little freedom to the women. Tom will inherit the estate and Edmund enjoy the livings under its patronage. Maria marries Mr Rushworth to win her freedom and enjoy the delights of a large income in the hands of a man she can manage. Julia marries Mr Yates as the only way to escape insupportable tutelage after Maria's elopement and disgrace. The absence of opportunity for women—only too obvious to the unmarried daughter of a relatively poor parson—was all too palpable, and is driven remorselessly home—not by rhetoric, of which there is none, but by plain exposition.

It is hardly surprising that Jane Austen had an exceptionally wide and incisive view of the role of women in her world—of their opportunities and restrictions. Here are two texts from *Mansfield Park*.

> About thirty years ago, Miss Maria Ward of Huntingdon, with only seven thousand pounds, had the good luck to captivate Sir Thomas Bertram, of Mansfield Park, in the county of Northampton, and to be thereby raised to the rank of a baronet's lady, with all the comforts and consequences of an handsome house and large income. All Huntingdon exclaimed on the greatness of the match, and her uncle, the lawyer, himself, allowed her to be at least three thousand pounds short of any equitable claim to it.

Some thought her two sisters as handsome as she, and 'did not scruple to predict their marrying with almost equal advantage. But there certainly are not so many men of large fortune in the world, as there are pretty women to deserve them'—so the eldest had to be content to marry a parson, and the third ran away with a Lieutenant of Marines.[32]

The second text describes Mrs Maria Rushworth's fate, after she has eloped and lived for a while with a man not her husband. Her father was determined that 'she should be protected by him, and secured in every comfort [in some meanings of the word], and supported by every encouragement to do right, which their relative situations admitted'—but he would not afford 'his sanction to vice, or . . . lessen its disgrace' by admitting her back home or 'be anywise accessary to introducing such misery in another man's family, as he had known himself'.[33] So she was incarcerated in a distant county in the company of Mrs Norris—a fearful punishment.

In the view of Sir Thomas, it was a woman's business to marry and live in fidelity to her husband: no profession, no alternative abode could take her from her home save to her husband's or to that of a respectable friend. Jane Austen herself spent all her early life with her parents—all her later life with her mother and sister: she had many friends, and visited them so far as difficulties of travel and her limited resources allowed. She was indeed the supreme professional writer of her age: yet it was not in contemporary eyes a profession. Brother Henry might tour the land proudly revealing his sister's achievement.[34] But a woman's place was with her family or her husband—though an educated woman without endowment, like Jane Fairfax, could be a governess; and there were many professions open to women artisans, none of them accessible to Miss Fairfax or Miss Austen.

Maria broke the rules, and received a harsh sentence—far more severe than Henry Crawford's.

> That punishment, the public punishment of disgrace, should in a just measure attend *his* share of the offence, is, we know, not one of the barriers, which society gives to virtue. In this world, the penalty is less equal than could be wished

—a thunderous understatement which gives the sentence infinitely more weight than if she had indulged in rhetoric—

> but without presuming to look forward to a juster appointment hereafter, we may fairly consider a man of sense like Henry Crawford, to be providing for himself no small portion of vexation and regret—vexation that must rise sometimes to self-reproach, and regret to wretchedness—in having so requited hospitality, so injured family peace, so forfeited his best, most estimable and endeared acquaintance [with Fanny Price], and so lost the woman whom he had rationally, as well as passionately loved.[35]

To be made to live secluded with Mrs Norris was Jane's version of hell. The comparison we have made elsewhere with Mr Bennet's treatment of Lydia in *Pride and Prejudice* underlines the point.[36] Even allowing that Lydia had broken no marriage vows—that Maria's sin was adultery—the difference is striking. The morality of Sir Thomas Bertram and his circle was stricter than that of the Bennets. They are indeed both examples of the remarkably wide variety of standards which obtained in Regency England. It was notoriously a time when what Sir Thomas would have regarded as exceedingly loose morals flourished in high society, and were widely condoned.[37] In the wide spectrum of differing views on sexual morality, we need not doubt that Jane Austen's own opinions were tolerably strict; but it would be a false assumption to presume she agreed wholeheartedly with Sir Thomas. It would be equally false to attribute her views or his to a specific religious affiliation: both were orthodox Christians according to their lights; neither was—in any strict sense—Evangelical.[38] Sexual morals were not necessarily a party matter at all; and if Jane was strict on Christian principle, Sir Thomas was stricter—as he is presented to us—because of the standards of his family and social order.

Rank and Status in *Persuasion*

Social comment in *Persuasion* offers a kind of summary, of characteristic subtlety, of the problems and attitudes expounded in the earlier novels.

'Good company requires only birth, education, and manners, and with regard to education is not very nice. Birth and good manners are essential; but a little learning is by no means a dangerous thing in good company, on the contrary, it will do very well.'

Thus Mr Elliot to his cousin Anne, who demurs. Mr Elliot tries again:

'My dear cousin, . . . you have a better right to be fastidious than almost any other woman I know; but will it answer? Will it make you happy? Will it not be wiser to accept the society of these good ladies in Laura-place [the Dowager Viscountess Dalrymple and her daughter, the Elliots' cousins], and enjoy all the advantages of the connexion as far as possible? You may depend upon it, that they will move in the first set in Bath this winter, and as rank is rank, your being known to be related to them will have its use in fixing your family (our family, let me say) in that degree of consideration which we must all wish for.'[39]

Even the devil can quote scripture, and it could on occasion serve Jane Austen's ironic turn to put good sense into the minds of her evil characters—and Mr Elliot is wicked, not foolish. But in all the many arguments in *Persuasion*, spoken and assumed, between snobbery and reasonable human feeling, the fools and knaves are for snobbery, Anne Elliot and the sailors against. The snobbery of Anne's sister Mary is of a special quality: it snubs even her admirable mother-in-law to whom she claims precedence as a baronet's daughter. Lady Russell bridges the gap between the enlightened and the fools. She is intelligent, well educated, had been a very close friend of Anne's mother—and sees with total clarity that Anne is the brightest and the most admirable of the family. She is a sensible, matter-of-fact person who tries to judge fairly by all. But she is more for rank and status than Anne, and judges too readily by a man's manner what he is worth—to the extent that she has been blinded to the virtues of Captain Wentworth and to the vices of Mr Elliot: so she condemned Captain Wentworth when she first encountered him—and was very quickly won by Mr Elliot's good manners even to think of him as Anne's future husband. Critics have made much ado of the delay in Anne telling Lady Russell the truth about Mr Elliot, as if it represents a change or weakness in Jane's plan—and we all know that she had much difficulty with the conclusion of *Persuasion*.[40] But the truth seems to be that Lady Russell's conversion was always intended to be a total conversion—an acceptance 'that she had been pretty completely wrong, and [a readiness] to take up a new set of opinions and of hopes'; this part of the conclusion was never altered.[41] Anne's objection to Lady Dalrymple is that this tedious old lady is subjected to obsequious behaviour by her father the Baronet—she whimsically laments his lack of pride. The sailors, all in some measure self made, act with far greater dignity than the Baronet. Anne admittedly has the ease of being a baronet's daughter, and does not have to struggle for status—but she is shown very clearly able to talk without condescension to every rank she encounters, including the poor of Kellynch.

Persuasion is not radical or subversive; it does not make a baron marry a chambermaid as did the original of *Lovers' Vows*; or the servants humiliate their masters, as in the *Marriage of Figaro*. The author had condescended to dedicate *Emma* to the Prince Regent, with every appearance of feeling he did her an honour in agreeing to it.[42] But *Persuasion* was not designed to bolster the fabric of society, if that might be supposed to depend in any degree on respect for rank. Does that mean that Jane Austen was a gentle revolutionary? In a very limited sense it does. But more truly it illustrates the ambiguity in social structure which we have pursued through the other novels. Her last novel gives no encouragement to the gentry or the aristocracy to believe that birth gives them any true superiority. What after all had birth given her?—She was a poor relation all her days—and it was not birth, but the happy accidents of human relations, which had made her brother Edward the squire of Godmersham and Chawton. And it is her talents alone which have set her in a place of honour above all the lords and ladies and right reverends and wrong reverends—above the Prince Regent himself—as the first citizen of Regency England.

Notes

1. *E* I, c. 16, p. 136.
2. Ibid.
3. *E* I, c. 1, pp. 5, 7; I, c. 3, p. 20; c. 7, p. 207; cf. III, c. 16, pp. 455-8.
4. *E* I, c. 7, p. 53.

5. *E* II, c. 6, p. 198.

6. *E* II, c. 7, pp. 207-8.

7. *E* I, c. 8, p. 62.

8. *E* III, c. 18, pp. 472, 475.

9. See p. 139.

10. Or influenced by the French Revolution: see above, p. 151.

11. Collins 1993, pp. ix-x, quoting 'Aunt Jane', *Cornhill Magazine* 163 (1947-49), 72-3.

12. Galatians 3:28.

13. *Troilus and Cressida* 1, 3, 109-10.

14. *MP*, p. 92. 'Either' in Jane Austen's usage can mean one of three or more.

15. See p. 16. On the two bishops, see *DNB*.

16. As happened to the duke of Bedford in 1478 (*Complete Peerage*, II, 72)—and to several peers in the reign of George III (Namier 1928, pp. 221-5).

17. *P* II, c. 9, p. 202.

18. See p. 84. For Mr Gardiner's 'line of trade', see *PP*, p. 28.

19. *All's Well that Ends Well*, esp. 5, 1, 25; 5, 3, 322.

20. N. S. Brooke, 1977.

21. See e.g. below, p. 162.

22. *SS*, p. 15. For landed investment, note that Robert was given £1,000 per annum from the Norfolk estate (*SS*, pp. 266, 269).

23. See *PP*, pp. 192, 367.

24. *PP* III, c. 14, p. 356: see p. 77. I have italicised '*so far we are equal*'.

25. See also p. 165.

26. *E* I, c. 1, p. 2.

27. See pp. 85-8.

28. *SS* I, c. 4, p. 4.

29. The even more unworthy Mr Rushworth may have inherited Sotherton from a relation none too close. *MP*, pp. 38-9, 76-7, 85-6 may seem to suggest this: see Chapman's note, p. 543. But they do not enforce it; and 'the late Mr Rushworth left [prayers] off' (*MP*, p. 86), though not free from ambiguity, points the other way. If the relationship had not been close, it is strange that Jane Austen does not make this explicit on p. 39. Nor is there any indication that he might have by-passed women heirs. For his £12,000 per annum, see *MP*, p. 40.

30. As anthropologists have noted in a number of different regions and cultures; for ultimogeniture in medieval England, see Pollock and Maitland 1895, II, 279-80.

31. *Letters*, L no. 157, p. 338; C no. 144, p. 491; and notes; M, F-445.

32. *MP* I, c. 1, p. 1.

33. *MP* III, c. 17, p. 465.

34. Jane Austen to her brother Frank, 25 Sept. 1813: *Letters*, L no. 90, p. 231; C no. 85, p. 340. Frank had kept the secret; Henry had revealed it on a visit to Scotland.

35. *MP* III, c. 17, pp. 468-9. Cf. Willoughby's fate, p. 171.

36. See p. 126.

37. See p. 199; *Letters*, L no. 82, p. 208; C no. 78, p. 504; M F-245-6.

38. See pp. 126-32.

39. *P* II, c. 4, p. 150.
40. See p. 45.
41. *P* II, c. 12, p. 249.
42. *Letters*, L nos. 125, 130-2, 138, pp. 296-7, 304-7, 311-12; C, nos. 113, 120-2, 126, pp. 429-30, 442-7, 452-3.

Works Cited

The Writings of Jane Austen
Quotations from the novels are from the first or second editions; reference is also made to the admirable editions of R. W. Chapman (1923) in their revised form, *The Oxford Illustrated Jane Austen* (based on Chapman's 3rd edn, 1932-4). Quotations from her other works are from ibid. VI, *Minor Works*, ed. R. W. Chapman, revised B. C. Southam (Oxford, 1969). For bibliographical details see Chapman's Introductory Notes to the novels, and esp. Gilson 1982.

E = *Emma*, 1st edn, 3 vols, John Murray, London, 1816

Letters, L = *Jane Austen's Letters*, ed. Deirdre Le Faye, Oxford, 1995

MP = *Mansfield Park*, 2nd edn, John Murray, London, 1816

P = *Persuasion*, 1st edn, *Northanger Abbey and Persuasion*, 4 vols, John Murray, London, 1818

PP = *Pride and Prejudice*, 1st edn, T. Egerton, London, 1813

SS = *Sense and Sensibility*, 2nd edn, T. Egerton, London, 1813

Other Books and Articles
Brooke, N. S., 1977, 'All's Well that Ends Well', *Shakespeare Survey*, 30, 73-84

Chapman, R. W., 1948, *Jane Austen, Facts and Problems*, Oxford

Collins, I., 1993, *Jane Austen and the Clergy*, London

Complete Peerage, The, ed. V. Gibbs *et al.*, 9 vols, London, 1910-59

DNB: *Dictionary of National Biography*

Gilson, D., 1982, *A Bibliography of Jane Austen*, Oxford

Namier, L. B., 1957, *The Structure of Politics at the Accession of George III*, 2nd edn, London

Pollock, Fredrick, and Frederic W. Maitland, 1895, *History of English Law Before the Time of Edward I*, vol 2, Cambridge

Roberts, W., 1979, *Jane Austen and the French Revolution*, London

Early Phase Versus Major Phase:
The Changing Feelings of the Mind_____

William Deresiewicz

Austen's career as a published writer was terribly short: *Sense and Sensibility*, her first publication, appeared on 30 October 1811, and the author was dead by 18 July 1817—just 2,088 days. It hardly seems a long enough career to be divided into "phases." But Austen was active as a writer well before her first novel appeared on booksellers' shelves. She wrote early versions of many of her novels late in the 1790s but, unable to find a publisher, she allowed them to languish before *Sense and Sensibility* was finally accepted. In this essay, William Deresiewicz pays attention to those early versions and compares them with the works published from 1811 to 1817. Of course, other critics have noted many of the changes, but Deresiewicz argues that earlier accounts "fail to add up to a coherent account of how Austen's art matured." He tries to offer that coherent account.

The years during which Austen worked were some of the most momentous in English cultural history. "Nature" was rediscovered and redefined; childhood assumed a new importance. It was an age of radical social change, and it marked a turning point in "the shaping of the self." Deresiewicz surveys the changes in sensibility during the Romantic age and concludes: "The late novels represent a complete transformation in Austen's understanding of time: not simply in the depths of time they involve, but in their rendering of physical and social processes, of memory, of loss, indeed, of change itself. As time in all its ramifications may be said to be Wordsworth's greatest and most persistent theme, so is it the great theme of Austen's mature work."   — J.L.

But seven years I suppose are enough to change every pore of one's skin, & every feeling of one's mind.

—Letters[1]

What did change, in Jane Austen's art, in those seven years and more between *Susan* and *Mansfield Park*? The few attempts to differentiate the second "trilogy" from the first have been general and brief, yielding, in sum, only a disconnected series of distinctions: "a more intensified sense of the influence of place and environment on personality and action, a broader and more thoughtful social critique, and a much greater power of imagining . . . figures within the social and geographical spaces they inhabit";[2] a greater focus on questions of bodily health;[3] a new emphasis on fulfillment through socially useful labor;[4] a new insistence on the claims of desire;[5] a deeper involvement with nature;[6] a new "sense of hazard to the larger community";[7] and a new consciousness of the Napoleonic War.[8]

While these characterizations are, by and large, unobjectionable, they fail to add up to a coherent account of how Austen's art matured. Nor do they go very far in explaining either our common readerly intuitions about the higher merits of the later novels—their greater emotional depth, artistic complexity, and psychological profundity—or our sense of the thematic developments and attitudinal shifts that mark those novels, as we note in critical shorthand, as belonging to the nineteenth rather than the eighteenth century.

A more thorough analysis is required. As the one I present in the ensuing pages argues, the differences between the novels of the major and early phases are both systematic, exhibiting a mutual coherence, and comprehensive, touching matters of narrative structure, characterization, language, and theme—touching, indeed, Austen's fundamental beliefs about those issues central to her art, the nature of personal growth and of the mind.[9] And my analysis indicates one more thing about these changes: that they are, to put it a bit too simply, Wordsworthian.[10] The influences of Scott, Byron, and, of course, Coleridge (not always distinguishable from that of Wordsworth) can also be recognized, but as we make our way through this system of changes, we will find that attribute after attribute bears the unmistakable imprint of Wordsworthian ideas and concerns. And those that do not will be seen to have grown out of those that do, to represent a development, within a novelistic framework that necessarily introduces aesthetic considerations of its own, of those same ideas and concerns.

For in those seven years and more, much, indeed, had changed. English poetry had changed, with the appearance of the new poetry of Wordsworth and Coleridge: a poetry of change, of the growth of the mind through the development of feeling; a poetry of memory and loss, interiority and solitude, ambivalence and openness—a poetry of process. And as the late novels make clear, Austen's beliefs had also changed, about those very questions, the most important questions with which her art, and especially her late art, concerns itself. In their form, language, and themes, but more, in the very sense of exploration with which they proceed, the novels of Jane Austen's major phase reflect her absorption of the new poetry.[11]

Of course, nothing of what follows should be taken as a disparagement of the early novels. Were they the only of Austen's works that we had, her place in the front rank of English fiction would still be secure; as it is, *Pride and Prejudice* in particular remains central both to her popularity and to her critical reputation, and in many respects nothing in the major phase surpasses its achievement. What is in question here is rather the greater overall merits of the late novels, merits that, as I began this study by noting, critics have sensed from the very first and that can be connected, as I will argue, to Austen's reception of the Romantic poets.

* * *

To begin with what has already been fairly well noted: Austen's late novels display an entirely new receptivity to nature and attitude toward natural contemplation.[12] In both *Sense and Sensibility* and *Northanger Abbey*, characters' observation of nature serves only to exhibit and ridicule stereotyped modes of response. Henry and Eleanor Tilney survey the country around Bath in strict accordance with the principles of the picturesque, and Catherine, their all-too-apt pupil, proves "so hopeful a scholar, that when they gained the top of Beechen Cliff, she voluntarily rejected the whole city of Bath, as unworthy to make part of a landscape" (99).

The more passionate Marianne Dashwood supplements picturesque conventions with effusions derived from Thomson, Cowper, and Scott, but she fares less well with her auditors, one of whom, Edward Ferrars, clearly represents Austen's approved way of evaluating a rural scene at that point in her career. "[M]y idea of a fine country," he says, is one that "unites beauty with utility. . . . I do not like crooked, twisted, blasted trees. I admire them much more if they are tall, straight, and flourishing. . . . I have more pleasure in a snug farm-house than a watch-tower—and a troop of tidy, happy villagers please me better than the finest banditti in the world."[13] Edward's ideal, in fact, is more than a union of beauty and utility, it is beauty understood in terms of utility, of the health and prosperity of a country's human inhabitants. As for *Pride and Prejudice*, it deliberately swerves away from an engagement with nature. Elizabeth and her uncle and aunt plan to visit the Lake District, for "[w]hat are men to rocks and mountains?"[14] But because their trip is delayed they can venture no farther than Derbyshire, where their attention is indeed brought back, willy-nilly, to "men."

The heroines of *Mansfield Park* and *Persuasion*, by contrast, display an attentiveness and spontaneous emotional responsiveness to nature that is in no way criticized or ironized. Though Anne, on the walk to Winthrop, "repeat[s] to herself some few of the thousand poetical descriptions extant of autumn," her response has a relationship to poetry the very reverse of Marianne's.[15] The earlier heroine projects onto the landscape feelings derived from verse; Anne recollects lines of verse to express feelings the landscape spontaneously evokes. In her farewell to Uppercross, as has been noted, she does more.[16] There, as in so many of Wordsworth's and Coleridge's best-known nature poems, observation and emotion, outer and inner worlds, interact dialectically.[17] A mood of melancholy turns her attention to the dreary outer scene (that she looks out through misty panes reinforces the sense of a semipermeable membrane between self and world), which in turn prompts memories of her whole sojourn at the place—memories of pain as well as of reconciliation, but both modified under the influence of the scene, the ones softened, the others made melancholy. As in Wordsworth and Coleridge, feeling and observation are mutually reinforcing, mutually deepening. In the words of one critic, landscape in *Persuasion* becomes "a structure of feeling which can express, and also modify, the minds of those who view it."[18]

Fanny Price's interludes of natural contemplation, while not exhibiting the dialectical complexity of Anne's, embody other important Wordsworthian-Coleridgian ideas. Gazing out at a brilliantly starlit night, "solemn and soothing, and lovely," she is roused to feelings of tranquility and rapture and moved to profess the conviction that "there certainly would be less" "wickedness [and] sorrow in the world" "if the sublimity of Nature were more attended to, and people were carried more out of themselves by contemplating such a scene" (94-95). We might smile at this, especially as Fanny's tone approximates the sentimental ardors of Marianne Dashwood, but neither here nor in connection with any of her other effusions (on memory, for example) does Austen give any hint of satiric intent. And we should remember that the morally healing power of immersion in nature is precisely Coleridge's theme in "The Dungeon," Wordsworth's in "The Convict," and Wordsworth's again in the passage in "Tintern Abbey" that speaks of the influence of "beauteous forms": "On that best portion of a good man's life,/ His little, nameless, unremembered, acts/ Of kindness and of love" (23, 33-35).

Sometime later, sitting in the Mansfield Parsonage shrubbery, enjoying the "sweets of so protracted an autumn," Fanny remarks on an example of the kind of human adaptation of nature that would have cheered Edward Ferrars—the fact that the spot had only three years before been "nothing but a rough hedgerow"—but her purpose is less to praise the utility or even the beauty of the transformation than to remark on the contrast between past and present: "and perhaps in another three years we may be forgetting—almost forgetting what it was before. How wonderful, how very wonderful the operations of time, and the changes of the human mind" (173-174). Alterations in nature, as Wordsworth explores most fully in "The Brothers," become the yardstick for measuring alterations in the self.[19] Indeed, as Austen has Fanny suggest—and this is an idea that lies at the heart of Wordsworth's poetic encounter with the natural world—the life of the mind and of vegetation are not only parallel phenomena, they are, equally, natural ones, alike subject to "the operations of time"—persistence and decay, remembering and forgetting.

They are interlinked phenomena as well. Thus while *Emma* contains no scenes of natural contemplation,[20] it embodies even more fully than the other late novels the more general principle of which the human interaction with nature—whether in *Mansfield Park* or *Persuasion*, Wordsworth or Coleridge, or Scott, for that matter—is ultimately only a particular instance: the shaping of the self by place.[21] The second scene discussed above in connection with each of the other late novels—Anne's leave-taking from Uppercross and Fanny's reflections in the shrubbery—exhibits this same principle. Anne's time at Uppercross has given new forms to her feelings and understandings, ones that—as that scene of mingled recollection and contemplation makes clear—are inseparably interwoven with the specific sensual textures of the place. Fanny's rootedness at Mansfield is even more heavily emphasized, especially since she first comes there having been shaped very differently by a different place and her ultimate inseparability from Mansfield is revealed to her precisely by a return to that same place. As Edmund tells her apropos of Henry Crawford, whose courtship threatens to take her away to yet a third place, "before he can get your heart for his own use, he has to unfasten it from all the holds upon things animate and inanimate, which so many years growth have confirmed" (288).

The shrubbery scene makes the point, as points about Fanny are often made, by contrasting her with Mary Crawford. Responding to

Fanny's effusions, Mary declares that "'If any body had told me a year ago that this place would be my home . . . I certainly should not have believed them!—I have now been here nearly five months!'" (175). Five whole months—hardly enough time for Fanny's tears to have dried. Mary—like her brother, a creature of mobility and instability—feels no such attachments as Fanny's; home, for her, is wherever she happens to be living at the moment. And yet, ironically, it is further evidence of the novel's investment in the idea of place as the shaper of self that that very instability, along with everything else about the Crawfords, is a product of their upbringing in London.

And *Emma*? Emma's rootedness to place is far less obvious than Fanny's or Anne's, because it receives no emphasis whatsoever. It does not have to: it is so fundamental that it helps constitute the very form of her novel itself. Alone among Austen's works, the scene of *Emma* never shifts from the place in which it is set. Alone among her heroines, Emma never ventures away from that place, never even thinks of doing so. Highbury and its environs are as essential to her constitution as a character as Dublin is to Leopold Bloom's; she is simply inconceivable without them, and everything she is she is because of them. Indeed, the story of the novel is, in one respect, the story of how Emma comes to recognize that very rootedness, her inseparability from and responsibility toward the community that includes Miss Bates, Robert Martin, and everyone else.

Elizabeth Bennet, by contrast, has no particular relationship to Meryton and its environs, owes nothing of herself to their influence, and is able to live very well without them. Much the same could be said of her novel; *Pride and Prejudice* could take place anywhere, or even nowhere—one of the reasons it has proven so adaptable to the stage. *Northanger Abbey* depends on certain social particularities of Bath and certain architectural ones of Northanger, but its characters have no essential relation to either locale, still less to Catherine's home village.

Of the early novels, *Sense and Sensibility* is the one most concerned with place, as it is most concerned with nature, but as with respect to the latter theme, that circumstance in fact allows it to serve in drawing a sharper contrast between the two groups of novels. Willoughby's moral failings, like the Crawfords', are associated with London, but they are, precisely, only associated with it. They are revealed there, but the city has played no role in creating them. As for the novel's depiction of the attachment to place, that attachment is purely a matter of sentiment and sentimentality. The Dashwood women are certainly sad to leave Norland, and Marianne apostrophizes it upon their departure in a storm of exclamation points, but it is essential neither to their constitution nor, as it turns out, to their happiness. Before long, both they and the novel have all but forgotten it.

As the foregoing discussion has already begun to make clear, the idea of place as the shaper of self is intimately connected, in Austen's late novels as in the four poets, with the idea of home. "If any body had told me a year ago that this place would be my home . . ."; home, for Mary Crawford, is anywhere. For the mature Austen, as for the poets, it is one place only—the place that has made you who you are.[22] Again, this is an idea essentially absent from the early novels. While each is intensely concerned with finding its heroine or heroines a suitable husband, in no case does that quest also involve finding them a suitable home, still less solacing them for the loss of a home they already have. Catherine Morland's home all but doesn't exist, while Elizabeth Bennet's is, if anything, something to get as far away from as possible. The Dashwoods' loss of Norland has just been discussed, and Barton Cottage, while a boon for them as a decent house, develops scarcely any resonance as a home. If anything, its proximity to Barton Park soon makes it almost as inhospitable to Elinor and Marianne as Longbourn is to Elizabeth.

The idea of home has similarly little relevance to the places in which the early heroines eventually settle. Henry's parsonage is as briefly touched upon as Catherine's childhood home. In settling Elinor and Marianne "almost within sight of each other" (323), *Sense and Sensibility* comes closest of the early novels to preserving for its heroines the home of their youth. Still, whatever Elinor's love for Marianne, re-lations between the sisters have never been easy, and the novel's final, disturbing note makes the mere absence of tension seem the highest blessing their relationship, and thus their common "home" (we never do get a glimpse of their actual houses), can hope for.[23] The best candi-date among the early novels for a house that is also a home may be thought to be Pemberley, the beauties and comforts of which are dwelt on at great length. But Pemberley functions in the novel as an estate, a socioeconomic unit whose condition bears witness to its master's char-acter. He has formed Pemberley, in other words; Pemberley has not formed him. At issue in its presentation is the way it has been managed, not the affective richness of the life that has grown up within it. For Eliz-abeth, it will be a place to be "mistress of," not, per se, to dwell in (201).

What is new in the late novels—and may be new in the European novel altogether, though it is at least as old as Homer—is the idea of home as a psychic necessity, together with the correlative idea of the loss of home as an irreparable psychic wound. That home is vital to the emotional health of each of the late heroines—as it is for Wordsworth and so many of his characters (Poor Susan, Leonard in "The Brothers"), for Scott's Lieutenant Brown in *Guy Mannering*, for Childe Harold—needs little additional emphasis. We have already seen how this is true for both Fanny and Emma, and for the former it is abundantly con-firmed by her acute misery, first at leaving Portsmouth for Mansfield, then at leaving Mansfield to revisit Portsmouth. In Anne's case the demonstration is almost wholly negative. As I will discuss more fully in my chapter on the novel, *Persuasion* is, to a great extent, a novel about homelessness and the effort to create a home away from home—for Anne, for the naval officers both at sea and upon their return to shore, even, in their own very limited way, for Anne's father and elder sister.

While Anne finally finds that home-that-is-not-a-home, Fanny and Emma never even have to leave their homes.[24] In Emma's case, home is only slightly less important than husband, as her husband quickly finds out. But Fanny almost seems to cling to Edmund just because he can guarantee her continuation at Mansfield. (The interlude at Thornton Lacey is, tellingly, virtually elided.) Or rather, her loves for him and for Mansfield are inextricable, emotions of a single growth, and it is not at all clear which is the more important. At the novel's close, we find her gazing not into her husband's eyes, but out at the estate; it is really that "union" that the novel finally celebrates. So important has the idea of home become, in this late novel at least, that it overshadows the romance plot altogether.

There is good reason why the ideas of place as the shaper of self and of home as the place where the self has been shaped are absent from the early novels. In the early novels, the self is not "shaped" at all. Elizabeth, Marianne, and Catherine all change during the course of their novels, but as I will discuss more fully below, their alterations each involve an abrupt change of consciousness rather than a continuous modification of personality. More to the point at hand, who they each are at their novel's outset is simply a given. Missing from the early novels, in other words, is another great Wordsworthian theme, that of childhood.[25] That Elizabeth even had a childhood we can only guess, for there is no evidence she had any life whatsoever prior to the opening of her novel; she simply pops into existence on its first page.[26] The opening chapter of *Sense and Sensibility* outlines the Dashwood family's past, including the sisters' childhoods, but those childhoods receive no elaboration and bear no relation to the characters sketched at the chapter's end. That Elinor, at nineteen, possessed "strength of understanding," "coolness of judgment," and "an excellent heart" and that Marianne, at sixteen, "was sensible and clever; but eager in every thing" remain unexplained and—in line with what the younger Austen apparently believed, for it is true of the Bennet sisters, as well—seem to be matters of innate disposition (6). Of the early heroines' childhoods, only Catherine's is sketched. We watch her pass rapidly from ten to fourteen to fifteen to seventeen, but her development is devoid alike of particularity and emotional significance, instead mingling and playing with two generalized developmental paradigms: the physical and attitudinal changes of puberty and the reading program of a "female Quixote."

At first glance, only *Mansfield Park* seems to differ from the early novels with respect to the significance of its heroine's childhood. Fanny's is dwelt on, not at the length that George Eliot, in her most Wordsworthian novel, would later devote to Maggie Tulliver's, but enough to show how the patterns of behavior and feeling established then shape her actions and responses throughout the rest of the novel. Her transplantation to Mansfield at age ten, placing her in the company of four older cousins vastly her superiors in knowledge, confidence, and social standing, makes her into the timid and self-doubting creature who creeps through the next three volumes, concealing her desires, doubting her choices, and suppressing her resentments. But Fanny is not the only one in the novel decisively shaped by the treatment she receives as a child; both her cousins and the Crawfords clearly are as well, each of the six in ways that reflect differences not only in place and parents, but also in gender and birth order.[27]

Of the childhoods of Emma and Anne nothing directly is shown, but the summary information Austen gives on the first two or three pages of each of their novels is enough to show how their early treatments, too, have produced the young women who appear at the start of their narratives proper. In Anne's case, this significant past includes not only her accession to Lady Russell's pressure not to marry, but extends back well into her adolescence and indeed helped give rise to that fateful choice at age nineteen. If Anne's life from nineteen to twenty-seven has been haunted by that choice, the previous six years had been haunted by her mother's death. Austen's presentation is uniquely understated here, but what she asks us to infer is clear: at a crucial point in her life, right around the onset of puberty, Anne, until then her mother's favorite, became the family member most disregarded and disdained by her emotionally frigid father and equally withholding elder sister.[28] That is, when she was at home at all, for the first consequence of that untimely death was Anne's removal to a Bath boarding school for three gloomy years. Not only did her mother's loss teach Anne an excessive reliance on Lady Russell's advice, then, it also established her voicelessness and powerlessness within her family, her melancholic disposition, her distrust of her own judgment, and her tendency to put her own needs and desires last.

Emma Woodhouse, handsome, clever, and rich, could hardly be more different from the meek and marginalized Fanny and Anne, but her upbringing was no less unfortunate than theirs, precisely for giving her so unshaken a confidence in her own powers and prerogatives. Again, as with the other late heroines, the early loss of a mother is decisive. The death of Mrs. Woodhouse in Emma's infancy left her younger daughter to the guidance of a weak father, a too-compliant governess, and a sister whom all acknowledge as her inferior.[29] Where Fanny and Anne must learn to speak, to desire, and to will, Emma must learn to do less of all three. The early lives of Austen's late heroines are not Wordsworth's happy childhoods in nature, but unfortunate childhoods in society. All three young women struggle throughout their novels with the legacies of a misshapen upbringing.

Two further developments follow from this new emphasis on childhood, one interesting but minor, the other of the very first significance. Children become more prominent in the late novels, if not quite as much as in Wordsworth and Coleridge,[30] and they acquire a specific new function relative to the heroine. The only children to appear in the first three novels, other than the Gardiners' in *Pride and Prejudice*, who figure very briefly, are Lady Middleton's brats in *Sense and Sensibility*, who seem to exist for the sole purpose of showing how revolting children can be. In each of the late novels, by contrast, the heroine has a significant care-giving relationship with a group of children within her own family—Emma's nieces and nephews, Anne's nephews, and Fanny's younger sisters in Portsmouth. Not only are these children shown in a more positive (though far from idealized) light—their feelings taken seriously, as in Wordsworth—the fact that the heroine cares for them, and cares for them well, counts as important evidence to the goodness of her character.

Far more significantly—another way in which her childhood or adolescence shadows her young adulthood—each heroine's life continues to be dominated by her relationship with a difficult, domineering father or surrogate father. (This is not a kind of relationship that much interested the poets, though Wordsworth's "Anecdote for Fathers" is an interestingly subtle portrait of paternal tyranny, but it shows Austen working out the logic of ideas she drew from them along the lines of her own concerns and within the framework of her own literary form.) In the early novels, relations between the heroine and her parents may be easy or strained, but they are never particularly important. Their emotional texture is thin, even in the strongest case, that of Marianne and her mother, and parents play little or no role in their daughters' courtship. Elizabeth may be embarrassed by her mother, but she is hardly influenced by her. These young women do more or less as they please, at least as far as their own families are concerned. Parental figures connected to the heroes do function more prominently in the early plots, but only as comedic blocking figures. Notwithstanding the subtle delineation of General Tilney's tyranny over his children, these relationships, too, acquire little or no depth. Indeed, the early novels overwhelmingly concern relationships among the heroine's coevals, be they siblings, friends, or potential lovers.

In the late novels, by contrast, parental and especially paternal relationships loom very large indeed. Fanny's relationship with her uncle and Emma's with her father are second only to those with their future husbands as their most important, emotionally fraught, and complexly negotiated. It is no surprise that at the end of their novels, they marry or settle in a way that very much pleases papa. For Anne, again, it is a matter of negatives. Deprived of her relationship, one way or another, with both parents, she clings to substitutes. Lady Russell is the obvious example, but the emotional pull Admiral Cross exerts within the narrative—on the reader as much as on Anne—points to his most significant symbolic function. He is the kind, loving, accepting father Anne has always lacked, and it is no accident that he replaces her real father as the caretaker of Kellynch, her lost home, as her protector (when she is taken into his carriage as well as when he escorts her through the streets of Bath) and—though this is far more pronounced in the first version of the novel's ending—as the person who symbolically "gives her away" to her husband.

It has been noted that the late novels' blocking figures all come from within the heroine's family, but more to the point, they are all parental and, for the most part, paternal figures: Sir Thomas, Mr. Woodhouse, Sir Walter, Lady Russell.[31] The early novels are, like Burney's *Evelina*, stories of "a young lady's entrance into the world." In the late novels, the young lady is already in the world (Anne), never gets there (Fanny), or has no larger "world" to enter (Emma). In this phase of her career, Austen discovers an even more compelling narrative: the family romance itself.

* * *

This new attention to the shaping of the self in early life is only the beginning of the largest and most important difference between the two phases of Austen's career. The late novels represent a complete transformation in Austen's understanding of time: not simply in the depths of time they involve, but in their rendering of physical and social processes, of memory, of loss, indeed, of change itself. As time in all its ramifications may be said to be Wordsworth's greatest and most persistent theme, so is it the great theme of Austen's mature work.

We can begin by noting that the early novels not only occupy less time than do most of the late ones—this is trivial—but that in the former the very nature of time is different. Two passages from *Pride and Prejudice* may be taken as emblematic. The Netherfield ball has been announced, but five days remain before the big event, days that prove sadly inclement: the "younger Miss Bennets," cut off from Meryton, are especially distressed, "and nothing less than a dance on Tuesday, could have made such a Friday, Saturday, Sunday and Monday, endurable to Kitty and Lydia" (75). Sometime later, with the Netherfield party gone, Charlotte married, and Jane in London, Elizabeth has little to do but write letters, and so, "with no greater events than these . . . and otherwise diversified by little beyond the walks to Meryton . . . did January and February pass away" (127). "Friday, Saturday, Sunday and Monday," "January and February": two stretches of time in which, narratively speaking, nothing happens: nothing changes, nothing develops, time itself has no effect on feelings, thoughts, or relationships.[32]

But there is nothing anomalous about these utterly blank intervals; rather, as I suggested, they are entirely characteristic of the younger Austen's handling of time. Events in the early novels occupy time like beads on a string; they function as discrete entities the intervals between which have no significance and could thus be made arbitrarily greater or smaller without materially affecting the narrative. Nothing changes in Elizabeth's story between Christmas and her arrival in Hunsford in March, and again nothing changes between her departure from Hunsford the following month and her visit to Pemberley in July. Had she and Darcy met in Hunsford in January and Pemberley in April, their story would have been the same. Austen clearly had aesthetic reasons for having both *Pride and Prejudice* and *Sense and Sensibility* occupy the space of twelve months, and there were circumstantial reasons, such as the winter season in London, for setting certain scenes at certain times of year, but nothing internal to the narratives, no matter of emotional development or personal change, would have prevented either novel from occupying two years or six months.

As for the deeper past in the early novels—for in each it eventually turns out that a crucial event took place during the prehistory of the narrative—it exists in a purely schematic relationship to the present, as if the time between it and the start of the narrative proper were as blank as the intervals we just looked at. At a certain point in each work, forward movement is suspended for the recounting of some lurid tale that, like the opening of a secret door in a Gothic mansion, throws a stark light on the dark recesses of the villain's character and the hero's hidden wounds: Darcy's story of Wickham and Georgiana, Colonel Brandon's of Willoughby and the two Elizas. (In *Northanger Abbey*, the one novel in which the secret story, that of Mrs. Tilney's death, actually is told in a Gothic mansion, the satiric point is that neither is it lurid nor does it reveal dark secrets about General Tilney or his son.) But in each case, no organic relationship, no sense of continuity, connects past event and present moment. Each tale is framed and offered for inspection like a painting hanging on a wall. Indeed, in *Pride and Prejudice*, paintings hanging on walls become another way of gaining access to an isolated moment from the deep past—Darcy and Wickham's appearance as they were eight years prior to the narrative present. The device suggests something I will deal with more extensively when considering the question of memory: that in the early novels, memory functions, as we might say today, like a camera, a recorder of isolated mental images that remain unchanged by intervening lapses of time. Again, time in the early novels progresses in discrete quanta, not along a continuum of constant change.

Any sense of the physical effects of time is similarly absent from the early phase. Wordsworthian examples include, most famously, Simon Lee's swollen ankles and other signs of age and hard times, but also any number of others, including those that mark the old Cumberland beggar and Ruth. The early novels, to be sure, contain characters of all different ages, but other than Colonel Brandon with his rheumatism— an ailment that proves, precisely, no impediment to his marrying a woman a generation his junior—none is shown to have been physically affected by the passage of time. The counterexamples in *Persuasion* are too numerous to mention, for what with illness, injury, and simple aging, they include most of the characters in the book. In *Mansfield Park*, they include both Sir Thomas, who returns thin and worn from his two-years-plus in Antigua, and Fanny herself, who has blossomed during the same interval into an attractive young woman. In *Emma*,

---

such effects are more subtle; we find no physical changes taking place during the span of the narrative, but we do find what we see nowhere else in Austen, the senescence of the elderly. Mr. Woodhouse is ostentatiously feeble. Mrs. Bates, as we are frequently reminded, is both hard of hearing and weak of vision. And Mrs. Churchill—continually ill, though no one will believe her, these past twenty-five years—bears witness to the ultimate effect of time on the human constitution and, doing what virtually no one else in the course of a Jane Austen novel does, dies.[33]

The late novels similarly display a new attention to social change. While such change is not absent from the early novels, it remains in the background. General Tilney's modernization of Northanger, John Dashwood's of Norland, the tension between Lady Catherine's old-fashioned understanding of the distance between aristocracy and gentry and Elizabeth's newer one—all these point to large-scale changes in English society that surround and contextualize the narratives. So too, at a smaller level, several of the novels' figures are themselves in the process of changing social position, but in each case the change lies outside the main action of the novel in question. The Dashwood women suffer a sharp decline in fortune as their story starts, but only as it starts, as a precondition of the narrative proper. So too, Elinor and Marianne enjoy an elevation of wealth and status when they get married—that is, as their novel ends. Their social positions, however, like those of everyone else in the early novels, remain static during the main course of their narratives. In the early phase, change both large and small happens around the edges; it is not an intrinsic property of the stories themselves.

In the late novels, change becomes pervasive at both the national and personal scales. Among the poets, Wordsworth registers social change particularly in his more extended portraits of the dispossessed rural poor—"The Female Vagrant," "Michael." But its leading exponent, of course, is Scott. Most of the great historical novels would come after Austen's death, but Scott anticipated their rendering of large-scale change in verse romances that likewise reflect on the passing away of old sociocultural orders and the rise of new ones, as the very title of the first of them, *The Lay of the Last Minstrel*, suggests—a point I will take up more fully in my chapter on *Persuasion*.

In *Mansfield Park*, the drama of small-scale change is embodied by the fortunes of Sir Thomas: imperiled enough before the start of the main action to necessitate his trip to Antigua to take personal charge of his estates; improving handsomely upon his return with the marriage of his eldest daughter to a wealthy young man and prospective marriages of his younger son and adopted niece to two more wealthy young folk; contracting suddenly at the end with the collapse of all three matches. As for larger-scale changes, the issue of the improvement of estates, peripheral to *Sense and Sensibility* and *Northanger Abbey*, becomes central. In *Persuasion*, social change involves both the rise and fall of personal fortunes—Wentworth's and William Walter Elliot's rising, Sir Walter's falling—and, as I will discuss at length in the relevant chapter, the larger changes rippling through English society as it makes the transition from war to peace and, concurrently, from the leadership of the aristocracy to that of the professional middle-class.

In the virtually self-enclosed world of *Emma*, large- and small-scale social change are hard to distinguish; what counts in the other novels as small feels momentous here. Austen's presentational techniques are at their subtlest in tracing these movements; by a myriad of small strokes, she charts the rise of Highbury's second-rank families to greater prominence: the Coles, beginning to give dinner parties; the Perrys, thinking of setting up a carriage; and of course, the Eltons, intruding everywhere and talking up their wealthy connections at every opportunity.[34] Add to them Mr. Weston, recent purchaser of an estate; Mrs. Weston, just risen from governess to mistress of that estate; Harriet Smith, learning new ideas about what she can aspire to; Robert Martin, a "gentleman farmer" "on his way," in Lionel Trilling's phrase, "to being a gentleman pure and simple";[35] and Miss Bates, sinking ever deeper into genteel poverty; and there scarcely seems a single person standing still in this supposedly timeless idyll. In *Emma*, then, as in all the late novels, change—continuous change—becomes the very groundwork of the narrative and of its characters' existences.[36]

Of all that gives these novels their increased complexity and density as compared to Austen's earlier works, this fact of continuous change is surely one of the most important. To use a mathematical analogy, a kind of narrative arithmetic sufficed for the sort of analysis that Austen undertook during the first part of her career, that of fixed characters within a fixed setting. For the novels of her maturity, in which both self and world exhibit continuous alteration, she had to devise a narrative calculus.

The corollary of the late novels' insistence on the inescapable fact of physical and social change is the prominence they give to characters who resist change both within and without, figures willfully stuck in time. (This is not a type prominent among the poets, though Byron's Giaour is an example.) Mr. Woodhouse—"a valetudinarian all his life"; "a much older man in ways than in years" (8)—seems never to have been young. Sir Walter Elliot, a freeze-dried version of what he was thirty years before, seems never to grow older. It is no accident that they both so vehemently reject the alterations going on around them; just as they stand still, so do they want their world to stand still. Sir Walter does his best to ignore the changes sweeping through English society in these "unfeudal" times, changes the most deplorable effect of which, in his view, is precisely the opportunity they give to persons of low birth to elevate their social status (152). Mr. Woodhouse resists all change whatsoever, but what he especially seeks to wish away are the changes consequent upon marriage. Having apparently never felt the longings of youth himself—for newness as little as for sex—he literally cannot seem to understand how anyone else could feel them.

The case of Sir Thomas, a more complex figure than these other two patresfamilias, is less obvious. Time has marked his body, his household, and his estates, and he does not seek to remain oblivious to these alterations. But his orientation is fundamentally conservative, and his way of dealing with these changes is to seek to reverse them: to restore his estates, recover his health, and, emblematically, remove every vestige of the theatricals that have so disrupted his household.[37] But Sir Thomas's desire to continue living in the past shows itself most importantly in his high-handed, authoritarian way of conducting himself as a father.[38] Written and set during the Regency, a time when the British national household was headed by a disreputable prince filling the place of a father who had lost his mind, *Mansfield Park* documents an evolution in family life that has weakened paternal authority and strengthened the willfulness of children in resisting it.

Admiral Crawford, Mr. Price: fathers here are not what they used to be, and even if they don't know it, their children do. Sir Thomas solemnly admonishes his eldest son for his extravagant ways, and Tom laughs in his sleeve. He cautions his eldest daughter not to enter into marriage with a man she cannot respect, and Maria practically cracks her gum in his face. Even Fanny, who buys into her uncle's retrograde notion of the obedience due one who stands in place of a father, resists his commandment to marry Henry in favor of her own hidden desires. And so, because his authority will not bend, it finally shatters, his daughters breaking into open revolt. Resisting change, all three of these proud men cut themselves off from the people around them. To place oneself beyond the realm of change, in the late novels, is to place oneself beyond the realm of human connection.

Three proud men, three stern fathers. Given what we have seen about the hold these figures have over their daughters' imaginations, it is no wonder that each of the late novels gives us a young woman with something of this same resistance to change. Each case is different. *Persuasion*'s is the least interesting, since the daughter in question is not the heroine, but her elder sister. Elizabeth Elliot's freeze-dried quality exactly resembles her father's. Emma is not nearly as bad as her own father, but as we have begun to see, much of what is wrong with the way she conducts herself—her snobbery, her obstruction of Harriet's marriage to Robert Martin, her refusal to take her proper place within her community—stems from her resistance to the very social changes outlined above. And while she herself does change gradually throughout the novel, as I will discuss below, she does not see that she does, and indeed thinks that no alteration will ever be necessary on her part: "I am not only, not going to be married, at present, but have very little intention of ever marrying at all. . . . I cannot really change for the better" (73). While the literal meaning of that last phrase refers only to a change of marital circumstances, its larger, unconscious implications point to the attitude embodied in Emma's every infuriating display of imperturbable self-possession—her belief that she has nothing to learn and no more growing up to do. Like Elizabeth Elliot, though in a very different respect, Emma is stuck at a certain stage of emotional development.

But what of Fanny? In her social values, as I have said, she emulates her uncle's conservatism, and in her visceral repugnance to any change in her personal circumstances, she approaches Mr. Woodhouse. If anyone would seem to constitute a counterargument to the idea that the late novels insist on the necessity of change, it is she. Doesn't she resist it in just the way Sir Thomas, Mr. Woodhouse, Emma, Sir Walter, and Elizabeth Elliot do? No, she does not. The resistance to change we find in those five figures is, as we have seen, a willful rejection of it: a refusal to acknowledge or yield to it. But Fanny's hatred of nearly every change that comes her way—her removal to Mansfield or, most poignantly, her recognition in Portsmouth that her parents no longer love her—is matched only by her resilience in accommodating herself to it.

The mature Austen does not insist that her characters like the changes happening to and around them, she only insists that they adjust to them. She never suggests that change is necessarily desirable, only that it is necessary. Each of the late novels, in fact, spends a great deal of energy exhibiting, examining, and evaluating the changes it documents. In each case, Austen chooses the middle way between the most radical agents of social change and its most conservative refusers: between Sir Thomas and the Crawfords, Mr. Woodhouse and Mrs. Elton,

Sir Walter and William Walter Elliot. And in each case, that middle way is embodied, finally if not initially, by the hero and heroine.

The idea of change leads in turn to perhaps the most profound and important Wordsworthian idea of all, one that is also of the first significance for Byron and Scott: loss. As criticism has shown on a massive scale, the fact of loss and the attempt to come to terms with it is everywhere in Wordsworth, be it the loss of youth and youthful powers or the loss of beloved individuals. The lamentation for the loss of childhood places, friendships, and loves is the principal subject of Byron's early lyrics, while the Turkish Tales are, one and all, stories of bereavement. Scott's romances—as the conspicuous framing devices of the first and best of them, *The Lay of the Last Minstrel* and *Marmion*, make clear—mourn the loss of the very cultural and narrative traditions they memorialize.

But absent a true consciousness of change, Austen's early novels are likewise innocent of loss. In each, the heroine must give up someone she once cared deeply about, but in every case, as she is made at great length to learn, the person in question turns out not to have been worth having in the first place. Even the pain of error is made perfectly good, and so happiness finally comes at no real cost whatsoever—surely one important reason the early novels, for all their splendors, feel so much less profound than do the later ones. For the later ones are saturated with loss. In fact, in two cases, the question of loss will be my main focus in the later chapters of this study. Fanny must give up nearly everything she loves, starting with her home in Portsmouth, and do without nearly everything she wants, being forced, in each case, to find substitute objects of affection or desire. Anne, like almost everyone else in *Persuasion*, is "widowed" of the person she most loves, and even if she retrieves him at novel's end, the lost time remains lost, so many years of happiness replaced by so many of loneliness and self-reproach. And while the very structure of *Emma* works to conceal its heroine's losses from us—precisely because she cannot see them herself—we should not doubt that they are heavy and continuous. Until her final release,

Emma's imprisoning egotism deprives her of nothing less than a full emotional life, true intimacy with those around her. That loss is embodied in Jane Fairfax, and by refusing to allow Emma a belated friendship with that young woman as the reward of her reformation, Austen tells us that things once lost cannot be recovered. In the late novels, time is real: too late is too late.

* * *

In discussing Austen's understanding of time in the later novels, my focus thus far has been on externals: physical appearance, social position, the loss of beloved objects. But the most important, pervasive, and subtle manifestations of this great new theme lie in the inner realm: in matters of feeling, reflection, recollection, relatedness, and personal transformation. It is also in these matters that we will find the grounds on which the new complexity and density of the late novels most significantly develop. I will turn to this large set of questions in a moment. First, though, I would like to touch on several other, strikingly Wordsworthian characteristics of the mature novels, ones that seem at first remote from these issues but will soon lead us back to them.

Few characteristics of Wordsworth's poetry in *Lyrical Ballads* and *Poems in Two Volumes* are more immediately striking than the attention it pays to the poor, the marginal, and the dispossessed. Many examples may be cited, including "Simon Lee," "The Old Cumberland Beggar," "Michael," "Resolution and Independence," and so forth. While such figures are entirely absent from Austen's earlier novels, they appear in all of the later ones, often with a great deal of emphasis. Fanny's family in Portsmouth may not be quite poor, but it is far down the economic scale from anyone in the early works. Miss Bates *is* poor, as is Mrs. Smith, and far poorer are the cottagers visited by Emma and Harriet.[39] Servants and dependents are newly visible, as well—nurserymaids, valets, laborers, tenant farmers, bailiffs—as are shopkeepers and the members of the less lucrative professions. In the late works, Austen opens her imagination to a whole world of economic realities that lies below the lives of the country gentry.[40]

As several of these examples suggest, this expansion of focus involves, in particular, a new attention to what Emma thinks of as "the difference of woman's destiny" (316). So too, most of Wordsworth's pictures of the poor and dispossessed are pictures of women, including "The Female Vagrant," "Goody Blake and Harry Gill," "The Thorn," "Her Eyes are Wild," "Alice Fell," and many others. Fanny, Jane Fairfax, Harriet, Miss Bates, Mrs. Smith, even Clara Brereton, *Sanditon*'s presumptive heroine ("[s]o low in every worldly view, as . . . to have been preparing for a situation little better than a nursery maid")[41]—all women in circumstances and with prospects far below even those of the Dashwood sisters, with their thousand-a-piece. It is to the pressures of such lives, not to the marriage plots of the relatively well set-up, that the late fiction gives the bulk of its attention.

These women share another, related characteristic: marginality within their family or community. Elizabeth Bennet, Jane, Elinor, Marianne, Catherine and her friends—all young and lovely, all cynosures of their circle, all avidly courted. But the late fiction gives most of its attention to young women whom no one regards: Fanny and Anne, of course, and—because *Emma* is told through the eyes of its heroine, who is herself fascinated by two more such women—Harriet and Jane. Yet because no one regards them, they (with the exception of Harriet) regard everything. As Fanny says, "I was quiet, but I was not blind" (300). Aside from Elinor's always-keen interest in Marianne, silent observation plays no significant role in the early heroines' lives. Scarcely more does silent contemplation, for the younger Austen tends to stage deliberative episodes as dialogues—Elizabeth with Jane or Charlotte, Elinor with Marianne, Catherine with Henry. The lives of these heroines are almost entirely absorbed by social activity; scarcely ever do we see them alone, their moment of transformation being in each case the one important exception. But the late heroines, including Emma, are frequently alone, and when alone are invariably immersed in introspection. Austen has discovered, in other words, the great Wordsworthian theme of solitude, essential to the flowering of a dynamic and ever-evolving inner life, a life of recollection and reflection. It is to that life that we now return.

The element of the inner life most obviously involved with time is that of memory. Memory plays only one role in the early novels, and though it is a crucial one, arising in connection with each novel's central scene; that of its heroine's transformation, it also exhibits the narrowness of Austen's conception of memory at this time in her career.[42] *Pride and Prejudice* provides the clearest instance, for its heroine's transformation, her self-recognition, is the most stunningly swift. Darcy's letter forces Elizabeth to reconsider all her judgments about him and Wickham, a reconsideration that in turn forces her to remember her impressions of the latter. The result proves distressing: "She tried to recollect some instance of goodness. . . . But no such recollection befriended her. . ." (169). She reads on, and her memory becomes more particularized: "She perfectly remembered every thing that had passed in conversation between Wickham and herself, in their first evening at Mr. Phillips's. . . . She was *now* struck with the impropriety of such communications to a stranger" (170, emphasis in the original). Her old judgments weaken, and only a paragraph later comes the catastrophe, the two dozen words on which the whole novel pivots: "She grew absolutely ashamed of herself.—Of neither Darcy nor Wickham could she think, without feeling that she had been blind, partial, prejudiced, absurd" (171). There are two things to note here. First, as I suggested above, the contents of memory undergo no change or decay from the moment of the event to the moment of recollection. Five months later, and Elizabeth still "perfectly remembered everything that had passed in conversation." It must be so, else the second and more important circumstance could not be true: the function of memory here—the only function it performs in the novel—is that of moral self-correction. The heroine remembers what she did, thinks about it, is heartily ashamed of it, and resolves to do better.

This is one of those instances in which an idea implicit in Austen, or at least in the early Austen, is identical to one explicit in Samuel Johnson: "Memory is the purveyor of reason, the power which places those images before the mind upon which the judgment is to be exercised, and which treasures up the discriminations that are once passed, as the rules of future action, or grounds of subsequent conclusions."[43] And so it is in *Northanger Abbey*, when Henry's rebuke opens Catherine's eyes to the "extravagance of her late fancies" (173). And so it is in *Sense and Sensibility*, for Marianne undergoes her transformation not because Willoughby jilts her, not because her grief over him makes her ill, but because her illness "has given me leisure and calmness for serious recollection": "I considered the past; I saw in my own behaviour . . . I saw that my own feelings . . . Whenever I looked towards the past . . . ," and so forth (293-294). Recollection, judgment, mortification, a resolution to judge and act better, and Marianne is cured in more than just the medical sense.

But because memory is confined to this one special role, its workings understood in so schematic a way, its potential impact on the sense of time in the early novels is negated. Time here is essentially Bergsonian *temps*—linear, unidirectional clock-time—with none of the thickening and deepening provided by those back-and-forth movements of consciousness that cause time present and times past to coexist in a complex temporal space. Compared with this mechanical understanding of memory's operations and limited view of its functions, the multifarious roles it plays in the late novels represent an immeasurable advance. From being Johnsonian, Austen's understanding of memory becomes Wordsworthian.[44]

So essential are the workings of memory to *Mansfield Park* and *Persuasion*, and so important will their exploration be to my chapters on these novels, that to give a full account of them here is neither desirable nor necessary. I will only touch on the most important points. We already began to see the ways in which memory operates for Fanny Price when we examined her response to nature in the shrubbery scene.[45] As opposed to what we find in the early novels, but very much like we see in Wordsworth and Coleridge's first-person lyrics, memory arises for her spontaneously. It also gives her a sense of rootedness in time, a way of understanding not only the past, but also the present. As in the greatest poems of memory Wordsworth published during Austen's lifetime— "Tintern Abbey," "The Brothers," "The Two April Mornings"—the present acquires significance because of the way it both echoes and alters the past. Memory thus makes palpable the distance between present and past, helping give time the weight it so lacks in the early works. Late in the novel, we find Fanny sharing the Portsmouth parlor with her father: "And the remembrance of her first evening in that room, of her father and his newspaper came across her. No candle was *now* wanted. The sun was yet an hour and half above the horizon. She felt that she had, indeed, been three months there" (362, emphasis in the original).

This passage, like the shrubbery scene, also shows memory connecting the temporal rhythms of Fanny's life to those of the life of nature, the passage of seasons and years ("five summers, with the length/ Of five long winters! and again I hear/ These waters . . ."). Another scene of recollection in Portsmouth suggests a deeper way in which the past gives meaning to the present through the action of memory. In a remarkable testament to the power of time to both alter and fix the affections, Fanny, greeting Mrs. Price for the first time in eight years, embraces a mother whose features she finds she "loved the more, because they brought her aunt Bertram's before her" (313). It is not that she so loves her aunt's features, as such; it is the electric charge of recognition, transmitted between memory's two poles of "then" and "now," that galvanizes her heart. The present is loved because it evokes the past, and the past is loved because it lives again in the present. Without the other, each is barren.[46]

But the supreme scene of recollection in *Mansfield Park*, as I mentioned in the previous chapter and will discuss at length in the next, is the first description of the East room, where Fanny, under the presiding emblem of Tintern Abbey, casts her glance about her and "could scarcely see an object in that room which had not an interesting remembrance connected with it.—Everything was a friend, or bore her thoughts to a friend." But what these beloved mementos speak of, in the first instance, are "the pains of tyranny, of ridicule, and neglect." Yet "almost every recurrence of either had led to something consolatory . . . and the whole was now so blended together, so harmonized by distance, that every former affliction had its charm" (126). Nothing could be more like Wordsworth, and especially the Wordsworth of "Tintern Abbey": memory's power, not to repeat the past, but to transform it, and in particular, to redeem experiences of suffering and loss.

In essence, the kind of temporal and therefore emotional depth Fanny experiences at particular moments undergirds the whole of *Persuasion*, constituting the affective ground bass of this, Austen's lushest orchestration of feeling. The whole narrative is a "now" shadowed by a "then," so that the novel itself may be said to remember: to possess a memory that grounds its sense of self, gives meaning to the present and weight to time, and finally redeems the past by bringing it again to life, immensely transformed. Of course, most of the novel's remembering is focused through the consciousness of its heroine, for whom, as for James in Wordsworth's "Brothers," memory becomes an almost physiological process.[47] Where Fanny courts memory, often her only friend, Anne has long suppressed hers, and so, when Wentworth's reappearance calls it forth, it seems to push its way to the surface from the very depths of her body. The mere mention of his name evokes blushes and sighs, effusions of blood and breath, that send her hastening out for a walk in an attempt to regain control of herself. With his actual approach, "a thousand feelings rushed on Anne,"[48] and with his appearance, her very senses rebel, rendering her scarcely able to hear or see (we can practically feel the blood pounding in her ears) and leaving her scarcely able to eat, her mind and body—if the distinction can still be maintained at this point—"resuming the agitation" that almost eight years "had banished into distance and indistinctness" (84-85).

We can scarcely speak of the past as being recollected here, because it seems never to have gone away. Both Anne's habit of suppressing her memories of Wentworth and the force with which those memories reassert themselves once that suppression is overborne arise, of course, from the grief she feels at having lost him. In this novel, whose central theme is loss and grief, memory is always closely allied to both. For what is grief but memory made visceral, memories felt in the body, and felt the more sharply for being only memories, for belonging to that which can never come back in another form?

Memory is clearly less important in *Emma* than in the other late novels, primarily because Emma is so different a figure from the melancholy, introspective Fanny and Anne. Where their thoughts tend to turn back to the past, those of Emma, a creature of energy and will, are busy striding forth into the future. But *Emma* is not unmarked by its author's new understanding of memory's place within a full human personality. Indeed, the narrative proper, which begins on Emma's governess's wedding day, begins in a manner that strikingly, if only lightly, anticipates *Persuasion*: "It was Miss Taylor's loss," we read, "which first brought grief" (7). Alone that same evening, Emma has "only to sit and think of what she had lost"—in other words, to remember. "She recalled [Miss Taylor's] past kindness—the kindness, the affection of sixteen years . . . but the intercourse of the last seven years . . . was yet a dearer, tenderer recollection" (8). Of the mother who had died in her infancy, we have already been told that Emma had no more "than an indistinct remembrance of her caresses" (7). As it is for Fanny and Anne, memory here is affective, even physical (those caresses seem more felt than anything else); helps ground the self by creating a sense of its history, including the different eras of that history ("sixteen years," "seven years"); and helps form, strengthen, and reform the affections. Already Emma dwells more deeply in time than do the early heroines, and in so doing, possesses herself more fully.

* * *

In discussing the quality of time in the early novels, I noted that the intervals between events possess no narrative significance, that time itself is a neutral medium. To say this is also to imply something about the nature of characters and relationships in the early works, of the feelings people have about each other and the ways they negotiate them—how these occupy and are affected by time.

In the early phase, feelings remain precisely as they are, with neither change nor growth nor decay, until some specific event, some confrontation or recognition, shocks them into a new, equally static condition. Darcy snubs Elizabeth, and from then on, she hates him; she reads his letter, and from then on she esteems him and regrets her behavior toward him; she meets him at Pemberley—perceiving what the estate says about its owner and what his behavior says about his feelings for her—and from then on, she loves him. The same analysis may be made of any of the less central feelings in the early novels (Jane, for example, has never stopped carrying a torch for Bingley, as we eventually learn, nor he for her), as well as of the major ones in *Northanger Abbey* and *Sense and Sensibility*: Catherine's for Isabella Thorpe and Henry Tilney, Marianne's for Willoughby—this last moving through sharply demarcated stages of passionate love endlessly dwelling on itself, passionate grief doing likewise, and finally a letting go of love and grief that happens, as we saw above, in the space of just a few days. True, Marianne's heart does "in time" become "as much devoted to her husband, as it had once been to Willoughby" (322), but this gradual transformation happens after the end of the narrative proper. The younger Austen may recognize that feelings can sometimes change with time and time alone, but she does not know how to dramatize that perception and for the most part disregards it. A graph of virtually any feeling in the early novels would resemble a set of stairs: a series of horizontal lines—steady states—linked by vertical jumps up or down—sudden shifts, as the personality that has hardened into one configuration is shattered by some dramatic event and instantaneously reassembles itself into a new one.

There are several implications and corollaries of this principle of sudden emotional transformation. Because changes in emotional state depend so much on confrontation and shock, melodramatic elements are much more prominent: stock events like Lydia's elopement, Catherine's ejection from Northanger, or those lurid tales Darcy tells of Wickham or Brandon of Willoughby; stock characters like the false, fortune-hunting female (Caroline Bingley, Lucy Steele, Isabella Thorpe) and the domineering dowager on the man's side (Lady Catherine, Mrs. Ferrars, Willoughby's Aunt Smith; General Tilney is a male version). We may also note, in this connection, how much more schematic are the early plots than the later ones, and how much greater is the family resemblance among them than among the later group. The younger Austen, having written out a certain narrative paradigm three times, had brought it to perfection; the mature writer clearly had no desire to repeat it, or in fact to repeat anything. Indeed, in trotting out Mrs. Clay, whose ambitions trouble Anne for about ten seconds, and William Walter Elliot, whose charms stand not the slightest chance of winning her over and whose perfidy she cannot finally be bothered to expose, *Persuasion* thumbs its nose at that very paradigm, with its lurid tales and its fortune hunters and its Mr. Wrongs.

With this relative simplicity of both emotional structure and narrative structure comes a relative simplicity of characterization. Complexity of character, to a great extent, *is* complexity of emotion. In many cases, in fact, figures in the early novels are not so much characters as caricatures, albeit brilliant ones. The late novels have their caricatures, too, but far fewer of them, and in far less prominent positions. We can see this deepening of characterization most clearly through a comparison of analogous figures. Collins and Miss Bates are both fools, but the latter is also a full human being, with complex feelings capable of being wounded, significant relationships, and a social role within her community, and that she is no mere figure of fun becomes, indeed, an extremely important idea at a certain point in the novel. John Thorpe and Yates are both "puppies," but while the first is a one-line joke, the latter is plausible as a real, albeit limited, young man. As a villain, John Dashwood's motives are as simple as his behavior is transparent; William Walter Elliot, to say nothing of Mrs. Norris, plays a more complex game, and for more complex reasons.

Just as the late novels are sparing of caricatures, so too do they abound in characters who are morally ambiguous. The early novels have none such; we know exactly what we are to think of everyone in them. But as the critical literature demonstrates, equivocal figures in the later works include, in *Persuasion*, Lady Russell, Mrs. Smith, and Captain Benwick; in *Mansfield Park*, the five most important figures at the very least—Fanny, Edmund, Mary, Henry, and Sir Thomas; and in *Emma*, pretty much everyone except Knightley and Mrs. Elton, the novel's moral poles.

Just as emotions and motives are so much less complex in the early novels, so too are relationships. That this is so, that relationships between characters are similarly unambiguous and shift in a similarly step-wise fashion, is already largely implicit in what I have said, but it bears on narrative form in ways well worth exploring. The younger Austen—it is one of her glories—is extremely fond of what might be called the narrative set-piece. So many of her most memorable scenes belong to this type: Catherine and Henry's teasing conversation during their first dance, Elinor and Lucy's set-to in the Middletons' parlor, Elizabeth and Darcy's sparring matches while Jane is ill as well as during the ball at Netherfield. We can recognize a general likeness between these scenes, as well as the great importance of each to their respective novels, but how can we characterize this likeness more precisely?

Most obviously, these episodes are all markedly performative. Austen constructs them like little plays, carefully setting the scene and disposing the characters in their places. (This is especially notable in Elinor and Lucy's encounter, where the break between chapters 23 and 24 functions as a kind of drumroll.) The scene set, she then withdraws, rendering the rest of the encounter almost entirely in dialogue. And the characters know they are performing—not for us, but for each other. The tension is high, because the stakes are high, too. Little plays, these set-pieces are also verbal fencing matches, impromptu debates—games, as Catherine and Henry's encounter makes clearest, albeit with unspoken rules. One more analogy: in their plotted, patterned, performed quality, their precise architectonics and balancing of opposed units, the set-pieces of the early phase are the scenic equivalents of the Johnsonian sentence, the syntactic form most favored by the younger Austen. As such, they may be said to spread out not so much in time as in space; their quality is pictorial rather than narrative. They do not advance their respective plots so much as reveal existing attitudes and the tensions between them. Indeed, as a game fences itself off from "real life," drawing a temporal boundary around itself, so do these scenes seem to arrest the narratives to which they belong, sticking out from their surface like rocks in a stream.

This last observation returns us to the relevance of the set-piece to the temporal quality of relationships in the early novels. Yes, Elizabeth and Darcy's relationship changes, in a very important sense, as a result of the sudden changes in their feelings about each other. But in another, equally important sense, their relationship never changes. The reason these set-pieces are so important, and much of the reason they are so memorable, is that each defines, once and for all, a central relationship. That is why each occurs early in its respective novel: the set-piece was the younger Austen's way of "pictorially" representing a certain crucial dynamic that would remain unchanged and would carry through the rest of the novel. This principle is less fully true in the case of Elinor and Lucy—their relationship is less central—but in the other cases the picture we get in those scenes—lighthearted, satiric Henry and wide-eyed Catherine; wickedly ironic Elizabeth and imperturbably forensic Darcy, at glittering daggers drawn—is the one we retain even after the narrative is over. However much these relationships may change during the course of their novels, what matters more is what they intrinsically, eternally are.

Set-pieces, stasis, sudden shocks and shifts—feelings and relationships in the late novels could hardly be more different. If events in the early works occupy time the way beads occupy a string, events in the later ones occupy time the way salt occupies water, so that it scarcely makes sense even to distinguish between "events" and "time."[49] Everywhere we find psychological states in continual flux, as characters respond to changing circumstances, not with stubborn rigidity or helpless collapse, but by means of gradual adjustments of feeling. This principle is everywhere in *Mansfield Park*, from Fanny's slow, painful, carefully documented adjustment to her initial removal to the way she copes with the arrival of Mary, with her own emergence as an attractive and desired young woman, with the several shocks of her return to Portsmouth, and with just about every other change that comes her way. This ability effortfully to bring her feelings to a new state is precisely what underlies her resilience in accommodating herself to change. Nor are all these adjustments willed; some take her by surprise, especially those having to do with the Crawfords. In Portsmouth, she finds herself ("Here was another strange revolution of mind!") glad to receive a letter from Mary (326); she even finds herself beginning to feel affection for Henry just as he, to his great surprise, had once found that a similarly undiscerned shift in feeling had brought him to the condition of loving her. The prospect of another letter, from Edmund, surprises Fanny by evoking terror rather than delight, occasioning what we might regard as the novel's thematic statement about change both inner and outer: "She began to feel that she had not yet gone through all the changes of opinion and sentiment, which the progress of time and variation of circumstances occasion in this world of changes" (309).

Emma and *Persuasion* take place in this same world. *Persuasion*, as we said, is about grief, a psychological process that by its very nature involves gradual adjustment, as we see most clearly, if perhaps too quickly, in the case of Captain Benwick. But such adjustments also lie at the very center of the narrative, in the slow dance Anne and Wentworth do toward each other. The process is not symmetric: because

Anne has never stopped loving him, her feelings are really about his, and we learn of his through her constant attempts to divine them: "Her power with him was gone forever" (86), she first sees; then a little while later, "She understood him. He could not forgive her,—but he could not be unfeeling" (113); then later still, she finds him "turning to her and speaking with a glow, and yet a gentleness, which seemed almost restoring the past" (134), and so the gradual transformation and gradual discovery go until she reads the note in which he passionately professes his love.

Emma, by unsurprising contrast, seeks frequently to measure the state not of a young man's feelings for her, but of hers for him, Frank Churchill. After his first departure from Highbury: "Emma continued to entertain no doubt of her being in love. Her ideas only varied as to the how much. At first, she thought it was a good deal; and afterwards, but little" (217). Later, hearing the news of his imminent return, she is set to "weighing her own feelings, and trying to understand the degree of her agitation, which she rather thought was considerable" (250), but a chapter later "[a] very little quiet reflection was enough to satisfy [her] as to the nature of her agitation on hearing this news of Frank Churchill. She was soon convinced that it was not for herself she was feeling at all apprehensive or embarrassed; it was for him" (261). Here not only do we see feelings changing day by day and even hour by hour, we see them changing under their own self-scrutiny, a minuteness of analysis on Austen's part, and a frequency of it on her heroines', absolutely foreign to the early novels.

Fanny and Anne experience no sudden recognition-cum-transformation—not, like Elinor, because they have nothing to reform, but because, like Wordsworth and Coleridge in their first-person lyrics, they practice a continual reappraisal of feeling and experience and are thus continually changing. Emma is not quite so heroic as these two creepmice, but her transformation is every bit as profound. Critics have long noted that, unlike those of the early heroines, hers involves not one but a series of recognitions, the moment when the truth of her love for Knightley darts through her constituting only the final one.[50] But to reduce Emma's transformation to her several moments of repentance and recognition is to flatten what is in fact a comprehensive maturation of personality by fitting it to the pattern of the mere changes of consciousness experienced by the heroines of the early works. When we read, for example, in the novel's penultimate chapter, that Emma now feels that "[i]t would be a great pleasure to know Robert Martin" (389), we recognize that her transformation has involved not just an illumination of the mind, but an opening of the heart, a supplanting of snobbery by generosity and humility, a fundamental change of character that has been gradually, continually coming over her throughout the entire novel.

Because continuously evolving inner lives make for continuously evolving relationships, the major phase replaces the set-piece with what might be called the "serial scene." If Darcy were the one who wanted to enter the ministry and Elizabeth the one who disapproved, the two would have one cracking go at it, one fireworks display, in which their antagonistic positions were fully set out, and that would be the end of it (until Elizabeth broke down, perhaps, and confessed how wrong she had been). Instead, Edmund and Mary worry the question over and over, at different lengths, in different contexts, from different angles, with different degrees of levity or vexation, and with differently adjusted feelings and hopes: in the Sotherton chapel (75), during the walk in the wilderness (77ff.), at Mansfield manor (91ff.), at the Parsonage (200ff.), at the ball (230), and so forth. Comparable serial scenes in *Emma* include Emma and Knightley's long wrangle about the propriety of her behavior to those around her as well as Frank's many-chaptered, subtly shifting game of double meanings and pretend-flirtation with her and Jane. *Persuasion*, as we just noted, is at its core a serial scene writ large, that of Anne and Wentworth's many tentative encounters with each other. Like feelings, relationships in the late novels are in a constant state of reexamination and recalibration, with characters constantly repositioning themselves relative to one another.

That is why both feelings and relationships are often so hard to define. In the early novels, we always know where people stand with each other. But what *is* Emma's relationship with Frank? And what is it with Knightley: brother and sister? friends? lovers? Wordsworth raises the same question about his relationship with his former schoolteacher in the Matthew poems. In fact, the issue of such "ambiguous relationships" will be the subject of my chapter on the novel. Again, how many shades of uncertainty and mutual misunderstanding must we account for in characterizing Fanny's relationship with Edmund at any given moment, and how many different ones at the next? About Anne and Wentworth's we needn't undertake such an investigation—as we've seen, Anne does it for us.

It is no wonder that just as relationships in the late novels are so often ambiguous, feelings are so often, what they never are in the early works, ambivalent. And, as in the Romantic poets—for whom ambivalent feelings are their favorite feelings of all—they are incomparably stronger for being so.[51] That this is the case in *Persuasion* has been noted more than once, specifically in connection with Byron as well as Keats and Shelley.[52] Again and again, Anne's encounters with Wentworth plunge her into agonizingly mixed states of mind, "compounded of pleasure and pain" (113) or of "agitation, pain, pleasure, a something between delight and misery" (185), the parade example occurring at the Musgroves' lodgings in Bath, where, waiting for the chance to open her heart to Wentworth, she finds herself "deep in the happiness of such misery, or the misery of such happiness" (233). Fanny's ambivalences tend to cluster around Edmund's attraction to Mary, as jealousy fights against guilt and hope against hopelessness. As she listens to the account of his final conversation with Mary, one that has crushed his own hopes, she cannot help but feel both "pain" and "delight" (375) and be "almost sorry" to have made him speak at all (377). Emma expresses similar feelings not only with respect to Frank, but also after the proposal scene, as her love for Knightley conflicts with feelings of duty toward her father and guilt toward Harriet.

About feelings in general in the late novels as opposed to the early ones, we can say that they are not only far stronger for being conflicted and far deeper for being rooted in a denser matrix of personal history, but also far more various. The early novels work with the limited repertoire of emotions proper to the marriage plot: love, humiliation, dejection, hope, happiness. But the later novels, while still ostensibly presenting pictures of courtship, in fact de-emphasize the marriage plot to such an extent that it becomes merely the vehicle of narrative resolution, and generally a hasty resolution, at that. The later novels spend almost no time on what almost exclusively concerns the early ones: the conversations and events of the hero and heroine's courtship. In the first two, in fact, the hero and heroine do not even discover that they are lovers until the very end, and in the third, they do not rediscover it until then.[53] Instead, each of these novels opens itself to a broad range of social situations and psychological states, which is why each traverses such a broad range of feelings. To take only Fanny, and only the first volume of her work, we watch her experience loneliness, despondency, gratitude, shame, guilt, jealousy, self-pity, terror, and moral revulsion. The rest of her story adds other feelings, the stories of Emma and Anne, others still.

In all this, then—the slow shaping of the self in childhood and adolescence, the multifarious operations of memory, the continuous conquest of self-knowledge, the gradual evolution of feelings and minute adjustment of relationships—we see how central was Austen's discovery of time in giving rise to the incomparably greater psychological complexity of her later novels. And we also see how unmistakably that discovery bears the imprint, in its central, structuring logic as well as in so many of its particulars, of the Romantic poets, and especially of Wordsworth.

* * *

We can go still further in delineating the impact of Austen's new understanding of time on her ideas and her art. The conceptual landscape of the early novels is dominated by the abstract moral vocabulary Austen inherited from the eighteenth century: "pride" and "prejudice," "sense" and "sensibility." It is fallacious, of course, to see Elinor as personifying sense and Marianne sensibility (we are twice told of the latter's sense in the very first chapter), but it is not fallacious to see the novel as organizing itself around a struggle between those two faculties. Pride and prejudice, in their novel, are rather mutually reinforcing than antagonistic, but they remain dominant terms of analysis. Nor are these the only important abstractions. In *Sense and Sensibility*, both characters and narrator spend a great deal of time identifying the story's various single men as "amiable," "agreeable," or the reverse. *Pride and Prejudice* simply cannot be fully understood without a grasp of what Austen means by such terms as "gentlemanliness," "respectability," "elegance," "dignity," "grace," "cordiality," and "warmth" (not to mention "address," "countenance," "manner," "air," and "features"). A powerful categorizing intelligence is at work.

But by the late novels, Austen's mind has grown into a far different shape. To be sure, the earlier mode of analysis has not been discarded, but it has receded into the background. The very titles point to the change, the paired abstractions having been replaced by names that may be understood as signifying, not collections of fixed qualities, but fields of possibility. How will Mansfield Park change? And famously, "[w]hat will become of" Emma? A phrase worth pondering, that: not only "What will happen to Emma," but also, "What will develop from Emma?" and "What will Emma become?" (35).[54] Become, indeed: from an artist of being, of static characters and abstract qualities, Austen becomes that most "Romantic" of creators, an artist of becoming.[55]

We can see it in her language. The greater "subtlety and flexibility of Jane Austen's mature prose" has long been noted.[56] At its worst, the language of the early Austen can practically drive itself dizzy with its Johnsonian juggling of paired and tripled abstractions. After Willoughby concludes his impassioned confessional monologue, "Elinor made no answer. Her thoughts were silently fixed on the irreparable injury which too early an independence and its consequent habits of idleness, dissipation, and luxury, had made in the mind, the character, the happiness, of a man who, to every advantage of person and talents, united a disposition naturally open and honest, and a feeling, affectionate temper" (280).

The late language displays its freedom most fully in the rendering of speech. Nothing can compare to Miss Bates's free-associative monologues of broken fragments, but a comparable freedom from syntactic order is often essential to the reporting of Fanny's speech, as well. This is a heroine whose first words are "'no, no—not at all—no, thank you'" (14) and who responds to the news that it was Henry who had arranged for her brother's promotion with, "'Good Heaven! how very, very kind! Have you really—was it by *your* desire—I beg your pardon, but I am bewildered. Did Admiral Crawford apply?—how was it?—I am stupefied'" (247; emphasis in the original).[57] Comparable examples from Anne's speech are harder to find, since she does so little speaking at all, but they are not at all scarce in Austen's notation of what passes through her mind. A scene discussed above, Anne's first meeting with Wentworth, provides what has become the best-known example: "Her eye half met Captain Wentworth's; a bow, a curtsey passed; she heard his voice—he talked to Mary, said all that was right; said something to the Miss Musgroves, enough to mark an easy footing: the room seemed full—full of persons and voices—but a few minutes ended it" (84-85).

As these last two examples suggest, the greater syntactic freedom of the late novels overwhelmingly serves one particular purpose: the moment-by-moment registration of feeling.[58] And this attention to the flux of feeling points, as we will see, to a development of the very first importance, nothing less than a revolution in Austen's conception of both the mind and the moral life. For even as we see the late characters' feelings develop moment by moment, so, very often, do we see their thoughts simultaneously doing likewise, evolving in snatches of half-formed and provisional formulations as their feelings search for expression. Nothing could be more like the poetic practice of Wordsworth and Coleridge, and often also of Byron, than this.[59]

The early novels know no half-formed thoughts, no feelings groping to understand themselves. Indeed, as we just saw with Elinor, thought in the early Austen tends to crowd out feeling, the diction and syntax of categorization asserting itself even at moments of intense passion, as if the only valid responses were rational ones.[60] But observe Emma's soliloquy as she tries to determine the exact degree of her love for Frank: "'I do not find myself making use of the word *sacrifice*. . . . I do suspect that he is not really necessary to my happiness. So much the better. I certainly will not persuade myself to feel more than I do. I am quite enough in love. I should be sorry to be more. . . . *He* is undoubtedly very much in love—everything denotes it—very much in love indeed!—and when he comes again, if his affection continue, I must be on my guard not to encourage it'" (217). This is thought evolving on the page as feeling seeks to discover itself—indeed, it is feeling itself evolving before our eyes through the effort of bringing itself to consciousness.

To cite examples from *Persuasion* would be arbitrary, since much of the novel takes this form. One of the most prominent instances in *Mansfield Park* enables us to make a closer comparison between the early and late works, for it occurs in Edmund's long, tormented letter to Fanny about his prospects with Mary, a letter analogous in important ways to that of Darcy to Elizabeth. In each case, a young man speaks his mind at a moment of intense feeling, and because he is writing, speaks it in a way that enables him to monitor his thoughts as they take shape on the page. After a short introduction, Darcy's letter begins thus: "Two offenses of a very different nature, and by no means of equal magnitude, you last night laid to my charge" (162). The passage offers a fair sample of the forensic language in which the whole letter is couched as well as of the forensic structure by which it is governed. Feelings may be at stake, but feelings are not permitted to enter into the letter itself; Darcy even makes a point of assuring Elizabeth that "my investigations and decisions are not usually influenced by my hopes and fears" (163).

Edmund's letter could not be more different. To cite a passage from the middle of it:

> I cannot give her up, Fanny. She is the only woman in the world whom I could ever think of as a wife. If I did not believe that she had some regard for me, of course I should not say this, but I do believe it. I am convinced, that she is not without a decided preference. I have no jealousy of any individual. It is the influence of the fashionable world altogether that I am jealous of. It is the habits of wealth that I fear. Her ideas are not higher than her own fortune may warrant, but they are beyond what our incomes united could authorize. There is comfort, however, even here. I could better bear to lose her, because not rich enough, than because of my profession. (348)

What we have here is not a structured argument but a spontaneous outpouring of emotions: determination, desperation, hope, jealousy, fear, comfort. Indeed, very shortly after this, Edmund interrupts himself to say, "You have my thoughts exactly as they arise, my dear Fanny; perhaps they are some times contradictory, but it will not be a less faithful picture of my mind. Having once begun, it is a pleasure to me to tell you all I feel." "Perhaps they are some times contradictory"—the mind is not, at bottom, a rational instrument. "You have my thoughts" as "[I] tell you all I feel"—it is, instead, constituted by emotion, with thought merely the form feeling assumes so that it may see itself.

The resemblance to the Romantics could not, again, be greater, and the change from Austen's early work could not be more complete.[61] In the early phase, feeling is dictated by reason, even (or especially), as Darcy's letter reminds us, in the most important instances. Elizabeth misjudges Darcy, therefore she hates him. Once her mind changes, her heart changes too. That is why this revolution in Austen's conception of the mental life is a revolution in her conception of the moral life. The ethical doctrine at the center of her early novels is the idea that feeling can and ought to be shaped, controlled, and educated by thought, a doctrine to which the flawlessness of their plots, the mercilessness of their irony, and the supreme self-assurance of their narrators give the inevitability of a mathematical demonstration. The errors of the early heroines are errors of reason; that is why each of the early novels can pivot on a single moment of clarified understanding, a sudden recognition of wrong thinking that opens the way for right feeling. The heroine changes by changing her mind: once, decisively, and forever.

But the late heroines, as we have seen, change continuously, and not by examining their judgments, but by discovering their feelings. The only sudden recognition the late novels give us is Emma's, and what darts through her with the speed of an arrow has nothing to do with realizing that she has been thinking wrongly and everything to do with realizing that all along she has been feeling rightly, only she hasn't known it. Elizabeth, Marianne, and Catherine must reform their minds; Emma must make herself "acquainted with her own heart" (335). And it is only then—right feeling opening the way for right thinking—that "[s]he saw it all with a clearness which had never blessed her before. How improperly had she been acting by Harriet! . . . What blindness, what madness, had led her on!" (335-336). In *Mansfield Park* and *Persuasion* the way is opened to the lovers' union in precisely the same fashion, only there it is the heroes who at last become acquainted with their hearts.

Does this mean that the mature Austen believes, "Romantically," that feeling, desire, is always right?[62] Clearly not, in the sense that feeling must still be guided by principle. But it is true that none of the late heroines has to sacrifice her feelings or alter her desires, at least with respect to the man she loves.[63] Other late characters clearly do have improper feelings and desires, but such matters no longer concern Austen much. The author of *Pride and Prejudice*, *Sense and Sensibility*, and *Northanger Abbey* gave her opinion very decidedly for so young a person, but the mature Austen is no longer an artist of what ought to be, but of what is. She has become an explorer of emotions, an observer of fields of relational possibility, a connoisseur of process. Twelve years after *Susan*, she has turned her attention to the changing feelings of the mind.

* * *

One final issue. With her new belief in change, Austen faced a crucial narratological problem. How to bring to closure narratives that embody the ever-evolving nature of all things human? The answer she found, as has been pointed out in various ways, was to not bring them to full closure, to resist closure.[64] This resistance takes three forms: the creation of interpretive confusion about how properly to judge characters and actions; the leaving open of narrative possibilities subsequent to the end of the action proper and/or the acknowledgment that possibilities have been left unexplored within it; and the construction of endings that create readerly dissatisfaction, the sense of the right outcome not having been achieved.[65]

The first of these figures only in *Mansfield Park* and *Emma* and has already been well explored in the critical literature. From the beginning, *Mansfield Park* has inspired a sharply polarized debate about whether its heroine embodies Austen's moral ideals or rather an infantile prudery that we are meant to criticize—a confusion related to the question of whom she and Edmund should marry and thus to those other two forms of resistance, as we will see in a moment. As for *Emma*, the interpretive confusion it generates may be represented by Trilling's observation that "[w]e never know where to have it," never know "what it is up to"—a fact we already glanced at in noting that the novel contains hardly a single character whose moral worth can be determined with certainty.[66]

The second form of resistance, the opening of alternative, unexplored narrative possibilities, is most obviously present in *Mansfield Park*, where Austen not only tells us, around the middle of the novel, that Henry's suit would have been successful had Fanny's heart not been elsewhere engaged, but also, at the novel's end, that it would have been anyway, especially once Edmund had married Mary. This news comes in the very last chapter, as Austen spins out the subsequent fates of her characters, and represents a stunning last-minute bifurcation of the plot: had Henry not eloped with Maria, everything would have turned out differently. And that does mean everything, since—to return to the issue of interpretive confusion—such an outcome would have required us to judge everything in the novel in a very different light. Of course, even the way things did turn out is left somewhat open, Austen famously "abstain[ing] from dates" (387) so that we may each imagine for ourselves the length of time required for the transfer of Edmund's affections from Mary to Fanny—a gesture of incompleteness explicitly related to the indeterminacies of emotional process. *Persuasion* achieves this kind of incompleteness by carrying its story up to the present, and in a sly narratological turn, leaving one of its possibilities to be worked out in the "future." Mrs. Clay and William Walter Elliot have run off together, "[a]nd it is now a doubtful point whether his cunning or hers may finally carry the day; whether . . . he may not be wheedled and caressed at last into making her the wife of Sir William" (252). We have already glanced at a different kind of unexplored possibility in *Persuasion*: that the novel leads us to expect that Anne will expose William Walter Elliot's scandalous behavior toward Mrs. Smith, only to drop that narrative line as quickly as it had developed it.

This kind of resistance to closure, like the others, is most subtle in *Emma*, the most highly wrought and architecturally perfect of Austen's late, indeed of all her novels. The first form it takes can be expressed by a question we looked at before, that of "what will become of [Emma]." As with none of her other heroines, Austen leaves us with the sense that even at the end of her novel, Emma still has a great deal of "becoming" to do—that *this* story is not the end of *her* story.[67] It is a sense reinforced by the fact that she has yet to settle in her permanent home when the novel ends. Neither, for that matter, have Frank and Jane, nor has it all been decided whether Emma or Mrs. Elton will play the leading role in the future life of their community. Quite likely, they will continue to struggle over it, just as we imagine Emma and Knightley continuing to struggle over Emma's behavior. But the novel's most compelling unexplored possibility is Jane herself. Any number of critics have testified to what most readers surely feel, the continually evoked, never fulfilled longing to see Emma become better friends, dear friends, with this beautiful and mysterious and fascinating young woman—a longing surely related to our desire to become "dear friends" with her, intimate with her, to know something, finally, about her. She is the Austen reader's great unrequited love.

As for the final form of resistance to closure, the arousal of feelings of dissatisfaction as to the correct outcome not having been achieved, I need hardly dwell on it in the case of *Mansfield Park*.[68] There is surely scarcely a reader who would not have preferred to see Fanny marry Henry and Edmund Mary, at least the first time through the novel. Not only did Austen clearly connive at this reaction, she seems to have shared it, at least in part. The bifurcated ending we just looked at suggests as much, that Austen's own heart tugged her at least part of the way in the other direction, as does her very rare use of the word "I" in the earlier of the two passages I alluded to in that connection: "although there doubtless are such incomparable young ladies of eighteen . . . as are never to be persuaded into love against their judgment . . . I have no inclination to believe Fanny one of them" (193).[69] In *Persuasion*, dissatisfaction of a different sort inheres in the sense that even if Anne and Wentworth have found each other, justice has scarcely otherwise been done, and that the world in which they will have to live is soured and bleak.[70] I will return to this point in my chapter on the novel; suffice it to note for now that the future of *Persuasion* is one in which Sir Walter will remain unshaken in his icy pride and vanity until his death, at which point Kellynch will be inherited by William Walter Elliot—and possibly, Mrs. Clay.

In *Emma*, we can hear the dark notes of the ending only if our ear has been properly tuned by the rest of the narrative. For who, at first glance, could see any reason for discontent in "the perfect happiness of the union" (396)? The only problem is that all three of those key words—"perfect," "happiness," and "union"—have been so ironized by the novel's handling of them as to make it a matter of very grave doubt whether they are not rather to be avoided.[71] The "union" of that last sentence echoes the language of the first, where "Emma Woodhouse, handsome, clever, and rich, with a comfortable home and a happy disposition, seemed to unite some of the best blessings of existence" (7). This first union, as we have seen, is in fact the start of all her woe: the vanity of being handsome, the willfulness of being rich and therefore independent, and the blind certainty of being clever, each trait the worse for being "united" to the others.

"Happiness" and its derivatives are words that—aside from also being compromised right from the beginning by that talk of Emma's "happy disposition"—belong, above all, to Miss Bates and Mrs. Elton. "Happy," for the first, is the slogan of her diminished, dependent existence. "And yet she was a happy woman," we are told upon first meeting her (20), and again, that "[s]he is a standing lesson in how to be happy" (210). This may sound admirable, but what is it but a pitiable making-do that forces her to lower her expectations to the level of her circumstances, no matter how far her circumstances have sunk? For Mrs. Elton, "happiness" is the name of the misery and false gaiety she inflicts on herself and everyone around her, with her "apparatus of happiness" at Donwell Abbey (296) and her outing to Box Hill, where, after the arrangements have been made, "nothing was wanting but to be happy when they got there" (303). Of the kind of happiness capable of being produced by the joint efforts of these two, by Miss Bates's abasement and Mrs. Elton's schemes, we get a fine sample in this picture of Jane after she accepts the position as governess: "She is as low as possible," says her aunt. "To look at her, nobody would think how delighted and happy she is to have secured a situation" (312).

As for "perfect," no word in the book is as insistently or emphatically undermined.[72] Of the dozens of times it or its derivatives appear,

almost none is without qualification or irony, the leading example being the conundrum devised by Mr. Weston, that moral imbecile, on the
very heels of Emma's cruelty to Miss Bates: "What two letters of the
alphabet are there, that express perfection? . . . M. and A.—Em—ma"
(306). To which Knightley gravely replies: "*Perfection* should not
have come quite so soon" [emphasis in the original]. No—for a novelist of process, perfection can never come late enough. "[P]ictures of
perfection," Austen wrote at around this time, "make me sick &
wicked."[73] Wicked indeed is the game Austen plays with us throughout
the novel, flattering us with our ability to see past Emma's blindness
about Elton only the better to rub our noses in our own blindness about
Frank, conjuring seductive appearances that continually give way to
hidden, hinted-at realities of a less pleasant nature. The logic of the
novel's language makes its final statement into just such another happy
deception, one that leaves us with a story in which nothing gets settled,
an apparently "perfect" work that terminates in nothing but loose ends,
a novel that refuses to stop playing games with us.

    In short, like poetry of Wordsworth and Coleridge, the novels of the
major phase are committed to notions of the ambiguous and continually evolving nature of human consciousness and human relationships,
as well as to the use of exploratory and opened-ended processes in their
own artistic construction. Indeed, in the major phase, as I noted above,
the center of Austen's attention has shifted away from the courtship
plot altogether. The narrative machinery that brings the lovers together,
then separates them and bars their way to each other, which in the early
novels occupies so much space, is in *Mansfield Park* and *Emma* entirely absent and in *Persuasion* relatively incidental.[74] The marriage
plot now functions merely as the framework for deeper explorations
from which the final unions emerge almost as epiphenomena. As my
final three chapters will seek to explain, each of the novels of the major
phase focuses its attention on one particular emotional structure or
mode of relatedness that seized Austen's imagination as essential to the
story she wished to tell. Or rather, the story she wished to tell seems in

Critical Insights

each case to have been constructed, in part, so as to enable her to explore that particular structure or mode. Again and again we can feel her improvising with language and emotions alike, groping her way toward new recognitions and new powers. The precocious certainties of the early phase have given way to the maturer wisdom of doubt.

Notes

1. *Letters*, p. 99 (8-11 April 1805).

2. John Wiltshire, "*Mansfield Park, Emma,* and *Persuasion,*" in *Cambridge Companion to Jane Austen*, p. 58.

3. John Wiltshire, *Jane Austen and the Body* (Cambridge: Cambridge University Press, 1992), p. 9.

4. Jane Nardin, "Jane Austen and the Problem of Leisure," in *Jane Austen in a Social Context*, p. 123.

5. Mary Poovey, *The Proper Lady and the Woman Writer* (Chicago: University of Chicago Press, 1984), pp. 208-209.

6. Litz, *Jane Austen*, p. 153.

7. Marilyn Butler, *Jane Austen and the War of Ideas* (Oxford: Clarendon Press, 1975), p. 123.

8. Warren Roberts, *Jane Austen and the French Revolution* (New York: St. Martin's, 1979), p. 105. To these more recent characterizations we can add the inaugural ones of Austen-Leigh—"a greater refinement of taste, a more nice sense of propriety, a deeper insight into the delicate anatomy of the human heart" (*Persuasion*, p. 374)—and Simpson—"in the former set the art is simpler, less concealed, more easily discovered: in the latter, both passion and humour are rather more developed" (in *Jane Austen: The Critical Heritage*, ed. Southam, pp. 253-254).

9. Although the ensuing discussion will cite specific works as points of reference, I will not be discussing poets or poems at any length. Apart from considerations of space, the characteristics in question are too well known as elements of Wordsworth's or the other poets' work to require additional demonstration, and the kind of influence I am considering here (as opposed to in my later chapters) is not such as is visible in one-to-one correspondences—allusions, echoes, rewritings—but rather involves the absorption of fundamental orientations.

10. Whether this also makes them "Romantic" I will leave the reader to decide, being anxious, for reasons I explained in the previous chapter (see notes 17 and 18), to avoid that term.

11. In making this argument, I will be drawing my lines of classification athwart

those of Julia Prewitt Brown and Susan Morgan, who have articulated two of the most valuable taxonomies of Austen's work. Brown, focusing on narrative structure, divides the novels into works of ironic comedy, *Northanger Abbey, Pride and Prejudice*, and *Emma*, and works of satiric realism, *Sense and Sensibility, Mansfield Park*, and *Persuasion*, identifying the former with the eighteenth century, the latter with the nineteenth (*Jane Austen's Novels*, pp. 37-45). I have no quarrel with this classificatory scheme, not even with Brown's assignment of each novel to its respective century, not only because she clearly does not mean us to take her temporal classifications literally (*Emma* is of course not literally a work of the eighteenth century) but also because her criteria relate not to the kinds of questions I will be taking up, but to unconnected matters of social setting and narrative dynamics (pp. 38-39). Morgan, focusing on modes of cognitive development, divides the novels into stories of crisis, *Northanger Abbey, Pride and Prejudice*, and *Emma*, and stories of passage, *Mansfield Park* and *Persuasion. Sense and Sensibility* splits between the two categories: Marianne's story is one of crisis, Elinor's one of passage (*In the Meantime*, pp. 7-8). Again, I have no quarrel with this. Still, it is worth noting that both Brown's and, to a slightly lesser extent, Morgan's groupings differ from mine with respect to the same two novels, *Sense and Sensibility* and *Emma*. These are indeed the two that present the most difficulty in seeing Austen's earlier work as uninfluenced by the Romantic poets and her later work as decisively shaped by them. *Sense and Sensibility*, to a cursory glance, does seem to present "Romantic" characteristics, while *Emma* seems to present few or none. I will accordingly focus on these two works whenever possible in the ensuing discussion.

12. The handling of nature in the late works has been discussed mainly in connection with *Persuasion*, though also occasionally with *Mansfield Park*. See chapter 1, note 15.

13. Jane Austen, *Sense and Sensibility* (London: Penguin, 1995), p. 85 (hereafter cited parenthetically).

14. Jane Austen, *Pride and Prejudice* (London: Penguin, 1996), p. 129 (hereafter cited parenthetically).

15. Jane Austen, *Persuasion* (London: Penguin, 1965), p. 107 (hereafter cited parenthetically).

16. Litz, "*Persuasion*: Forms of Estrangement," in *Bicentenary Essays*, p. 228.

17. As discussed, classically, in M. H. Abrams's "Structure and Style in the Greater Romantic Lyric" (in *From Sensibility to Romanticism*, ed. Frederick W. Hilles and Harold Bloom [New York: Oxford University Press, 1965], pp. 527-560). This is not to say that this or any scene in Austen reproduces the structure or possesses all the features of Abrams's model. But by the same token, many of Wordsworth and Coleridge's nature poems that also do not fully fit the model exhibit the dialectic in question, which is indeed fundamental to their approach to the perception of nature.

18. Litz, *Jane Austen*, p. 153. See also his "*Persuasion*: Forms of Estrangement," p. 228.

19. See especially ll. 91-99 and 146-166.

20. Though, as Litz points out, it shows a much greater sensitivity toward the natural world than any of the early novels, working the annual cycle into the fabric of the

narrative by keying Emma's moods to the passage of the seasons, so that, to take only the most obvious examples, her frosty reception of Elton's proposal accords with the weather outside the carriage, while she and Knightley declare their mutual warmth on a midsummer afternoon (*Jane Austen*, p. 151).

21. Much of Wordsworth's most important poetry of place not having yet been published, the most obvious example available to Austen would have been "The Brothers," in which this theme is central. It is also essential to "Tintern Abbey," of course, as well as to Coleridge's peroration in "Frost at Midnight" ("For I was reared . . . ," ll. 51ff.). In Scott's verse, the theme receives its most emphatic expression in the title character of "The Lady of the Lake"; in his early fiction, in the figure of Brown in *Guy Mannering*, especially upon that character's return to Ellengowan at the start of vol. III. But it is also an idea that, in an expanded form, informs virtually everything Scott wrote: that national character—whether of Highlanders, Lowlanders, or Englishmen—is shaped by the land in which it took root.

Wiltshire, as I noted above, also mentions the idea of place as among the differences between the first and last three novels ("*Mansfield Park*, *Emma*, and *Persuasion*," p. 58). For the view that character is formed in relation to place in all six of the novels, see Ann Banfield, "The Influence of Place: Jane Austen and the Novel of Social Consciousness," in *Jane Austen in a Social Context*, pp. 28-48.

22. Byron expresses the sentiment in two early poems on his school days, "On a Distant View of the Village and School of Harrow on the Hill, 1806," and "Lines Written Beneath an Elm in the Churchyard of Harrow," but his fullest expression of it is negative: Childe Harold's self-tormenting self-exile from his native land.

23. For Elinor's love for Marianne as the emotional center of the novel, see Eve Sedgwick, "Jane Austen and the Masturbating Girl," *Critical Inquiry* 17 (1991): 818-837; and George E. Haggerty, *Unnatural Affections* (Bloomington: Indiana University Press, 1998), pp. 72-87. The passage in question reads, "among the merits and the happiness of Elinor and Marianne, let it not be ranked as the least considerable, that though sisters, and living almost within sight of each other, they could live without disagreement between themselves, or producing coolness between their husbands" (322-323).

24. Gene W. Ruoff discusses the tendency of the last three novels to be about "coming home," as opposed to going out ("The Sense of a Beginning: *Mansfield Park* and Romantic Narrative," *Wordsworth Circle* 10 [1979]: 184-185).

25. Austen did not know *The Prelude*, of course, but she would have known any number of Wordsworth's other poems that show the self as formed during childhood, most obviously the Intimations Ode and "My heart leaps up when I behold," which makes explicit the doctrine that "The Child is father to the Man."

26. In Ruoff's words, "Elizabeth seems in some peculiar fashion to have been born yesterday" ("Sense of a Beginning," p. 178).

27. Wiltshire traces this shaping of character by upbringing in the cases of Fanny and Mary ("*Mansfield Park*, *Emma*, and *Persuasion*," pp. 59-66).

28. That Anne was her mother's favorite is implied by the fact that she becomes Lady Russell's, her mother's closest friend's, but even more by the fact that "it was only in Anne that [Lady Russell] could fancy the mother to revive again," for it is a rule in Austen's world that a parent will love the child most like them, as Mr. Bennet does

Elizabeth, Mrs. Bennet Lydia, Mrs. Dashwood Marianne, and Anne's own father his Elizabeth.

29. The novel's opening also sketches the histories of several other characters in such a way as to show that their present patterns of behavior are the outgrowth, if not of their childhoods, then still of their pasts. Mr. Weston and Miss Taylor/Mrs. Weston are thus characterized in chapter 2, Miss Bates in chapter 3. Emma's argument to Knightley about Frank in chapter 18 rests on the same logic.

30. Any number of examples may be cited, including "We are Seven," "The Idiot Boy," "Anecdote for Fathers," "Lucy Gray," "Alice Fell," and Coleridge's "The Foster Mother's Tale."

31. Morgan, *In the Meantime*, p. 134.

32. Another, silent example is the gap between the reception of Collins's initial letter, dated 15 October, and his arrival a month later on 18 November, an interval indicated by nothing more than a paragraph break. It took me many years to notice just how long this gap is, probably because, as is not the case with these other two intervals, it does occur at a point in the plot when something important is supposedly in progress, Jane's romance with Bingley. Nevertheless, this interval, too, remains blank, devoid of development.

33. Two peripheral figures, Mr. Norris and Dr. Grant, die during the course of *Mansfield Park*. It is no coincidence that Mrs. Churchill's death precipitates the cascade of changes that results in the novel's culminating unions by releasing a whole raft of characters from the situations in which they had been frozen: Frank and Jane, Emma and Knightley, Harriet and Robert Martin—even, in a comic touch, Mr. Churchill himself, finally able to pay his very old friend the visit he had been promising these ten years.

34. I am indebted to Karl Kroeber for this insight.

35. Lionel Trilling, "*Emma*," *Encounter* 8 (June 1957): 53.

36. The same is also true, more massively and emphatically than ever before in Austen's work, for *Sanditon*.

37. For a different view, see Trumpener, *Bardic Nationalism*, p. 179, who argues that his experiences in Antigua leave Sir Thomas a fundamentally changed man.

38. Particularly illustrative is his remark to Fanny during their dialogue about Henry's proposal, where he rails against the "willfulness of temper, self-conceit and . . . tendency to that independence of spirit, which prevails so much in modern days, even in young women" (262-263).

39. For a reading of this visit that sees it as implicitly critical of Emma's contempt for the poor, see Brown, *Jane Austen's Novels*, pp. 114-117.

40. This development is clearly related to Wiltshire's observation that the later novels undertake a much broader and deeper social critique (see note 2 above). Mary Evans, arguing that Austen criticizes capitalist morality in all her novels, notes that they all present pictures of desperate or potentially desperate financial circumstances (*Jane Austen and the State* [London: Tavistock Publications, 1987], pp. 4-7). (For a similar view, see Judith Lowder Newton's reading of *Pride and Prejudice* in *Women, Power, and Subversion: Social Strategies in British Fiction, 1778-1869* [Athens: University of Georgia Press, 1981], pp. 55-85.) But there is an important difference between a des-

perate situation and one that is merely potentially so. It is worth noting in this connection that while all three of Brown's "ironic comedies" maintained their lightness of tone by shielding their heroines from financial pressures, *Pride and Prejudice* and *Northanger Abbey* simply wave those pressures away (her mother may worry about the future, but Elizabeth doesn't, and neither does the narrator), whereas in *Emma* the importance of money is confronted squarely, the heroine simply being fortunate enough to have a lot of it.

41. *Lady Susan/The Watsons/Sanditon*, p. 168.

42. I regard Marianne's story as *Sense and Sensibility*'s principal narrative line, with Elinor present mainly to provide contrast and a point of view.

43. *Rambler* 41, *The Yale Edition of the Works of Samuel Johnson*, 16 vols., ed. W. J. Bate (New Haven: Yale University Press, 1969), III:223.

44. For a discussion of the difference between the Johnsonian and Wordsworthian conceptions of memory very much along these lines, see Margery Sabin, *English Romanticism and the French Tradition* (Cambridge, Mass.: Harvard University Press, 1976), pp. 78-80.

45. Stuart M. Tave provides the most extensive analysis heretofore of the theme of memory in *Mansfield Park*, primarily comparing Fanny's strong memory to the Crawfords' weak ones (*Some Words of Jane Austen* [Chicago: University of Chicago Press, 1973], pp. 194-204). For other discussions, see my chapter on the novel.

46. "The Two April Mornings" presents a particularly complex intertwining of past and present moments through the uniting power of memory. In a striking effect not dissimilar from what we see here, Matthew recollects how, coming upon his daughter's grave some time after her death, he "loved her more./ For so it seemed, than till that day/ [he] e'er had loved before" (ll. 38-40). The key to this striking statement seems to be the fact that Matthew had come upon the grave inadvertently; as in Fanny's experience with her mother, memory acts the more powerfully when acting unexpectedly.

47. In one of Wordsworth's most striking images of the power of memory over the body—its physical dwelling within it—the priest says of James that "often, rising from his bed at night,/ He in his sleep would walk about, and sleeping/ He sought his brother Leonard" (ll. 351-353).

48. Austen is driving home here the closeness of the word "feeling"'s two senses, just as Wordsworth, in Karl Kroeber's account, "prefers the word 'feeling' to 'emotion,' in part because he wants to exploit the dual relevance of 'feeling,' which by its ambiguity emphasizes the inseparableness of emotion and sensation" (*Romantic Landscape Vision* [Madison: University of Wisconsin Press, 1975], p. 35).

49. As Ruoff puts it in connection with *Mansfield Park*, "Life is continuous, without sharply demarcated beginnings and endings; revelations are not sudden, and genuine turning points are not dramatically vivid" ("Sense of a Beginning," p. 181). Thus, "[i]n place of a mode of romance that had enhanced dramatic occurrences—first meetings, flirtations, misapprehensions, quarrels, and conquests—we must substitute one that exemplifies continuity of feeling, the growth of emotion so slow that its very stages are virtually undetectable" (p. 183).

50. Litz notes that Emma's reformation occupies the entire course of the novel, contrasting it to Elizabeth Bennet's (*Jane Austen*, pp. 133-134), while Brown remarks that

"Emma has had three enlightenments, and we expect that she will experience more" (p. 123).

51. In Karl Kroeber's analysis, "[f]or the romantics, the highest human achievement is to achieve and sustain intensely contradictory feelings" (*Ecological Literary Criticism* [New York: Columbia University Press, 1994] p. 5). Examples from Wordsworth include the "aching joys" of "Tintern Abbey" (l. 84), the "discontent/ Of pleasure" of "To the Daisy" (ll. 2-3), and "That sweet mood when pleasant thoughts/ Bring sad thoughts to the mind" of "Lines Written in Early Spring" (ll. 3-4); from Coleridge, the disposition of Genevieve in "Love," who "Loves me best, whene'er I sing/ The songs that make her grieve" (ll. 19-20); from Scott, his claim that "When, musing on companions gone,/ We doubly feel ourselves alone,/ Something, my friend, we yet may gain;/ There is a pleasure in this pain" (*Marmion*, Introduction to canto II). For Byronic instances, see the following note.

52. For Byron, see Knox-Shaw, "*Persuasion*, Byron, and the Turkish Tale," p. 69, who gives examples of "feelings that simultaneously smart and enchant." For Keats and Shelley, see Nina Auerbach, *Romantic Imprisonment* (New York: Columbia University Press, 1985), p. 54.

53. As Ruoff notes of *Mansfield Park*, "[I]n conventional terms Edmund begins to love Fanny three pages from the end of the story—so much, the novel tells us, for those conventional terms" ("Sense of a Beginning," p. 185).

54. Austen's intended title for *Persuasion*, *The Elliots*, also fits this model, especially when understood as referring not just to the nuclear family of Sir Walter and his daughters, but, as the opening paragraph makes clear it should be, to the family conceived of as a lineage. *Catherine*, her title for *Northanger Abbey*, is clearly a parody of such titles as "Cecilia, or Camilla, or Belinda" (34) rather than a field-of-possibility title like *Emma*.

55. See Peckham, "Toward a Theory of Romanticism" in *Triumph of Romanticism*. See also Peter Thorslev, "German Romantic Idealism," in *Cambridge Companion to British Romanticism*, who remarks that for Wordsworth and Hegel, to modify Pope, "Whatever's about to be is right" (p. 82).

56. Butler, *Jane Austen and the War of Ideas*, p. 261. Butler cites studies by Howard Babb (*Jane Austen's Novels: The Fabric of Dialogue*), K. C. Phillips (*Jane Austen's English*), Kroeber (*Styles in Fictional Structure*), and Page (*The Language of Jane Austen*).

57. In "The Two Voices of Fanny Price," Moler notes how inarticulate Fanny is in the face of passion (*Jane Austen: Bicentenary Essays*, pp. 172-179). In this "schoolgirlish" voice, among other things, "sentences are often loosely structured. Thought is lost and caught up with by means of repetition, left incomplete, revised in mid-sentence" (p. 175).

58. Knox-Shaw speaks of "[a]n unusually direct registration of thought and emotion" in *Persuasion*, noting that Anne's feelings "are given comparatively raw, and seem to belong to the moment" ("*Persuasion*, Byron, and the Turkish Tale," p. 53).

59. As Geoffrey Hartman puts it in reference to Wordsworth, "here is a man whose mind moves as he writes, who thinks aloud in verse" (*Wordsworth's Poetry: 1787-1814* [New Haven: Yale University Press, 1964], p. 209). In "Nature and the Human-

---

ization of Self in Wordsworth," Hartman further remarks that Wordsworth's was a radically new "consciousness of consciousness," for he shows us feeling moving in "natural rather than fictionally condensed time" (in *English Romantic Poets*, ed. M. H. Abrams [2nd ed.; New York: Oxford University Press, 1975], p. 125). In Kroeber's formulation, Wordsworth's "attitude toward language is apparent in his characteristically long sentences of loose syntactic structure, which permit development of thought, expansive treatment of emotion, and—above all—a fluid interplaying of perceptual fact with mental fancy" (*Romantic Landscape Vision*, p. 128). Hartman and Kroeber clearly have in mind such explicitly introspective first-person poems as "Tintern Abbey," "Resolution and Independence," and the Intimations Ode (as well as *The Prelude*), to which we can of course add Coleridge's conversation poems, but some of the same characteristics—thought moving in real time as emotion finds itself through language—can be seen in such Wordsworthian "dramatic monologues" as "The Complaint of the Forsaken Indian Woman," "The Affliction of Margaret—," and "The Emigrant Mother." For Byron, see Jerome J. McGann, "On Reading Childe Harold's Pilgrimage," where McGann discusses how the poem's tonal fluctuations trace the moment-by-moment reactions of the poet's mind (in *Critical Essays on Lord Byron*, ed. Robert F. Gleckner [New York: Maxwell Macmillan International, 1991], pp. 33-36).

60. As Knox-Shaw notes, "Elinor's feelings are mediated to the reader through the measured language of the narrator, or frequently through a reflective kind of self-report" (*"Persuasion*, Byron, and the Turkish Tale," p. 53).

61. According to Kroeber, all six canonical Romantic poets "tended to regard thought as constituted of emotions" (*Ecological Literary Criticism*, p. 5).

62. Mary Poovey, as I mentioned above, does indeed see the late novels as insisting more on the claims of desire (see note 5). Knox-Shaw, citing Thomas Lockwood, argues that "there is truth in his contention that Jane Austen exposes the chasm that separates reason from the life of feeling in *Persuasion*, setting their respective claims at jar" (*"Persuasion*, Byron, and the Turkish Tale," p. 53).

63. Fanny must surrender her desires in nearly every other respect, as I will discuss in detail in my chapter on *Mansfield Park*, but that she must do so is presented as a deplorable consequence of the nature of the novel's social world, not as something endorsed by Austen as ethically desirable. As for Emma, it is not her feelings that are wrong but her imagination; if anything, as Trilling notes, her feelings tend to set her right after she has seen what her imagination has led her into (*"Emma,"* p. 55). And as for her desires—again, it is a matter of discovering what they are rather than what they ought to be.

64. Roger Sales notes that all three novels have unresolved endings (*Jane Austen and the Representation of Regency England* [London: Routledge, 1994], p. xxi). For discussions of individual novels, see below. For the view that all six of the novels resist closure, see Richard Handler and Daniel Segal, *Jane Austen and the Fiction of Culture* (2nd ed.; Lanham, Md.: Rowman and Littlefield, 1999), pp. 130-134, who argue that all of them call into question any one construction of reality by characters or author; Robin Grove, "Austen's Ambiguous Conclusions," in *Jane Austen*, ed. Bloom, pp. 179-190, who claims that, contrary to popular opinion, Austen never takes clear moral positions, that her endings are always qualified or ironic or self-conscious; and also, of

course, D. A. Miller, *Narrative and Its Discontents: Problems of Closure in the Traditional Novel* (Princeton: Princeton University Press, 1982), pp. 3-106.

65. None of the early novels exhibits any of these forms of resistance to closure, with one obvious exception. The forced marriage of Marianne to Brandon at the end of *Sense and Sensibility* arouses as much readerly dissatisfaction as does the marriage of Fanny to Edmund. But by the same token it serves to point out the difference between the early and late works. While the late Austen goes out of her way to incite questions about the ending of *Mansfield Park*, as we will soon see, the younger one does her best to shove the ending of *Sense and Sensibility* down our throats. Austen deliberately designed *Mansfield Park* to create interpretive indeterminacy, but *Sense and Sensibility*, her weakest novel in quite a number of ways, simply seems to have gotten away from her. The moral implicit in its ending—and none of her other novels comes close to being as didactic—is at odds with the readerly emotions and desires that had been aroused up to that point. To use terms I developed in the previous chapter, while Austen loved Marianne, she only esteemed Elinor, and so while the novel quite effectively makes us love Marianne as well, makes us wish to see her as happy at the end of the novel as she had once been with Willoughby, it does not move us to assent to the triumph of Elinor's way of being in the world. Our minds may be convinced, but our hearts aren't persuaded—just as is the case with Marianne herself. (For a different discussion of the problem of closure in the novel, see Laura Mooneyham White, "Jane Austen and the Marriage Plot: Questions of Persistence," in *Jane Austen and the Discourses of Feminism*, pp. 77-78.)

66. Trilling, "*Emma*," p. 51.

67. Along these lines, Claudia L. Johnson argues that Emma is "*not* fully contained within the grid imposed by the courtship plot" (*Equivocal Beings* [Chicago: University of Chicago Press, 1988], p. 195; emphasis in the original), while Brown notes that Emma's dialectical relationships—with herself, with Knightley, and with Highbury—never move to "the death of total resolution" (p. 106).

68. A feeling so widespread in the critical literature as to make particular citation arbitrary. Even George Levine, who believes the novel to be teleological, acknowledges that the ironies of the happy ending represent a tug against telos (*Darwin and the Novelists* [Cambridge, Mass.: Harvard University Press, 1989], p. 69), while Ruth Bernard Yeazell suggests that even Fanny's final happiness is meant to be taken ironically, as a "fiction" (*Fictions of Modesty* [Chicago: University of Chicago Press, 1991], p. 168).

69. We find the same apparent ambivalence and same rare appearance of the first-person pronoun in another passage that bespeaks the possibility of Fanny's ultimate attachment to Henry. Mortified at running into her vulgar father on their walk through Portsmouth, Fanny laments that Henry will undoubtedly "soon give her up, and cease to have the smallest inclination for the match; and yet, though she had been so much wanting his affection to be cured, this was a sort of cure that would be almost as bad as the complaint; and I believe, there is scarcely a young lady in the united kingdoms, who would not rather put up with the misfortune of being sought by a clever, agreeable man, than have him driven away by the vulgarity of her nearest relations" (p. 333).

70. For an extensive discussion of this negativity, see Brown, *Jane Austen's Novels*, pp. 127-150.

71. Swingle, though arguing that this famous final phrase should be taken without irony, sees the ending as "a sort of miracle": "We see a fragile construct, which our sense of the laws of life (at least the novel's laws of life) tells us should not be able to exist, but it is existing" ("Perfect Happiness of the Union," p. 318).

72. For other discussions of the notion of perfection in *Emma*, see Joseph Litvak, "Reading Characters: Self, Society, and Text in *Emma*," in *Jane Austen's Emma*, ed. Harold Bloom (New York: Chelsea House, 1987), p. 134, and Tave, *Some Words of Jane Austen*, p. 241.

73. *Letters*, p. 335 (23 March 1817).

74. Ruoff makes this point about *Mansfield Park* ("Sense of a Beginning," pp. 184-185).

Works Cited

Abrams, M. H. "Structure and Style in the Greater Romantic Lyric." In Frederick W. Hilles and Harold Bloom, eds., *From Sensibility to Romanticism*, pp. 527-560. New York: Oxford, 1965.

Auerbach, Nina. *Romantic Imprisonment*. New York: Columbia University Press, 1985.

Austen, Jane. *Emma*. London: Penguin, 1996.

——————. *Lady Susan/The Watsons/Sanditon*. London: Penguin, 1974.

——————. *Mansfield Park*. London: Penguin, 1996.

——————. *Northanger Abbey*. London: Penguin, 1995.

——————. *Sense and Sensibility*. London: Penguin, 1995.

——————. *Persuasion*. London: Penguin, 1965.

——————. *Pride and Prejudice*. London: Penguin, 1996.

Banfield, Ann. "The Influence of Place: Jane Austen and the Novel of Social Consciousness." In David Monaghan, ed., *Jane Austen in a Social Context*, pp. 28-48. Totowa, N.J.: Barnes and Noble, 1981.

Brown, Julia Prewitt. *Jane Austen's Novels: Social Change and Literary Form*. Cambridge, Mass.: Harvard University Press, 1979.

Butler, Marilyn. *Jane Austen and the War of Ideas*. Oxford: Clarendon Press, 1975.

Byron, George Gordon, Lord. *The Poetical Works of Lord Byron*. Reprint 1972. London: John Murray, 1905.

Coleridge, Samuel Taylor. *The Works of Samuel Taylor Coleridge*. Ware, Hertfordshire: Wordsworth Editions, 1994.

Copeland, Edward, and Juliet McMaster, eds. *The Cambridge Companion to Jane Austen*. Cambridge: Cambridge University Press, 1997.

Evans, Mary. *Jane Austen and the State*. London: Tavistock Publications, 1987.

Grove, Robin. "Austen's Ambiguous Conclusions." In Harold Bloom, ed., *Jane Austen*, pp. 179-190. New York: Chelsea House, 1986.

Haggerty, George E. *Unnatural Affections: Women and Fiction in the Later Eighteenth Century*. Bloomington: Indiana University Press, 1998.

Handler, Richard, and Daniel Segal. *Jane Austen and the Fiction of Culture*. 2nd ed. Lanham, Md.: Rowman and Littlefield, 1999.

Hartman, Geoffrey. "Nature and the Humanization of Self in Wordsworth." In M. H. Abrams, ed. *English Romantic Poets*, pp. 123-132. 2nd ed. New York: Oxford University Press, 1975.

_____. *Wordsworth's Poetry: 1787-1814*. New Haven: Yale University Press, 1964.

Johnson, Claudia L. *Equivocal Beings: Politics, Gender and Sentimentality in the 1790's: Wollstonecraft, Radcliffe, Burney, Austen*. Chicago: University of Chicago Press, 1995.

Johnson, Samuel. *The Yale Edition of the Works of Samuel Johnson*. 16 vols. W. J. Bate, ed. New Haven: Yale University Press, 1969.

Knox-Shaw, Peter. "*Persuasion*, Byron, and the Turkish Tale." *Review of English Studies*, n.s. 44 (1993): 47-69.

Kroeber, Karl. *Ecological Literary Criticism: Romantic Imagining and the Biology of the Mind*. New York: Columbia University Press, 1994.

_____. *Romantic Landscape Vision*. Madison: University of Wisconsin Press, 1975.

_____. *Styles in Fictional Structure: The Art of Jane Austen, Charlotte Brontë, and George Eliot*. Princeton: Princeton University Press, 1971.

Le Faye, Deirdre, ed. *Jane Austen's Letters*. Oxford: Oxford University Press, 1995.

Levine, George. *Darwin and the Novelists*. Cambridge, Mass.: Harvard University Press, 1988.

Litvak, Joseph. "Reading Characters: Self, Society, and Text in *Emma*." In Harold Bloom, ed., *Jane Austen's* Emma, pp. 119-134. New York: Chelsea House, 1987.

Litz, A. Walton. *Jane Austen: A Study of Her Artistic Development*. New York: Oxford University Press, 1965.

_____. "*Persuasion*: Forms of Estrangement." In John Halperin, ed., *Jane Austen: Bicentenary Essays*, pp. 221-232. Cambridge: Cambridge University Press, 1975.

McGann, Jerome J. "On Reading Childe Harold's Pilgrimage." In Robert F. Gleckner, ed., *Critical Essays on Lord Byron*, pp. 33-58. New York: Maxwell Macmillan International, 1991.

Miller, D. A. *Narrative and Its Discontents: Problems of Closure in the Traditional Novel*. Princeton: Princeton University Press, 1981.

Moler, Kenneth. "The Two Voices of Fanny Price." In John Halperin, ed., *Jane Austen: Bicentenary Essays*, pp. 172-179. Cambridge: Cambridge University Press, 1975.

Monaghan, David, ed. *Jane Austen in a Social Context*. Totowa, N.J.: Barnes and Noble, 1981.

Morgan, Susan. *In the Meantime*. Chicago: University of Chicago Press, 1980.

Nardin, Jane. "Jane Austen and the Problem of Leisure." In David Monaghan, ed., *Jane Austen in a Social Context*, pp. 122-142. Totowa, N.J.: Barnes and Noble, 1981.

Newton, Judith Lowder. *Women, Power, and Subversion: Social Strategies in British Fiction, 1778-1860.* Athens: University of Georgia Press, 1981.

Peckham, Morse. *The Triumph of Romanticism.* Columbia: University of South Carolina Press, 1970.

Poovey, Mary. *The Proper Lady and the Woman Writer: Ideology as Style in the Works of Mary Wollstonecraft, Mary Shelley, and Jane Austen.* Chicago: University of Chicago Press, 1984.

Ruoff, Gene W. "Anne Elliot's Dowry: Reflections on the Ending of *Persuasion*." *Wordsworth Circle* 7 (1976): 342-351.

_____. "The Sense of a Beginning: *Mansfield Park* and Romantic Narrative." *Wordsworth Circle* 10 (1979): 174-186.

Sabin, Margery. *English Romanticism and the French Tradition.* Cambridge, Mass.: Harvard University Press, 1976.

Sales, Roger. *Jane Austen and Representations of Regency England.* London: Routledge, 1994.

Sedgwick, Eve. "Jane Austen and the Masturbating Girl." *Critical Inquiry* 17 (1991): 818-837.

Southam, B. C., ed. *Jane Austen: The Critical Heritage.* London: Routledge and Kegan Paul, 1968.

Swingle, Larry J. "The Perfect Happiness of the Union: Jane Austen's *Emma* and English Romanticism." *Wordsworth Circle* 7 (1976): 312-319.

Tave, Stuart M. "Jane Austen and One of Her Contemporaries." In John Halperin, ed., *Jane Austen: Bicentenary Essays*, pp. 61-74. Cambridge: Cambridge University Press, 1975.

Thorslev, Peter. "German Romantic Idealism." In Stuart Curran, ed., *The Cambridge Companion to British Romanticism*, pp. 74-94. Cambridge: Cambridge University Press, 1993.

Trilling, Lionel. "*Emma*." *Encounter* 8 (1957): 49-59.

Trumpener, Katie. *Bardic Nationalism.* Princeton: Princeton University Press, 1997.

White, Laura Mooneyham. "Jane Austen and the Marriage Plot: Questions of Persistence." In Devoney Looser, ed., *Jane Austen and the Discourses of Feminism*, pp. 71-86. New York: St. Martin's, 1995.

Wiltshire, John. *Jane Austen and the Body.* Cambridge: Cambridge University Press, 1992.

_____. "*Mansfield Park, Emma*, and *Persuasion*." Edward Copeland and Juliet McMaster, eds., *The Cambridge Companion to Jane Austen*, pp. 58-82. Cambridge: Cambridge University Press, 1997.

Wordsworth, William. *Poems*, vol. 1. London: Penguin, 1977.

Yeazell, Ruth Bernard. *Fictions of Modesty.* Chicago: University of Chicago Press, 1991.

Conjecturing Possibilities:
Reading and Misreading Texts in
Jane Austen's *Pride and Prejudice*_____

Felicia Bonaparte

Pride and Prejudice, writes Felicia Bonaparte, is "a map of misreading." She starts with a letter—the letter from Darcy to Elizabeth Bennet that marks the novel's turning point—and uses it to argue that the novel actually engages with important philosophical questions having to do with the nature of interpretation itself. "Austen," she writes, "is highly philosophical," even if she rarely resorts to the abstractions in which philosophy is usually debated. For Bonaparte, the point of this letter is to give Elizabeth "a philosophic understanding of the epistemological grounds that allow us to read at all." By looking at the use of words such as *suspect, presume, conjecture, guess*, and *detect*, Bonaparte demonstrates that Austen brings to her narrative a real sophistication in discussing the ways we all make sense of our world.   — J.L.

Precisely halfway through the novel (almost to the very letter by a computer count of words), Elizabeth Bennet, the central character of Jane Austen's *Pride and Prejudice*, is the recipient of a letter. She is forced to read it twice. The letter is from Fitzwilliam Darcy, the man she will eventually marry, but still in the grip of those two flaws from which the novel takes its title, Elizabeth at first misreads it. Only when she reads it again in a different frame of mind is she able to arrive at a closer estimation of the meaning of its words and the intention of its author. In a novel initially written in the epistolary style, it is not, of course, remarkable that letters should be received and sent, and indeed there are quite a few coming and going on its pages. Yet this one, so centrally placed, functions not only as a turning point in the progress of events but as the focal point of a theme that is devoted only in part to the ways of courtship and marriage and—for it is important to note the incident Austen picks as her image—far more to the reading of texts. Kelly and Newey are right to argue that in this novel the reading of texts stands as both a fact and a metaphor, for Austen often speaks here of "reading" the world as well as the word (e.g., 90, 95). But Austen is actually more precise. What she wants to teach Elizabeth, and the reader along with her, is, in the strictest sense of the word, a philosophic understanding of the epistemological grounds that allow us to read at all.

We have not typically thought of Austen as a novelist much disturbed by such philosophical questions, although a number of excellent studies have sought to dislocate this prejudice.[1] These, and the work of Martha Satz and Zelda Boyd, to whom I shall return in a moment, have not, however, yet succeeded in changing the general impression that if Austen has an interest in anything but human affairs, it is in social manners and history, not in philosophic issues. Even critics like Gilbert Ryle, who takes her to be a serious moralist and to be interested in the theory as well as the practical end of morality, begins his analysis of her views by stating that she is not a "philosopher" (168). Yet Austen is highly philosophical, alert both to ideas in general and to the currents of her time. What is deceptive is that rarely does she present these theoretically. Mostly her conceptual world is so fully dramatized in her characters and her plots that it can only be inferred from the nature of the action and the language of the narrative. But once in a while we do, in fact, find a moment so abstract as to convince us beyond doubt that Austen's purpose is philosophical. Thus, for example, in *Mansfield Park*, Mary Crawford, the embodiment of the skeptical point of view, measures the distance and the duration of her walk in the woods with Edmund in subjective and relative terms. He, the voice of another age, proposes an objective criterion. Consulting his watch, he tries to show her she has mistaken both space and time. But this means nothing to Mary Crawford. "'A watch,'" she protests, exasperated, "'is always too fast or too slow. I cannot be dictated to by a watch'" (95). The presence of such a striking scene and the central place of these characters indicate that the human relationships that stand at the fore-front of Austen's action, important as they are in themselves, serve as illustrations as well of a philosophic theme. Austen seems to be asking here, is there such thing as truth? Can it be known? And by what means? And with what degree of certainty?

These same epistemological questions lie at the heart of *Pride and Prejudice*. Its vocabulary—and Austen, as I shall show, uses lexical devices to guide the reader through her argument—relies heavily on such words as "suspect," "presume," "conjecture," "guess," "detect," "surmise," "infer," "trust," "perceive," "believe," "construe." "Suppose," her favorite of this kind, turns up ninety times in the novel. Such words stress not only the importance of epistemological questions but also the absolute uncertainty of epistemological grounds. The novel's famous opening sentence—"It is a truth universally acknowledged that a single man in possession of a good fortune, must be in want of a wife"—immediately introduces the question of truth, however only to interrogate it by the irony of its tone. Truth is not to be had so easily, if it is to be had at all. Elizabeth, saying to Miss Bingley "'Your conjecture is totally wrong'" (27), utters words that would be appropriate almost anywhere in the book. The novel is a map of misreading. Even its comedy often depends on the misconstruing of texts.

Two very fine essays have already laid some groundwork for my inquiry. Arguing that "problems of knowledge" are highlighted on every page (171), Martha Satz has demonstrated that there is often in *Pride and Prejudice* "a salient gap" in the minds of the characters "between evidence and conclusion," that what they take as reliable knowledge is in fact a "fragile edifice" (172). And writing on *Sense and Sensibility*, Zelda Boyd has shown that Austen uses modal auxiliaries to suggest that knowledge rests not on certainty but on "hypothesis" (149).[2] I agree with both these claims but believe we must go further. In *Pride and Prejudice* Austen enters the great debate on epistemological questions raging at that very moment between the empiricists and the rationalists, that she sides not with the rationalists, with whom she has always been associated (see, for example, Farrer, Simpson, Meyersohn, and Held)[3], but rather with the empiricists.[4] But realizing that empiricism is an epistemological minefield, she sets out to chart a path that will make the reading of texts, of the word or of the world, not an utter impossibility. For even as with David Hume himself, who concedes that in actual life we cannot function on absolute skepticism, Austen knows that human existence requires some approximation of truth. Elizabeth's destiny is tied to her being able to read both the letter and its sender. The narrative is thus a quest for an epistemological principle on which a suitable hypothesis of reality can rest. And while there is never any question that we are looking at a work rooted in its time and place, in the process of this quest Austen foreshadows many issues central to modernism and postmodernism, even to current critical theory—all rooted, if we look back far enough, in that very empiricism Austen was one of the first to embrace.

In this essay I explore the particulars of her epistemological inquiry, in itself and as it shapes the plot, the characters, the language, and the very act of narration, the last of which, as I shall show in my concluding paragraphs, offers an encompassing frame that encapsulates the problems Austen addresses in this novel and the manner in which she resolves them. I should also like, in passing, to take note of the many points at which Austen anticipates questions we are still asking today, to delineate, as I do so, ways she suggests these in her narrative, and to identify her conclusions, many of which could still be argued as defensible positions, some of which would not be alien to contemporary thought. Such a project has its dangers. It may pull Austen out of her time and project her into ours. But it has advantages also. Looking back from our perspective, knowing the questions we currently pose, helps us to discern the outlines of similar questions in Austen's work. But looking forward from her text, where these questions are conceived in their embryonic forms and have not yet the names and histories they have acquired in our era, we come to realize that these questions may be formulated differently, that, while they cannot be answered definitively—as Austen herself is well aware—they are not incapable of some tenable solutions.

Repeatedly in *Pride and Prejudice* Austen negates the possibility of anything like genuine knowledge. The very word is considered suspect. Rarely do characters say "I know" without being shown to be wrong. "'I know it must be a scandalous falsehood,'" Lady Catherine says, for instance, on being told that Elizabeth might be inclined to marry Darcy (353). "'No, no,'" says Jane on being informed that the marriage is to take place. "'I know it to be impossible'" (372). "Conviction" also, as a rule, heralds an erroneous conclusion, as when Darcy writes to Elizabeth that having carefully observed Jane, he felt secure in his "'conviction'" that she did not care for Bingley (197). Although she will finally decide that it is not completely impossible to approximate reality, by destabilizing words that rest on epistemological certainty, Austen clearly undermines the idea that human knowledge can ever be sure and absolute. Sometimes we are only ignorant of the unknown, not the unknowable, but one of Austen's notable modernisms is her sense that human events always occur in a temporal context. What we are ignorant of at the moment at which we need to make a choice that hinges on that specific knowledge, however knowable it might be in some putative universe, is, in its effects on us, much the same as the unknowable. The very genesis of the plot turns on such a moment exactly. Hearing Darcy, at the beginning, say of her that he does not find her "'handsome enough'" to entice him to dance (12), Elizabeth takes an instant disliking to him, "unaware" that a moment later, catching sight of her playful manner, Darcy quickly changes his mind (23). She has already conceived that prejudice by which the rest of the novel is driven.

Much of the structure of the narrative, including its characters and action, is as consciously calculated to explore the means of knowing as to offer the realistic social and psychological portraits we have mostly thought it aimed for. Each of the sisters, for example, is an experiment in the question of what it is we can rely on for the knowledge we require. Lydia, the slave of passion and instinct, proves, by the future predicted for her, that we cannot count on nature for an intuitive sense of truth. Nor can we rely on others to interpret reality for us. Many in this novel do, each in a somewhat different fashion, with the deviations illustrating variations on this theme. Kitty, for instance, who shadows Lydia and generally does what her sister urges, is psychologically suggestible, a characteristic that can be dangerous when the influence is bad but one that can be beneficial when the influence is good. Swayed by Lydia, she is reckless. But when her "elder sisters" take "charge," at the conclusion of the novel, she exhibits "great" "improvement" (385). Bingley, who is Kitty's double in being susceptible to influence, differs, however, in one respect. While Kitty is psychologically malleable, Bingley is malleable intellectually. The power Darcy has over him is not the power of personality but the power to persuade. When Darcy explains to Elizabeth the events that separated Bingley from Jane, he characterizes Bingley as "'modest'" and speaks of the "'diffidence'" that prevented him from "'depending on his own judgment'" (371). Mary, whose primary function lies in connection with a point I shall turn to in a moment, belongs also to this group, although she relies not on people but books. Jane, the sweetest of the sisters, is, from a practical point of view, epistemologically the worst. Disinclined to "'see a fault'" (14), hers is the wiser course undoubtedly when she refuses to believe the stories Wickham has told of Darcy. But later she refuses equally to conclude that Wickham has lied. She will make no decision at all. Her favorite attitude, which is summarized in her phrase "'I hope and trust'" (305), makes her a very pleasant young woman but not a very useful guide through the complexities of life. Elizabeth only, of the sisters, will learn, as she learns to read that letter, the skill required to read the world. Her arriving at this skill is the *bildung* of the novel. But Austen's development of her heroine is essentially philosophic, all her other acquisitions being ancillary to this end. And what she develops in Elizabeth is a practical empiricism. Almost the first thing we learn about her is that her dominant attribute is her "quickness of observation" (15). And Austen so conceives the plot as to turn this characteristic, the first requirement of the empiricist, into the basis of what becomes Elizabeth's philosophic perspective.

It is Austen's perspective too. What Austen had or had not read on the subject of empiricism cannot be ascertained. But in the preface he appended to the posthumous publication of *Persuasion* and *Northanger Abbey*, her brother Henry does insist that her reading was extensive, in history and *belles lettres* especially, and we know that serious reading in the later eighteenth century and early nineteenth routinely included works that today would be classified as philosophy. It would not have been unusual for a family like the Austens to have had in its library the standard works of Locke and Hume. We know that Austen read some Hume, for her nephew James Edward Austen-Leigh reports that she was well acquainted with Hume's *History of England* (88), to which indeed she herself refers on the pages of *Northanger Abbey* (109). But whether or not she had read Hume's more philosophical publications, empiricism was in the air and the subject of much discussion, disagreement, and debate. Indeed, as Austen was growing up, empiricism was the philosophy that was displacing rationalism as the modern point of view. It would have been difficult for Austen to avoid exposure to it.

Austen makes the empirical method explicitly central to her concerns. "'We all love to instruct,'" says Elizabeth, "'though we can teach only what is not worth knowing'" (343). The obvious corollary to this is that whatever is worth knowing we must discover for ourselves, and the prominence in this novel of the empiricist vocabulary—particularly "perceive" and "observe"—implies that we must discover these things chiefly through the empirical method.

Austen, indeed, takes visible pains to discredit other assumptions, especially the faith in reason still left over from the Enlightenment. She is intent on setting limits, in the text of the novel itself, on the nature and function of reason and on redefining the term entirely in empiricist terms, as a mere logical operation designed to sift through empirical data. Characters who turn to reason as a tool for acquiring knowledge turn out invariably to be wrong. Elizabeth herself begins with the assumption that what is reasonable must, by that very token, be true. Wickham's "account" of the relationship between Darcy and Lady Catherine, seeming to be "rational," seems to her therefore implicitly right (84). It will be part of her education to learn that the rational may be false. Compared to her empirical language, which is extensive, as we have seen, Austen uses very few words that point to the uses of rational thought. Her favorites are "deduce" and "conclude," and both are operational terms. Even "reason" and "rational"—except when the former is used to mean "ground"—are employed, with one exclusion on which I will comment below, primarily to describe the logic through which we need to filter data. Indeed, in one of those abstract moments in which the argument turns philosophical, Austen even provides a tutorial on the need to differentiate between the knowledge we can acquire and the reason that helps us use it, between what David Hume would have called matters of fact and matters of logic, the first to be derived empirically and only the latter to be determined by the rules of rational thought. Jane and Elizabeth have been speculating on why Bingley has left the neighborhood:

> "You persist, then, in supposing his sisters influence him."
> "Yes, in conjunction with his friend."
> "I cannot believe it. . . . They can only wish his happiness, and if he is attached to me, no other woman can secure it."
> "Your first position is false. They may wish many things beside his happiness." (136)

Jane is perfectly right in her reasoning. She is wrong in her conclusion because she has started from the wrong premise. The premise is a matter of fact and cannot be reached through a rational process. By arranging it so that Jane can be right about the one and yet wrong about the other, Austen tells us we must distinguish between the tools that give us knowledge and the tools that help us use it.

Equally, Austen in this novel rejects the idea of authority, the notion that there are truths to be had from the wise, or from the past, from our elders, or from religion, attacking, almost systematically, virtually every conventional site—parents, social standing, clerics—held in eighteenth-century culture, by traditionalists at least, as the venue of authority. Most of those who claim authority or on whose behalf it is claimed are objects of contempt or derision. Never indeed is Austen's humor broader or less subtle than here. It is, for instance, Lady Catherine, presented as nearly a farcical character, whose manner is said to be "authoritative" (58) and Mr. Collins, the novel's fop, who entertains a high opinion of his "authority as a clergyman" (48). Similarly, the authority imputed to Mr. and Mrs. Bennet in their roles as parental figures—as when Collins feels sure Elizabeth will accept his proposal of marriage as soon as she realizes it has been "'sanctioned'" by the "'authority'" of her parents (109)—is shown to be without justification and, even more to the point, without merit. Even when an authority is not manifestly ludicrous, Austen shows it is not possible to rely on it as truth. When Elizabeth and the Gardiners are taken through Pemberley, for instance, Elizabeth is so greatly impressed by what the housekeeper says of Darcy that she thinks they might have been wrong in not thinking well of him. Having known Darcy all his life, the woman is clearly an "authority" (264). But the Gardiners disagree. Having no grounds as yet to doubt Wickham, they take him as an "'authority,'" too (249). What Austen is saying is plain enough. Looking to someone else's authority only postpones the final question since in the end we must determine which authority to believe, and the only way to do that is to turn again to experience, for it is only by being witnesses to what Wickham and Darcy do that everyone comes at last to realize which authority is to be trusted.

This is not to say that Austen necessarily wants to jettison what might be called traditional wisdom. It may contain some kernels of truth, but to know whether or not it does it must be tested again and again, in every conceivable circumstance, against the evidence of experience. It is this critical distinction Mary is designed to illustrate. Despite her pomposity, which inclines us to discredit what she says, Mary's remarks, it should be noted, usually turn out to be true, true in the general run of things and true in a general sort of way within the events of the novel itself. "'Every impulse of feeling,'" for instance, she pronounces at one point, "'should be guided by reason'" (21), and these are words her sister Lydia might well have heeded for her good. The problem Austen sees with Mary is not that her opinions are wrong but that she enunciates them as though they were *a priori* postulates. In reality they are not. In fact, the opinions Austen gives Mary, like the one just quoted above, are almost always generalizations that would have been garnered from experience, experience codified over the ages into quotable principles. But this is the very thing that Mary seems unable to comprehend. For Mary, these are eternal verities to be accepted without question. Austen is stressing that unless—and this is surely one of the reasons she dwells so persistently on the concrete that she often succeeds in convincing us she has no philosophical purpose— they are merely informing frames on which we draw to form our insights, general truths are nothing more than empty and meaningless clichés, as they always are with Mary. Tradition, that is, may be wise or not. But whether it is we can only know by putting it to the test ourselves. It is this ability, in the exclusion I mentioned above, to find exactly the right relationship between the codified principle that generalizes from experience and the particular situation to which the principle is applied that Austen normally calls "common sense" and its possessor "reasonable."

That Austen's empiricism cannot be taken as a mere casual inclination to look for insights in experience is plainly shown in the philosophic sophistication of her analysis, which structures the action so as to demonstrate its implications and limitations.

She is acutely aware of both. She knows, for instance, as well as

Hume, that empiricism can yield only that limited body of knowledge that is accessible to the senses. Every other kind of reality is completely beyond its ken. Religion is not a concern in this novel, as it will be in *Mansfield Park*, but social, moral, psychological, and philosophic questions are, and even the simplest of these, she shows us, cannot be answered through sensory knowledge. Darcy's failure, once again, to perceive, by watching Jane, that she was in love with Bingley testifies to the limitation of even the strictest observation. Similarly, Austen knows that, restricted to the phenomenal, empiricism can only speak of how things look, not what they are. Her constant use of "appear" and "seem" in relating the conclusions to which her characters arrive acknowledges an unbridgeable gap between perception and reality. The fact, indeed, that some of the characters are shown to be consciously engaged in manufacturing appearances—when Jane does not wish to be "perceived" as being affected by Bingley's return (337-38), when Charlotte argues that women must show more affection than they feel to induce proposals of marriage (21-22)—illustrates how intensely conscious Austen is of the degree to which appearance is capable of being dissociated from reality. Through Wickham and Darcy, who appear the opposite of what they are, deliberately in Wickham's case, this discrepancy becomes a central question in the book.

The very existence of reality is obviously problematic to Austen. Although in the end she seems to accept, at least hypothetically, the idea that, however inaccessible, there is some kind of reality somewhere, there are moments in the novel, especially in Wickham's story, in which she appears to toy with the notion that, as Nietzsche once expressed it in a passage that has gained currency in modern theory, reality must be considered only another "piece of fiction" (Section 521). Wickham, as he exists in the minds of the characters of the novel almost until the very end, and even in the mind of the reader, is entirely fictional. Both his character and his history are fabrications of his own. Some might say he should be seen, as invariably he has been, simply as an old-fashioned liar, but it is not without importance that the stories

Wickham tells do not appreciably alter the details of what we later hear from Darcy. From the beginning, Wickham admits to his "'imprudence'" and "'extravagance'"; he even concedes he did not deserve the kindness Darcy's father bestowed on him (79). It is not lying Austen emphasizes. What she emphasizes is construction, the fact that the identical data may serve to construct quite different truths. It is to this that she draws our attention in her typically ironic way when Wickham is made to say of Darcy what is actually true of himself, namely that "'the world . . . sees him only as he chuses [sic] to be seen'" (78).

Hence, whatever she may be willing to assume in some ultimate sphere, Austen's view of the reality to which observation admits us is very much in the empiricist realm, epistemologically a realm less detected than construed. This is prodigiously clear in her language. Rarely, unless she is being ironic, does Austen use words like "discover" or "find" when she describes what a character learns. What little we do learn in her novel about the realities of the world, we must rather "credit," "trust," "believe," "imagine," "fancy," "conceive," "presume," "surmise," "suspect," "suppose," "infer," "guess," "conjecture," and "construe." The paradigm scene—another one of those philosophic moments that call our attention to the abstract—is to be found when Colonel Fitzwilliam, summarizing a conversation in which he has had, characteristically, to infer what the speaker meant, closes by saying, "'It was all conjecture'" (185). Inference, the Colonel reminds us, is the sum total of our knowledge.

And Austen is well aware that inference is nothing more than interpretation.[5] It is interesting that the word "fact," except as part of the phrase "in fact" used as an intensifier, appears in the novel only six times. Observation does not yield facts. The heavy inferential vocabulary through which conclusions are presented, of which the words I cited above are but a small representation, suggests that, like a good empiricist, Austen looks on sense impressions as a mere dustheap of raw data, out of which reality must be conceptually constructed, much like those puzzles we find in newspapers made up of individual dots that can only produce a picture if we draw connecting lines from one number to the next. Austen repeatedly shows us Elizabeth engaged in attempting to draw those lines. "'I cannot make him out,'" for instance, she remarks on hearing her father read a letter Collins has sent (64). Asking Darcy a series of questions, she says she is trying to "'make . . . out'" his character (93). When she hears of Bingley's return, she does "not know what to make of it" (332). In each of these cases, Elizabeth uses a common colloquialism, but it is not perhaps an accident that the word "make" appears in each. Austen is showing Elizabeth in the act of making reality, not because she is fabricating it in the way that Wickham does but because she has no choice. That is the nature of empirical knowledge. Often, indeed, such knowledge rests not on a single inference only but on layers of supposition. Believing she has understood him, Elizabeth does not, for example, say that she knows what Darcy means, rather that she has surmised what his words *"seemed* to *imply"* (182; italics mine).

One of the things that makes it difficult to interpret in empiricism is that there are no paradigms to guide us in ordering our data. The picture in the newspaper puzzle is predetermined by the numbers that are pre-assigned to the dots. The dots of observation, however, do not come with sequential numbers. We can connect them in many ways. Austen's epistemological language leaves no doubt that she is aware that the right picture, if there is one, not only lies beyond our reach, but that many pictures are possible, and that the ones we form in our minds depend on the patterns we make of our data. Frequently Austen foregrounds the hurdles that stand in the way of interpretation and when she does so she places her emphasis not on the fictional dilemmas her characters are attempting to solve but, metafictionally, on the act of decipherment itself. Different characters, for example, often make totally different pictures out of the identical dots. Thus, to Bingley speed in writing signifies ease and fluency; to Darcy it shows carelessness (48). Bingley's departure from the neighborhood means to Jane he does not love her; to Elizabeth it proves that his sisters know he does and are whisking him away to avoid his marrying her (118). And as she reads that central letter trying to evaluate Darcy's version of events but recalling Wickham's story, it dawns on Elizabeth that there must be, the versions being incompatible, duplicity on "one side or the other" (205). But nothing in the data itself can tell her where the duplicity is.

Error is therefore unavoidable. Most of the blunders in the novel are made through faulty interpretation. Austen does not use many words to suggest this kind of flaw—"mistake" and "error" are her favorites—but she uses these words often. "'I am much mistaken,'" says Jane when she first meets Caroline Bingley, "'if we shall not find'" her "'charming'" (15). "'You can hardly doubt,'" says Collins, confident that Elizabeth is expecting his proposal, "'the purport of my discourse; ... my attentions have been too marked to be mistaken'" (105). In every case the speaker is wrong. As Collins remarks on the only occasion he turns out to be right in the novel, "'we are all liable to error'" (114). Error often compounds error. While we are trying to interpret, we are being ourselves interpreted, and being interpreted, sooner or later we are bound to be misread. It is a sign of Elizabeth's growing philosophical consciousness that she recognizes this fact. Listening to Darcy, Austen writes as she layers once again multiple levels of supposition, Elizabeth notes "a sort of smile" that she *fancied* she understood; he *must* be *supposing* her to be thinking of Jane" (179; italics mine). Here is one small empirical fact, a sort of smile on Darcy's face. Elizabeth takes it to be the result of his interpreting her thoughts; but her own thoughts, she is aware, are an interpretation of his, or at least of what she thinks he has interpreted her to mean.

Nor is the chance of misunderstanding limited to our reading of others. In a striking, postmodern, way, Austen suggests we are not always subjects even to ourselves. Often we are, no less than others, objects to our own understanding and must attempt to read ourselves in the same way we read others. Time and again we find her characters waking suddenly to the thought that they have wrongly construed themselves.

Only near the end of the book does Darcy, for instance, come to recognize that his first letter had been written in a state of "'dreadful bitterness,'" though at the time he had believed himself to be perfectly "'calm and cool'" (368). This is a point so important to Austen that Elizabeth's striking words, spoken after she comes to see that it had been her pride and prejudice that had led, in her first attempt, to the misreading of Darcy's letter—"'Till this moment, I never knew myself'" (208)—are the pivotal point of the book.

The only way in Austen's novel we can know whether or not we have interpreted well or ill is, pragmatically, by seeing the results of our actions. But such a test, as Austen knows, puts us at the mercy of time. As, often, we lack the knowledge we need at the time we really need it, before we commit ourselves to action, so we have no way of knowing, at the time we need to know it, whether we are right or wrong in the reading of our data. An enlightening gloss on this question is to be found in the act of deception. Another subject Austen explores in the language of her narrative—characters, thus, are "duped," "misled," "deceived," victims of "misrepresentation," "self-deceived" and much "imposed on"—is the idea that deception would at first appear to be a moral or psychological problem, a question more of human relationships than of epistemological truth. But that is not how Austen presents it. Her point is not that people lie and that other people believe them but rather that truth is hard to detect and falsehood hard to distinguish from it. The Wickham affair is once more an instance—on his part a deliberate lie but simulating truth so well that those who hear him cannot tell, until much later, which it is.

And even when consequences suggest which interpretation is right, conclusions always remain contingent. Austen never lets us forget that, however true they seem, interpretations are only hypotheses, resting on so many assumptions that we can never be certain about them. When Darcy admits he may have been wrong in his estimate of Jane's feelings, he does not say he had misread her, but offers instead a conditional statement: "'If *you* have not been mistaken here, I must have been in error'" (197). Someone had to have been wrong, but which of the two he is not prepared, even now, to stipulate.

Austen's extraordinary grasp of the motives of her characters makes not only for the novel's shrewd psychological analysis, it stresses yet another aspect of its epistemological inquiry, namely the problem of premises. The recurrent use of words like "assume," "presume," and "suppose," as well as small periodic lessons—as when Darcy tells Elizabeth she was right that his "'behavior'" merited nothing but "'reproof'" but that her "'accusations'" were, nevertheless, completely "'ill-founded'" because they were "'formed on mistaken premises'" (367)—remind us that everything hinges on premises, that if our premises are wrong, we cannot count on our conclusions, however good our logic may be. The chief example here is Collins when he proposes to Elizabeth. On the premise that she intends to accept his proposal of marriage, Collins interprets her refusals in every conceivable way but one: it is her modesty that prevents her from accepting him initially, although in the end she means to do so; this is how "elegant" women behave; she wishes to increase his passion by prolonging his suspense. Although she repeatedly tells him so, it never occurs to him that Elizabeth has no desire to marry him (106-09).

It is a premise of this kind that is the prejudice of the title. The term has generally been taken in its psychological sense to the exclusion of all others. But this is precisely where psychology and philosophy intersect. Elizabeth's bias towards Wickham because he flatters her vanity and her prejudice against Darcy because he has insulted her pride are the false premises on whose basis she misinterprets both their stories. Nothing, indeed, is worse than premises produced by psychological flaws. Hidden as they are from our consciousness, these are the very last assumptions we subject to scrutiny. But every premise, Austen reminds us, is in the strictest sense a prejudice—something for which we have no evidence; if we did it would be a conclusion—and is capable, if mistaken, as in the case of Collins above, of rendering both empirical proof and the strictest logic useless.

These many and radical qualifications Austen places on what we can know and how well we are able to know it come very close to the total skepticism inherent in the empiricist view, but never, at least in *Pride and Prejudice*, does Austen retreat from this position. Indeed, what makes her epistemology not only modern but postmodern is the fact that, on the contrary, she seeks an answer not beyond but within this skepticism and that she is prepared, in the end, to accept a hypothesis in which knowledge and understanding are partial, imperfect, and indistinct. It would be fruitful to compare Austen's views here to Arthur Fine's in current philosophic thought. Fine repudiates, on the one hand, philosophic realists like Larry Laudan and Ian Hacking who, in an Aristotelian way, believe that there is a correspondence between perception and reality, but, on the other, also is averse to the ideas of antirealists like Bas Van Fraassen and T. H. Morgan who deny such a correspondence and accept or reject a theory on internal coherence alone. Fine thus turns away from all global statements in favor of a more conditional and a more open-ended approach, one that "picks out . . . interpretations, locally, as it goes along," satisfied to find a small, temporary, and relative truth and ready to rescind its inferences if new discoveries contradict them (148).[6] Although we can never know with certainty, Austen appears to say in this novel, that although we can never be really sure about reality and our conclusions, we can, in a small and provisional way, locate islands of possibility on which thought and action may rest.

And these local, tentative answers are to be found through probability, in *Pride and Prejudice* without question the most important aid we have. Not surprisingly, probability as the means of gaining access, however imperfectly, to reality, so much in our statistical age the contemporary view, was popular, in the wake of empiricism, as early as the eighteenth century. In *The Analogy of Religion, Natural and Revealed, to the Constitution and Course of Nature*, published in 1736, Joseph Butler, for example, while attempting to defend Christianity against the deists and yet unable to escape the impact on his thought of Locke, argues not for the truth of his creed but only for its probability, probability being for him the best of the available tools. The word itself and synonyms for it appear well over a hundred times in the progress of Austen's novel. Austen knows that probability, as an interpretation itself, is not without serious snares and pitfalls, and over and over again she illustrates the difficulties of calculating what is likely and what is not. Often the probable seems improbable. When Elizabeth learns that Darcy chose to be present at Lydia's wedding, it strikes her that she might have been the reason. Of course, she is absolutely right. But, recalling their recent history, she decides that that is "improbable" (320). On the other hand, the improbable may appear probable to some. Mrs. Bennet considers it "'likely'" that the new tenant of Netherfield will "'fall in love with'" one of her daughters (4), although, since the parties have not even met, she has no grounds for thinking so. And the fact that Mrs. Bennet miraculously turns out to be right tells us that sometimes it is not the probable but the improbable that occurs.

Nevertheless, interpretation through the sifting of probabilities is not a totally hopeless task, and chiefly in Elizabeth's efforts to read the novel's central letter Austen shows us how to steer through the perilous obstacles of realities and of texts.

That there is a verbal text to be deciphered in the letter Austen is not prepared to deny, any more than she is prepared to deny that some reality, however unknowable, exists, although, precisely as she questions our ability to apprehend objective truth with certainty, she questions the degree to which verbal realities can be grasped. The very circumstance that one text can yield two utterly different readings plainly indicates that Austen knows how uncertain meanings can be.

Further, that the verbal text refers to the world and not to itself Austen similarly insists on. Language is not here self-referential, although this is yet another idea she appears to be toying with, for during the period that Elizabeth cannot determine which reality, Darcy's or Wickam's, is the true one, the language of each, as it creates rival constructs in her mind, seems, as Austen is well aware, to point only to itself. Reading, in that crucial letter, Darcy's account of past events and recalling Wickham's version, Elizabeth does not know which is true. "On both sides," she is made to say in words that might well have appeared in a Saussurean argument, "it was only assertion" (205). For the moment, she is standing merely between two rival texts, each, as Perry Meisel might put it, a reality that for her, being ontologically "groundless," is linguistically tautological. Yet Austen contends that, hard as it is, we must not decline to attempt a conclusion.

Meanwhile, she does suggest that in one respect there can be a good in not insisting on one final point of view. For the contrary temperaments of Elizabeth and Jane have a beneficial effect as they correct each other's excesses. Jane is too flexible, too gullible, far too trusting for her own good, Elizabeth too suspicious and stubborn. But that is just as well, hints Austen, considering that Jane was right to believe the best of Darcy and Elizabeth was wrong. If human beings will make mistakes, it is just as well that there should be errors on all sides of a question. This is what makes of social exchange a vital epistemological instrument, that in the barter of opinions individual biases can hope to cancel each other out. But ultimately a choice must be made. Those who do not make a choice invariably find themselves the victims of accidental circumstances or of truths selected by others, as we see in the case of Jane, whose passivity nearly costs her marriage to the man she loves. Furthermore, not taking action, again in a postmodern way, is merely another kind of action. When new information is learned about Wickham, Jane and Elizabeth, for example, decide not to broadcast it to the neighborhood. "'Wickham will soon be gone,'" says Elizabeth, and "'it will not signify to anybody here, what he really is'" (226). Of course, they are wrong, as they come to know (277, 291), since their silence allows Lydia just enough time to elope with Wickham. In certain circumstances, indecision is not even an alternative. This is the case with Darcy's letter. Elizabeth must believe him or not. She cannot choose to suspend judgment. Unless she actively believes and accepts Darcy's apology, she has as much as disbelieved it. In the phrasing of

William James, indecision in this instance does not exist as a live option.

And most importantly, Austen insists, unlike Derrida and others who dissociate the text from the pen that has engendered it, that the letter has an author, one whose character and intentions Elizabeth must attempt to decipher, the decipherment of which is in fact the very point of reading it. For each of Elizabeth's two readings produces the picture in her mind of a very different man. It is for the sake of determining which of these two is really Darcy that she must interpret his words, because one she would marry and one she would not. And on that choice will rest her happiness.

The process that takes her through this reading, while it constitutes instructions not remarkable in themselves in the context of empiricism, is remarkable in that it shows, drafting a virtual course in the management of empirical observation, how completely Austen requires herself to stand within the empiricist framework and how thoroughly she understands what that framework allows and entails.

The primary focus is on evidence, on its nature, on its sources, on its proper interpretation. Until the moment she reads that letter, the most basic of all prerequisites, namely that evidence is necessary for the making of a judgment, simply does not occur to Elizabeth. Her sense of Darcy had been nothing but the expression of an antipathy, which she had, however, accepted as a valid base for her view. Only now does she realize that she had had no "'reason'" at all for the opinion she had formed of him (225). Not only is Austen stressing the need here for substantiating evidence, she is also differentiating between a reason and a cause, between a psychological motive and a philosophic ground. A cause Elizabeth had had for her disinclination toward Darcy: the mortification of her pride. What she had not had was the evidence that could function as a reason. In yet another of those moments that make a philosophic point, Austen illustrates the difference. Earlier, when Wickham had told her that Darcy had accused him of forfeiting his claim to the family's good will by his "'extravagance'" and "'imprudence,'" Elizabeth had protested indignantly, certain that Darcy's charges were slanderous (79). Now, in a clearly parallel scene, she comprehends that she has "no proof" that Darcy is wrong to speak in his letter of Wickham's "extravagance" and "profligacy" (205). Rehearsing her history with both men as she reconsiders that letter, Elizabeth furthermore comes to see not only that evidence is essential but that it must be relevant evidence. She had formed her conception of Wickham by taking his appealing "countenance" and his delightful "manner" and "voice" as indications of his character (206). But now, beginning to discern what to accept and what to question in making a particular judgment, Elizabeth dismisses these factors as entirely irrelevant and becomes in turn aware of others, others she had ignored before. She recalls how freely Wickham had spoken to her of himself, how quickly he had confided to her what should have been his private thoughts, how unreservedly he had complained that Darcy had treated him unfairly. She had been flattered by his confidences. Only now is she finally "struck" by the astounding "impropriety" of his making "communications" of this kind to a total "stranger," struck even more that this impropriety had completely "escaped her before" (206-07). Austen, moreover, requires Elizabeth to take full responsibility for the discovery of evidence. Until this moment, Elizabeth has allowed herself to be only a passive recipient of whatever accidental intelligence was directed her way. Now, as she upbraids herself for blindly putting her trust in Wickham, a man about whom nothing was known by anyone in the neighborhood, she understands that she should have made the effort to learn something about him, to acquire "information" by "enquiring" into his character (206).

Had she done so, had she inquired in the neighborhood about Wickham, she would have acquired what Austen calls "second-hand intelligence" (9), a major subject in this novel. For the most part Austen distrusts it. In the form of rumor, gossip, and the general opinion, it becomes in *Pride and Prejudice* a chorus transmitting misinformation, voicing, for instance, the popular view that Wickham is charming and

Darcy cold (206). Austen is so much indeed the empiricist that she is always highly suspicious of any opinion that is not rooted not only in actual observation but in a specific observer. The passive voice in verbal constructions—such as Wickham's "'it is believed'" that Darcy intends to marry his cousin (83)—is always in Austen a warning signal precisely because it names no source. Individual observation often counters what rumor claims. When Elizabeth has a chance to rely on her own "observation," she realizes that Darcy's sister, whom everyone considers "proud," is nothing more than "exceedingly shy" (261). But it is frequently the case that such intelligence is the only knowledge that is available, and Austen is at pains to teach Elizabeth as well as the reader how to assess it judiciously. The critical moment in this connection comes when Elizabeth suddenly realizes that everything she has known about Wickham, or everything she thought she knew, was only "what he had told" her "himself" (206). Darcy, by contrast, suggests in his letter that she inquire into his character by consulting the "'testimony'" of his cousin, Colonel Fitzwilliam. Their "'near relationship,'" Darcy explains, and their "'constant intimacy,'" as well as his role as an executor of the elder Darcy's will, renders him thoroughly "'acquainted with every particular'" of his story (202). The key to this passage is the word "testimony." Austen uses this word again when Elizabeth at Pemberley ponders the housekeeper's "testimony" in regard to Darcy's character (265). David P. Demarest, Jr., has stressed that, not only in *Pride and Prejudice* but in *Emma* and *Mansfield Park*, Austen uses legal language to suggest a legal paradigm for the investigation of evidence. And that is just what she means here. Colonel Fitzwilliam and the housekeeper are being offered as character witnesses, as though Darcy were on trial. Whatever we cannot observe ourselves, Austen appears here to be saying, we may have to accept from others, but we must give it credence only if it is the kind of evidence acceptable in a court of law.

Finally, we must understand, in handling the evidence we acquire of whatever sort it is, that, like all empirical data, the picture that evidence gives us of reality is an interpretation only, never certain or absolute. Until she rereads Darcy's letter, this too does not occur to Elizabeth. And for this her pride is to blame. For if it is as a faulty premise that the prejudice of the title has its most important function, pride here functions as an obstacle to our seeing that even at best our conclusions are only conjectures. Elizabeth's pride not only inclines her to a prejudice against Darcy, it engenders an arrogant certainty that her reading of events is the only possible one. Had she considered at the start, as she was forming her first impressions of the characters of the two men, that other interpretations were feasible, it would not have been so difficult for her to detect errors in her thoughts. Convinced, however, that there could be one interpretation only, she persisted in her blindness to every other possibility. Only as she rereads that letter and considers what Darcy tells her does she suddenly realize that the very information that had led her to favor Wickham was equally "capable of a turn which must make" Darcy utterly "blameless" (205). "Capable of a turn," of course, is the crucial language here. The focus is not on new information. The focus is on interpretation and the many ways in which evidence can be construed.

It is in connection with such blunders that Austen invokes the power of reason. Although it cannot provide us with knowledge, as it might for a rationalist, reason, in a functional sense, can, for Austen as for Hume, help us manage empirical evidence in an intelligent, fruitful way. It can help us judge and evaluate it. This is the process that takes Elizabeth from her first reading to her second. Both of her readings are impressions in the strictest empiricist sense, as are both her readings of Darcy. That is why the novel's first title—and we should note that for this title Austen chose an empiricist term—is not *Impressions* but *First Impressions*. Impressions are not what Austen rejects. What she rejects are those first impressions Elizabeth forms without reflecting on whether or not they are defensible. And to make impressions defensible we need the critical power of reason. Rereading that letter, for example, Elizabeth now begins to compare, as she had failed to do before, Wickham's actions to his words. He had boasted that facing Darcy was not something he had to fear. But he had not appeared at the ball at which Darcy was expected. He had told tales to everyone who was inclined to listen to him that Darcy had mistreated him. But he had only told those tales after Darcy had left the neighborhood. He had assured her that he respected Darcy's father far too much to speak a word against his son. And yet he had spoken ill of Darcy at every available opportunity. Each of these empirical tidbits she had held separately in her mind. Reason is what brings them together. It is what helps her now to draw those lines that connect the disparate dots. Having "weighed" now "every circumstance" of the particulars of the letter, she is able to see a picture that had not emerged before. Austen is still not prepared to say that Elizabeth has arrived at knowledge. But the connecting of those dots has at last enabled her to estimate a "probability" (205-06).

Reason, furthermore, is essential in helping correct those errors of will that often prevent the mind from consenting to these various operations. These errors are highlighted all through the novel. When Elizabeth, for example, attempts to send Mary silent signals not to offer to play the piano for the hapless assembled guests, Mary, Austen pointedly writes, simply *would not* understand them" (100; italics mine); when Darcy accuses Elizabeth of misapprehending everyone, he insists that she does so "'wilfully'" (58). The condition is psychological, but it is evident that Austen comes at her psychology here from a philosophic angle, for her interest in these errors is primarily epistemological, not as a limitation of character, although that is of interest too, but as an obstacle to knowledge. Again and again, as she takes Elizabeth through the rereading of that letter, Austen brings her to recognize not only that she has misread but that she has chosen to do so. Even when she had been compelled, on her first reading of the letter, to see some merit in Darcy's words, she had been so averse to believing him that she had repeatedly cried "'This must be false! This cannot be! This must be the grossest falsehood!'" not because his words were not credible but because "if" she granted them "true," they would "overthrow," she realized, "every cherished opinion" she held. Her "prejudice" had engendered a will to "discredit" what he said (204-05). What Austen keeps underscoring here is that the words, the signs on the page, plain enough before her eyes, have little to do with Elizabeth's reading. Reading is done with the mind, not the eye. Until Elizabeth utters those words that mark the turning point of the novel, "'Till this moment, I never knew myself'" (208), she is not ready psychologically to form her philosophic view.

Some of what Austen raises here concerning the state of mind of the reader and the nature of reading itself seems to anticipate the idea that it is the reader's response that makes the meaning of a text. The very fact that the different readings of that letter are made to depend not on changes in the text but in the reader's state of mind indicates that Austen is conscious of the philosophic issues that have led to this critical theory. Having conceded that objectivity lies forever beyond our grasp, Austen could hardly have failed to realize that reading was a subjective act. Yet this is precisely the conclusion on which she cannot come to rest. To accept a reader-response interpretation of that letter would make the reading of it useless. The only point of reading the letter is for Elizabeth to know whether or not to marry Darcy. The meaning has to be tied to the text even as the text to its author. Yet, although she is clearly repudiating its most radical ramifications, Austen does not altogether reject even this postmodern idea. She seeks a less global middle position. As Wayne Booth conceives of a figure whom he calls the "implied reader," "created by the work" itself and functioning as the "ideal interpreter" (138), as Umberto Eco imagines an *intentio operis* that places a set of defined parameters around what the reader may infer as the meaning of a text, creating a kind of model reader (see especially 64 ff.), and as Walter Slatoff insists that readers have to come to the text with a degree of self-awareness of their own subjective locations (171), so Jane Austen tries to find, within the unavoidable limits of our subjective relationship to the meaning of a text, a position that will allow the possibility of a reading.

And the position she adopts is precisely the position offered by David Hume himself in his essay "Of the Standard of Taste," his most important contribution to the subject of aesthetics and, incidentally, to the problems inherent in the act of reading. Austen might well have known this work. Published in 1757, this was precisely the kind of essay that was read in homes like Austen's. Admitting, as he hardly cannot, the subjectivity of perception, Hume, nonetheless, insists in this essay that there are worse and better readings, and, precisely as Austen does, offers advice on how a critic can distinguish between the two. His focus, very much like Austen's, is on the state of mind of the reader. In each of us there is potentially a "sound" and a "defective" state, but only in a "sound" condition can we formulate a "true standard" that will permit us to read well. To reach that standard, we must seek to divest ourselves of bias, of our moods, of idiosyncrasies. We must seek to bend our "fancy" to the "situation" at hand and give "due attention to the object" (232). As we would not choose to judge "flavors" while suffering from a "fever" or "colours" with a jaundiced eye, so we should not attempt to read when subject to certain "internal" states (233-34). And of these the most pernicious, as for Austen so for Hume, is the state in which we harbor a particular "prejudice" (244). To "produce its due effect," a "work of art" must be "surveyed in a certain point of view" (239); "prejudice" destroys "sound judgment, and perverts all operations of the intellectual faculties" (240). What Hume is saying here in essence is that even in empiricism there are two kinds of subjectivity, one implicit in the philosophy, the other the distinctive prejudice of the individual mind. The first is impossible to escape. The second, however, can be corrected once we recognize its existence and take measures to counteract it. And, like Austen, Hume believes that the means of correcting our prejudices are the "operations" of "reason" (240-41).

Hume is speaking here, of course, of a reader of literature. But Austen not only, as we have seen, uses the concept and language of reading for every kind of interpretation, she clearly intends, as she trains Elizabeth, to educate her readers as well, to teach them to read both the world and her novel. The novel is a *bildungsroman* as much for the reader as for Elizabeth. Partly we learn in the usual way, by identifying with the heroine. But partly our education is wrought through the narrator of the novel. Satz has shown that this narrator assumes the epistemological task of pointing out the interpretations to which events and characters lend themselves (171). But narrators and the making of narratives are even more central in this book that is full of rival narrators engaged in making rival narratives. Wickham's story, for example, is told to Elizabeth in many versions through a series of narrators. First, she hears it from Wickham himself (77 ff.), then from Miss Bingley, whom she believes to be prejudiced against him (94), then from Jane who is not prejudiced but who is only, it turns out, repeating the story she heard from Bingley (95-96), who, in his turn, we then discover, did not know Wickham at all but only had his account from Darcy (96). Obvious in this tangle of narratives is not only Austen's emphasis on narration as an activity but, since these narratives do not differ very much in the data they offer but only in how it is interpreted, an emphasis too on the fact that narrative is always tied to a narrator, that every tale, like every fact, is only an interpretation reflecting the narrator's view or purpose, and that both narrator and narrative must, in consequence, be considered objects to be interpreted.

And it is exactly this fact that the chief narrator of the novel is designed to make us realize. The very first words are so constructed, in the irony of their tone, as to require interpretation. The narrator either intends what is written or its absolute opposite. But nothing in the words themselves tells us which of the two is meant. Many ironists have, we know (Jonathan Swift, whose "A Modest Proposal" was held by some to be suggesting that the Irish eat their children), lamented literal-minded readers who have taken them at their word and have so misread their meaning. A reader of Austen's opening sentence might well understand the words themselves and yet wholly miss their point. Austen thus positions her narrator and the reader of her text in a dialogue not of words but of meanings and intentions. The bond so created is complex and makes an epistemological statement. It gives us experiential evidence that, despite the skepticism of the empiricist position, despite the profoundly reflexive reality of its subjective point of view, and despite the relative nature of any truth it claims to find, reading, even if only feasible by conjecturing possibilities, is nonetheless, though always precarious, not entirely impossible.

From *Studies in the Novel* 37, no. 2 (Summer 2005): 141-161. Copyright © 2005 by The University of North Texas. Reprinted by permission.

Notes

1. Janis Stout, for example, has demonstrated that Austen is often more interested in her themes than in her action, Butler that her moral perspective rests on a solid base of ideas, and Susan Morgan that Austen's novels are not only firmly grounded in an "intellectual position," but that it is this very position that, in fact, unifies her works (3-4). Daniel Gunn shows that the rhetoric of her fiction is frequently ideological, Frederick Keener that she is the genuine heir of the "philosophical tale" that prevailed in the eighteenth century, and Stone that it is misleading to think that the limited scope of her action limits her philosophic dimensions.

2. While she holds that Austen's fiction cannot "release a theory of knowledge formed fully enough to be a systematic epistemology," and while she believes that Austen rejects "the inheritance of Locke" (3-4), Susan Morgan does conclude that Austen shares with her contemporaries a sense that the question of "how we perceive" can no longer be assumed but is a "dilemma" she must resolve (5).

3. This overwhelming conviction that Austen is, if anything, a rationalist in her epistemological views arises, in part, I think, from the fact that there is so much in her fiction that is essentially Augustan, from her dislike of excessive emotion to her well-balanced, sculptured sentences. The tendency has always been to assume she is of a piece with every aspect of the age, including its mainstream rationalism. But sitting on the line that divides the age of reason from the age of empiricism, she takes her imprint from both.

4. While no one has ever, as far as I know, taken her to be an empiricist—and some like Ryle insist she was never touched even by "echoes" of Butler and Hume (182)—a few have argued that Austen allows sentiment to temper reason in the making of moral choices (see, for example, Kearney) and, as Chillman has rightly claimed, sentiment in the Romantic period is largely grounded in empiricism. Zelda Boyd has, furthermore, argued that Austen and Hume share one thing, namely the view, as Hume expressed it, that one cannot derive an "ought" from an "is" (149).

5. This question of interpretation is foregrounded again in *Emma*. Here the "enig-

mas," "riddles," "charades" and "conundrums" the characters play (especially in Chapter 9) act as metaphors for the difficulties inherent in interpretation.

6. I owe my acquaintance with Arthur Fine's book to George Levine's discussion of it in his essay "Looking for the Real." In the literary field, antirealism, suggests Levine, might be said to acquiesce in the final "impossibility of unmediated knowledge" without entailing "a refusal to accept the conditions of 'homely' truths" (13). Susan Morgan says something similar. Rejecting the view of those who speak, as most of Austen's readers have done, of her novels in terms of "finalities," Morgan characterizes Austen as one who chose rather "to speak of the possible, the continuous, the incomplete" (80).

Works Cited

Austen, Henry. "Biographical Notice of the Author." *The Novels of Jane Austen.* 3rd ed. V. 3-8. Ed. R. W. Chapman. Oxford: Oxford UP, 1933.

Austen, Jane. *Mansfield Park.* 3rd ed. 1934. Ed. R. W. Chapman. Oxford: Oxford UP, 1988.

_____. *Northanger Abbey.* In *Northanger Abbey and Persuasion.* 1934. Ed. R. W. Chapman. Oxford: Oxford UP, 1988.

_____. *Pride and Prejudice.* 3rd ed. 1932. Ed. R. W. Chapman. Oxford: Oxford UP, 1988.

Austen-Leigh, James Edward. *A Memoir of Jane Austen.* London: Richard Bentley, 1870.

Booth, Wayne. *The Rhetoric of Fiction.* Chicago: U of Chicago P, 1961.

Boyd, Zelda. "The Language of Supposing: Modal Auxiliaries in *Sense and Sensibility.*" *Women and Literature* 3 (1983): 142-54.

Butler, Marilyn. *Jane Austen and the War of Ideas.* Cambridge, England: Clarendon P, 1975.

Chillman, Dawes. "Miss Morland's Mind: Sentiment, Reason, and Experience in *Northanger Abbey.*" *South Dakota Review* 1 (1963): 37-47.

Demarest, David P., Jr. "Legal Language and Situation in the Eighteenth-Century Novel: Readings in Defoe, Richardson, Fielding, and Austen." DAI 24 (1964): 2907. U of Wisconsin P.

Derrida, Jacques. *Of Grammatology.* Trans. Gayatri Chakravorty Spivak. Baltimore: Johns Hopkins UP, 1977.

Eco, Umberto. *Interpretation and Overinterpretation.* With Richard Rorty, Jonathan Culler, Christine Brooke-Rose. Ed. Stefan Collini. Cambridge: Cambridge UP, 1992.

Farrer, Reginald. "Jane Austen." *Quarterly Review* CCXXVIII (1917): 11-12, 16-18.

Fine, Arthur. *The Shaky Game: Einstein, Realism, and the Quantum Theory.* 1986. 2nd ed. Chicago: U of Chicago P, 1996.

Gunn, Daniel P. "In the Vicinity of Winthrop: Ideological Rhetoric in *Persuasion.*" *Nineteenth-Century Literature* 41.4 (1987): 403-18.

Hacking, Ian. *Representing and Intervening*. Cambridge: Cambridge UP, 1983.

Held, Leonard Edgar. *The Reader in* Northanger Abbey. DAI 38 (1977): 805A. U of New Mexico.

Hume, David. "Of the Standard of Taste." *Essays Moral, Political, and Literary*. 1757. Ed. Eugene F. Miller. Indianapolis, IN: Liberty Fund, Inc., 1985. 226-49.

James, William. "The Will To Believe." *The Will To Believe and Other Essays in Popular Philosophy and Human Immortality*. New York: Dover, 1956. 1-31.

Kearney, J. A. "Jane Austen and the Reason-Feeling Debate." *Theoria* 75 (1990): 107-22.

Keener, Frederick M. *The Chain of Becoming: The Philosophical Tale, The Novel, and a Neglected Realism of the Enlightenment: Swift, Montesquieu, Voltaire, Johnson, and Austen*. New York: Columbia UP, 1983.

Kelly, Gary. "The Art of Reading in *Pride and Prejudice*." *English Studies in Canada* 10.2 (1984): 156-71.

Laudan, Larry. *Science and Relativism*. Chicago: U of Chicago P, 1990.

Levine, George. "Looking for the Real." *Realism and Representation: Essays on the Problem of Realism in Relation to Science, Literature, and Culture*. Ed. George Levine. Madison: U of Wisconsin P, 1993. 3-23.

Meisel, Perry. "Everything You Always Wanted to Know About Structuralism but Were Afraid to Ask." *National Village Voice* 30 Sept. 1976: 43-45.

Meyersohn, Marylea. "A Habermas Speech-Act Model: Modes of Rationality in Jane Austen." *Language and Style* 24.3 (1991): 271-88.

Morgan, Susan. *In the Meantime: Character and Perception in Jane Austen's Fiction*. Chicago: U of Chicago P, 1980.

Morgan, T. H. *The Theory of the Gene*. 1929. New York: Hafner, 1964.

Newey, Katherine. "What Think You of Books?": Reading in *Pride and Prejudice. Sydney Studies in English* 21 (1995-1996): 81-94.

Nietzsche, Friedrich. *The Will to Power*. Trans. A.M. Ludovici. Vol. 16 of *The Complete Works of Friedrich Nietzsche*. Ed. Oscar Levy. New York: Russell & Russell, 1964.

Ryle, Gilbert. "Jane Austen and the Moralists." *English Literature and British Philosophy: A Collection of Essays*. Ed. S. P. Rosenbaum. Chicago: U of Chicago P, 1971.

Satz, Martha G. "An Epistemological Approach to *Pride and Prejudice:* Humility and Objectivity." *Women and Literature* 3 (1983): 171-86.

Saussure, Ferdinand de. *Cours de linguistique générale*. Ed. T. de Mauro. Paris: Payot, 1972.

Simpson, Richard. "Jane Austen." *North British Review* 52 (1870): 131-140.

Slatoff, Walter. *With Respect to Readers: Dimensions of Literary Response*. Ithaca: Cornell UP, 1970.

Stone, Donald D. "Sense and Semantics in Jane Austen." *Nineteenth-Century Fiction* 25.1 (1970): 31-50.

Stout, Janis P. "Jane Austen's Proposal Scenes and the Limitations of Language." *Studies in the Novel* 14 (1982): 316-26.

Pride and Prejudice and
the Beauty of Justice _____

Sarah Emsley

The history of Austen criticism is filled with people who have un-
derestimated the author's engagement in the serious questions of her
day. Austen's works do not seem on first reading to be politically engaged, and they are therefore easily dismissed as less than serious.
But as Sarah Emsley points out here, "Austen should also be taken
seriously as a philosophical and religious writer in the context of the
tradition of both men and women who wrote before her time."

In keeping with that principle, Emsley makes an argument about
the place of Christian humility in several of Austen's novels. It features large in *Sense and Sensibility*, but in *Pride and Prejudice*—a
more complicated novel, Emsley says—"There is more at stake," and
"Austen takes on the problems of anger and prejudice, investigating
how they work in relation or opposition to the principles of virtue." All
this leads her to conclude that *Pride and Prejudice*—though Austen
herself called it "light, & bright, & sparkling"—was in fact "intensely
serious, even the most serious of Austen's novels, despite and often
in places because of its comedy."   — J.L.

. . . perfect happiness the just reward of their virtues.

—Jane Austen, "Evelyn," Volume the Third (*MW* 191)

Like *Sense and Sensibility, Pride and Prejudice* is concerned with
the social virtue of amiability and the problem of how to be truthful and
civil simultaneously. Like Elinor, Elizabeth Bennet must negotiate
ways to keep her judgment independent while she behaves politely to
her family, her neighbors, and her enemies. But she has much more
spirit than Elinor, and thus has a great deal more trouble behaving civ-
illy when she is insulted or exasperated by others. In *Pride and Preju-*
dice, the tensions in Jane Austen's exploration of competing virtues are

heightened, yet it is not simply because Elizabeth has a harder time than Elinor at balancing amiability and civility. There is more at stake, the questions are more complicated, and the action is more dramatic in this novel because Austen takes on the problems of anger and prejudice, investigating how they work in relation or opposition to the principles of virtue.

A number of critics have read *Pride and Prejudice* as the humiliation of Elizabeth Bennet, objecting to the way in which the novel seems to require the subjection of Elizabeth's assertiveness to Darcy's better judgment.[1] The underlying assumption of such critics is, as Claudia L. Johnson says explicitly in *Jane Austen: Women, Politics, and the Novel*, that original sin is what Mary Bennet calls "thread-bare morality" (*PP* 60).[2] In addition to the tendency to see *Pride and Prejudice* as a story of humiliation, another trend of much longer standing has been to accept too readily as critical fact Austen's playful comment in a letter to Cassandra that *Pride* and *Prejudice* really is too "light, & bright, & sparkling" (*Letters*, February 4, 1813; 203).[3] A number of critics attempt to demonstrate Austen's seriousness by showing how the novel is "marked, even scarred, by history," or by arguing that Austen was a political subversive hiding behind conservative forms, because "the family of readers that Austen posited did not necessarily exist" in her own time.[4] Julia Prewitt Brown has argued convincingly that "Jane Austen's stature has declined with the rise of feminist literary criticism," suggesting that while feminist critics such as Mary Poovey, Nina Auerbach, Carolyn Heilbrun, and Sandra M. Gilbert and Susan Gubar read Austen as complicit in bourgeois ideology and see marriage in her novels as an inadequate substitute for independence, the criticism of men including F. R. Leavis, Ian Watt, Lionel Trilling, George Steiner, and Alasdair MacIntyre reads Austen as serious and internationally important.[5] I agree with Brown that the decline in Austen's reputation is a serious one, but whereas she would like to see Austen taken seriously primarily in the context of a feminism based on the works of Mary Wollstonecraft and George Eliot, I think Austen should also be taken seriously as a philosophical and religious writer in the context of the tradition of both men and women who wrote before her time.

In contrast to critics who focus on either humiliation or the scars of history in *Pride and Prejudice*, then, I argue first of all in this chapter that the change in Elizabeth is not due to repression and humiliation, but to a liberating process of education that leads to Christian humility. Humility in *Pride* and *Prejudice* is not abject self-abasement, but a right sense of one's own fallibility, and it is not just something Elizabeth learns in order to submit herself to Darcy, but something that they both learn so that they may together submit to God in the context of Christian marriage. In the second part of my argument, I defend some of the language—including the words *anger, prejudice*, and *judgment*—that Austen uses to describe the education of Darcy and Elizabeth, in order to demonstrate that *Pride and Prejudice* is intensely serious, even the most serious of Austen's novels, despite and often in places because of its comedy. It is serious not primarily because it is political in a historical sense—by which most critics mean that it participates implicitly in the debates surrounding the French Revolution and the Napoleonic Wars—but because it deals with the issues of courage and justice.[6] It is thus in fact highly political, insofar as Aristotle says that the question of "how shall our life together be ordered?" is the central issue of politics.[7] Both the seriousness and the beauty of *Pride and Prejudice* arise out of Austen's concern with how to get from sin to justice. Part of the answer to the question of this process has to do with humility, part of it also has to do with anger, and most of it has to do with love.

Sparkling or Serious?

There has always been a suspicion among readers—and especially among nonreaders—of Jane Austen's novels, that love is not quite a serious enough topic, even for a novel. Janeites are often caricatured as escapist readers indulging in a guilty pleasure, reading Jane Austen in a dream-world of fantasy, wish-fulfillment, Regency ball gowns, lace, and perfectly happy marriages. The real world, even the real world of other kinds of fiction, it is suggested, is much more serious than that. Even the best of the recent film adaptations do little to counteract the assumption that Austen novels are preoccupied with the perfect wedding as the culmination of every woman's dream.[8]

Pride and Prejudice, perhaps because it is one of the best-known and best-liked of the novels, is particularly vulnerable to the criticism that it is mere fantasy. Johnson calls the novel "almost shamelessly wish-fulfilling," Judith Lowder Newton describes it as "Austen's fantasy of female autonomy," and Isobel Armstrong says that its explorations of class privilege are limited, which is why "the assuaging and energizing dreamwork of its comedy have no parallel in Jane Austen's other novels." Armstrong defends Austen by saying that she was "no dreamer" because in *Mansfield Park* she next "constructed a text which would challenge" the dream of *Pride and Prejudice*. Attempting to defend the political seriousness of this novel, Marilyn Butler first of all writes that "It would not be in keeping with the serious mindedness of modern scholarship to rest content with the popular view of *Pride and Prejudice* as having no meaning at all," and goes on to suggest that "If in nothing else, a clue to the conservatism of the novel lies in the original title, 'First Impressions,'" which may indicate that "the early version was more dogmatic" than the later version with its revolutionary heroine.[9]

Even critics who are unwilling to accept the view that *Pride and Prejudice* has "no meaning at all," have had trouble reading it as politically engaged and therefore as serious writing. Thus, it remains read by many as irredeemably romantic or insufficiently political. Ironically, the barrier to taking *Pride and Prejudice* seriously has been that it is easy to accept Austen's own comments on her work as a serious statement of artistic fact.[10] If we are to take her seriously we need to read the whole "light and bright and sparkling" sentence closely. Austen writes of *Pride and Prejudice* that

The whole work is rather too light, & bright, & sparkling; it wants shade; it wants to be stretched out here & there with a long Chapter—of sense if it could be had; if not, of solemn specious nonsense—about something unconnected with the story; an Essay on Writing, a critique on Walter Scott, or the history of Buonaparte, or anything that would form a contrast & bring the reader with increased delight to the playfulness and Epigrammatism of the general stile. (*Letters*, February 4, 1813; 203)

These lines are clearly ironic: she may be modest here but it is widely agreed by now that she was not an unconscious artist, and if she really thought her novels needed extra long chapters of sense (Chapter 17 of Eliot's *Adam Bede* comes to mind) she could have added them. As she well knew, sense is pervasive throughout her novels—it is never an aside. In this sentence she anticipates the objections of some of her readers; she is not speaking as a serious critic of her novel, because the novel could speak for itself. Regrettably, the uncritical tendency to believe what writers say of their work, whether their intention is serious or ironic, has meant that many of Austen's readers think that she too thought *Pride and Prejudice* was "light."

Tragedy is never far away in *Pride and Prejudice*, and the brilliance of Austen's heroine is that Elizabeth can see the materially disastrous consequences of acting according to conscience and the good, yet she does the right thing anyway, refusing both Mr. Collins's modest competence and Mr. Darcy's powerful consequence because both men are, among other things, self-interested and self-important.[11] Mr. Collins is clearly ineducable; Darcy, however, is capable of improving the education of his judgment. The questions of judgment and education are not frivolous, nor is the problem of how to bring about the right kind of learning. Austen's question throughout *Pride and Prejudice* is Plato's question in the *Meno*: "Can virtue be taught?"

This is a sensible question and a serious one. As to the question of whether *Pride and Prejudice* is "too light, & bright, & sparkling" because "it wants . . . a long Chapter . . . of solemn specious nonsense," it is clear from Austen's use of the word specious that the novel does not want it at all. And the novel's intensely serious comedy is very much connected with its story. D.W. Harding is right that "The people who feel that her work would have been in some way more significant if she had dealt directly with contemporary great events are coming perilously close to the Prince Regent's Librarian with his suggestion" that she consider writing "any Historical Romance illustrative of the History of the august house of Coburg" (*Letters*, March 27, 1816; 311). Harding makes a useful distinction between being preoccupied with "abstract social questions" and being intelligently aware of them.[12] Those who are preoccupied with them will have little room for art; those who are oblivious to them will have little idea of the larger significance of their work; those who write with an awareness of history, society, and human nature will be able to achieve much more than either of the former kinds of writers.

"Regulated Hatred"

Although Harding is right that Austen's novels are not less significant for their lack of chapters of historical solemnity, his well-known interpretation of the novels as the author's way of achieving ironic distance from society because of her "regulated hatred" of society's vulgarities is too extreme. His understanding of Austen is that as a novelist "part of her aim was to find the means for unobtrusive spiritual survival, without open conflict with the friendly people around her whose standards in simpler things she could accept and whose affection she greatly needed."[13] The "subversive school" of Austen criticism takes its cue from Harding's pioneering reading between the lines of her novels, and ranges from such critics as Marvin Mudrick and John Halperin, who see Austen as bitterly ironic toward other human beings, to Johnson and Poovey, who see Austen's subversiveness as selective hatred directed against social structures and strictures rather than against vulgar people.

But the problem with the first version, by Harding and Mudrick, of the sharply satiric and subversive view of Austen, is that it may tempt readers to cultivate Mr. Bennet's kind of ironic detachment, reserve, and sense of his own superiority, rather than engaging even with difficult people and characters. Proponents of Austen as a proto-feminist political subversive ironically are in the same position as these critics: arguing, as Poovey does, that Austen only appeared to uphold conservative values in common with readers because she could not speak subversively in her own time, suggests that only a small group of enlightened readers today can understand the novels.[14] As Wayne C. Booth says in *The Rhetoric of Fiction* of many conservative Austen readers through the years, they have the "illusion of traveling intimately with a hardy little band of readers whose heads are screwed on tight and whose hearts are in the right place."[15] Thus even writers who celebrate Austen as a subversive feminist cultivate a small band of superior readers who can now understand Austen, even if her contemporary readers could not.

The idea that what Austen sought through her novels was "unobtrusive spiritual survival" is also problematic. In suggesting that Austen wanted to remain unobtrusive, Harding anticipates the feminist argument articulated by Johnson that she found silence empowering; that given her social situation as a single woman without wealth or status, the most effective thing she could do was to go along with the forms of "conservative myths" while silently objecting and plotting subtle ways to communicate her message of political change. In life it may be true that Austen wanted, to some extent, to remain unobtrusive—that she required seclusion for her writing, did not seek out literary circles, and tried not to offend her neighbors with overt criticisms of their vulgarities. But in her novels spiritual survival is not unobtrusive. It may be temporarily hidden or reserved, as in the case of Fanny Price seeking refuge in her room or Anne Elliot playing the piano in order to deflect attention from herself, but it eventually is shown to assert itself in various ways, as Fanny insists on not marrying Henry Crawford and Anne demonstrates her instincts for survival when she directs the response to Louisa's fall. And in *Pride and Prejudice* especially, precisely because of its bright and sparkling heroine, spiritual survival is shown to be central, as survival requires being actively engaged even with the most impossible people in order to address the pressing political problem of how our collective life should work. The unobtrusive survivor is Mr. Bennet, hiding in his library. Spiritual survival in Austen's novels, as it is exemplified by her most virtuous characters, requires not the rejection of the vulgar world (as in the ascetic Christian extreme or the eighteenth-century model of the discontented man of the world withdrawing from social life), but courageous engagement with the world in the service of justice. Harding's theory, therefore, that hatred is the driving force behind the novels, does not account for the positive energy they possess and inspire.

Righteous Anger

Hatred, even well-regulated, is still hatred, still negative. The idea that Austen's novels are powered by bitter hatred whether of people or institutions does not adequately explain the positive exuberance or the joy of her vision of human happiness. Austen writes with ironic humor and criticism and with sharp satire, but she also writes with pleasure and hope. To emphasize the joy in the novels is not in any way to lessen their seriousness or downplay their satire: it is in her comprehensive judgment of both good and bad that the powerful and the positive aspects of her work reside. Judgment, while it cannot coexist even with well-regulated hatred, does require the naming of evil. But it is the naming of evil in the service of love, not of hatred, and that is the important distinction for understanding Austen's novels. Distinguishing between good and evil is a central concern for her characters, and in order to do it they must learn to exercise judgment; they need to examine their prejudices and their principles, and doing so will unavoidably involve anger, whether it is anger at something that is evil in someone or something else, or anger at something in themselves. This is righteous anger, but it is temporary, because in the novels, as in the Christian tradition, love triumphs. It cannot do so, however, if no one recognizes what is wrong, becomes angry, and makes the effort to set things right; that is, makes an effort to establish justice.

What is central to *Pride and Prejudice* is not wish-fulfillment or fantasy, but justice, and how to get there. Readings of the novel that rely on the politics of the state or the politics of gender in Austen's time or our own in order to explain this novel are bound to demonstrate that women were required to be unobtrusive. But some of the very concepts that trouble Austen's readers because the words seem so negative, so humiliating, such as anger, prejudice, and judgment, are actually integral to the cause of virtue and justice. Integral, I must stress, only when rightly used and rightly understood. They are powerful concepts, and it is the difficult business of Austen's characters, in the novels generally and in *Pride and Prejudice* in particular, to learn exactly how to use them with courage and with love. Not all her characters are capable of learning this; not all her virtuous characters do it consistently well. But her analysis of how her characters think about social and political life together is what makes the novels so fascinating. It is righteous anger, not "regulated hatred," that is the source of Austen's ironic and artistic power, and that helps her characters determine how to act and how to live.

Anger is, strangely enough, closely tied to the practice of amiability. Those who never get upset at anything, who tolerate or even praise everyone and everything, are inevitably excessively amiable. More extreme than Mrs. Jennings in this excess is Mr. Collins. According to Aristotle, as I noted in the previous chapter, the excess of amiability is obsequiousness.[16] Mr. Collins is insufferably obsequious, and his attempts at civility are invariably excessive, as his confession to Mr. Bennet about his habit of "'arranging such little elegant compliments as may be adapted to ordinary occasions'" suggests (*PP* 68). Far from offering compliments that occur to him naturally in social situations, he contrives stock phrases to offer up, much like greeting-card verses kept in readiness for any emotional occasion.[17] This preparation saves him the trouble of actually assessing the abilities or charms of the individual ladies he meets, and ensures that he will never be astonished at the beauty of any one woman. And, as we know, it is not the individual woman he thinks of in his schemes of marriage, it is his own happiness.

When Elizabeth realizes that his "affections," such as they are, have been transferred to her, she "observed his increasing civilities toward herself, and heard his frequent attempt at a compliment on her wit and vivacity" (*PP* 88). His civilities are increasing to excess, and, significantly, it is a repeated attempt at one compliment. The unfortunate Mr. Collins aspires to the virtues of civility and humility, and it would be impossible to say that he falls short of them, for he far exceeds the mean in both cases. So much so, in fact, that Austen describes his walk into Meryton with the Bennet girls as passing "[i]n pompous nothings on his side, and civil assents on that of his cousins" (*PP* 72). Excessive civility turns into pompous behavior, while the sisters somehow manage to be appropriately civil in response. Civility is to amiability what manners are to morals: ideally the outward manifestation of real goodness, politeness based on respect, tolerance, and understanding.

The defective form of amiability is cantankerousness, churlishness, or contentiousness;[18] it involves a lack of manners and understanding, and is exemplified by Lady Catherine's cantankerous behavior and interference in the business of those around her. At Rosings in conversation with Elizabeth—really more of an interview than a real conversation—she is always exclaiming, one imagines, quite loudly, at the answers Elizabeth makes to her intrusive questions: "'Five daughters brought up at home without a governess!—I never heard of such a thing'" (*PP* 164); "'All!—What, all five out at once? Very odd!—And you only the second.—The younger ones out before the elder are married!'" (*PP* 165). At cards, "Lady Catherine was generally speaking—stating the mistakes of the three others, or relating some anecdote of herself" (*PP* 166). She does not aspire even to the most basic civilities of conversation, and instead criticizes other people without the least attempt to understand or respect them. She and Mr. Collins are indeed opposites, but neither is anywhere near virtue. Criticism and anger come too easily to Lady Catherine; Mr. Collins is not nearly critical enough.

Mr. and Mrs. Gardiner are often singled out as a rare example of the happily married couple, at ease with each other, their family, and their relations in society—whatever Miss Bingley and Mrs. Hurst may think of their position—and they serve as a good illustration of the mean, the center at which the virtue of amiability may be found. They fulfill Aristotle's criterion for true amiability, which is that they behave "alike towards those [they know] and those [they do] not know, towards intimates and those who are not so." Aristotle specifies that "in each of these cases" the virtuous person "will behave as is befitting; for it is not proper to have the same care for intimates and for strangers."[19] They are neither too defensive nor too generous. The civil behavior of the Gardiners to their relatives and to strangers is founded on a complex understanding of human nature; by offering respect and politeness to all, they leave open the possibility that even those who appear undeserving may turn out to be better than they seem, as Darcy in fact does. Yet when Lydia and Wickham elope the Gardiners are sufficiently angry to take action: once an individual has demonstrated that he or she is undeserving, even the amiable person is entitled to become angry—to a point. The contemplation of anger in the cause of justice is extremely difficult, and the action that follows such contemplation is even more difficult, because justice without mercy, without charity, is scarcely justice at all. Figuring out how anger is related to amiability, then, is something that can be learned only through practice.

The virtue of amiability is complicated for Mr. Darcy, and he is aware that it is: his problem, as he himself describes it, is that he does not have "'the talent which some people possess . . . of conversing easily with those I have never seen before. I cannot catch their tone of conversation, or appear interested in their concerns, as I often see done'" (*PP* 175). Elizabeth, describing her own performance at the piano, implies that like her, he does not "'take the trouble of practising'" (*PP* 175). Soon after this conversation, Elizabeth herself is called on to do what Marianne Dashwood calls "'practis[ing] the civilities'" (*SS* 347), as Lady Catherine makes comments on Elizabeth's piano-playing, "mixing with them many instructions on execution and taste"; Austen says, "Elizabeth received them with all the forbearance of civility" (*PP* 176). Civility clearly has a great deal to do with decorum, with maintaining social niceties even when one does not feel like being polite, but its practice is also shown to be closely related to morality.[20] By not responding rudely or angrily to Lady Catherine, Elizabeth is not merely doing what Mr. Collins asks her to when he tells her to dress simply because Lady Catherine "'likes to have the distinction of rank preserved'" (*PP* 161). This would be following the rules. Instead, by putting up with the incivility of others, she learns to practice and preserve her own amiability.

The Excuse for Incivility

The crucial moment in *Pride and Prejudice* in which the anger of both Darcy and Elizabeth is demonstrated is the first proposal scene. When Darcy finds his proposal rejected, he accuses Elizabeth of incivility: "'I might, perhaps, wish to be informed why, with so little *endeavour* at civility I am thus rejected'" (*PP* 190). Struggling for composure despite his anger, he feels that she has been rude in saying that if she "'could *feel* gratitude,'" she would thank him (*PP* 190). But of course she cannot feel it, and so she chooses not to pretend that she is grateful for his affections. Despite the fact that he will soon explain his own behavior and his struggles over his regard for her by avowing that "'disguise of every sort is my abhorrence'" (*PP* 192), he does seem to wish that she had disguised her frank statement that she cannot feel obligation or gratitude. Here again, the virtues are shown to be dramatically interesting, as it just is not possible to practice all the virtues at the same time, because they compete with one another. This is exactly what happens to both Elizabeth and Darcy in this scene. Both attempt to be civil: despite losing "all compassion in anger" when Darcy first speaks of the inferiority of her position, Elizabeth "tried, however, to compose herself to answer him with patience, when he should have done" (*PP* 189). Darcy likewise becomes "pale with anger," yet he speaks "in a voice of forced calmness" and "with assumed tranquillity [*sic*]" (*PP* 190-91).

But in spite of their efforts at first to be, or at least to seem, civil, the virtue of amiability comes into direct conflict with the virtue of truthfulness. Neither likes to lie; thus under pressure they tell each other the truth, Darcy that he loves her even though her relations are inferior, and Elizabeth that she cannot feel gratitude and therefore cannot even thank him for his proposal. And Elizabeth, when he accuses her of incivility, counters with her own implied accusation: by asking "'why with so evident a design of offending and insulting me, you chose to tell me that you liked me against your will, against your reason, and even against your character?'" she argues that he transgressed against civility first, and so she feels justified in asking "'Was not this some excuse for incivility, if I *was* uncivil?'" (*PP* 190). When she seeks an excuse for her own reaction, she is not simply searching for something that will explain her transgression against a rule of virtue, a code of conduct, but she is reaching for a tradition in which, as I suggested in chapter three, the virtue of civility exists in tension with the virtue of honesty.

In this scene, neither character can exist for long within that tension, and both are overcome by anger, but, as I have been suggesting, anger is not necessarily always a bad thing. It is important that Elizabeth and Darcy struggle not with politeness as it is tested against the temptation to become rude or angry, but instead they wrestle first with two competing virtues, amiability and truthfulness, before they become truly angry. It is hard to be virtuous, but it is even harder when the virtues will not exist equally and simultaneously. The outbursts of honesty and anger that follow are brief but powerful. With respect to anger, Aristotle calls the excessive form irascibility or revengefulness, and says that the deficiency has no real name, but the right disposition is something like patience, or good temper. He says, "The man who is angry at the right things and with the right people, and, further, as he ought, when he ought, and as long as he ought, is praised."[21] Neither Elizabeth nor Darcy gives in to anger completely, as they reveal, honestly, why they are angry, and yet they are both trying to be patient and civil. Elizabeth again tries "to the utmost to speak with composure" (*PP* 192) and Darcy, leaves her, with "incredulity and mortification," true, but with civil parting words: "'Forgive me for having taken up so much of your time, and accept my best wishes for your health and happiness'" (*PP* 193). The apology may be narrow—he does not apologize for anything he has said or for injuring her feelings, but his wish for her welfare shows that he can pay attention to what is apart from himself.

Practicing Amiability and Civility

It is not until Elizabeth and the Gardiners meet him at Pemberley that Darcy begins to demonstrate that he is learning to practice the virtue of amiability. Elizabeth is surprised that he wishes to be introduced to her uncle and aunt—"This was a stroke of civility for which she was quite unprepared" (*PP* 254)—and yet she then hears him invite her uncle, "with the greatest civility, to fish there as often as he chose" (*PP* 255). Darcy is practicing civility even toward those he does not know—this is in sharp contrast to his remarks on his first meeting with Elizabeth. While Mr. Gardiner suspects that "'perhaps he may be a little whimsical in his civilities,'" Elizabeth explains to them that Darcy's "character was by no means so faulty, nor Wickham's so amiable, as they had been considered in Hertfordshire" (*PP* 258).

Wickham's manners, his civil behavior and pleasing address, convinced many that he was amiable; Darcy's manners, on the other hand, convinced many that he was guilty of pride, conceit, and even perhaps cantankerousness. Wickham's character demonstrates that it is possible to be civil without being truly amiable. The civilities, then, are lesser virtues; though it is still possible to behave in excess or defect of the virtue of civility, this virtue is more a matter of form. Even Miss Bingley can be civil, though hers is often described as "cold civility" (*PP* 42). Politeness and etiquette may reflect an amiable character and a complex moral life, but they clearly cannot substitute for them. Here the civilities are more like a set of rules to follow, rules that may give the appearance of goodness, and may contribute to the preservation of decorum, but which in isolation from other virtues can be dangerous. Civility often disguises anger, and often should. Yet there are no rules for exactly when and how anger should be concealed or repressed, and when it should be spoken. Once again, the pressure is on the individual to learn, to feel, to know, to judge, and to accept responsibility for mistakes. As Henry Tilney puts it in *Northanger Abbey*, "'When properly to relax is the trial of judgment'" (*NA* 134). Prudence and wisdom are essential to the pursuit of justice and the practice of amiability.

Righteous anger is a tremendously difficult concept, and is next to impossible to practice in a virtuous way, and yet in the first proposal scene both Elizabeth and Darcy are justified to some extent in their anger with each other. There is no easy way to be reconciled in a polite compromise. They are trying to find the truth, and they are right to be angry with each other when they suspect deviations from truth. As Aristotle suggests, however, it is important to control anger, and to be sure that one is only angry with the right people, for the right length of time. Near the end of *Pride and Prejudice*, when she and Darcy are discussing that first proposal and he exclaims, "'How you must have hated me after that evening,'" Elizabeth registers her awareness of the changes in her level of anger: "'Hate you! I was angry perhaps at first, but my anger soon began to take a proper direction'" (*PP* 369). To understand how anger may work toward justice it will be necessary to consider the difficult questions of prejudice and judgment.

Prejudice in Favor of the Good

How can prejudice possibly be defensible? To the extent that it is an unthinking bias against someone or something, it is not; but the idea of having preconceived opinions warrants further consideration. When one is predisposed in favor of something that is good, like fairness, or beauty, or kindness, one's prejudices prevent one from giving equal weight to things that are opposed to them. If prejudice is understood as prepossession, or adherence to principle, it is quite different, and much more acceptable, than the idea of judging adversely in advance of the situation or the facts.[22] While Jane Austen does not by any means advocate all prejudice as good, it is worth thinking about prejudice as a complex word and a complex issue in her novels, especially, for obvious reasons, in *Pride and Prejudice*.

For example, Elizabeth is prejudiced in favor of good sense; judging Mr. Collins by that principle, not only in advance of his arrival at Longbourn, but also during his visit there, she finds him deficient. Although she has prejudged him during the conversation with her father and sisters at breakfast when they analyze his letter, her prejudice is borne out by her later observation of his behavior. Her prejudice in favor of good sense leads to a prejudice against, and then a judgment of Mr. Collins's foolishness, and when his lack of sense threatens to impinge on her own freedom she rejects his offer of marriage in the name of principle. Jane, who has fewer prejudices and is more greatly disposed to approve of everyone—Elizabeth says she is "'a great deal too apt you know, to like people in general'" (*PP* 14)—might have accepted him.

Good judgment always relies to some extent on prejudices in favor of the good—the difficult thing is determining when a judgment is too hastily made. Judgment involves discrimination, another unfashionable word, in order to make sure that it is good judgment. Tolerance, compassion, and sympathy invoked without limits are just as dangerous as prejudice, discrimination, and judgment made without reason. Just as a virtue is better understood as a quality with limits and degrees

---

rather than as the diametric opposite of a vice, judgment is better understood as incorporating aspects of anger, prejudice, and discrimination, as well as incorporating understanding, mercy, and love, than as a rigid system of negative pronouncements.

The problem, then, for Elizabeth and Darcy, is that although both have understandable and defensible prejudices in favor of civility and good breeding, they both judge each other too quickly as offending against those ideals. That they are apt to judge others is not in itself a bad thing—their judgment is independent, in contrast to Mr. Bingley's preference of relying on his friends to judge for him, and it is intelligent, in contrast to Jane's too-generous candor and subsequent susceptibility to Miss Bingley's guile—but their tendency to judge others before they judge themselves is a serious problem for both Elizabeth and Darcy. Their potential, then, to exercise good judgment is superior, but as yet uneducated, and both make mistakes. As Darcy says of Bingley in his letter to Elizabeth, "'Bingley has great natural modesty,—with a stronger dependence on my judgment than on his own.—To convince him, therefore, that he had deceived himself [with regard to Jane's affection], was no very difficult point'" (*PP* 199). Darcy is confident in his own powers of perception, and does not stop to question his own judgment. Likewise, Elizabeth is certain that Charlotte would never act so foolishly as to show more affection than she feels in order to secure a husband, and of course is soon obliged to reexamine her convictions. With respect to each other, their judgments are premature, as Darcy pronounces Elizabeth tolerable, but not handsome enough to tempt him, before he has thought very much about her looks or had a chance to see what effect her liveliness has on her looks, and Elizabeth establishes her inflexible view that Darcy is proud and disagreeable before she has even spoken to him. Their prejudices are founded on first appearances, not even on first impressions of conversation; neither has an adequate basis for good judgment.

While early on they make wrong decisions, Darcy soon revises his under the influence of love, and the education he receives from the moment he begins to love Elizabeth is a difficult one. Love is beautiful, but education can be painful, as it is hard to come to terms with one's own mistakes. The fear of shame, however, as Plato has Phaedrus suggest in the *Symposium*, can inspire the individual to learn more and to be more virtuous. The pursuit of love and the pursuit of the beautiful involve openness to error. Elaine Scarry writes in *On Beauty and Being Just* that beauty "ignites the desire for truth by giving us, with an electric brightness shared by almost no other uninvited, freely arriving perceptual event, the experience of conviction and the experience, as well, of error."[23] Scarry suggests that the love of the beautiful, far from distracting us from what is just, can instead drive us to seek justice.

In Darcy's case, by the time he writes his letter to Elizabeth, in the aftermath of the anger over injustices in the proposal scene, he has realized that judgment and justice are more difficult than he had previously thought. In describing why he convinced Bingley of Jane's indifference, he shows a new openness to reconsidering his own judgments on the basis of better information: he writes, "'If *you* have not been mistaken here, *I* must have been in an error. Your superior knowledge of your sister must make the latter probable.—If it be so, if I have been misled by such error, to inflict pain on her, your resentment has not been unreasonable'" (*PP* 197). He also recognizes that she has not had enough information to judge Wickham correctly: "'Ignorant as you previously were of every thing concerning either, detection could not be in your power, and suspicion certainly not in your inclination'" (*PP* 202). Just as the truths of the proposal scene were painful to both, sorting out the truth in the letter is painful; the difference is that when he was proposing and then being rejected, Darcy thought only of himself—"'And this . . . is your opinion of me! This is the estimation in which you hold me!'" (*PP* 192). When he is writing the letter to Elizabeth he is thinking of the pain that the truths he tells will give her: "'Pardon me.—It pains me to offend you'" (*PP* 198). In the letter, in addition to explaining his own actions, he is trying to establish what is right: he asks if he has been mistaken regarding Jane, he reveals the reasons for his adverse judgment of Wickham, and he is at pains to judge correctly.

Learning the Art of Judgment

In their book *The New Idea of a University*, Duke Maskell and Ian Robinson argue that in Jane Austen's fiction "There is no saying in advance how we ought or ought not to speak, no prescribing the best style. There are judgements to be made but no rules to follow, no skills to be exercised."[24] While it is true that there are no prescriptions for speech or behavior, judgments are not made without reference to principle. In his letter Darcy appeals to his observation of Jane, which he acknowledges to be incomplete, and his experience of Wickham, which he maintains is a solid basis for judgment. Prejudice formed on superficial observation is shown to be faulty: Darcy needs to learn to look more closely before judging others, to let Bingley judge for himself, and most importantly, to judge himself more strictly than he judges others, and to do that first, while leaving open the possibility that others will behave better than he expects them to. Yet with Wickham, he has greater reason to judge his character because he has seen him deceive again and again. While the Bible would tell Darcy to forgive his brother seventy times seven, or to welcome the prodigal son home again, Wickham is neither Darcy's brother nor his son, and he is not repentant. And forgiveness does not necessarily mean Darcy has to continue to let Wickham take advantage of him. Judgment is not a skill that can be taught by obeying rules; it is an art. And art is harder to achieve than the correct execution of technical skill.

By writing the letter, Darcy demonstrates some of the ways in which he is learning this art. Reading it, and rereading it, Elizabeth exemplifies Austen's model for the art of education. Maskell and Robinson suggest that *Pride and Prejudice* provides a framework by which we can understand what education should be. But they point to Mr.

Bennet's breakfast seminar on the textual analysis of Mr. Collins's letter as the ideal model, with a learned man offering to young students a piece of writing for discussion.[25] Mrs. Bennet's response focuses more on her projections for the future than on the matter at hand, saying, "'There is some sense in what he says about the girls however; and if he is disposed to make them any amends, I shall not be the person to discourage him'" (*PP* 63). Two of his other listeners, preoccupied with other things, decline to comment, as "To Catherine and Lydia, neither the letter nor its writer were in any degree interesting" (*PP* 64). Each of the other three offers her opinion of the text, with one determined to like it (Jane), one commenting pedantically on style (Mary), and one (Elizabeth) arriving at something resembling the seminar leader's own opinion, thereby at once demonstrating her critical capacities and pleasing her teacher. The idea of the seminar discussion represented here is a useful comment on education, but it is not the best model for it.

For one thing, Maskell and Robinson give Mr. Bennet too much credit for wisdom. They write that "As Mr. Bennet, without aiming to, just in the ordinary course of domestic life, educates his daughter Elizabeth, so Elizabeth reeducates the formally educated Darcy, and is educated by him in turn."[26] In the ordinary course of domestic life, Mr. Bennet is usually in his library, ignoring the education of all his daughters, including Elizabeth. And in the breakfast seminar scene, he gives no guidance to his students: he simply offers them a text to think about and then prepares to enjoy laughing at their responses to it. He teaches only his own prejudices. That Elizabeth responds intelligently owes nothing to the powers of the seminar leader (except in this case, perhaps genetic inheritance), and everything to her own judgment: "'He must be an oddity, I think,' said she. 'I cannot make him out.—There is something very pompous in his stile.—And what can he mean by apologizing for being next in the entail.—We cannot suppose he would help it, if he could.—Can he be a sensible man, sir?'" (*PP* 64). In asking this question she is not seeking confirmation of her suspicion, but drawing out the reluctant participant at the table and forcing him to give his own opinion to the group, which he has hitherto concealed from his students just as he has concealed the very fact of the letter and of Mr. Collins's visit for a month. In both cases he enjoys the concealment and the resulting attention he gets when he does reveal something. At Elizabeth's prompting, he offers his opinion, which reveals more about his anticipation of entertainment than about his judgment of Mr. Collins's lack of sense; thus he does not address Elizabeth's question adequately. He replies, "'No, my dear; I think not. I have great hopes of finding him quite the reverse. There is a mixture of servility and self-importance in his letter, which promises well. I am impatient to see him'" (*PP* 64).[27]

Elizabeth's Education

Like Maskell and Robinson, Susan Fraiman sees Mr. Bennet as the source of Elizabeth's initial intellectual power; however, while they argue that Elizabeth goes on to educate Darcy, Fraiman argues that Elizabeth loses that power: she writes that "Enabled by her father, this unique Bennet daughter sets out with a surplus of intellectual confidence and authority which, in the course of the novel, she must largely relinquish."[28] Mr. Bennet does recognize Elizabeth's intellectual superiority, but he is not responsible for her education. When Lady Catherine speculates that if the Bennet girls had no governess—"'I always say that nothing is to be done in education without steady and regular instruction, and nobody but a governess can give it'"—their "'mother must have been quite a slave to your education'," Elizabeth answers that "that had not been the case": "'but such of us as wished to learn, never wanted the means. We were always encouraged to read, and had all the masters that were necessary. Those who chose to be idle, certainly might'" (*PP* 164-65). In the past Mr. Bennet may have encouraged reading, and provided other instructors or tutors from time to time, but he did not undertake the formal education of his daughters.

No more does he contribute to the education of Elizabeth's judgment in the course of the novel. Elizabeth's education comes from her own self-examination, and the beginnings of that process arise from her contemplation of Darcy's letter. This is not to say, as Fraiman does, that Darcy becomes the agent of her education—Fraiman describes "a darker, downward vector" in what she sees as "the narrative that passes Elizabeth from one father to another and, in doing so, takes her from shaping judgments to being shaped by them"[29]—with his letter offering its judgment of her, but that the letter provides the occasion for her to educate herself.

If Elizabeth were to attempt to maintain her self-esteem by persisting in her initial impression of the letter, that would indicate a dark and downward vector. At first she reads "with a strong prejudice against every thing he might say" (*PP* 204)—clearly the wrong kind of prejudice, as it makes learning impossible. She is "too angry to have any wish of doing him justice" (*PP* 204). But although "for a few moments, she flattered herself that her wishes did not err"—that is, that her judgment of Wickham is intact and infallible—and although if she were to do what she intends to do with the letter and "never look in it again" (*PP* 205) she would indeed confirm her previous judgments and blindly proceed with the vain assurance of her own confidence, she does not put the letter away, and she does not leave her opinions unquestioned. When she "protest[s] that she would not regard" (*PP* 205) the letter, it is because she suspects that it will challenge her. At this point, she has not read the whole letter anyway: she "put it hastily away" even "though scarcely knowing any thing of the last page or two" (*PP* 205). She is not in a position to judge the letter because she has not read the whole text. Reading the whole thing is the first part of education.

The second part is to read it all over again: "when she read, and re-read with the closest attention, the particulars immediately following of Wickham's resigning all pretensions to the living, of his receiving in lieu, so considerable a sum as three thousand pounds, again she was forced to hesitate" (*PP* 205). She puts down the letter, deliberates, and then rereads again and again. It is not just the information Darcy provides that makes it possible for her to reformulate her judgment, but the fact that this information prompts her to think more carefully about other things she already knows about Wickham and about Darcy. As she rereads Darcy's account of Wickham, she finds that "she could bring no proof of its injustice" (*PP* 205). It is not the revelation that Wickham tried to elope with Georgiana Darcy that causes her to change her mind; she does not rely as others do on Darcy's judgment alone. The key to her education is the way in which new knowledge enlarges, revises, and enlightens previous knowledge. Elizabeth thinks on the past and focuses on her conversations with Wickham: "She was *now* struck with the impropriety of such communications to a stranger, and wondered it had escaped her before" (*PP* 207).

Elizabeth's education comes from an intense engagement with a significant text that does not tell her how to think or how to live, but inspires her to rethink what she thinks of herself. The consequence of that education is that she is reminded that it is human to be wrong, not always but often, and that in order to know anything she must be humble and careful. In recognizing the extent of her error, she does find it humiliating, but in addition to the humiliation inherent in the situation it is important to note that she sees the justice of her new assessment of herself "'How humiliating is this discovery!—Yet how just a humiliation!— Had I been in love, I could not have been more wretchedly blind'" (*PP* 208). To persist in errors that occurred because she had "courted prepossession and ignorance, and driven reason away" (*PP* 208) would be further folly. It is necessary for her to recognize her fault so that she can turn from it; she has to go to one extreme in order to rise to the other. It is not possible to learn anything if one cannot learn from one's mistakes.

Elizabeth does not dwell on her humiliation once she has recognized that "'Till this moment, I never knew myself'" (*PP* 208), but moves on to further consideration of other things, this time, like Darcy, thinking of the pain of others rather than of herself. "From herself to Jane—

from Jane to Bingley, her thoughts were in a line which soon brought to her recollection that Mr. Darcy's explanation *there*, had appeared very insufficient; and she read it again" (*PP* 208). Once she knows herself, she does not focus on herself, because she is no longer humiliated: she is free to think of others, and "Neither could she deny the justice of his description of Jane" (*PP* 208). Again, the model of her education means that she reads, thinks, and rereads. This process as Austen dramatizes it in this passage is a more detailed, more imaginative, more serious, and more effective example of how education works than the seminar scene with Mr. Bennet. Mr. Bennet's method of instruction is self-serving: his goal is his own entertainment, not the advancement of his students. As Elizabeth says to Jane in Volume Three, Chapter Twelve, "'We all love to instruct, though we can teach only what is not worth knowing'" (*PP* 343). Virtue is not easily taught, as the example of Mr. Bennet's attempt at instruction demonstrates. Some people, in fact, are incapable of learning much anyway. But the process of revising judgment on the basis of better information reveals, in the scene in which Elizabeth comes to terms with Darcy's letter and with her own mind, that virtue can be learned.

Good judgment does not by any means come easily to Elizabeth following this scene. In fact, she is wary of judgment or action, as is apparent in her decision not to reveal Wickham's character to anyone but Jane, and her subsequent lament after Wickham and Lydia elope that, as she says to Darcy, "'Oh! had I known what I ought, what I dared, to do! But I knew not—I was afraid of doing too much'" (*PP* 277-78). Once Wickham involves Lydia in his escapades, Elizabeth is firm in her revised judgment of him—"'Wickham will never marry a woman without some money. He cannot afford it'"—but she is also careful to acknowledge the limits of her knowledge: "As to what restraint the apprehension of disgrace in the corps might throw on a dishonourable elopement with her, I am not able to judge; for I know nothing of the effects that such a step might produce" (*PP* 283).

Although her judgment is moderated, as I argued in the introduction, it has not disappeared and it is still her own. Fraiman argues that "Darcy woos away not Elizabeth's 'prejudice,' but her judgment entire."[30] This reading is based primarily on the passage in the novel in which Elizabeth begins

> to comprehend that [Darcy] was exactly the man, who, in disposition and talents, would most suit her. His understanding and temper, though unlike her own, would have answered all her wishes. It was an union that must have been to the advantage of both; by her ease and liveliness, his mind might have been softened, his manners improved, and from his judgment, information, and knowledge of the world, she must have received benefit of greater importance. (*PP* 312)

Fraiman objects to this passage, saying that "What may surprise and sadden us, . . . and what the novel surely registers with a touch of irony, is that a heroine who began so competent to judge should end up so critically disabled, so reliant for judgment on somebody else."[31] But Austen does not say that Elizabeth would adopt Darcy's judgments; she would benefit from his wider experience, which is simply a way to gain access to some of the aspects of more formal education that have been denied her as a woman. Their marriage will be a marriage of equals, as Mr. Bennet's warning to Elizabeth about avoiding an unequal marriage indicates. Elizabeth does not see it as marriage to a superior any more than she sees it as marriage to an inferior, as I have discussed in the introduction. By the time she marries Darcy she has already helped him to reeducate his own judgment, and so for him to share his knowledge of the world with her does not mean she will be subservient to all his views.

Courage and Love

The process of learning good judgment, virtuous judgment, in *Pride and Prejudice* is extremely difficult. How does one know how to judge without excessive prejudice, excessive anger, and without arrogance, self-righteousness, and rigid intolerance? The answer implicit in the novel is through the prudence and wisdom to adhere to good principles in the first place, but also through the courage to learn, accept, and revise the places where one goes wrong. *Pride and Prejudice* is about cultivating the courage to be open to education through a constant revision of self-knowledge in order to try to understand one's principles better and to act according to them. Paradoxically, courage requires humility. Those who resist Austen's insistence that after Elizabeth learns what Darcy has done to bring about Lydia's marriage, "For herself she was humbled; but she was proud of him," do not give full weight to the next sentence: "Proud that in a cause of compassion and honour, he had been able to get the better of himself" (*PP* 327). This passage highlights the paradoxical interdependence of virtues, for in order to act courageously in the name of honor, Darcy has had to humble his pride and act with compassion, not condescension. And Elizabeth is humbled not because he has condescended to help her family, but because she feels anew the injustice of her early treatment of him: "Oh! how heartily did she grieve over every ungracious sensation she had ever encouraged, every saucy speech she had ever directed towards him" (*PP* 327). This echo of the general Confession in the Book of Common Prayer points to the Christian nature of the humility with which both Darcy and Elizabeth therefore approach marriage.[32] Both of them repent and confess, and resolve to act better in future: this pattern represents the eternal quest of the Christian soul to reach a state of grace. It is because Darcy and Elizabeth discover humility that they are both able to submit to each other in Christian marriage.

Justice and Memory

Jane Austen is interested in how characters can act courageously in the service of truth and justice. Part of that service involves sympathy, as Darcy learns to see where he gives pain to others, and Elizabeth's knowledge of her self makes it possible for her to think more of others. David E. Gamble compares Elizabeth's education in sympathetic judgment with the process Adam Bede goes through when he learns he has misjudged Hetty Sorrel, and he concludes that "In the end, Lizzie and Adam both show that sympathy is not so much a matter of truth as it is a practical necessity for dealing with others and the world." Invoking George Eliot's image of the pier-glass from Chapter 27 of *Middlemarch*, Gamble writes that "Our sympathy is itself a light which distorts its objects—the only difference is that it seems to work a little better than egoism." Although this may be true of how sympathy works in Eliot's novels, Gamble bases his argument about Austen on Elizabeth's injunction to Darcy to "'Think only of the past as its remembrance gives you pleasure'" (*PP* 369), and he suggests that Elizabeth is willing to forget the past "for the sake of the future amiability.[33] Like Gamble, Claudia L. Johnson reads this as a serious statement of Elizabeth's, and Austen's, philosophy about "the wish for and experience of happiness and pleasure."[34] Austen is not sending Elizabeth in pursuit of the freedom of pleasure, however, but in pursuit of happiness as a good. And Darcy does not believe Elizabeth believes what she calls her philosophy—"'I cannot give you credit for any philosophy of the kind,'" he says (*PP* 369). Elizabeth does not really believe this philosophy, given how much time she has spent in the course of the narrative going over the past, spending more time remembering painful things than pleasant, because she wishes to learn from the most difficult things.[35] The characters in *Pride and Prejudice* who do think on the past only as it gives them pleasure are Lydia and Wickham: on their visit to Longbourn following their wedding, "They seemed each of them to have the happiest memories in the world. Nothing of the past was recollected with pain" (*PP* 316).

In the first proposal scene, the writing of the letter, and Elizabeth's reading of the letter and her subsequent reassessment of her memory of the past, both Elizabeth and Darcy have experienced pain. They have had to acknowledge their mistakes, and they have had to revise their memories of past events. Darcy has had to admit that Elizabeth is probably right about Jane, and he later acknowledges to Bingley that he made a mistake in keeping from him the news that Jane was in London. Both Darcy and Elizabeth examine their memories, and both of them find the process painful. Yet when it is over, they do not then forget. They forgive each other, and their memories of the pain of having their pride humbled will fade with time. But they do not seriously advocate the beauty of forgetting as the solution to being overburdened with memories. The justice that comes with remembering and examining memory is far more beautiful than the playfulness of selective forgetting could ever be.

Learning to Practice the Virtues

Austen suggests in *Pride and Prejudice* that we need not all remember everything all of the time, and we may need to forgive and forget, but the balance between memory and forgetting must be negotiated at the right time, in the right manner, for the right length of time, and so on. It will not do to create new memories based on inclination and pleasure. This is not Austen's idea of freedom. Freedom will only come with a just understanding of the past, present, and future, and for that her heroines need to examine and reexamine their memories, their motivations, and to act in future with an understanding based on just memories of the past.

In their discussion following the second proposal, Darcy says to Elizabeth about his letter that "'I knew . . . that what I wrote must give you pain, but it was necessary'" (*PP* 368). Justice is difficult and judgment of character and action can be painful, but the difficulty and the pain are sometimes necessary. Darcy regrets the bitterness of the beginning of the letter, but Elizabeth assures him that "'The adieu is charity itself'" (*PP* 368). In the same way that he limited his anger at the end of the first proposal by offering his best wishes for her health and happiness, he concluded the letter by saying, "'I will only add, God bless you'" (*PP* 203). Darcy's own education, though not represented in the same detail as Elizabeth's, arises equally from his gradual conviction of the rightness of her criticism of his conduct. Especially in her attack on the fact that he did not behave as a gentleman, he has received a shock, and he says that her words "'have tortured me;—though it was some time, I confess, before I was reasonable enough to allow their justice'" (*PP* 367-68). "Gentleman-like" behavior is here not only manners, but morals, as Darcy, like Elizabeth, must recognize how to change in order to behave justly. Just behavior is not simply the kind of restorative justice that Darcy brings about in the case of Lydia's marriage to Wickham, either. Before either Darcy or Elizabeth can act to restore justice, they must reach a philosophical standpoint from which they can appraise their own minds justly.

In *Pride and Prejudice*, justice is achieved through education, and education is possible only through courage, humility, and love. As Maskell and Robinson rightly observe, "Without love education will not get far." Integral to education is the ability to make good judgments about the world, a text, another person, and especially one's self, in order to move beyond the self and enter into engagement with the world, through reading and through sympathizing with other people. Maskell and Robinson are right that "Jane Austen goes further" than Socrates does in his suggestion that "'The unreasoned life . . . is not worth living'": for Austen, "a life without judgement . . . would not be a human life at all."[36] To be truly virtuous, civility must be accompanied by genuine amiability (which Wickham does not have), and amiability must be exhibited through the forms of civility (which Darcy learns). Virtues may be thrown into competition with each other (as Elizabeth and Darcy discover when they try to uphold the virtues of civility, honesty, and patience), but although they don't always coexist peacefully and simultaneously, they are nevertheless dependent on one another.

It is in the education of judgment that virtue can flourish; courage and justice and love are the serious ideals of *Pride and Prejudice*. The novel brilliantly outlines ways to know what virtue is and how to prac-

---

tice it, and in doing so, *Pride and Prejudice* exemplifies Austen's fullest expression of the range of the virtues. Yet it is not an ethical manual or treatise, but a serious and comic novel of morals and manners. In its investigation of the serious questions of anger, prejudice, and judgment, and of the way in which these concepts may be seen as integral to the tradition of the virtues of justice and love, *Pride and Prejudice* is, I think, Austen's most accomplished novel. At the conclusion of the novel, Elizabeth writes to her aunt Mrs. Gardiner, uniting the ideals of justice and happiness in the announcement of her union with Darcy: she writes that "'I am the happiest creature in the world. Perhaps other people have said so before, but not one with such justice'" (*PP* 382-83).

From *Jane Austen's Philosophy of the Virtues*, 83-106. Copyright © 2005 by Palgrave Macmillan. Reprinted by permission of Palgrave Macmillan.

Abbreviations

NA = Northanger Abbey
SS = Sense and Sensibility
PP = Pride and Prejudice
Letters = Jane Austen's Letters

Notes

1. See e.g., Judith Lowder Newton, *Women, Power, and Subversion*; Mary Poovey, *Proper Lady*; and Susan Fraiman, *Unbecoming Women*. The argument that Austen's heroines are forced into humiliating submission stems from Sandra M. Gilbert's and Susan Gubar's influential *The Madwoman in the Attic*, which argues that Austen's imaginative heroines are "mortified, humiliated, even bullied into sense" (159), and that "the happy ending of an Austen novel occurs when the girl becomes a daughter to her husband, an older and wiser man who has been her teacher and her advisor, whose house can provide her with shelter and sustenance and at least derived status, reflected glory" (154).

2. Johnson sums up the attitude of many recent critics of Austen when she argues that "*Pride and Prejudice* invites us not to chide Elizabeth with threadbare morality about original sin, but on the contrary, if not actually to flatter people's pride as Wick-

ham and Collins do, then at least to honor it" (*Jane Austen: Women, Politics, and the Novel*, 83).

3. For example, in their biographies of Austen, both David Nokes and Carol Shields miss the irony of Jane Austen's comments about adding "shade" and stretching out the novels with "a long chapter of sense."

4. Armstrong, Introduction to *Pride and Prejudice*, ix; Johnson, *Jane Austen: Women, Politics, and the Novel*, 75; Poovey, *Proper Lady*, 115.

5. Brown, "Feminist Depreciation," 303.

6. Unlike most critics who argue that Austen is political, Roger Gard sees Austen as politically representative precisely because her work is not overtly political: "Unpolitical, she is *therefore* the realistic novelist of an evolving national democracy" (*Jane Austen's Novels: The Art of Clarity*, 17).

7. See Aristotle's *Politics*. Austen's heroines begin with the ethical question "How should I live my life?" and the novels also open up political questions about how our collective life should be lived, in the context of a civil society.

8. Andrew Davies's 1995 miniseries based on *Pride and Prejudice*, though well-done and for the most part faithful to the spirit of the novel, is particularly guilty of reinforcing the image of the wedding as the climax of the story, with its focus on costumes, carriages, and kissing forming a sharp contrast to Austen's single-sentence reference to the weddings of Jane and Bingley, Elizabeth and Darcy: "Happy for all her maternal feelings was the day on which Mrs. Bennet got rid of her two most deserving daughters" (*PP* 385). One-line weddings do not translate well to the screen. The wedding scene in Emma Thompson's version of *Sense and Sensibility* (1995) is just as elaborate. Ironically, it is the scripts that invent wholly new concluding scenes that are more successful at conveying the spirit of Austen's conclusions. Davies does better in his 1996 *Emma* than in his version of *Pride and Prejudice*. This film version of *Emma* concludes with an invented country dance that celebrates the engagement of Emma and Mr. Knightley, but more prominently symbolizes the harmonious future of the community. Despite the fact that it too departs from the novel, Nick Dear's 1995 film version of *Persuasion* also offers a satisfactory solution by briefly showing Anne and Wentworth together on board ship. This conclusion suggests that their life lived together, in its resemblance to the marriage of Admiral and Mrs. Croft, is far more important to Austen than the mere wedding ceremony. For an overview of the relation between the novels and the recent films, including the various approaches to the endings, see Sue Parrill, *Jane Austen on Film and Television*; Linda Troost and Sayre Greenfield, eds., *Jane Austen in Hollywood*; and Gina Macdonald and Andrew F. Macdonald, eds., *Jane Austen on Screen*.

9. Johnson, *Jane Austen: Women, Politics, and the Novel*, 73; Newton, *Women, Power, and Subversion*, 74; Armstrong, Introduction to *Pride and Prejudice*, xxx; Butler, *Jane Austen and the War of Ideas*, 197; 212-13.

10. The difficulty of taking Austen both seriously and lightly simultaneously is nicely summarized by Park Honan, who says that "As the twentieth century ends, Jane Austen's power is credited, though her lightness disguises her profundity" (*Jane Austen*, 420).

11. Dorothy Van Ghent remarks that Jane Austen, like Cervantes and Molière,

knew how closely comedy and tragedy are related. Van Ghent cites the ending of Plato's *Symposium*, in which Socrates tells Aristophanes and Agathon that the genius of tragedy is the same as the genius of comedy (*English Novel*, 195).

12. Harding, "Social Habitat," 52; 65.

13. Harding, "Regulated Hatred," 12.

14. Poovey writes that "It is precisely the latitude of interpretations permitted by this compromise of ethical and moral absolutes that finally imperils the didactic design of *Pride and Prejudice*. For the family of readers that Austen posited did not necessarily exist; even in her own day, the consensus of values she needed to assume was as wishful a fiction as Elizabeth Bennet's marriage to Darcy" (*Proper Lady*, 207).

15. Booth, *Rhetoric of Fiction*, 266. For a useful discussion of some of the dangers of assuming that Austen's readership is limited to a select few in either her time or ours, see Gard, *Jane Austen's Novels: The Art of Clarity*, 2-7.

16. Aristotle, *Nicomachean Ethics*, 1126b.11-15.

17. He does, at least, compose them himself. The reason he looks so foolish here is not so much that he studies in preparation for delivering compliments, as that he reveals this, proudly, to another.

18. Aristotle, *Nicomachean Ethics*, 1126b.15-17.

19. Ibid., 1126b.25-27.

20. For a discussion of the importance of speech to the practice of politeness in *Pride and Prejudice*, see Patricia Howell Michaelson, *Speaking Volumes*, 203-08.

21. Aristotle, *Nicomachean Ethics*, 1125b.32-34.

22. Compare the *OED* definition of *prejudice* as "Preconceived opinion; bias or leaning favourable or unfavourable; prepossession; when used *absolutely*, usually with unfavourable connotation." As an example of prejudice as a favorable leaning, the *OED* cites Edmund Burke's use of the word in his *Reflections on the Revolution in France* (1790): "Prejudice renders a man's virtue his habit. . . . Through just prejudice, his duty becomes a part of his nature."

23. Scarry, *On Beauty and Being Just*, 52.

24. Maskell and Robinson, *New Idea*, 60.

25. Ibid., 36-37.

26. Ibid., 45.

27. This desire for entertainment means that Mr. Bennet resembles his wife: she too is anxious for entertainment and some kind of excitement. For him, however, the entertainment has little point. For her at least it is constructive, because the goal of her entertainment is to find husbands for her daughters and solve the problem of the entail.

28. Fraiman, *Unbecoming Women*, 63.

29. Ibid.

30. Ibid., 81.

31. Ibid.

32. In the words of the Confession, "We acknowledge and bewail our manifold sins and wickedness, Which we from time to time most grievously have committed, By thought, word, and deed, Against thy Divine Majesty, Provoking most justly thy wrath and indignation against us. We do earnestly repent, And are heartily sorry for these our misdoings." Margaret Doody suggests that the *Book of Common Prayer* was probably

a stronger influence than the style of Samuel Johnson on the rhythm and balance of Austen's sentences ("Jane Austen's Reading," 347).

33. Gamble, "Pragmatic Sympathy," 360; 359.

34. Johnson, *Jane Austen: Women, Politics, and the Novel*, 78. See also Margaret Doody, "'A Good Memory Is Unpardonable,'" 93.

35. Her statement here therefore indicates that Darcy was right to point out in one of their conversations at Rosings that she finds "'great enjoyment in occasionally professing opinions which in fact are not your own'" (*PP* 174). The fact that Darcy is right about this does not belittle Elizabeth, however, because she is speaking in hyperbole.

36. Maskell and Robinson, *New Idea*, 172; 54.

References to Jane Austen's Works

References to Jane Austen's works are to the following editions:

The Novels of Jane Austen. 5 vols. 3rd ed. Ed. R. W. Chapman. London: Oxford University Press, 1932-1934.

Minor Works. Vol. 6 of *The Works of Jane Austen*. Ed. R. W. Chapman. London: Oxford University Press, 1954; rpt. with revisions by B. C. Southam, 1969.

Jane Austen's Letters. 3rd ed. Ed. Deirdre Le Faye. Oxford: Oxford University Press, 1997.

Works Cited

Aristotle. *Nicomachean Ethics*. Trans. J. A. K. Thomson. Harmondsworth, Middlesex: Penguin, 1955.

_____. *Nicomachean Ethics*. Trans. W. D. Ross. *The Basic Works of Aristotle*. Ed. Richard McKeon. New York: Random House, 1941. 935-1112.

_____. *Politics*. Trans. Benjamin Jowett. *The Basic Works of Aristotle*. Ed. Richard McKeon. 1113-316.

Armstrong, Isobel. Introduction to *Pride and Prejudice*. By Jane Austen. Oxford: Oxford University Press, 1990. vii-xxx.

Auerbach, Nina. "Jane Austen's Dangerous Charm: Feeling as One Ought about Fanny Price." *Jane Austen: New Perspectives*. Ed. Janet Todd. New York: Holmes and Meier, 1983. 208-23.

_____. "O Brave New World: Evolution and Revolution in *Persuasion*." *ELH* 39 (1972): 112-28.

Austen, Jane. *Emma*. 1816. *The Novels of Jane Austen*. Vol. 6. 3rd ed. Ed. R.W. Chapman. London: Oxford University Press, 1932-34.

_____. *Jane Austen's Letters*. 3rd ed. Ed. Deirdre Le Faye. Oxford: Oxford University Press, 1997.

_____. *Mansfield Park*. 1814. *The Novels of Jane Austen*. Vol. 3.

_____. *Northanger Abbey*. 1818. *The Novels of Jane Austen*. Vol. 5.

_____. *Persuasion*. 1818. *The Novels of Jane Austen*. Vol. 5.

_____. *Pride and Prejudice*. 1813. *The Novels of Jane Austen*. Vol. 2.

_____. *Sense and Sensibility*. 1811. *The Novels of Jane Austen*. Vol. 1.

The Book of Common Prayer and Administration of the Sacrament and Other Rites and Ceremonies of the Church. Oxford: Printed by John Baskett, 1737.

Booth, Wayne C. *The Rhetoric of Fiction*. Chicago: University of Chicago Press, 1961.

Brown, Julia Prewitt. "The Feminist Depreciation of Jane Austen: A Polemical Reading." *Novel* 23.3 (1990): 303-13.

Butler, Marilyn. *Jane Austen and the War of Ideas*. Oxford: Clarendon Press, 1975; rpt. with a new introduction 1987.

Doody, Margaret. "'A Good Memory Is Unpardonable': Self, Love, and the Irrational Irritation of Memory." *Eighteenth-Century Fiction* 14.1 (2001): 67-94.

_____. "Jane Austen's Reading." *The Jane Austen Handbook*. Ed. J. David Grey. 347-63.

Eliot, George. *Adam Bede*. 1859. Ed. Stephen Gill. London: Penguin, 1980.

_____. *Middlemarch*. 1871-72. Ed. Bert G. Hornback. New York: Norton, 1977.

Fraiman, Susan. *Unbecoming Women: British Women Writers and the Novel of Development*. New York: Columbia University Press, 1993.

Gamble, David E. "Pragmatic Sympathy in Austen and Eliot." *CLA Journal* 32.3 (1989): 348-60.

Gard, Roger. *Jane Austen's Novels: The Art of Clarity*. New Haven, CT: Yale University Press, 1992.

Gilbert, Sandra M., and Susan Gubar. *The Madwoman in the Attic: The Woman Writer and the Nineteenth-Century Literary Imagination*. New Haven, CT: Yale University Press, 1979; rpt. with a new introduction 2000.

Halperin, John. *The Life of Jane Austen*. Baltimore, MD: Johns Hopkins University Press, 1984; rpt. 1996.

Harding, D. W. "Regulated Hatred: An Aspect of the Work of Jane Austen." *Scrutiny* 8.4 (1940): 346-62. Rpt. in *Regulated Hatred and Other Essays on Jane Austen*. Ed. Monica Lawlor. London: Athlone Press, 1998. 5-26.

_____. "The Social Habitat in Jane Austen: Distant and Nearer Contexts." *Regulated Hatred and Other Essays on Jane Austen*. Ed. Monica Lawlor. 48-68.

Honan, Park. *Jane Austen: Her Life*. London: Weidenfeld and Nicolson, 1987.

Johnson, Claudia L. *Jane Austen: Women, Politics, and the Novel*. Chicago: University of Chicago Press, 1988.

Leavis, F. R. *The Great Tradition: George Eliot, Henry James, Joseph Conrad*. 1960. New York: New York University Press, 1973.

Macdonald, Gina, and Andrew F. Macdonald, eds. *Jane Austen on Screen*. Cambridge: Cambridge University Press, 2003.

MacIntyre, Alasdair. *After Virtue: A Study in Moral Theory*. 1981. 2nd ed. Notre Dame, IN: University of Notre Dame Press, 1984.

Maskell, Duke, and Ian Robinson. *The New Idea of a University*. London: Haven Books, 2001.

Michaelson, Patricia Howell. *Speaking Volumes: Women, Reading, and Speech in the Age of Austen*. Stanford, CA: Stanford University Press, 2002.

Mudrick, Marvin. *Jane Austen: Irony as Defense and Discovery*. Princeton, NJ: Princeton University Press, 1952.

Newton, Judith Lowder. *Women, Power, and Subversion: Social Strategies in British Fiction, 1778-1860*. Athens: University of Georgia Press, 1981.

Nokes, David. *Jane Austen: A Life*. New York: Farrar, Straus and Giroux, 1997.

Parrill, Sue. *Jane Austen on Film and Television: A Critical Study of the Adaptations*. Jefferson, NC: McFarland, 2002.

Plato. *Meno*. Trans. W. K. C. Guthrie. *The Collected Dialogues*. Ed. Edith Hamilton and Huntington Cairns. Princeton, NJ: Princeton University Press, 1961. 353-84.

_____. *Symposium*. Trans. Michael Joyce. *The Collected Dialogues*. Ed. Edith Hamilton and Huntington Cairns. 526-74.

Poovey, Mary. *The Proper Lady and the Woman Writer: Ideology as Style in the Works of Mary Wollstonecraft, Mary Shelley, and Jane Austen*. Chicago: University of Chicago Press, 1984.

"prejudice, *n.*, II.3.a." *The Oxford English Dictionary*. 2nd ed. 1989. OED Online. Oxford University Press. January 6, 2005. http://dictionary.oed.com.ezp2.harvard.edu/cgi/entry/50187167.

Scarry, Elaine. *On Beauty and Being Just*. Princeton, NJ: Princeton University Press, 1999.

Shields, Carol. *Jane Austen*. New York: Viking Penguin, 2001.

Trilling, Lionel. "*Mansfield Park*." *The Opposing Self: Nine Essays in Criticism*. New York: Harcourt Brace Jovanovich, 1955. 181-202. Rpt. in *The Moral Obligation to Be Intelligent: Selected Essays*. Ed. Leon Wieseltier. New York: Farrar, Straus and Giroux, 2000. 292-310.

Troost, Linda, and Sayre Greenfield, eds. *Jane Austen in Hollywood*. Lexington: University Press of Kentucky, 1998.

Van Ghent, Dorothy. *The English Novel: Form and Function*. New York: Rinehart, 1953.

Watt, Ian, ed., *Jane Austen: A Collection of Critical Essays*. Englewood Cliffs, NJ: Prentice-Hall, 1963.

_____. "On *Sense and Sensibility*." Introduction to *Sense and Sensibility*. 1961. Rpt. in *Jane Austen: A Collection of Critical Essays*. Ed. Ian Watt. 41-51.

Wollstonecraft, Mary. *A Vindication of the Rights of Woman*. 1792. Ed. Miriam Brody. London: Penguin, 1992.

RESOURCES

1775	Jane Austen is born on December 16 in the village of Steventon, Hampshire, to George Austen and Cassandra Leigh Austen.
1785-87	Austen attends Abbey School at Reading.
1787-93	Austen writes various pieces that are later collected in three volumes of juvenilia.
1793-97	Austen writes her first novel, an epistolary titled *Lady Susan*. She begins work on another epistolary, "Elinor and Marianne," which will later become *Sense and Sensibility*.
1796-97	Austen completes and tries to publish "First Impressions," an early version of *Pride and Prejudice*.
1798	Austen finishes "Susan," an early version of *Northanger Abbey*.
1801-02	George Austen retires and moves the family to Bath.
1803	Austen sells "Susan" to a publisher, but it is never published.
1803-05	Austen begins work on *The Watsons* but eventually abandons it.
1805	George Austen dies.
1808	With her mother and sister, Austen moves to Southampton.
1809	With her mother and sister, Austen moves to Chawton, in Hampshire. The house is provided by her brother Edward.
1811	Austen publishes *Sense and Sensibility* anonymously.
1813	*Pride and Prejudice* is published.
1814	*Mansfield Park* is published. Austen begins work on *Emma*.

1815-16	*Emma* is published in December 1815, although the work is dated 1816. Austen begins work on *Persuasion*.
1817	Austen begins work on *Sanditon*. She becomes ill and moves to Winchester for treatment. On July 18, Jane Austen dies. She is buried in Winchester Cathedral.
1818	*Persuasion* and *Northanger Abbey* are published together posthumously.

Works by Jane Austen

Juvenilia, written 1787-1793
Sense and Sensibility, 1811
Pride and Prejudice, 1813
Mansfield Park, 1814
Emma, 1816
Northanger Abbey, 1818
Persuasion, 1818
The Watsons, 1871, written 1803-1805
Sanditon, unfinished at her death

Bibliography

Auerbach, Emily. "'A Barkeeper Entering the Kingdom of Heaven': Did Mark Twain Really Hate Jane Austen?" *Virginia Quarterly Review* 75.1 (1999): 109-20.

_____. *Searching for Jane Austen*. Madison: University of Wisconsin Press, 2004.

Bander, Elaine. "The Other Play in *Mansfield Park*: Shakespeare's *Henry VIII*." *Persuasions* 17 (Dec. 1995): 111-20.

_____. "*Sanditon*, *Northanger Abbey*, and *Camilla*: Back to the Future?" *Persuasions* 19 (Dec. 1997): 195-204.

Beer, Patricia. "Elizabeth Bennet's Fine Eyes." *Fair of Speech: The Uses of Euphemism*. Ed. D. J. Enright. Oxford: Oxford University Press, 1985. 108-21.

Benedict, Barbara M. "Jane Austen's *Sense and Sensibility*: The Politics of Point of View." *Philological Quarterly* 69.4 (1990): 453-70.

Benson, Robert. "Jane Goes to *Sanditon*: An Eighteenth Century Lady in a Nineteenth Century Landscape." *Persuasions* 19 (Dec. 1997): 211-18.

Bloom, Harold, ed. *Jane Austen*. New York: Chelsea House, 1987.

_____. *Jane Austen's "Pride and Prejudice."* New York: Chelsea House, 1987.

Breunig, Hans Werner. "Jane Austen: Romantic? British Empiricist?" *Re-mapping Romanticism: Gender-Text-Context*. Ed. Christoph Bode and Fritz-Wilhelm Neuman. Essen, Germany: Blaue, Eule, 2001. 163-81.

Bristow, Catherine. "Unlocking the Rape: An Analysis of Austen's Use of Pope's Symbolism in *Sense and Sensibility*." *Persuasions* 20 (1998): 31-37.

Brown, Lloyd W. *Bits of Ivory: Narrative Techniques in Jane Austen's Fiction*. Baton Rouge: Louisiana State University Press, 1973.

Burdan, Judith. "*Mansfield Park* and the Question of Irony." *Persuasions* 23 (2001): 118-29.

Castellanos, Gabriela. *Laughter, War, and Feminism: Elements of Carnival in Three of Jane Austen's Novels*. New York: Peter Lang, 1994.

Clay, George R. "In Defense of Flat Characters: A Discussion of Their Value to Charles Dickens, Jane Austen, and Leo Tolstoy." *Italia Francescana* 27.1-2 (2000): 20-36.

Clifford-Amos, Terence. "Some Observations on the Language of *Pride and Prejudice*." *Language and Literature* 20 (1995): 1-10.

Copeland, Edward. "Virgin Sacrifice: Elizabeth Bennet After Jane Austen." *Persuasions* 22 (2000): 156-94.

Copeland, Edward, and Juliet McMaster, eds. *The Cambridge Companion to Jane Austen*. New York: Cambridge University Press, 1997.

Correa, Delia Da Sousa, ed. *The Nineteenth-Century Novel: Realisms*. London: Routledge for Open University, 2000.

Cowley, Malcolm, and Howard E. Hugo. *The Lesson of the Masters: An Anthology of the Novel from Cervantes to Hemingway.* New York: Charles Scribner's Sons, 1971. 80-97.

Craig, G. Armour. "Jane Austen's *Emma*: The Truths and Disguises of Human Disclosure." *Defense of Reading: A Reader's Approach to Literary Criticism.* Ed. R. A. Brower and R. Poirier. New York: E. P. Dutton, 1962. 235-55.

Curry, Mary Jane. "'Not a Day Went by Without a Solitary Walk': Elizabeth's Pastoral World." *Persuasions* 22 (2000): 175-86.

Dabundo, Laura. "The Devil and Jane Austen: Elizabeth Bennet's Temptations in the Wilderness." *Persuasions* 21 (1999): 53-58.

DeForest, Mary. "Jane Austen: Closet Classicist." *Persuasions* 22 (2000): 98-104.

Deresiewicz, William. *Jane Austen and the Romantic Poets.* New York: Columbia University Press, 2004.

Duckworth, William C., Jr. "Misreading Jane Austen: Henry James, Women Writers, and the Friendly Narrator." *Persuasions* 21 (1999): 96-105.

Emsley, Sarah. "Practising the Virtues of Amiability and Civility in *Pride and Prejudice*." *Persuasions* 22 (2000): 187-98.

Ferguson, Frances. "Jane Austen, *Emma*, and the Impact of Form." *Modern Language Quarterly* 61.1 (2000): 157-80.

Fischer, Doucet Devin. "Byron and Austen: Romance and Reality." *Byron Journal* 21 (1993): 71-79.

Fletcher, Loraine. "Emma: The Shadow Novelist." *Critical Survey* 4.1 (1992): 36-44.

Fraiman, Susan. "Jane Austen and Edward Said: Gender, Culture, and Imperialism." *Critical Inquiry* 21.4 (1995): 805-21.

_____. *Unbecoming Women: British Women Writers and the Novel of Development.* New York: Columbia University Press, 1993.

Frye, Northrop. *The Secular Scripture: A Study of the Structure of Romance.* Cambridge, MA: Harvard University Press, 1976.

Fullerton, Susannah. *Jane Austen and Crime.* Madison, WI: Jones Books, 2006.

Galperin, William. "Byron, Austen and the 'Revolution' of Irony." *Criticism: A Quarterly for Literature and the Arts* 32.1 (1990): 51-80.

_____. "The Picturesque, the Real, and the Consumption of Jane Austen." *Wordsworth Circle* 28.1 (1997): 19-27.

_____. "The Theatre at *Mansfield Park*: From Classic to Romantic Once More." *Eighteenth-Century Life* 16.3 (1992): 247-71.

_____, ed. *Re-reading Box Hill: Reading the Practice of Reading Everyday Life.* College Park: University of Maryland, 2000.

Giles, Paul. "The Gothic Dialogue in *Pride and Prejudice*." *Text and Context* 2.1 (1988): 68-75.

Gilman, Priscilla. "'Disarming Reproof': *Pride and Prejudice* and the Power of Criticism." *Persuasions* 22 (2000): 218-29.

Goldstein, Philip. "Criticism and Institutions: The Conflicted Reception of Jane Austen's Fiction." *Studies in the Humanities* 18.1 (1991): 35-55.

Gross, Gloria Sybil. *In a Fast Coach with a Pretty Woman: Jane Austen and Samuel Johnson*. New York: AMS Press, 2002.

Halperin, John. "Inside *Pride and Prejudice*." *Persuasions* 11 (16 Dec. 1989): 37-45.

Harmsel, Henrietta Ten. "The Villain-Hero in *Pamela* and *Pride and Prejudice*." *College English* 23 (Nov. 1961): 104-8.

Havely, Cicely Palser. "*Emma*: Portrait of the Artist as a Young Woman." *English: The Journal of the English Association* 42.174 (1993): 221-37.

Hermansson, Casie. "Neither *Northanger Abbey*: The Reader Presupposes." *Papers on Language and Literature* 36.4 (2000): 337-56.

Heydt-Stevenson, Jill. *Austen's Unbecoming Conjunctions: Subversive Laughter, Embodied History*. New York: Palgrave Macmillan, 2005.

_____. "Liberty, Connection, and Tyranny: The Novels of Jane Austen and the Aesthetic Movement of the Picturesque." *Lessons of Romanticism. A Critical Companion*. Ed. Thomas Pfau and Robert F. Gleckner. Durham, NC: Duke University Press, 1998.

Hill, Reginald. "Jane Austen: A Voyage of Discovery." *Persuasions* 19 (Dec. 1997): 77-92.

Irvine, Robert P. *Jane Austen*. New York: Routledge, 2005.

"Jane Austen, 1775-1975" [special issue]. *Nineteenth-Century Fiction* 30.3 (Dec. 1975).

Jenkyns, Richard. *A Fine Brush on Ivory: An Appreciation of Jane Austen*. New York: Oxford University Press, 2004.

Johnson, Gregory R. "The Great-Souled Woman: Jane Austen as Public Moralist." *The Moral of the Story: Literature and Public Ethics*. Ed. Henry T. Edmondson III. Lanham, MD: Lexington, 2000. 123-33.

Jones, Darryl. *Jane Austen*. New York: Palgrave Macmillan, 2004.

Kaplan, Zoe C. "Emma and Her Influence on Future Self-Deceiving Literary Heroines." *Persuasions* 22 (2000): 87-97.

Katz, Richard A. "The Comic Perception of Jane Austen." *Voltaire, the Enlightenment, and the Comic Mode: Essays in Honor of Jean Sareil*. Ed. Maxine G. Cutler. New York: Peter Lang, 1990. 65-87.

Kearney, J. A. "Jane Austen and the Reason-Feeling Debate." *Theoria* 75 (May 1990): 107-22.

Kliger, Samuel. "Jane Austen's *Pride and Prejudice* in the Eighteenth-Century Mode." *University of Toronto Quarterly* 16 (July 1947): 357-70.

Kramp, Michael. *Disciplining Love: Austen and the Modern Man*. Columbus: Ohio State University Press, 2007.

Lambdin, Laura Cooner, and Robert Thomas Lambdin, eds. *A Companion to Jane Austen Studies*. Westport, CT: Greenwood Press, 2000.

Lau, Beth. "Jane Austen, *Pride and Prejudice*." *A Companion to Romanticism*. Ed. Duncan Wu. Oxford, England: Blackwell, 1998. 219-26.

Lawrence, Joseph P. "Poetry and Ethics: Their Unification in the Sublime." *Southern Humanities Review* 24.1 (1990): 1-14.

Lee, Judith. "'Without Hate, Without Bitterness, Without Fear, Without Protest, Without Preaching': Virginia Woolf Reads Jane Austen." *Persuasions* 12 (16 Dec. 1990): 111-16.

Lee, Miae. "What Makes Us Read Jane Austen? The Narrative Development in Austen's Works." *Journal of English Language and Literature* 46.4 (2000): 1197-1220.

Looser, Devoney, ed. *Jane Austen and Discourses of Feminism*. New York: St. Martin's Press, 1995.

Loveridge, Mark. "*Northanger Abbey*: Or, Nature and Probability." *Nineteenth-Century Literature* 56.1 (1991): 1-29.

Lucas, John, ed. "Jane Austen and Romanticism" [special issue]. *Critical Survey* 4.1 (1992).

Lynch, Deidre, ed. *Janeites: Austen's Disciples and Devotees*. Princeton, NJ: Princeton University Press, 2000.

McMaster, Juliet. "Talking about Talk in *Pride and Prejudice*." *Jane Austen's Business: Her World and Her Profession*. Ed. Juliet McMaster and Bruce Stovel. New York: St. Martin's Press, 1996. 81-94.

McMaster, Juliet, and Bruce Stovel, eds. *Jane Austen's Business: Her World and Her Profession*. New York: St. Martin's Press, 1996.

Marsh, Nicholas. *Jane Austen: The Novels*. New York: St. Martin's Press, 1998.

Mellor, Anne K. "Why Women Didn't Like Romanticism: The Views of Jane Austen and Mary Shelley." *The Romantics and Us: Essays on Literature and Culture*. Ed. Gene W. Ruoff. New Brunswick, NJ: Rutgers University Press, 1990. 274-87.

Miller, D. A. *Jane Austen, or, The Secret of Style*. Princeton, NJ: Princeton University Press, 2003.

Millgate, Jane. "*Persuasion* and the Presence of Scott." *Persuasions* 15 (Dec. 1993): 184-95.

Morini, Massimiliano. *Jane Austen's Narrative Techniques: A Stylistic and Pragmatic Analysis*. Burlington, VT: Ashgate, 2009.

Morris, Ivor. *A Jane Austen Quintet: Critical Inquiries into the Novels' World*. Winchester, Hampshire, England: Sarsen Press, 2008.

Morris, Pam. "Reading *Pride and Prejudice*." *The Realist Novel*. Ed. Dennis Walder. London: Routledge for Open University, 1995. 31-60.

Newman, Karen. "Can This Marriage Be Saved: Jane Austen Makes Sense of an Ending." *ELH* 50.4 (1984): 693-710.

Newton, Judith Lowder. *Women, Power, and Subversion: Social Strategies in British Fiction, 1778-1860*. Athens: University of Georgia Press, 1985.

Olsen, Stein Haugom. "Appreciating *Pride and Prejudice.*" *The Nineteenth-Century British Novel.* Ed. Jeremy Hawthorn. Baltimore: E. Arnold, 1986.

Ortells, Elena. "Bridging the Gap Between Linguistics and Literary Criticism: The Role of the Narrator in the Presentation of Characters in Jane Austen's *Pride and Prejudice* and Henry James's *The American.*" *SELL: Studies in English Language and Linguistics* 2 (2000): 161-70.

Poovey, Mary. *The Proper Lady and the Woman Writer: Ideology as Style in the Works of Mary Wollstonecraft, Mary Shelley, and Jane Austen.* Chicago: University of Chicago Press, 1984.

Robertson, Leslie. "Changing Models of Juvenilia: Apprenticeship or Play?" *English Studies in Canada* 24.3 (1998): 291-98.

Rogers, Deborah D. *Two Gothic Classics by Women: "The Italian" by Ann Radcliffe and "Northanger Abbey" by Jane Austen.* New York: Signet, 1995.

Roth, Barry. "Jane Austen Bibliography for 2000." *Persuasions* 23 (2001): 222-28.

Roulston, Christine. "Discourse, Gender, and Gossip: Some Reflections on Bakhtin and *Emma.*" *Ambiguous Discourse: Feminist Narratology and British Women Writers.* Ed. Kathy Mezei. Chapel Hill: University of North Carolina Press, 1996. 40-65.

Rowen, Norma. "Reinscribing Cinderella: Jane Austen and the Fairy Tale." *Functions of the Fantastic: Selected Essays from the Thirteenth International Conference on the Fantastic in the Arts.* Ed. Joe Sanders. Westport, CT: Greenwood Press, 1995. 29-36.

Ruoff, Gene W. *Jane Austen's "Sense and Sensibility."* New York: St. Martin's Press, 1992.

Sabor, Peter. "'Finished up to Nature': Walter Scott's Review of *Emma.*" *Persuasion* 13 (16 Dec. 1991): 88-99.

Scheuermann, Mona. *Reading Jane Austen.* New York: Palgrave Macmillan, 2009.

Shaffer, Julie A. "The Ideological Intervention of Ambiguities in the Marriage Plot: Who Fails Marianne in Austen's *Sense and Sensibility*?" *A Dialogue of Voices: Feminist Literary Theory and Bakhtin.* Ed. Karen Hohne and Helen Wussow. Minneapolis: University of Minnesota Press, 1994. 128-51.

Shaw, Harry E. *Narrating Reality: Austen, Scott, Eliot.* Ithaca, NY: Cornell University Press, 1999.

Simons, Judy. *"Mansfield Park" and "Persuasion."* New York: St. Martin's Press, 1997.

Spacks, Patricia Meyer. "Ideology and Form: Novels at Work." *Ideology and Form in Eighteenth-Century Literature.* Ed. David H. Richter. Lubbock: Texas Tech University Press, 1999. 15-30.

Stovel, Bruce. "Jane Austen and the Pleasure Principle." *Persuasions* 23 (2001): 63-77.

"Symposium: Jane Austen." *Philosophy and Literature* 23.1 (Apr. 1999): 96-137.

Tandon, Bharat. *Jane Austen and the Morality of Conversation.* London: Anthem, 2003.

Tauchert, Ashley. *Romancing Jane Austen: Narrative, Realism, and the Possibility of a Happy Ending.* New York: Palgrave Macmillan, 2005.

Tave, Stuart M. *Some Words of Jane Austen.* Chicago: University of Chicago Press, 1973.

Todd, Janet. *The Cambridge Introduction to Jane Austen.* New York: Cambridge University Press, 2006.

Tuite, Clara. *Romantic Austen: Sexual Politics and the Literary Canon.* New York: Cambridge University Press, 2002.

Waldron, Mary. *Jane Austen and the Fiction of Her Time.* New York: Cambridge University Press, 1999.

Wallace, Tara Ghoshal. *Jane Austen and Narrative Authority.* New York: St. Martin's Press, 1995.

Wilkie, Brian. "Structural Layering in Jane Austen's Problem Novels." *Nineteenth-Century Literature* 46.4 (1992): 517-44.

Wiltshire, John. *Jane Austen: Introductions and Interventions.* New York: Palgrave Macmillan, 2006.

_____. "Mrs. Bennet's Least Favorite Daughter." *Persuasions* 23 (2001): 179-87.

Wisenforth, Joseph. "The Case of *Pride and Prejudice*." *Studies in the Novel* 16 (Fall 1984): 261-73.

_____. "The Revolution of Civility in *Pride and Prejudice*." *Persuasions* 16 (Dec. 1994): 107-14.

CRITICAL INSIGHTS

About the Editor_____

Jack Lynch is Associate Professor of English at Rutgers University in Newark, New Jersey. He has published both scholarly and popular books and essays, mostly on British and American culture in the long eighteenth century. He is the author of *The Age of Elizabeth in the Age of Johnson* (2003), *Becoming Shakespeare: The Unlikely Afterlife That Turned a Provincial Playwright into the Bard* (2007), and *Deception and Detection in Eighteenth-Century Britain* (2008). He is also the editor of *The Age of Johnson: A Scholarly Annual* and coeditor of *Anniversary Essays on Johnson's Dictionary* (2005). His essays and reviews have appeared in such scholarly forums as *Eighteenth-Century Life*, *The Review of English Studies*, and *Studies in Philology* as well as in *The American Scholar*, *The New York Times*, and the *Los Angeles Times*.

About *The Paris Review*_____

The Paris Review is America's preeminent literary quarterly, dedicated to discovering and publishing the best new voices in fiction, nonfiction, and poetry. The magazine was founded in Paris in 1953 by the young American writers Peter Matthiessen and Doc Humes, and edited there and in New York for its first fifty years by George Plimpton. Over the decades, the *Review* has introduced readers to the earliest writings of Jack Kerouac, Philip Roth, T. C. Boyle, V. S. Naipaul, Ha Jin, Jay McInerney, and Mona Simpson, and published numerous now classic works, including Roth's *Goodbye, Columbus*, Donald Barthelme's *Alice*, Jim Carroll's *Basketball Diaries*, and selections from Samuel Beckett's *Molloy* (his first publication in English). The first chapter of Jeffrey Eugenides's *The Virgin Suicides* appeared in the *Review*'s pages, as well as stories by Edward P. Jones, Rick Moody, David Foster Wallace, Denis Johnson, Jim Shepard, Jim Crace, Lorrie Moore, Jeanette Winterson, and Ann Patchett.

The Paris Review's renowned Writers at Work series of interviews, whose early installments include legendary conversations with E. M. Forster, William Faulkner, and Ernest Hemingway, is one of the landmarks of world literature. The interviews received a George Polk Award and were nominated for a Pulitzer Prize. Among the more than three hundred interviewees are Robert Frost, Marianne Moore, W. H. Auden, Elizabeth Bishop, Susan Sontag, and Toni Morrison. Recent issues feature conversations with Salman Rushdie, Joan Didion, Stephen King, Norman Mailer, Kazuo Ishiguro, and Umberto Eco. (A complete list of the interviews is available at www.theparisreview.org.) In November 2008, Picador will publish the third of a four-volume series of anthologies of *Paris Review* interviews. The first two volumes have received acclaim. *The New York Times* called the Writers at Work series "the most remarkable and extensive interviewing project we possess."

The Paris Review is edited by Philip Gourevitch, who was named to the post in 2005, following the death of George Plimpton two years earlier. Under Gourevitch's leadership, the magazine's international distribution has expanded, paid subscriptions have risen 150 percent, and newsstand distribution has doubled. A new editorial team has published fiction by Andre Aciman, Damon Galgut, Mohsin Hamid, Gish Jen, Richard Price, Said Sayrafiezadeh, and Alistair Morgan. Poetry editors Charles Simic, Meghan O'Rourke, and Dan Chiasson have selected works by Billy Collins, Jesse Ball, Mary Jo Bang, Sharon Olds, and Mary Karr. Writing published in the magazine has been anthologized in *Best American Short Stories* (2006, 2007, and 2008), *Best American Poetry*, *Best Creative Non-Fiction*, the Pushcart Prize anthology, and *O. Henry Prize Stories*.

The magazine presents two annual awards. The Hadada Award for lifelong contribution to literature has recently been given to William Styron, Joan Didion, Norman Mailer, and Peter Matthiessen in 2008. The Plimpton Prize for Fiction, given to a new voice in fiction brought to national attention in the pages of *The Paris Review*, was presented in 2007 to Benjamin Percy and to Jesse Ball in 2008.

The Paris Review won the 2007 National Magazine Award in photojournalism, and the *Los Angeles Times* recently called *The Paris Review* "an American treasure with true international reach."

Since 1999 *The Paris Review* has been published by The Paris Review Foundation, Inc., a not-for-profit 501(c)(3) organization.

The Paris Review is available in digital form to libraries worldwide in selected academic databases exclusively from EBSCO Publishing. Libraries can contact EBSCO at 1-800-653-2726 for details. For more information on *The Paris Review* or to subscribe, please visit: www.theparisreview.org.

Contributors

Jack Lynch is Associate Professor of English at Rutgers University in Newark, New Jersey. He is the author of *The Age of Elizabeth in the Age of Johnson* (2003), *Becoming Shakespeare: The Unlikely Afterlife That Turned a Provincial Playwright into the Bard* (2007), and *Deception and Detection in Eighteenth-Century Britain* (2008). He is also the editor of *The Age of Johnson: A Scholarly Annual.*

Rosemary M. Canfield Reisman was Professor of English and Department Chair at Troy University and is now Adjunct Professor at Charleston Southern University. She coauthored *Contemporary Southern Women Fiction Writers* (1994) and *Contemporary Southern Men Fiction Writers* (1998) and has published numerous essays. She has presented lectures on British and American literature at the University of Hanover, Germany, at the American University in Cairo, and throughout the southeastern United States.

Radhika Jones is a senior editor at *Time* magazine and Time.com, covering the arts. She holds a Ph.D. in English and comparative literature from Columbia University.

Neil Heims is a writer and teacher living in Paris. His books include *Reading the Diary of Anne Frank* (2005), *Allen Ginsberg* (2005), and *J. R. R. Tolkien* (2004). He has also contributed numerous articles for literary publications, including essays on William Blake, John Milton, William Shakespeare, and Arthur Miller.

Bonnie Blackwell is Associate Professor and Director of Graduate Studies at Texas Christian University. She has published articles in *Literature and Medicine* and *Camera Obscura.*

Dominick Grace is Associate Professor of English at Brescia University College. His research interests are eclectic, and his publications range from work on Chaucer and Shakespeare to work on contemporary literature and popular culture.

Bernard J. Paris is Professor Emeritus at the University of Florida. His books include *Experiments in Life: George Eliot's Quest for Values* (1965), *A Psychological Approach to Fiction: Studies in Thackeray, Stendhal, George Eliot, Dostoevsky, and Conrad* (1974), *Character and Conflict in Jane Austen's Novels* (1978), *Bargains with Fate: Psychological Crises and Conflicts in Shakespeare and His Plays* (1991), *Character as a Subversive Force in Shakespeare: The History and the Roman Plays* (1991), *Imagined Human Beings: A Psychological Approach to Character and Conflict in Literature* (1997), *The Therapeutic Process: Essays and Lectures* (1999), *The Unknown Karen Horney: Essays on Gender, Culture, and Psychoanalysis* (2000), *Rereading George Eliot: Changing Perspectives on Her Experiments in Life* (2003), *Conrad's Charlie Marlow: A New Approach to* Heart of Darkness *and* Lord Jim (2005), and *Dostoevsky's Greatest Characters: A New Approach to "Notes from Underground,"* Crime and Punishment, *and* The Brothers Karamazov (2008).

Robert W. Uphaus is Professor Emeritus at Michigan State University. His books include *American Protest in Perspective* (editor, 1971), *The Impossible Observer: Reason and the Reader in Eighteenth Century Prose* (1979), *Beyond Tragedy: Structure and Experience in Shakespeare's Romances* (1981), *William Hazlitt* (1985), *The Idea of the Novel in the Eighteenth Century* (1988), and *The Other Eighteenth Century: English Women of Letters, 1660-1800* (editor, with Gretchen Foster, 1991, 2000).

Susan Morgan is Distinguished Professor of English at Miami University of Ohio. She has published several books, including *In the Meantime: Character and Perception in Jane Austen's Fiction* (1980), *Sisters in Time: Imagining Gender in Nineteenth-Century British Fiction* (1989); a reading edition of Anna Leonowens's 1873 *The Romance of the Harem* (1991), a reading edition of Marianne North's 1892 *Recollections of a Happy Life* (1993), *Place Matters: Gendered Geography in Victorian Women's Travel Books About Southeast Asia* (1996), and, most recently, *Bombay Anna: The Real Story and Remarkable Adventures of the* King and I *Governess* (2008).

Jill Heydt-Stevenson is Associate Professor of English and Humanities at the University of Colorado. Her essays have appeared in edited volumes and journals, including *European Romantic Review, Nineteenth-Century Literature, Eighteenth-Century Fiction*, and *Studies in the Humanities*. Her books include *Austen's Unbecoming Conjunctions: Subversive Laughter, Embodied History* (2005) and *Recognizing the Romantic Novel: New Histories of British Fiction, 1774-1824* (with Charlotte Sussman, 2008).

Sarah R. Morrison is Professor of English at Morehead State University. She is a specialist in Restoration and eighteenth-century British literature. She has published essays in *SEL: Studies in English Literature, 1500-1900, Biography: An Interdisciplinary Quarterly*, and *The Age of Johnson: A Scholarly Annual*, as well as in the volume *Milton's Legacy* (2005).

Christopher Brooke is Dixie Professor Emeritus of Ecclesiastical History at Gonville and Caius College. Among his many published books are *The Medieval Idea of Marriage* (1989), *A History of the University of Cambridge* (1993), *A History of Gonville and Caius College* (1985), and *Jane Austen: Illusion and Reality* (1999).

William Deresiewicz taught English at Yale University and is a regular contributor to *The American Scholar, The Nation, The London Review of Books*, and *The New York Times*. His book *Jane Austen and the Romantic Poets* was published in 2004.

Felicia Bonaparte is Professor of English and Comparative Literature at the Graduate Center of the City University of New York. Her essays have appeared in *Clio, International Journal of the Classical Tradition, New Vico Studies*, and the *Notre Dame English Journal*. She has published several books, including *Will and Destiny: Morality and Tragedy in George Eliot's Novels* (1975), *The Triptych and the Cross: The Central Myths of George Eliot's Poetic Imagination* (1979), and *The Gypsy-Bachelor of Manchester: The Life of Mrs. Gaskell's Demon* (1992).

Sarah Emsley taught at Harvard University. Her book *Jane Austen's Philosophy of the Virtues* was published in 2005.

Acknowledgments

"Jane Austen" by Rosemary M. Canfield Reisman. From *Dictionary of World Biography: The 19th Century.* Copyright © 1999 by Salem Press, Inc. Reprinted with permission of Salem Press.

"The *Paris Review* Perspective" by Radhika Jones. Copyright © 2010 by Radhika Jones. Special appreciation goes to Christopher Cox and Nathaniel Rich, editors for *The Paris Review.*

"*Emma*" by Bernard J. Paris. From *Character and Conflict in Jane Austen's Novels: A Psychological Approach*, 64-95. Copyright © 1978 by Bernard J. Paris. Reprinted by permission.

"Jane Austen and Female Reading" by Robert W. Uphaus. From *Studies in the Novel* 19, no. 3 (1987): 334-345. Copyright © 1987 by The University of North Texas. Reprinted by permission.

"Why There's No Sex in Jane Austen's Fiction" by Susan Morgan. From *Studies in the Novel* 19, no. 3 (1987): 346-356. Copyright © 1987 by The University of North Texas. Reprinted by permission.

"Liberty, Connection, and Tyranny: The Novels of Jane Austen and the Aesthetic Movement of the Picturesque" by Jill Heydt-Stevenson. From *Lessons of Romanticism: A Critical Companion*, eds. Thomas Pfau and Robert F. Gleckner, 261-279. Copyright © 1998 by Duke University Press. All rights reserved. Used by permission of the publisher.

"Of Woman Borne: Male Experience and Feminine Truth in Jane Austen's Novels" by Sarah R. Morrison. From *Studies in the Novel* 26, no. 4 (1994): 337-349. Copyright © 1994 by The University of North Texas. Reprinted by permission.

"Rank and Status" by Christopher Brooke. From *Jane Austen: Illusion and Reality*, 151-166. Copyright © 1999 by Boydell & Brewer Ltd. Reprinted by permission of Boydell & Brewer Ltd.

"Early Phase Versus Major Phase: The Changing Feelings of the Mind" by William Deresiewicz. From *Jane Austen and the Romantic Poets*, 18-55. Copyright © 2004 by Columbia University Press. Reprinted by permission.

"Conjecturing Possibilities: Reading and Misreading Texts in Jane Austen's *Pride and Prejudice*" by Felicia Bonaparte. From *Studies in the Novel* 37, no. 2 (2005): 141-161. Copyright © 2005 by The University of North Texas. Reprinted by permission.

"*Pride and Prejudice* and the Beauty of Justice" by Sarah Emsley. From *Jane Austen's Philosophy of the Virtues*, 83-106. Copyright © 2005 by Palgrave Macmillan. Reprinted by permission of Palgrave Macmillan.

Index

and knowledge, 264; language and vocabulary, 239, 262, 271, 275, 281, 298; and memory, 225; publication of, 9, 42, 53; and reading, 31, 38, 106, 311; and social hierarchy, 165, 186, 188; and time, 214; turning point, 64, 225, 260, 274, 280; writing process, 10

Radcliffe, Ann, 33, 171
Reeve, Clara, 33
Repton, Humphry, 139, 152, 155
Rhetoric of Irony, A (Booth), 5, 49
Richardson, Samuel, 32, 126
Robinson, Ian, 308, 318
Rogers, Katharine M., 165
Rozema, Patricia, 46
Ruoff, Gene W., 251, 253
Rushdie, Salman, 17
Ryle, Gilbert, 261, 287

Sales, Roger, 158, 255
Sanditon (Austen), 120, 252
Satz, Martha G., 262, 286
Say, Elizabeth A., 168
Scarry, Elaine, 307
Scott, Sir Walter, 16, 42, 119, 217
Seduction, 122, 172, 187
Sense and Sensibility (Austen), 39, 117, 226, 250, 253; critical interpretations, 165, 170; ending, 256; film adaptations, 320; and knowledge, 262; language and vocabulary, 239; and place, 208; publication of, 11; and reading, 110; reviews (contemporary), 42; and social hierarchy, 189; writing process, 10
Seward, Anna, 152
Seymour, Juliana-Susannah, 114
Shame, 44, 57, 62, 96, 225, 307

Shields, Carol, 320
Showalter, Elaine, 44, 175, 178
Sister relationships, 166, 209, 265
Slatoff, Walter, 284
Smith, Adam, 113, 118
Snobbery, 73, 180, 190, 197, 220
Social status, 57, 65, 85, 165, 180, 184, 186, 189, 192, 217
Spacks, Patricia Meyer, 169
Status. *See* Social status
Stern, G. B., 79
Stout, Janis P., 287
Sulloway, Alison, 157
Sutherland, John, 50
Swingle, Larry J., 257

Tanner, Tony, 65
Tave, Stuart M., 253
Themes; change, 64, 75, 77, 214, 219, 234, 239; education, 72, 77, 267, 286, 292, 294, 307, 310, 313, 318; humility, 79, 236, 292, 315; integrity, 21; justice, 298
Tilney, Henry (*Northanger Abbey*), 38, 44, 108, 304
Tom Jones (Fielding), 32
Tomalin, Claire, 39, 47
Tompkins, J. M. S., 124
Trilling, Lionel, 244, 255
Trumpener, Katie, 252

Van Ghent, Dorothy, 320
Vindication of the Rights of Woman, A (Wollstonecraft), 113
Vocabulary. *See* Language and vocabulary

Walpole, Horace, 33
Watsons, The (Austen), 11
Watt, Ian, 42
Wealth, 40, 60, 185, 190

LIBRARY
BUNKER HILL COMMUNITY COLLEGE
CHARLESTOWN, MASS. 02129

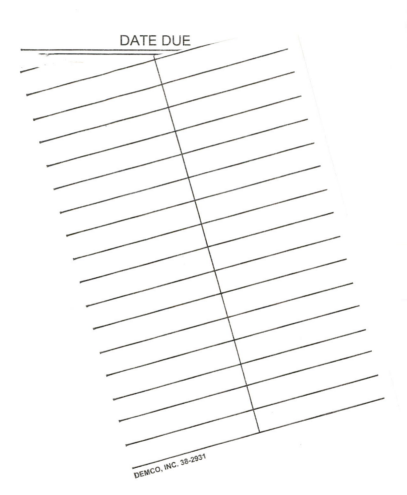

DATE DUE